WordPress®:
Pushing the Limits

Rachel McCollin

WILEY

This edition first published 2013

Registered office

John Wiley & Sons Ltd, The Atrium, Southern Gate, Chichester, West Sussex, PO19 8SQ, United Kingdom

For details of our global editorial offices, for customer services and for information about how to apply for permission to reuse the copyright material in this book please see our website at www.wiley.com.

A catalogue record for this book is available from the British Library.

ISBN 978-1-118-59719-4 (paperback); ISBN 978-1-118-59717-0 (ebook); 978-1-118-59718-7 (ebook); 978-1-118-59715-6 (ebook)

Set in 9.5 Myriad Pro by Wiley Indianapolis Composition Services

Printed in United States by Bind-Rite

Publisher's Acknowledgements

Some of the people who helped bring this book to market include the following:

Editorial and Production

VP Consumer and Technology Publishing Director: Michelle Leete

Associate Director–Book Content Management: Martin Tribe

Associate Publisher: Chris Webb

Associate Commissioning Editor: Ellie Scott

Project Editor: Tom Dinse

Copy Editor: Luann Rouff

Technical Editor: Mike Little

Editorial Manager: Jodi Jensen

Senior Project Editor: Sara Shlaer

Editorial Assistant: Annie Sullivan

Marketing

Associate Marketing Director: Louise Breinholt

Marketing Manager: Lorna Mein

Senior Marketing Executive: Kate Parrett

Marketing Assistant: Tash Lee

Composition Services

Compositor: Jennifer Goldsmith

Proofreader: Wordsmith Editorial

Indexer: Potomac Indexing, LLC

About the Author

Rachel McCollin is a keen (if sometimes slow) cyclist, amateur photographer, and mother of two budding boy geeks.

She first discovered WordPress in 2010 when a client asked for a CMS to manage their site, and hasn't looked back since. She attended her first WordCamp a few months later and is now a regular fixture at WordCamp UK, having been declared "'the best speaker wearing red shoes" in 2012.

She contributes to *Smashing Magazine* and wptutsplus and is the author of two WordPress-related Beginners Guides for Packt Publishing. She also runs Compass Design, a WordPress web development agency in Birmingham, UK.

About the Technical Editor

Mike Little is the co-founder of WordPress and founder and CEO of zed1.com ltd, a WordPress specialist web development consultancy.

He is a 100% WordPress specialist providing WordPress development, consultancy, training, and tech editing services.

He has developed many web sites for his clients including a number of UK government web sites and the award-winning I'm a Scientist, Get Me Out of Here (http://imascientist.org.uk) educational science engagement site. All in WordPress, of course. He is a long-term software developer (25+ years), with many programming languages, many disciplines, and many years under his belt, most at senior levels. He is a published author and technical editor.

He runs his local Manchester WordPress User Group, and serves on the WordCamp UK organising committee.

He lives with his family in Stockport, UK.

Acknowledgements

I'd like to thank all those in the WordPress community who have helped me develop my own use of WordPress, in particular the organizers of WordCamp UK, without whom I wouldn't have had the opportunity to meet many of the developers I'm now pleased to call friends.

I'd also like to thank Birgit Gruber (formerly of Wiley) for bringing me on board with this project, and Chris Webb, Tom Dinse, Luann Rouff, Sara Schlaer, and Ellie Scott for their professionalism and support. A huge thanks goes to Mike Little for his enthusiasm and feedback—having a co-founder of WordPress involved with this book is a pleasure and an honor. Members of my team at Compass Design provided feedback on the initial ideas for this book, inspired some of the content and contributed code used in the case studies—thanks to Mark Wilkinson, Tammie Lister, Scott Evans, and Nivi Morales.

My husband, Pete, spent many hours keeping two small boys calm while I disappeared to quiet rooms, libraries, or coffee shops to write, and I thank him for his continuing and unwavering support and patience.

Finally, I'd like to thank Jonny Allbut, whose input in planning this book made it much better than it would have been without him—I hope we manage to work on another writing project together sometime.

Contents

Introduction

WordPress is the world's most popular content management system (CMS), and it continues to grow in popularity. There's an increasing trend for owners of websites of all descriptions to move to WordPress as their needs scale, along with their frustration with other customized or unintuitive CMSs that they may be using. As Matt Mullenweg said in 2012:

> *"We might not always be the platform people start with, but we want to be what the best graduate to."*

WordPress is now far more than a blogging platform. Enhancements such as custom post types and taxonomies, as well as improvements to the Dashboard such as the Menus screen added in version 3.0, and the new Media Manager enhancements in version 3.5, mean that developers can push WordPress further and users can quickly create beautiful, customized websites. If you're prepared to write custom functions and hook into the WordPress APIs, then there's very little you can't do.

WordPress is free and open source, with a large and dedicated community of users and developers, which is one of its strengths. It's also a platform on which you can build a career and a business. As a WordPress developer you may be considering setting up your own agency building WordPress-powered sites, or you may have already done this and want to take your skills to the next level so you can meet the needs of larger clients with more complex requirements.

This book will help you advance your WordPress skills so you can become a sought-after WordPress professional—working with teams and clients to create unique and powerful projects.

Who This Book Is For

This book is for WordPress developers. It won't teach you how to set up a WordPress installation and add themes, plugins, and content to create a basic site. You can find many other books out there that do that.

The book is aimed at people who have experience with web development and developing with WordPress. You might be an experienced plugin or theme developer, or you may have built sites for a handful of clients. You could be working as part of an agency team using WordPress, or in the web department of an organization whose own site is powered by WordPress. Or you could simply be an enthusiastic WordPress developer who wants to take things further.

Most of the examples in this book will teach you how to code custom PHP to make WordPress do what you want—you won't learn how to use the WordPress admin screens here. Although some screenshots of the admin are included, you won't learn which button to click or which menu to select—it is assumed that you already know this.

To get the most from this book, then, you should have a solid understanding of HTML, some CSS experience, and be capable of writing your own PHP. All the PHP in the examples is explained in detail but the book does not provide an introduction to PHP (again, there are other books that do that).

What This Book Covers

As WordPress becomes more popular and more widely accepted as a serious CMS, there is an increasing need for skilled developers who can use it to build custom websites that are much more than a blog or simple "brochureware."

In addition, as large organizations switch over to WordPress, there is a need for WordPress developers who can manage large-scale web development projects, understand client needs, lead teams of developers, and develop robust, future-proof sites.

This book focuses on both of these. In the first part you will learn about WordPress as a professional tool, and about the skills you need to manage WordPress projects. You won't get a complete primer on business or management, but you will be prompted to think about how your WordPress skills need to be complemented by project management, planning, and team management skills. In the subsequent parts you will learn techniques for pushing WordPress to create powerful, customized sites. You will learn how to customize the admin and enhance security, as well as how to build mobile or responsive sites and make the best use of JavaScript and CSS alongside PHP. You'll learn when to add functionality via themes and when to use plugins, and make use of conditional tags for styling and content. Finally, you'll learn about releasing your code to the public, so you can test, submit, and market your themes and/or plugins and prepare them for translation.

How This Book Is Structured

This book isn't designed to be read from cover to cover (although please feel free to do so!). You can dip into chapters relevant to your expertise and learning needs, as each chapter stands alone. However, the book is divided into four related parts.

Part I: Professional WordPress Development

If you're an experienced WordPress developer but have little experience using WordPress professionally or managing WordPress projects, this part of the book will introduce you to the relevant considerations and skills.

- **Chapter 1: "WordPress As a Professional Web Development Tool"**—Why WordPress is great tool for professional web development and for building a career. Learn about the potential for professional WordPress development—it isn't just about client work.
- **Chapter 2: "Kicking Off a WordPress Project"**—How to begin WordPress projects in a way that gives you the best chance of success, including planning, writing a technical brief, and setting up your development environment.

Part II: Content and Administration

This part explains how WordPress manages content and data, and it will provide the skills you need to customize the WordPress admin for your clients.

- **Chapter 3: "Content Organization and Relationships"**—An analysis of how WordPress uses tables to store different kinds of content and the relationships between these tables, and what it means for development.

Chapter 4: "Customizing the WordPress Admin for Client Sites"— How to customize the admin screens to make things easier for your clients and give them access to settings and options. This chapter also covers the Settings API.

Part III: Practicalities of Developing and Hosting WordPress Sites

As covered in this part, ensuring that you have robust hosting and development environments and can protect your code from security attacks or other problems enhances your reputation as a developer and saves you a lot of time.

Chapter 5: "Development and Hosting Environments"—How to identify the most appropriate development and hosting environments for your projects, set them up, and configure them.

Chapter 6: "Avoiding and Dealing with Disaster"— Everyone dreads a site being hacked or breaking after a WordPress update. This chapter shows you how to anticipate potential problems and avoid them, as well as how to deal with disaster if it does strike.

Part IV: Pushing the Limits: The Best Tools for Site Development

One of WordPress' many strengths is that you often have more than one way to accomplish a task. Using specific areas of development, this part of the book looks at the different options you have to achieve your objectives. Sometimes there is a "better" approach, but on other occasions it comes down to the specifics of the project or to your own, your client's, or your team's experience and preferences.

Chapter 7: "Theme Building: Frameworks, Standalone Themes, or Child Themes?"—There are a few valid approaches to developing themes, and none of them is necessarily the "best" one. In this chapter you'll learn about the different approaches and when each might be most useful; how to interact with the popular theme frameworks; and how to build your own framework using custom action hooks and filter hooks.

Chapter 8: "Conditional Content: Functions, Template Files, and Styling"—Different sections within a site may need to work in very different ways, either functionally or visually. In this chapter you'll learn how to use a variety of methods to achieve this.

Chapter 9: "Custom Functionality in Theme Functions and Plugins"—Sometimes it's appropriate to add functionality to your theme's functions file, but in many cases writing a plugin will be better. In this chapter you'll learn how to identify which approach to use and how to build plugins to add commonly required functionality.

Chapter 10: "Making a Site Soar: HTML, JavaScript, and CSS"— WordPress sites don't run on PHP alone. To build interactivity, styling, and media into your projects you'll need to work with CSS and JavaScript, and no theme will function without HTML. In this chapter you'll learn how to use these languages within WordPress and how to add animations, enhance the use of media, and customize navigation menus.

Chapter 11: "Device Compatibility: Responsive and Mobile Development"— Responsive design has now entered the mainstream. In this chapter you'll learn how to add a responsive layout to your themes, how to work mobile first, and when to use a separate mobile theme for custom mobile sites.

Chapter 12: "Releasing Your Code to the Public"—There are many opportunities for developers to share their code, either free or for payment. This chapter explores requirements for themes and plugins in the WordPress repository and how to submit them, and looks at the practicalities of selling your code for money, including how to identify a need and how to market and distribute your code. Finally, you'll learn how to prepare your code for translation.

What You Need to Use This Book

All examples in this book have been developed using WordPress version 3.5. In some cases the Twenty Twelve theme (`http://wordpress.org/extend/themes/twentytwelve`) has been used to power sites used in the examples.

In order to follow along, you'll need the following:

- A local or remote installation of WordPress 3.5 or later (preferably the latest version)
- A text editor (with FTP access if you're working remotely)
- A modern browser

You'll have your own preferred text editor and browser, so I won't make recommendations.

WordPress Documentation

The best source of documentation on WordPress is the codex at `http://codex.wordpress.org/`. Each chapter also contains a "Further Reading" section at the end, and in many cases the links quoted are to pages in the Codex. Codex pages are continually edited and added to, so if you can't find any of the resources listed, a search of the Codex is your best bet.

Source Code

As you work through the examples in this book, you may choose either to type in all the code manually or to use the source code files that accompany the book. All of the source code used in this book is available for download at `www.wiley.com/go/ptl/wordpress`. For example, you will find the following sample code online in the Chapter 10 folder, in the `Example` project, and the `example.php` file.

Example.php

```php
<?php
function wpptl_call_scripts3() {
 wp_enqueue_script( 'example_script', plugins_url('/js/example-script.js',
__FILE__), , , true );
}
add_action('wp_enqueue_scripts', 'wpptl_call_scripts3' );
?>
```

Some source code snippets shown in the book are not comprehensive, as they are meant to help you understand a particular concept in the chapter. For these instances, you can refer to the files available on the website for the complete source code.

Part I

Professional WordPress Development

Chapter 1

WordPress As a Professional Web Development Tool

WordPress was originally established as a tool for bloggers, aimed at the growing community of people writing personal, technical, or business blogs, and providing them with a platform they could use to host that blog on their own server. But WordPress has evolved—significantly. It is no longer simply a blogging tool, but a fully fledged content management system (CMS), with a myriad of features that enable developers to experiment with the structure and functionality of a site, customize the dashboard and admin screens for users, and install plugins to enable whatever additional capabilities the site needs.

WordPress, to put it simply, is now a professional web development tool, used by thousands of web professionals to build sites for themselves, their clients, and other users. It's a tool on which you can build a business.

This chapter looks at the WordPress features you can harness as a professional web developer, and identifies how your working practices may need to change if you're scaling up your WordPress practice. You'll learn some techniques for improving your working and coding practices when collaborating as part of a larger team, and find out how to manage large web design and development projects, including the skills you'll need and the people you can expect to work with. You'll also look at the implications of building and possibly selling WordPress themes and plugins for release to other users and developers.

What It Means to Be a Professional WordPress Developer

If you're reading this book, there's a good chance that you already use WordPress on a professional or semi-professional basis. Maybe you work for an agency that builds client sites in WordPress, or for a company with a WordPress site that you maintain. You could be a freelance WordPress developer, or perhaps you're starting out as a fully fledged WordPress professional, setting up your own agency and building WordPress-powered sites for your own clients.

If you're going to do this professionally, you'll have to adapt your working style and practices, as well as your approach to development and coding. As a bare minimum, you'll need to do the following:

- Ensure that you understand WordPress well enough to build a diverse range of complex sites with it.
- Change the way you code so that people you're working with can understand what you've done and work with your code.

- Start thinking imaginatively about WordPress development, and in particular about how you can harness WordPress to solve your clients' real-world problems.

- Develop the skills needed to explain to your clients how WordPress, and the site you design and develop using it, can benefit them.

- Come to grips with the more commercial aspects of WordPress—using it to enhance your clients' SEO, seeing the potential to maximize your earning potential from WordPress, and possibly start selling themes or plugins.

As you work through this book you'll see that there is no one-size-fits-all approach to being a WordPress professional, but there are some practices and capabilities all WordPress professionals need, and others that will be more relevant to you depending on exactly how you work with WordPress. We'll be revisiting this theme throughout the book, particularly in Part IV, "Pushing the Limits: The Best Tools for Site Development."

Professional Coding Practices

The first thing you need to do if you want to scale up your approach to WordPress is review the way you code. Ask yourself: Who else looks at or works with your code at the moment?

The answer will vary according to where and how you work. If you're not running your own agency, you are probably not the person with ultimate responsibility for the quality and robustness of your code. Conversely, you might be the only person who works with your code.

Professional coding practices are about more than writing valid, standards-compliant code, although that is essential—and hopefully you already do this. It's about writing code that other developers can happily work with and develop further. If you're developing themes or plugins for other WordPress users to install, then you may need to focus on writing code that is resistant to the kind of hacking a WordPress novice might subject it to.

There are a few aspects to professional coding practices:

- Make sure your code is valid and standards-compliant.
- Use up-to-date coding methods.
- Comply with the WordPress coding standards.
- Make your code tidy.
- Structure your files well.
- Be consistent.
- Use comments liberally.

The following sections describe what these guidelines mean in practice.

Valid and Standards-Compliant Code

Yes, I've already said this, but it is absolutely fundamental. If you haven't run the HTML in your themes or plugins through a validator, do it! The most popular method for validating your code is to use the W3C validator at `http://validator.w3.org`. This is the most widely used approach and the first place to start. However, validating your code involves more than just this. It includes (but is by no means limited to) the following:

- Validating against accessibility standards, including WAI, or the Web Accessibility Intitiative
- Checking links
- Validating feeds
- Cross-browser compatibility checking (including handheld and tablet devices)

For a long list of validation tools and techniques, take a look at the guidance on the WordPress codex at `http://codex.wordpress.org/Validating_a_Website`.

Up-to-Date Coding Methods

If others are going to be working with your code, especially if they're going to be paying for it, it's imperative that you write code that is up to date. For example:

- Don't use tables for layout (we really hope you stopped doing this a while back, but it bears repeating).
- Use the most recent versions of the main coding languages—HTML5 and CSS3.
- Avoid using deprecated code—although browsers are generally forgiving, your users may not be.
- Accept that you can't keep up to date with everything, but make sure you read web development blogs, journals, and magazines so you're not completely out of the loop.
- If a project involves something you haven't done for a while (or at all), do some research before starting— or hire a specialist as a freelancer or staff member.

WordPress Coding Standards

The WordPress codex details a set of standard coding practices, designed to help enhance consistency in WordPress code structure. This includes standards for PHP, HTML, and CSS.

Get to know these standards and use them. Even if you come across code that doesn't adhere to them, it's good practice to use them yourself and to expect members of your team to do so. The consistency and clarity that this brings to your code will help others who work with it, including your team—and your clients if you are selling themes or plugins.

Tidy Code

If other people are going to be working with your code, especially if they aren't advanced developers themselves, your code has to be easy to understand. Adhering to the following best practices will result in code that is easier to work with and harder to break:

- Use line breaks and indentation to help others see how your code is structured in one glance.
- Avoid empty divs and other elements added purely for styling—try to keep your markup lean and use CSS to style it, including the use of CSS pseudo-elements where appropriate.
- Rationalize your stylesheets to avoid duplication—if two or more elements or classes have the same styling, code it once instead of doing it repeatedly for each one.

Well-Structured Files

Files that have a clear structure are much easier for other developers to work with.

Your markup should be written in the order it appears on the page, even where you're using CSS to position it outside that flow. So if your layout shows the header first, then the content and sidebar followed by a footer, code it in that order. This will not only help other developers, but also improve accessibility, as screen readers read the code in the order in which it's written.

Structure your stylesheets in sections, with a summary of the structure at the beginning. For example, the Twenty Eleven theme (`http://wordpress.org/extend/themes/twentyeleven`) is split into no less than 21 sections, which include the following:

- CSS reset (this should always come first)
- Structure (for overall page layout)
- Global (for global elements such as fonts, list styling, and colors)
- Header (specific styling for the header layout)
- Menu (for the navigation menu)
- Content (for page or post content)
- Link (for links, including links in text and page titles)
- Image (for images within the content)
- Widgets
- Footer
- Media queries

Your themes may not need so many sections, but if you are developing themes for others to download and use, you'll need to cover all the bases.

Consistency

People who need to work with your code don't want any surprises, so consistency is essential.

For example, when coding HTML within PHP files, use a consistent method.

Some developers prefer to write opening and closing PHP tags every time they need to add markup, as shown in the following very simplified extract from the WordPress loop:

```php
<?php if ( have_posts() ) while ( have_posts() ) : the_post(); ?>
  <article>
    <?php the_content(); ?>
  </article>
<?php endwhile; ?>
```

Other developers prefer to stay in PHP, and use `echo` instead:

```php
<?php if ( have_posts() ) while ( have_posts() ) : the_post(); ?>
  echo "<article>";
    the_content();
  echo "</article>";
endwhile; ?>
```

The first approach is probably the most commonly used, and it is preferable if the people who will be working with your code are more familiar with HTML than they are with PHP. Whichever you choose, make sure you stick with it.

You should also use and format comments consistently. For example, you might prefer to add comments to your PHP on the same line as the code:

```php
<?php the_content(); ?> // this is a comment
```

Conversely, you might prefer adding comments on separate lines:

```php
<?php
/* this is a multiline comment
which spans more than one line */
?>
```

Again, whichever you do, be consistent and use the correct syntax.

CSS styles comments in the same way. HTML, however, uses only one kind of commenting syntax:

```html
<article><!-- comments here --></article>
```

You already know how you prefer to code, and don't need us to tell you how to do it—but it's important to consider your preferences when other people will be working with that code, to ensure consistency and ease of understanding. You may also want to specify some coding practices and habits for other members of your team so you're all working in the same way.

Avoiding Duplication of Function and File Names

Whenever you write a new function, it's essential that you give that function a unique name to void any conflicts with WordPress functions or functions in other plugins or the active theme. It's normal practice to add a prefix to each function that corresponds to the name of your theme or plugin.

A function such as the following runs the risk of not being unique:

```php
<?php
function name_of_function(){
 // function contents
}
?>
```

Instead, it should have a prefix, as follows:

```php
<?php
function prefix_name_of_function(){
 // function contents
}
?>
```

In this book I prefix all functions with `wpptl_`:

```php
<?php
function wpptl_name_of_function(){
 // function contents
}
?>
```

This also applies to any the names of any hooks you register and of files you create in plugins. It doesn't apply to theme template files—these need to adopt the standard filenames for template files if they're going to work.

Liberal Use of Comments

Still on the topic of comments, it's worth stressing how important they are when working with other developers. Try to anticipate any places in your code where a comment could be useful to someone unfamiliar with it. This will help other developers understand at a glance what your code is designed to achieve.

As I discuss later in this book, there is almost always more than one way to achieve something in WordPress, and in code. The next person to work on your files may have a different way they prefer to code something, so what you've done may not make sense to them. By adding a comment, you're telling them what your code does and where it applies.

Commenting liberally will also help you when you revisit some code you wrote a year ago on a client site that now needs updating. The chances are good that this will happen at 4:00 p.m. on a Friday when the client's site has hit a problem and you need to edit some offending code fast. Good commenting can mean the difference between finding the problem straightaway, making the edit, and being home in time for the weekend, versus slogging through thousands of lines of code and missing your kid's soccer game.

Following are some tips for good comments:

- Use comments at the beginning of your file to explain what the file does. For example, in template files include a note about what data it displays and any customizations you've made to the loop or other parts of the file; and in plugin files add a note regarding its functionality. For example:

```
/**
 * Template Name:    sidebar-products.php
 *
 * The include file used for the sidebar on pages using the
   single-product.php template. Displays a gallery of product images
   (omitting the featured image which is displayed in the content).
 *
 * @package WordPress Pushing the Limits
 * @since 1.0
 */
```

This comment tells users the name of the template file, what it does, the theme it is part of (@package), and which version of the theme it has been in place since (@since). You should use a similar system for plugin files.

- Use comments to demarcate the sections of your code, not only in stylesheets but also in your theme template files and functions file.
- Comment anything that is nonstandard.
- Comment anything that took you a while to work out—use detailed comments so when you come back to it, you don't have to think it through again.
- Comment anything that you know someone else will be working on—for example, if your theme files contain scripts that you'll be asking a JavaScript developer to perfect, add comments explaining where they apply in the site.
- Use wording in your comments that you can find using a search later—so don't abbreviate, and use terms others would understand.
- Whenever you comment out some code, add a comment to yourself containing the reason. That way, if you forget to remove the code after you've finished, or want to add it back in the future, you'll know what's going on.
- When in doubt, add a comment!

Approaching Large-Scale Site Design

So, now that you're running a professional WordPress business (or planning to), you're going to want to attract big clients—clients with exciting, complex requirements for their website, and the budget to match.

The reality, of course, is that not all of your clients will be like this—indeed, if you're new to this game, the chances are good that smaller clients will be your bread and butter in the early years, but it's a good idea to set your sights high and develop working practices in line with this goal.

You may have worked on large, complex sites before, perhaps as an employee in an organization's web team. However, you may not have had overall responsibility for the site, for managing its development, and for working with its stakeholders.

To work with clients and manage the completion of large-scale web design projects, you need some key skills:

- The ability to work with a range of stakeholders
- A balance between technical capability and business sense
- Communication skills
- Planning and project management skills
- Problem-solving skills

The following sections take a look at how each of these skills applies to large-scale site development.

Working with a Range of Stakeholders

When managing large-site builds, you typically work with a range of stakeholders who have hugely varying expectations and different levels of understanding regarding what you're trying to achieve. Some stakeholders you might need to work with include the following:

- **The client's project manager or website manager.** This may well be the person who commissioned the work (but may not have approved it). He or she will have a sufficient level of technical capability but may know little or nothing about WordPress, especially if the client is moving to WordPress for the first time. This individual is an important ally for you as someone with an interest in the project's successful completion but may not have the authority to make important decisions.

- **The client's senior managers or managing director.** These people will be less closely involved in the project but have the power to make key decisions, including pulling the plug on your project or drastically changing its direction. Not involving these individuals at key stages in the project can be a big risk—if you complete most of the work before you present the website to them and they don't like it, you may have to start again from scratch.

- **The client's technical staff or website editors.** The client may have employees whose job it will be to maintain and edit the site once it is launched—unless they require you to do this. If not, you may have to train these employees to use WordPress and/or work collaboratively with them on some of the code. They are unlikely to be decision-makers.

- **Your own team.** You may have one or more partners in your agency, and a team of developers and designers, either freelance or employed by you. Your role is to ensure that they know their role in any project you're managing, they have the information and resources they need to do the work, they get feedback on that work, and they know what the deadlines are. You also need to oversee the quality of their work and intervene if it is not up to scratch.

As you can see, you could be working with some very different people; therefore, in order to ensure that your projects are successful, you'll likely have to adopt a different approach with each group—something you may never have done before if you're used to spending most of your time on development. You'll need to use the set of skills described in the following sections to make it work.

Balancing Technical Capability and Business Sense

Technical capability is essential. If you weren't already proficient in WordPress, you wouldn't be setting up a WordPress business. But you also need business sense, which comes into play not only when you're dealing with clients, but also when you're managing your own business. Obviously, it's beyond the scope of this book to teach you how to manage your accounts, form a business plan, and so on—you can find hundreds, if not thousands, of resources to help you with that—but it's worth noting that having or developing a business sense will help you choose the right WordPress projects and make a success of them.

When you're talking to a client about their website build, it's important to be able to step back from the details of a project to see the bigger picture—so you can translate technical knowledge into something that has a tangible benefit. For example, you may be great at building responsive sites, but if you can't explain the benefits to your client, they won't pay you to do it.

Communication Skills

"Code is poetry," or so the saying goes, and it is—well-written code can make a website soar, in terms of content, functionality, and performance. However, most clients don't understand code—and they probably don't understand web development or WordPress, at least not as well as you do. They may have some knowledge of web design and some fixed ideas about what their site should look like, and some of these may be good—we would caution against challenging the client on every design decision on the basis of your superior experience. Some of them may not be so good, however, and you'll need the communication skills to explain why—and then work together to find a resolution that will meet the client's needs.

Following are some of the scenarios in which you need to ensure effective communication with clients and your team:

- **Client pitches.** If you're lucky, all your work will come from referrals and you'll never have to do this, but most agencies need to do a client pitch at some point. Even if you are the only agency in the running, you still have to convince the client to hire you. At these meetings you need to be able to explain what you can offer in terms that the client understands and can identify with—in other words, a combination of business benefits and enough technical background to convince them of your expertise.

- **Project and planning meetings.** After landing a project, you will be working closely with the client to identify their requirements and determine how to implement them using WordPress. It's important to fully understand the requirements before diving straight into solutions, to avoid going down the wrong track. You need to both be a good listener and ask the right questions in order to extract the relevant information and probe for more detail. You should also be sure you confirm your understanding with the client— preferably in writing after meeting, to avoid any potential disagreements later.

- **Dealing with disagreement.** If you work well with your client and have a collaborative style, disagreements should be rare, but they do happen to most web designers at some point or other. If your client disagrees with something you've done, try not to get defensive. Remember that the site is theirs, and that they understand their business and its needs better than you do. If you don't think their idea will get the best results for the project or their business, explain it in those terms—"This is what I think will achieve the most conversions for your website and this is why," rather than "I've designed hundreds of websites and I know what works." For a definitive guide to working well with clients and avoiding conflict, you could do a lot worse than reading Paul Boag's *Client Centric Web Design*, or see his blog at `http://boagworld.com`.

- **Managing your team.** If you are working with a team of designers or developers, whether you personally employ them or not, you need to effectively communicate with them. At a minimum they need to know the following:

  - What you are hiring them to do

  - Your expectations in terms of quality and working style (e.g., how they code, what browsers or devices they should use for testing)

  - Deliverables and deadlines

  - The consequences of not delivering

  It's important to build a solid relationship with your team if you want them to give you their best work—especially when the team is made up of your own employees, who you want to feel a real sense of loyalty toward your agency. Part of your management effort may also include occasions when they don't deliver work on time or to standard, or when they're unavailable.

There is a reason why you can find plenty of resources out there to help you manage and communicate with a team: It's crucial to the success of your agency. We've listed some of these, along with other relevant resources, in the "Additional Resources" section at the end of this chapter.

Planning and Project Management Skills

This is a biggie! If you will be managing large-scale web development projects, and hopefully more than one at a time, you need to plan thoroughly and hone your project management skills.

The strongest technical skills and the smoothest relationships with your clients and your team won't offset a lack of planning and effective project management. Managing large projects with teams of developers means spending a lot of your time doing the following:

- **Planning projects.** Large-scale web development projects need to have a project plan. Depending on your preferences and experience, you have a few options for creating this: project management software, a simple spreadsheet, or an online project management and collaboration tool. Whatever you choose, you need a plan that at the very least specifies the following:

  - What needs to be done

  - Who needs to do it

  - When it must be completed

    In addition, you might include dependencies—stages of a project that can't start until another one is compete (for example, you can't add content to a site until your client has provided it).

    Make sure all stakeholders, including everyone with tasks to perform (and their managers if relevant), have provided their input to the plan and are committed to completing their actions within the deadlines agreed upon. Don't just sit down and write a plan yourself and expect everyone to stick to it—check everyone's availability before selecting any deadlines.

- **Monitoring progress.** As the project progresses, you need to keep on top of things. Check progress against deliverables and milestones on a regular basis—not just your own actions. If a delay seems likely, talk to the people involved to determine what can be done to get back on track. Do this as early as possible to avoid renegotiating deadlines when milestones aren't met because problems were communicated with only a few days left to deal with them.

- **Communicating progress to stakeholders.** Make sure anyone involved with the project knows what is expected of them next and what they can expect from you. This applies particularly to the client, who is likely to be focused on other things—for example, when sending the client work for review, specify the date by which you expect their feedback.

  If you suspect that the client may struggle to complete necessary tasks, make success more likely by scheduling time to work with them on site. For example, schedule meetings to plan the site's content together and agree how it will be structured, rather than expect them to do it in a vacuum. Most clients will appreciate your expertise about planning website content and find that this starting point makes it easier for them to complete the work.

- **Dealing with problems or delays.** Most large website builds come up against a problem at some point. Try to spot problems early and have the courage to deal with them, rather than hope they'll go away. That way, they'll remain small problems instead of turning into messy, large ones.

  - If you think you or your team won't be able to meet a deadline, deal with it early—either find a way to meet it by bringing in more resources, or negotiate the deadline or deliverables with the client well in advance.

- If the client changes their mind about something, use your communication skills to work out the best solution collaboratively. Avoid potential issues related to extra work by including a clause in your contract clearly stating what happens if the project brief changes along the way.

- If you suspect that a senior manager in the client organization is not entirely positive about the project, try to have a conversation about what you're trying to achieve in terms that make sense to him or her. Ask for any objections and concerns, and be able to demonstrate how you're addressing them. Try to ensure that all senior stakeholders have input early on, so they don't have it later by changing everything!

- If the client asks you to do something not outlined in the brief, explain that you can do so but only after the current project is complete. Put the new request on a wish list that you can review with the client later and agree on deadlines and costs.

Problem-Solving Skills

Creating a website for a client is a form of problem-solving. They have a problem (typically, not having as many customers as they'd like), and you are brought in to help them solve it. Any effective website will be an answer to a problem, rather than an end in itself, and the site needs to evolve and grow to continually address that problem throughout its lifetime—a good reason to use WordPress, whose flexibility enables a site to grow after launch.

All the areas we've already discussed involve solving problems—such as dealing with delays or disagreements—but the very process of designing and developing sites, themes, or plugins for clients involves problem-solving skills. If you get into this mindset of viewing your job as solving a problem, you can create solutions that truly benefit your clients, whether they're hiring you to build them a website or buying themes or plugins from you.

Before planning any project, consider what problems it has to address. What are the objectives? What does the client want people to do when they visit the site? What do the visitors expect when they are navigating the site? What does success look like?

This approach applies on both a large scale, when looking at a site's overall objectives, and on a small scale, when deciding exactly how to approach a given part of the site. For example, suppose the client wants to sell something online. Do they need a full-blown e-commerce solution, a subscription-based site, or a simple form linked to PayPal? In order to provide the client with the best solution, you first need to understand the client's problem (goal) and what they need to achieve.

Developing Your WordPress Skills: It Never Stops

You've already learned about some of the ways you can develop your WordPress skills by getting involved in the WordPress community. As someone selling WordPress services to others, be they clients or other WordPress users, you need to remember the following important point: Keep developing—continually. WordPress (like web design and development in general) never stands still—ongoing releases and updates mean you need to keep current with changes to the platform itself. In addition, methods for working with WordPress and extending it are constantly developing, so in order to remain competitive you have to keep up.

Set aside time every day, or at least every week, to learn about WordPress developments or techniques. Some of this time should be spent reading blogs, magazines, and journals to keep abreast of new developments, while some time should be spent expanding the range of WordPress skills in your armory.

Identify any gaps in your skills and the areas you need to improve on in order to win the kind of contracts you want, meet your clients' needs better, expand your services, or simply feel more confident in your own ability. Identify experts in those areas and follow their blogs or articles. Buy, read, and work through the growing library of WordPress books. Follow the blog at http://make.wordpress.org to keep abreast of changes, updates, and issues.

Set aside a budget for your own (and your team's) development. This should include money for books, conferences, and other events. As well as a monetary budget, you'll need a time allocation. When do you learn best—reading RSS feeds and blogs over your cornflakes, poring over a book in the wee small hours, or experimenting with new technologies at a hackday? Identify your own style and then block out some suitable time.

There will inevitably be occasions when personal development has to take a back seat to client work—if your business is successful, you'll struggle to juggle these. Don't let these periods of time last too long. If you get out of the habit of developing your WordPress skills and knowledge, you'll start to lose your edge—and if you lose your expertise, you'll start losing potential clients.

I recommend that every WordPress professional attend at least one WordCamp every year. This is where you'll meet other like-minded developers, pick up new techniques, make contact with potential partners, clients, or staff, and get out from behind your desk and mix with some real people.

Giving Something Back to the WordPress Community

Becoming a WordPress professional isn't just about filthy lucre. Because WordPress is an open-source platform, its continued evolution and success depends on a broad, highly committed community of developers who contribute to WordPress in a variety of ways.

Becoming part of this community helps you develop your WordPress skills, network with other WordPress developers, and raise your profile in the community. It also helps WordPress to evolve so that it continues to meet the needs of users, designers, and developers—including you!

Contributing to the Development of WordPress

WordPress has a team of core developers, but they aren't the only people involved—hundreds of developers contribute code, without whom WordPress couldn't survive. Areas you can contribute to include the following:

- Submitting patches
- Raising tickets
- Contributing to UI and design development
- Translating WordPress
- Reviewing themes

If you are going to be involved in core development, we recommend taking some time to understand what's involved and what's expected. Talk to other WordPress contributors if you can, or ask questions on the Make WordPress site at http://make.wordpress.org. The site also describes how to contribute, including detailed guidelines on submitting patches.

Testing

In addition to needing developers to contribute to WordPress core, WordPress also seeks people to help with testing. This isn't limited to developers. To get started, you need to install the WordPress beta tester plugin and set it up to work with one of two types of build—point release nightlies or bleeding edge nightlies. Point release nightlies tend to be more stable, and are useful for testing your own themes and plugins against beta versions of WordPress, while bleeding edge nightlies represent the very latest code and are what you would use as a WordPress tester.

You can also report bugs you find while testing beta versions of WordPress or already released versions.

Writing Free Plugins and Themes

Writing code for release to the public is a great way to develop your WordPress skills, even if you've never written a plugin or theme in your life. By making your code available free on the WordPress repository, you are helping other developers and giving them the opportunity to contribute to and improve your code, which helps you learn.

If you're a theme developer, why not try releasing a free plugin? Similarly, plugin developers can extend their knowledge by creating a theme. Other developers will help you to improve upon what you've written, and it gives you a chance to work with WordPress from a new angle.

> **This book has a whole chapter dedicated to releasing your code to the public (both free and paid). If this is something you want to do, take a look at Chapter 12.**

Contributing to the WordPress Website

The content of the WordPress site at `http://wordpress.org` is contributed by developers just like you, and if you're good at answering questions or decsribing how code works, you can help.

Contributing to the Codex

The Codex (`http://codex.wordpress.org`) is the place most WordPress users and developers go to for information on how WordPress works. You can volunteer to contribute to the WordPress Codex, helping to improve the quality of the documentation. As WordPress evolves, there will always be functions and features that need documenting, or you could improve, add to, or update existing documentation. To find out how to get involved, see `http://codex.wordpress.org/Codex:Contributing`.

WordPress Support Forums

Open-source communities depend on the active participation of their members. If you know the answer to a question that another user has posted on a forum, please add your reply; it could help many other developers. You can use tags to access forum threads on a specific topic that you have expertise in—for example, if you're a CSS developer, visit `http://wordpress.org/tags/css` to find questions you might be able to answer.

Getting Involved in WordPress Groups or WordCamps

Local WordPress Groups and WordCamps are an invaluable source of support, informaiotn and advice for WordPress users and developers. Around the world, people meet up to talk about WordPress, to hear about techniques from speakers, and to discuss the work they're doing with WordPress—as well as to make friends!

Helping with Organization

If you've got experience of organizing events, or you'd like to have a go, you can volunteer to help organize your local WordPress group of the WordCamp in your country or region. Taking on this role will introduce you to a broad community of other WordPress users and developers, and you will gain a lot of respect and gratitude from your peers. But most importantly, it could mean an event can take place in your locality that otherwise wouldn't—which will benefit many WordPress developers and users.

You can find out more about becoming a WordCamp organizer at `http://central.wordcamp.org/become-an-organizer/`.

Contributing as a Speaker

If you have WordPress knowledge or experience that others could find useful and you don't mind talking in front of an audience, speaking at a WordCamp is a great way to share your expertise, learn from other participants and speakers, and get some public speaking experience in front of a generally friendly audience. I've done this and gained a lot from it.

How much and exactly what you're able to take on will depend on your experience, areas of expertise, and availability, but getting involved in the WordPress community is a great thing to do if you are truly serious about using the platform. By being connected in this way, you'll learn about the latest developments in WordPress itself, you'll meet people from whom you can learn a huge amount and with whom you may be able to work in the future; and you'll be introduced to a potential source of WordPress developers you can later hire when you need more resources.

The Potential for Professional WordPress Development

At this point, we've already established that WordPress isn't just for bloggers anymore; it's a fully fledged, grown-up web development tool being used across the board—from the smallest of startups to major multinational corporations.

As a WordPress developer, however, you need to understand just how you can harness WordPress to meet your clients' needs and help them build their business, as well as your own. This is about more than simply building custom WordPress sites, or developing themes or plugins. It's about understanding the benefits that WordPress can bring to your clients, and being able to communicate this in language that makes sense to them—in plain English.

It's also about recognizing opportunities and gaps in the market, particularly if you're developing themes or plugins—if you fill a niche, you'll be much more successful than if you produce yet another Twitter plugin.

Harnessing WordPress As a CMS

At some point, a client will utter those dreaded words:

"WordPress – but I thought that was just for blogs?"

Resist the temptation to groan or roll your eyes in mockery. Unfortunately, WordPress is still perceived as a tool used exclusively by mommy bloggers and geeks to fill the Internet with personal impressions and ideas (not that we have anything against anyone doing that!). In order to sell WordPress to your clients, you need to be ready to explain that WordPress is much more than that. In particular, you need to develop arguments supporting the use of WordPress as a CMS—indeed, that it's in fact better than any custom CMS another agency may try to sell them.

The obvious arguments are about WordPress's development and credibility:

- WordPress is used by major organizations with huge, complex sites containing data they absolutely don't want to lose, such as CNN, the Daily Telegraph, and more. For some great examples, see the showcase page on the WordPress site at `http://wordpress.org/showcase/`.

- WordPress is much more secure than many people assume, and it can be made more secure. It is used by organizations and public entities that go to great lengths to avoid being hacked—1600 Pennsylvania Avenue and 10 Downing Street, anyone?

- As a tool used by thousands of developers, WordPress is a platform your client can stick with even if you stop working with them. Don't be afraid to tell your clients this; we believe that reassuring your clients that their site can be developed by another developer or agency in the future enhances their trust in both WordPress and you. If you have ever had a client who was switching from their old agency's custom CMS and could no longer update their site, you'll know how much of a problem this can be.

As well as the arguments in favor of WordPress, you should also be prepared to explain your ability to modify WordPress for your client's specific scenario, effectively turning it into a custom CMS but without the drawbacks:

- You can configure the WordPress installation to increase its security and avoid any potential problems related to hacking or server problems.

- You can structure the site content in any way the client needs using custom post types, taxonomies, and fields, resulting in a unique site that is very different from standard WordPress.

- You can design and code a custom layout and design that is in harmony with the client's branding, it can be as innovative as necessary, and it doesn't need to have a traditional blog layout unless they want that.

- You can add plugins, scripts, and more to the site to give it extra functionality, creating a better user experience—changing the site from one that merely enables users to consume content to one that encourages them to interact with the site in new ways.

- You can customize the WordPress admin to make editing and managing the site quick and easy for the client, to point them in the direction of the relevant content and to reflect their brand if necessary.

- You can configure the client's site to be lean and fast to load, stripping out unwanted functionality and using caching and other techniques to improve performance.

- You can install and configure SEO plugins (and teach your client to do so), which will enhance the site's search engine rankings.

- You can create a responsive site or web app for your client, providing them with another way to reach and potentially sell to their customers.

Of course, you may not be able to do all these things—yet. Nonetheless, they represent a cross-section of the ways in which you can push, stretch, and customize WordPress—and you will be able to do them after you've finished this book!

WordPress for SEO and Site Conversions

Developing a fabulous site won't help your client much if people can't find it. This is obviously essential for a business—attracting the right customers to a site will increase the amount of sales. But even sites that don't sell anything or offer a service, such as community sites, need to attract the right visitors in order to be successful, as their purpose is to spread information or affect public opinion.

Some clients will have their own techniques for pulling visitors to their site, but the majority will be reliant on search engines, via either organic search (i.e., free) or fee-based search listings such as Google AdWords.

The great news is that WordPress gives you and your clients a head start in Search Engine Optmization(SEO). This isn't just about the use of plugins:

- WordPress (when paired with a well-written theme) uses valid, standards-compliant code, which is a fundamental starting point for SEO as well as for good web development.

- If you write your theme in HTML5 (which you should), you'll have access to semantic elements that help search engines index your code.

- WordPress can be configured to be fast, using off-the-shelf plugins and your own customization.

- WordPress automatically generates search-engine-friendly page titles based on your site title and page or post title.

- Permalinks can be configured to enhance URLs within the site for an SEO boost.

- The image uploader makes adding `<alt>` tags and titles for images easy, which enhances not only SEO but also accessibility.

- By installing a plugin such as SEO by Yoast, you or your client can specify titles and descriptions site-wide or for individual pages or posts, and analyze how well a page is likely to perform.

- Other plugins let you link a Google analytics account to the site, displaying statistics in the dashboard that clients can view every time they work on the site.

Developing Themes and Plugins You Can Sell

Using WordPress to build sites for clients is just one way to make a living from the platform. You could also develop plugins or themes that you can then sell to other WordPress users.

This isn't as easy as you might think. A lot of people are reluctant to part with their hard-earned cash for themes, frameworks, or plugins when so many are available free. If you hope to make any sales, you have to offer something that is of very high quality, gives developers or users something they really need, and fills a need not currently being met by another product. You may have a great idea for a Twitter plugin, for example, but with so many already available, is it really a good idea to put all your efforts into competing in such an overcrowded market?

To make a success of this, you need to do your R&D first:

- Research the market. Does your idea fill a gap or provide something that is of considerably higher quality than what's already out there?

- Talk to developers and users, and find out what they want from a plugin or theme like yours. Identify influential WordPress bloggers and experts and ask them for their views. If they like what they see they may recommend it to their followers.

- If you are developing a theme, research the avenues for selling them. The easiest way is via a large theme vendor. If you go that route, find out what percentage of your sales they take and the price of similar themes.

- If you're developing a plugin, you'll have to find your own ways of marketing it and making it available. You might consider releasing a free version on the WordPress plugin repository, with a premium version for people who want extra features. Take care to make your free version useful to a respectable proportion of your audience, however, or you may inspire frustration instead of a loyal following.

- If you're developing a framework, you need to familiarize yourself with those already available. Until you understand what they do and how they work, you can't offer something new to fulfill a different need.

You also need to think about the way you build your product:

- It nearly goes without saying that your code must be reliable, bug free, compatible with the latest release of WordPress (and ideally the previous release too), accessible, and standards compliant.

- Consider the number of options you'll make available via the WordPress admin. Buyers of premium themes and plugins expect to be able to make their own customizations. You can also provide developers with documentation on customizing the code.

- If you're building a premium product, other developers won't help you improve upon and develop it (unlike a free one). You'll need to budget for the time or expense of doing this, and make updates available when new versions of WordPress are released.

- Ensure that your plugin or theme is robust and not liable to hacking—you don't want to be responsible for hundreds of WordPress sites going down because of a vulnerability in your code!

There's a lot more to think about and take into consideration when developing themes, frameworks, or plugins for release or sale. For more details, see Chapter 12, "Releasing Your Code to the Public."

Summary

Hopefully I've convinced any skeptics out there that WordPress is a great platform on which to build a business. It's evolved way beyond its humble beginnings as a blogging platform, and now offers the capable developer myriad ways to extend, push, and customize it to power large, complex sites that would be hardly recognizable as a typical WordPress site.

As a web development professional, you can use WordPress to develop websites for a range of clients, as well as release and maybe sell products that will help other users and developers to extend and work with WordPress themselves, in the form of plugins and themes.

WordPress is at a hugely exciting stage in its development, and it's rapidly becoming the mainstream CMS of choice for clients, developers, and users. If you're ready to take advantage of WordPress, there's a lot you need to learn, so read on…

Further Resources

Professional WordPress Development

"How to become a top WordPress developer"
`http://wp.smashingmagazine.com/2012/08/23/how-to-become-a-top-wordpress-developer/`

"Do's and don'ts for WordPress startups"
`http://wp.smashingmagazine.com/2012/06/21/dos-donts-wordpress-startups/`

Client Centric Web Design by Paul Boag (Boagworld)
`http://amzn.com/B007QUTLQ6`

How to Start Your Own Business for Entrepreneurs by Robert Ashton (Pearson Business, 2012)
`http://www.amazon.co.uk/dp/0273772171`

Coding Practices

W3C validator
`http://validator.w3.org`

Web standards project
`http://webstandards.org`

Web accessibility standards
`http://www.w3.org/WAI/`

WordPress coding standards
`http://codex.wordpress.org/WordPress_Coding_Standards`

WordPress guidance on validating your site
`http://codex.wordpress.org/Validating_a_Website`

Designing with Web Standards by Jeffrey Zeldman and Ethan Marcotte (Voices That Matter)
`http://amazon.com/0735712018`

"Top 15 Best Practices for Writing Super Readable Code"
`http://net.tutsplus.com/tutorials/html-css-techniques/top-15-best-practices-for-writing-super-readable-code/`

Giving Something Back to the WordPress Community

Contributing to WordPress
http://wordpress.org/Contributing_to_WordPress
http://make.wordpress.org

Aaron Campbell and Andy Stratton on getting involved (video)
http://wordpress.tv/2011/09/08/aaron-campbell-and-andy-stratton-getting-involved-contribution-and-courtesy/

WordPress Core Contributor Handbook
http://make.wordpress.org/core/handbook/

Guide to WordPress beta testing
http://make.wordpress.org/core/handbook/beta-testing/

WordPress beta tester plugin
http://wordpress.org/extend/plugins/wordpress-beta-tester/

WordCamps
http://central.wordcamp.org

WordPress meetups
http://wordpress.meetup.com

The WordPress Codex
http://codex.wordpress.org

WordPress support forums
http://wordpress.org/support/

WordPress trac
http://core.trac.wordpress.org

WordPress support forums
http://wordpress.org/support

Make WordPress site
http://make.wordpress.org

Developing Your WordPress Skills

WordPress TV: Videos from WordCamps and other events
http://wordpress.tv

WordPress blog
http://wordpress.org/news/

The WordPress Codex
http://codex.wordpress.org

Smashing Magazine's WordPress section
`http://wp.smashingmagazine.com`

Roundup of professional WordPress development tools
`http://wp.tutsplus.com/articles/general/professional-wordpress-development-tools-2/`

WordPress for SEO

All in One SEO Pack plugin
`http://wordpress.org/extend/plugins/all-in-one-seo-pack`

SEO by Yoast plugin
`http://wordpress.org/extend/plugins/wordpress-seo`

WordPress SEO tutorial
`http://yoast.com/articles/wordpress-seo`

Developing Themes and Plugins You Can Sell

Professional WordPress Plugin Development by Brad Williams, Ozh Richard, and Justin Tadlock (Wrox, 2011)
`http://amazon.com/0470916222`

WordPress Plugin Developer Center
`http://wordpress.org/extend/plugins/about/`

Theme review guidelines
`http://codex.wordpress.org/Theme_Review`

Chapter 2

Kicking Off a WordPress Project

So, you've landed a plum WordPress project or you have big plans for a personal project that's going to make your fortune. The way you get started will have a huge impact on the success of your project, the satisfaction of your client, or the number of sales you make.

Before diving into code or opening a design tool, you need to spend time setting the project up and communicating to all stakeholders what will happen and what's expected. You also need to set up your development environment, agree where the development site will be hosted, and configure WordPress for your client and team.

You need to take time to consider the site content and how best to display and structure that content—for example, by identifying areas of the site that need to a different layout. You need to identify where you plan to use custom post types and taxonomies, and then proof them for reuse, so if clients or users add more content later (and you hope they will), it will be displayed as beautifully as the content added during the site build.

This chapter describes the necessary aspects of starting a project, including all the preliminary research you should do before embarking on the site build and a detailed checklist of tasks to complete.

> **Getting started on a project to develop your own themes or plugins entails some extra steps—I cover these in detail in Chapter 12.**

Setting Up Development Hosting and Domains

The first step is to set up your development installation of WordPress. You want to put a system in place that both works for you and your team and enables the client to review the site as you go along. If you're working closely with the client, this review may be continuous, not just at key stages.

Selecting the Best Hosting and Domain Setup for Your Project

Consider whether you want to use a local development installation or a remote one; and if you use a remote one, determine where to host it. Table 2-1 shows the pros and cons of each development option.

Table 2-1: Development Options

Option	Pros	Cons
Local installation	This option is the fastest and easiest to work with and doesn't require an Internet connection. It's also the most secure—barring a lost or stolen machine, no one will see your work until you're ready to put it online.	If multiple team members are working on the site and can't access the same local installation, there could be versioning problems. Clients won't be able to see progress as you work on the site.
Remote installation on the client's server	Some clients may require this because they are more comfortable with the security or accessibility of their own server. Migration is easier because the site is being developed in the same environment it will be hosted on at launch (assuming it will be hosted on the client's server). It's easy for clients to see progress (although this does run the risk that they could look at the site when you don't want them to, e.g., if it's temporarily broken).	You have no control over access to the server. You may need to jump through some access or security hoops with the client to be able to set up a development installation of WordPress (although you may have to do this later anyway). You have to ensure that security measures are in place to prevent members of the public from accidentally landing on the development site when browsing the client's existing live site.
Remote installation on your server	You have control over the environment in which the site is installed. All members of the team can access the site, and so can the client. You can control the client's access to the site. Useful when the client doesn't have an existing site or server and you are in the process of setting this up for them.	You have to put in place security measures to ensure that members of the public don't inadvertently access the site. The client may be less comfortable with the security or privacy of the site.

Your approach will likely vary according to the nature of the project. In scenarios in which a team is working on a project, working remotely on your own server is the easiest way to give everyone access while retaining full control. Conversely, when only one individual is working on a project, it might be best to develop locally, uploading the site at key stages to show colleagues or the client. The right approach for the project should be agreed upon by all parties involved—you, your team, and your client.

What's important is finding a balance between making development as smooth as possible for you and your team and meeting any client concerns about access to the site, ownership of content, and security.

Agreeing What to Put in Place During Development

As part of the initial planning phase, you and the client need to agree about exactly what should be put in place during development. This includes considerations such as the following:

▪ Setting up a holding or teaser page, to act as a preview of the new site, to provide contact and other information and to gather data about potential customers. Setting up teaser pages is covered in more detail in the next section.

- If the client has an existing site, do they want a teaser page for the new site or are they happy keeping their old site live? This will depend on the quality of their old site and the reason they are developing a new one—for example, if their business has changed significantly they may prefer to use a teaser page to provide information about their new venture and to gather data about prospective customers.

- How will you approach revision control? Options include using Subversion, Git, or making backups of theme files and the database at key stages. Subversion is covered in more detail in Chapter 12, and Git is covered in Chapter 3.

- How do you want to give the client access to the site? Some plugins allow you to create a "secret" URL for the client to access a protected site without logging in, which makes life easier for clients. Alternatively, if you want to track client activity on the site, you may need to set up a user account for the client organization or individual members of staff. In our experience, clients are sometimes irritated by this need to log in to view their site, and it does increase the risk of an inexperienced client accessing the admin screens and doing something to break the site. (Of course, they will deny doing this strenuously and expect you to fix the problem!) If the site is on the client's own server, they may have their own methods for setting up access to directories on that server, which could provide automatic access to users accessing the site from their network or IP address, for example.

SEO During Site Development

If your client has an existing domain with no content or a site they want to take down during development, you need to proactively prevent any negative impact on the site's search engine optimization (SEO).

If you remove all the existing content and simply replace it with a holding page, any internal links will break—both for humans and for search engines. It won't take long for SEO rankings to start to slide, and for human visitors to become irritated. In addition, if you are developing the site on the same domain and haven't properly set up privacy, there is a risk that someone accessing a broken link will find themselves on the 404 page in the development site—not something you want to happen!

A better alternative is to add a temporary redirect to your holding page from all other pages. To do this, you need to create a 503 page, as a 503 error tells search engines (and humans) that the site is temporarily unavailable. This means that search engines won't crawl your site while it's down, but nor will they drop it from search results.

> **Warning:** Avoid keeping a 503 error message up for too long on a site. Eventually, search engines will interpret this to mean that the site is permanently unavailable and stop indexing it.

Setting Up a 503 'Service Unavailable' Status

The simplest way to do this on a WordPress site is by using a plugin. Plugins such as Site Maintenance (`http://wordpress.org/extend/plugins/wet-maintenance/`) and Ultimate Coming Soon (`http://wordpress.org/extend/plugins/ultimate-coming-soon-page/`) include the option to set up a 503 redirect, which directs visitors to your teaser page and informs search engines that the site is temporarily unavailable and has not disappeared in a puff of smoke.

What if you don't want to use a plugin, or you're developing a teaser page or site outside of WordPress? It's still pretty simple—follow these steps:

1. Create a blank file called `503.php` in the root directory of your domain.

2. Type the following code into the blank file:

```php
<?php
    header("HTTP/1.1 503 Service Temporarily Unavailable");
    header("status: 503 Service temporarily Unavailable");
    header("Retry-After: Mon 1 April 2013 00:00 GMT");
?>
```

The preceding code tells search engines that the site is temporarily unavailable and specifies when to crawl the site again. This information is output in the HTTP response headers before any page content is returned and won't be visible to visitors.

3. Open the `.htaccess` file in your root directory (if you don't have one, create one), and add the following to it:

```
<IfModule mod_rewrite.c>
ErrorDocument 503 /503.php
RewriteEngine on
RewriteBase /
RewriteCond %{ENV:REDIRECT_STATUS} !=503
RewriteCond %{REMOTE_HOST} !^111\.111\.111\.111$
RewriteCond %{REQUEST_URI} !robots\.txt$ [NC]
RewriteRule ^ - [L,R=503]
</IfModule>
```

4. Save both files and access your site in a browser. You will see a blank screen.

5. You need to tell visitors what's going on. To do this, simply add some markup to the `503.php` file, such as the following:

```html
<!DOCTYPE HTML>
<html>
<head>
<title>Error 503 service temporarily unavailable</title>
</head>
<body>
<h1>This site is being redeveloped</h1>
<p>Please come back soon to see our fabulous new site!</p>
</body>
</html>
```

6. Save the file, return to your site, and refresh the browser. You'll now see something more useful, as shown in Figure 2-1.

Figure 2-1 The 503 message

Using Teaser Pages and Gathering Data Prior to Launch

A 503 page is all very well but it won't do much to enhance the client's brand or encourage visitors to come back when the site is live. For clients who don't have an existing site they want to keep in place, or for a new product launch, a *teaser site* or *teaser page* is a great way to give visitors advance notice about what's coming, and to gather data that you or your client can use to drive traffic to the site following launch and communicate directly with prospects.

There are two approaches to developing a teaser site:

- Build a completely separate site to host on the client's domain during development, using either a simple WordPress installation or a collection of one or a few static pages of HTML.
- Use a WordPress plugin to display a teaser page.

Determining which approach to take depends on a few factors:

- **Budget**—How much does your client have to spend on the teaser site? If it's an important part of their marketing campaign, they may have the budget for a standalone WordPress site; but if they have little or no budget for this, a static page or a plugin will be the better approach.
- **Hosting**—If you have access to the client's domain and hosting, then installing WordPress and making use a of a plugin is a possibility. If you don't have these yet, you may need to create a static page and send the HTML file for this, plus the stylesheet and any images, to the client's IT department to upload to their server.
- **Time**—If you have little time to create a teaser site (a factor probably linked to the budget), then the plugin approach is the quickest.
- **Branding**—If the client has an existing brand with design elements, including possibly a logo, then any of the preceding options are possible. If the client hasn't developed their branding yet, or you're doing it for them, then it will be difficult to style a standalone site, in which case using a plugin is likely the most effective option.
- **Visitors**—If the domain is already getting a steady stream of visitors, it's essential to provide them with something both useful and of high quality. Most clients will want to gather data about those visitors, tell them when the new site goes live, and be able to add them to their mailing list, in which case the best approach is a WordPress site with a contact form or a plugin that includes data gathering.

Installing and Configuring a Teaser Page Plugin

The teaser page plugin I tend to use is called Ultimate Coming Soon (`http://wordpress.org/extend/plugins/ultimate-coming-soon-page/`). Both a free version and a paid version are available—it's worth upgrading to the paid version if you will be creating a lot of teaser pages, as it includes advanced features for styling the teaser page and gives you the option to create a special URL for clients so they can review their development site without having to log in to WordPress.

In this section you work with the free version of the plugin, which still gives you a perfectly adequate teaser page.

Install the plugin using your preferred method—either via upload or using Plugins➪Add New in the WordPress admin. The plugin is configured via a screen in the Settings menu. The configuration options for the plugin are fairly straightforward, especially for the free version, which doesn't have too many. Here are some of the more interesting options:

- **Email signup**—With the free version, this is possible only using the FeedBurner address for your RSS feed:

  1. For this example test site, a feed was set up at FeedBurner and named appropriately. You can do this by visiting `http://feedburner.google.com` and entering your feed address, as shown in Figure 2-2. Your RSS feed address is normally `http://siteaddress.com /?feed=rss2`.

Figure 2-2 Setting up the feed in FeedBurner

  2. For the notifications to work, you need to set up e-mail notifications in FeedBurner. Click the Publicize tab near the top of the FeedBurner screen, and then click the Email Subscriptions link in the left side menu to see the dialog shown in Figure 2-3.

  3. Click the Activate button. FeedBurner will present you with the Subscription Management page, which is designed for users who are pasting a FeedBurner widget into their website. As this doesn't apply here, just click Save to finish this step.

Figure 2-3 Adding e-mail subscriptions in FeedBurner

4. Back in the Coming Soon screen in your site's WordPress admin, type the last part of the FeedBurner address for your feed in the Feed Address field—in this case it's **WordPressPushingTheLimits**. Click the Save Changes button.

5. When visitors sign up for the e-mail notification, they will see a pop-up from FeedBurner asking them to complete a CAPTCHA form, as shown in Figure 2-4, after which they will receive an e-mail with a verification link. Assuming they click that link to verify their subscription, they will automatically receive an e-mail notification when you turn the Coming Soon plugin off and make the site live.

Figure 2-4 The FeedBurner e-mail subscription request pop-up

If you select the premium version of the plugin, you also have the option to link the notifications to your preferred e-mail service, which is useful if your client is already using a service such as MailChimp, AWeber, or CampaignMonitor for their e-mail list. In that case, you don't need to set up a feed in FeedBurner, but instead need to link the plugin to the e-mail service account.

- **Custom HTML**—You can add whatever custom HTML you want to the Coming Soon page. For example, to add a link to a Facebook page that the client might be using to communicate with customers while the site is down, add code similar to the following:

```
<a href="http://facebook.com/yourpage">
  <img class="fb-logo" src="http://example.com/
  wp-content/uploads/2012/11/facebook-logo.jpg" />
</a>
```

This displays a Facebook logo link to visitors, as shown in Figure 2-5.

Figure 2-5 Visitors will see a link to the client's Facebook page

- **Custom CSS and images**—The current teaser page is functional, but a bit drab. You have the option to upload a background image and a logo, which will be displayed above the heading. You can also customize the CSS from the Settings screen and add custom CSS if you wish. After uploading a background image, the following code sets the text color to white, adds a font for the heading from the available list (which is sourced from Google fonts), and adds some custom CSS:

```
p#teaser-description {
background-color: rgba(0, 0, 0, 0.4)
}
a:link, a:visited {
color: #ccc;
}
a:hover, a:active {
color: #fff;
}
```

The resulting teaser page, shown in Figure 2-6, may not be a work of art, but at least it now looks a little more distinctive.

Figure 2-6 The customized teaser page

The options you can tweak with the free version of the plugin have the capability to quickly create a professional-looking teaser page with data capture. The premium version offers additional options to make your teaser pages work harder, such as the following:

- Integrate with e-mail services such as MailChimp, CampaignMonitor, and Aweber.

- Set a "secret" URL for clients to view the site, or specific IP addresses that display the development site instead of the teaser page.

- Include the `<head>` code required to provide search engines with a 503 status.

- Embed photos from Flickr or videos from YouTube—the latter can be an effective way to increase engagement with the site prior to launch. However, there's no reason you couldn't do this with the custom HTML in the free version.

- Offer an incentive such as a free eBook or PDF for visitors who sign up for e-mail notifications.

- Add a countdown timer to launch.

Content Planning and Structure

Now that you and your client have agreed upon where the development site will be hosted and what will be put in place while it's being developed, the next, and crucial, step is to plan the content.

It's tempting to jump straight into installing WordPress and firing up a code editor, or into designing the site layout, without taking the time to consider what the site should contain. Avoid that temptation. Keep in mind that a website's success depends on its content, so you need a very solid understanding of what content will be displayed on the site, how it will be structured, and how users will interact with it.

A thorough understanding of the content requirements will help you plan the site's structure and determine which WordPress content types you will use (such as custom post types and taxonomies). Getting this right at the beginning of the project will save countless headaches and the risk of rework later.

Identifying How to Structure Content: Questions for Clients

When first meeting with clients, some will not have given much thought to the site's content yet, whereas others will have a detailed content plan. Either way, there are specific questions you can ask that will help you work together to ensure both that the correct content is added and that it is displayed in a manner that works best for the client and the site users. This also makes the site build smoother and quicker, and the site itself faster.

▪ **What are the site objectives and how will the content help to meet them?** Before you can determine the site's content, you need to know what the website hopes to achieve. Ask your client why they want a website. If the answer is vague ("To get more customers," for example), ask probing questions to get more specific answers. What sort of customers do they want? What do they want those customers to do on the site? How many customers do they need? Are they reaching out to existing customers or targeting a new group of people?

▪ **What do site visitors expect? How does this overlap with the client's objectives?** E-commerce sites are a great example of how the user's objectives and the owner's objectives are different but overlap. On Amazon, for example, many users access the site to buy books; but Amazon would like you to also buy a Kindle, or stock up on household items, clothes, or gifts. Figure 2-7 provides hardly any clues to Amazon's beginning as a bookseller, and the site's design highlights the diversity of products available, making it very easy for you to view and buy them.

Your client may have a new product or service that they want to encourage visitors to buy or contact them about—something that may be different from what visitors are expecting. If you understand this, you can ensure that the design, layout, and content meet the client's objectives while not making things too unfamiliar or difficult for visitors.

▪ **Who is the target audience?** The answer to this will influence the kind of content needed and its tone. Different audiences will have different expectations in terms of ease of navigation, tone of voice, and quantity of content, such as a site for professional programmers versus a site for bank customers.

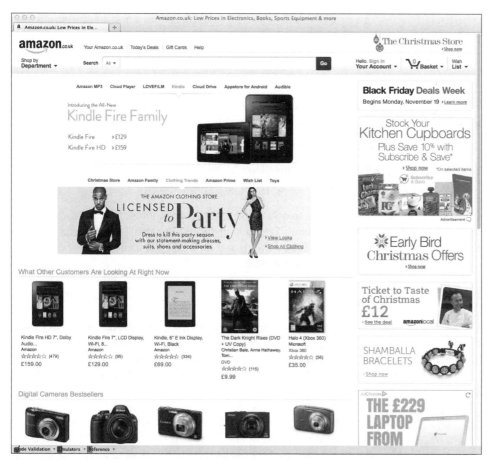

Figure 2-7 Amazon would like to sell us more than books!

- **How is the content structured?** This is crucial to a smooth site build. If your client wants to showcase products or case studies, you will need a custom post type for them. If these custom post types need to be categorized in the same way as each other, this will affect the taxonomies you set up—sometimes one for each custom post type, sometimes one for multiple post types.

  As part of the content planning, be sure to identify what content type(s) will apply to it. When planning a site, consider creating a spreadsheet with the following columns:

  - Page (this refers to a web page, not a WordPress page)
  - Level in navigation/hierarchy
  - Section(s) of site
  - Content type (page, post, custom post type, attachment, or archive—in which case archive of what post type)
  - Content summary

- Content to be generated by (this can include responsibilities for the content or a note indicating where the content will be generated automatically)
- Deadline for content generation
- Deadline for page creation

- **Where is content coming from?** Obviously, you need to identify who is generating site-specific content, but you also need to identify any content that is generated elsewhere or already exists. For example:
  - If there is an existing site, what content is being used from it, and will it be edited first?
  - Is any content being pulled in from external sources such as social media or RSS feeds?
  - Does content need to be obtained from third parties? If so, what permissions are needed?

Asking your client these questions will enable you to determine exactly what content to expect and from where. In particular, clients with an existing site should be thinking about the extent to which they want to change, restructure, and update their content. Even if they're not replacing the content, a new website design is a good opportunity to overhaul what's already there.

Planning Content Generation

One of the most common causes of delays to a site build is generating content. Clients may underestimate the amount of work involved in creating or writing content and how long this will take them. You need to work content generation into your project plan with realistic schedules that have been agreed upon with the people doing the actual work. Try to generate content in batches as the site build progresses, avoiding the temptation to leave it all until the last minute.

You'll also need to agree upon how content will be added to the site. Will the client have access to the site to add content themselves or will you be expected to do it? If you will be doing it, make it clear in what form you need the content in order to be able to upload it. Written content needs to be clearly labeled with its location in the site, and media needs to be provided in the right format and at the appropriate level of quality.

Sometimes it is best to treat content generation as a different project altogether. In this case, you build a site with the necessary pages, posts, widgets, and so on, and set it up to display the content but without all of the content in place. You make it clear to the client that the site build is complete when the structure is built, and that you will then hand the site over for them to finish adding content. If you both agree to this plan, make sure it's in your contract; otherwise, the client could be disappointed when asked to pay for a site that hasn't been completely populated.

A better approach with larger site builds is to see content generation as an ongoing process. The first phase of the project is to build and launch a site with essential content. You then continue to work with the client to support the generation and addition of more content, adding widgets, custom post types, and whatever else is needed as the site evolves. This approach reflects the fact that any website should always be seen as a work in progress, and it has the additional advantage of ensuring a continuing, or at least a longer, relationship with the client after the site goes live. That means better service for the client and a better bottom line for you. Again, if you do adopt this approach, work it into your contract, with specific clauses covering site support and development after launch.

Matching Content to the Best WordPress Page or Post Type

At this point, you know what content the client needs to include in their site, and you've agreed on a site structure that will achieve their goals most effectively. You now need to identify what WordPress content type to use to store each piece of content.

Depending on the site, this will typically be a mix of pages, posts, and custom post types; but you may also need to use custom fields, taxonomies, and other post types that could be provided by plugins. For example, if the site needs to list any content, it will need to be contained in a post, attachment, or custom post type. Even if the site won't have a blog or a news section, it's a good idea to set up a custom post type for other listings, in case a blog is added later. You may need to use more than one custom post type, or you may find that using categories or taxonomies for your custom post type does the job. Plan out all of the instances where you will need to display an archive of your custom posts to help you identify any taxonomies you might need, and consider any changes that may affect them in the future.

Having identified custom post types, the next stage is to identify any relevant taxonomies. If your different post types need to be categorized in a similar way, then using categories or one custom taxonomy will suffice. However, if you need a more granular listing of taxonomies, and need to be able to categorize each item in more than one way, you'll need more than one taxonomy.

In some cases, you may find that custom fields or post metadata are more useful than custom post types, when applied to posts or to custom post types. Post metadata can be useful in the following scenarios:

▪ You want to display additional data relating to a post separately from the post content itself.

▪ You want the custom data to be kept separate so there is no risk of it being deleted or changed if the client edits the post content.

▪ You want to list multiple instances of the same custom field separately from the post content.

For example, a company site might include the following custom fields for each custom post type of "staff member":

▪ Experience

▪ Specialisms

▪ Twitter name

▪ Interesting fact

By using custom fields, you could, for example, display a list of all the twitter names of staff members. You could also display the custom fields separately from the content of the job posting, perhaps in the sidebar.

> **For more details about using custom post types, fields, and taxonomies, see Chapter 3, "Content Organization and Relationships."**

Planning Content Display

This isn't about styling or design just yet, but rather where content will be displayed on the site, including the use of archive listings and widgets. A clear understanding of which widgets and listings will be used and where they will appear on the site will help you to identify where you need separate template files or conditional code. This is covered in detail in Chapter 8.

For each section of the site, identify what content will be displayed on the page and where. This includes the following:

- **Headers and banners**—Be sure to consider different elements for different areas of the site (for example, it's common to have a slideshow or large banner image on the home page).

- **Navigation**—Will the navigation be structured using both main navigation and secondary navigation in specific sections of the site? If so, will the secondary navigation be displayed as part of the main navigation or in the content or sidebar? If the latter, how will this be set up?

- **Widgets**—What widgets need to be displayed and where? This need not be limited to sidebar and footer widgets—widgets can be useful in the header or above or below the content.

A good way to summarize this information is by creating a grid with the content type on one axis and the section of the site on the other, as demonstrated in Table 2-2.

Table 2-2: Planning the Location of Content

Content	Home	Static pages	Posts	Blog	Products section
Banner image	x				
Main nav	x	x	x	x	x
Sidebar menu					x
Sidebar Call To Action (CTA)	x	x	x	x	x
Sidebar category listing				x	
Sidebar twitter feed	x				
Footer blog listing	x	x	x	x	x
Footer map	x	x	x	x	x
Footer CTA	x	x	x	x	x

Writing a Technical Brief

After you and the client have agreed upon what's required, you need to write a technical brief. This is essential if a team will be working with you on the project, but it can also be useful if you are working alone. A good technical brief helps everyone understand what the deliverables are, what's expected of them, the methods they should use for development, and the schedules agreed upon. This can help to avoid later problems due to lack of clarity or communication.

An effective brief provides four benefits:

- It clarifies exactly what's expected.
- It helps to identify anything that changes after quoting a price for the job, so you can discuss any additional costs with your client.
- It provides documentation regarding what has been agreed upon.
- It gives your team a detailed explanation of what they are expected to do.

Key Elements of an Effective Brief

Your technical brief should have a core section that is relevant to everyone involved in the project. It may also have additional sections or appendices that apply to individuals.

Your brief should include the following:

- **Overview**—A summary of the project and the website being created
- **Client**—The client's name and some brief information about them
- **Team members**—Names of team members working on the project and their roles (in brief)
- **Background and site objectives**—A summary of the client's objectives from the site
- **Schedules**—An overview of the project's main milestones. You may choose to include just the final delivery date here, putting milestones and detailed delivery dates in a separate project plan.
- **Site content**—A summary of the content to be included in the site, followed by a detailed grid along the lines of the spreadsheet described earlier. This may be in the body of the brief or it may be an appendix or attachment.
- **Site structure**—This contains details about how the site will be structured, which may or may not be part of your site content section.
- **Page layouts**—An overview of how each section of the site should be laid out. This may include wireframes if these have been developed, and will include a grid similar to the one shown earlier in Table 2-2.
- **Design**—If the design work has already been done, developers will need mockups, or code if the design is done in the browser, plus a list of key design elements such as fonts, colors, and images.
- **Technical specifications**—This is an important part of the brief and should include specifications such as the following:
  - Browser and/or device compatibility
  - Accessibility requirements
  - Coding standards (e.g., use of comments, scripts, etc.)

- Theme frameworks to be used where relevant
- Any custom WordPress setup such as security enhancements
- Details regarding where the development site and live site are to be hosted
- Any core plugins that should be used for the site build
- Any other specifications that reflect the particular way you or your client works

■ **Additional notes**—Anything team members need to know that is not covered elsewhere

Tailoring Briefs to Different Stakeholders

Your client won't need all the information outlined in the preceding technical brief—for example, the client doesn't need to know your standards for commenting code. Similarly, not everyone on your team will need all the information provided, especially if you are working team members who specialize in different aspects of the site build.

For the client, you may not need to include the technical specifications, or you might only need to include some of them, such as browser or device compatibility, to avoid any unhappy surprises—such as the site layout breaking after launch because you aren't supporting IE6 (you aren't, are you?).

For team members, it's helpful to provide them with the full brief so each member knows what the others are doing, especially if they will be working closely together. However, clearly indicate which parts of the brief apply to whom.

You also need to provide the client with details about costs and payment terms—and to any contractors you may be using. In the case of the client, this should be covered in a separate contract. For contractors, you may find it more efficient to have a general contract that applies to all projects, and a project-specific agreement for each project, with details regarding the project deliverables, rates of pay, and payment terms. This could take the form of an appendix to the brief, which is unique to each contractor.

Technical Briefs That Prevent Later Problems

A good technical brief will avoid all sorts of problems further down the line, in much the same way that a good contract will—in fact, the technical brief forms part of your contract with both your client and any contractors.

To avoid later misunderstandings or disagreements, make sure you include the following:

■ **Responsibilities**—For example, if the client will be adding content to the site, make this clear. Conversely, if they are providing the content for you to upload, make this clear as well, to prevent misunderstandings later if they question why the site is empty and you haven't magically filled it with content.

■ **Deadlines**—Team members need to know when they are expected to deliver their work. Clients need to know when they will be expected to review the site and provide content. Encourage everyone to let you know well in advance if they cannot meet a deadline; and include information on the consequences of deadlines not being met. You should have this in your contracts, too.

■ **Standards**—For team members, it's important to specify the standards you expect in terms of code, delivery of work, saving backups, commenting, accessibility, browser compatibility and anything else that is relevant. This clarifies exactly what they have to do—and if they don't do it, you have the documentation to prove it.

Configuring WordPress for the Team and the Client

You have your plan, everyone knows what's going on thanks to your outstanding technical brief, and you and the client have agreed upon how the site will be built. Before starting the build, you—or one of your team— must set WordPress up so everyone can use or access it for site development.

Planning Access and User Capabilities

The first step, of course, is to install WordPress, adding any necessary customizations for security or for your or your client's setup.

After WordPress is installed, each member of the team needs a user account with the appropriate user role:

- Team members working on the site build will need Administrator accounts.
- If client staff are adding content, they'll need an Editor or Author account.
- The client may also need a Subscriber account for viewing and interacting with the site.
- It's a good idea to set up a Subscriber account for testing so your team can see how the site will work for users without Administrator access.
- If the site requires custom roles, you need to set up dummy examples of these for testing, plus one for the client to use to review and interact with the site as it is developed.
- You may also want to password protect the server or directory if you are developing on a remote testing server.

Keep a note of all the permissions, roles, and users you set up. Someone is bound to forget his or her username at some point; and when the site goes live, you may need to delete or amend user accounts or disable some. You'll learn more about this in Chapter 5 when you look at site launch.

Tools and Plugins to Help the Team

There are two main types of tool that help the team with the site build: tools that facilitate communication and project collaboration, and tools that help you set WordPress up so that the development process is smooth. This section describes both of these.

Project Collaboration Tools

Dozens of good project management and collaboration tools are available, and I don't intend to tell you which to use. However, there are some WordPress-specific tools that can help make your life easier, including the following:

- **P2 Theme** (http://wordpress.org/extend/themes/p2)—A WordPress theme designed to help teams communicate and keep each other updated. The theme is inspired by Twitter and enables you to post short updates on the front page. You can also view updates by tag or category, make use of threaded comments, and set up notifications to alert team members about a new comment. There are also some add-on plugins for P2 to enhance its use for project collaboration such as P2 Resolved Posts (http://wordpress.org/extend/plugins/p2-resolved-posts/).

■ **CollabPress** (`http://wordpress.org/extend/plugins/collabpress/`)—This plugin adds project collaboration to your site. Its capabilities include multiple project management, task lists, BuddyPress integration, file upload for projects, task lists and tasks, and due dates with a calendar view. It goes a step further than the P2 theme and can be useful as an alternative to a subscription-based online project management tool.

■ **bbPress** (`http://wordpress.org/extend/plugins/bbpress/`)—The WordPress forum plugin, this can be useful as an alternative to the P2 theme for team communications. It could also be used for site development and support with the client after a site is launched.

Development Tools

A comprehensive list of all the great developer plugins in the plugin repository is beyond the scope of this section, but the following should get you started if you don't already have your own favorites:

■ **Developer** (`http://wordpress.org/extend/plugins/developer/`)—Provided by Automattic, this plugin ensures that you have "all the essential tools and plugins" installed. The plugins it can install for you include the following:

- Debug Bar Cron (`http://wordpress.org/extend/plugins/debug-bar-cron/`)

- Rewrite Rules Inspector (`http://wordpress.org/extend/plugins/rewrite-rules-inspector/`)

- Log Deprecated Notices (`http://wordpress.org/extend/plugins/log-deprecated-notices/`)

- VIP Scanner (`http://wordpress.org/extend/plugins/vip-scanner/`)

- Grunion Contact Form (`http://wordpress.org/extend/plugins/grunion-contact-form/`) (only recomende for wordpress.com VIP sites)

- Monster Widget (`http://wordpress.org/extend/plugins/monster-widget/`)

- Beta Tester (`http://wordpress.org/extend/plugins/wordpress-beta-tester/`)

You have the option to select or deselect any of these—for example, if you're using a different forms plugin, such as Gravity Forms, you wouldn't want to turn on the Grunion Contact Form plugin.

■ **WP-DB-Backup** (`http://wordpress.org/extend/plugins/wp-db-backup/`)—Enables you to quickly take a backup of your database and either e-mail it to yourself or download it

■ **Members** (`http://wordpress.org/extend/plugins/members/`)—Enables you to quickly set up multiple member roles and capabilities

■ **Custom Post Type UI** (`http://wordpress.org/extend/plugins/custom-post-type-ui/`)—Provides an interface for creating custom post types and taxonomies. It gives you access to the post type generation code generated by the plugin, so you can paste it into your theme's `functions.php` file and work with that code later if desired.

You can replicate the functionality of some of these plugins by coding your own functions, either in your theme's `functions.php` file or in your own plugin, a topic covered in detail in Chapter 9. The plugins can be useful for speed or ease of use, however.

Summary

You've already done a lot of work on your WordPress site development even though you've hardly touched a line of code yet. Planning and preparation are vital first steps to ensure that a site build runs smoothly and results in success, especially a large one with multiple stakeholders. For each project you work on, make sure you have each of the following covered:

- **Site hosting and development**—Where will the site be hosted and developed?

- **SEO and teaser pages**—Create a 503 page or use a plugin to set up a teaser page to tell visitors about the new site and collect data.

- **Content planning**—Understanding exactly what content will be included in the site and how it needs to be stored and structured helps you make quick progress when it comes to development—and avoid any misunderstandings later.

- **Technical briefs**—Members of your team need to know exactly what's expected of them and when. The client needs to know exactly what you are promising to deliver. A good technical brief communicates this in order to avoid problems.

- **WordPress configuration**—Users and roles may need to be created, and tools set up, to ease the process of site development.

After completing the steps outlined in this chapter, you will be well prepared to begin working on your project, whether it's small and simple or large and intricate. Proceed to the next chapter to start the site build!

Further Resources
SEO and Teaser Pages

- SEO during site development
  `http://www.seomoz.org/blog/how-to-handle-downtime-during-site-maintenance`

- Site Maintenance plugin
  `http://wordpress.org/extend/plugins/wet-maintenance/`

- Ultimate Coming Soon plugin
  `http://wordpress.org/extend/plugins/ultimate-coming-soon-page/`

- FeedBurner
  `http://feedburner.google.com`

- Setting up e-mail notifications using FeedBurner
  `http://www.peachpit.com/articles/article.aspx?p=693646`

Project Collaboration: Themes and Plugins

- P2 Theme demo
  `http://p2demo.wordpress.com`

- P2 Theme
  `http://wordpress.org/extend/themes/p2`

- CollabPress
  http://wordpress.org/extend/plugins/collabpress/

- bbPress
  http://wordpress.org/extend/plugins/bbpress/

Site Development Plugins

- Developer
  http://wordpress.org/extend/plugins/developer/

- WP-DB-Backup
  http://wordpress.org/extend/plugins/wp-db-backup/

- Members
  http://wordpress.org/extend/plugins/members/

- Shortcode Developer
  http://wordpress.org/extend/plugins/shortcode-developer/

- Custom Post Type UI
  http://wordpress.org/extend/plugins/custom-post-type-ui/

Part II

Content and Administration

Chapter 3
Content Organization and Relationships

Having planned your WordPress project and identified exactly what you will building and how you will approach it, the next step is to plan how you will handle site content. It's worth taking some time for this—as you'll know, WordPress uses different types of content and different kinds of metadata, and getting this right before you start to code will save you a lot of headaches and some potential rework further down the line.

In Chapter 2 you looked at a basic content planning grid, which serves to identify the key content in a site and assign content types to it. In this chapter you will learn how WordPress stores content in detail and identify ways in which you can harness and build on core capabilities to make your content work for you. By the end of this chapter you will be familiar with the following topics:

- **Rationalizing your content**—How to identify the structure of your site's content, breaking each part of the site into content types and looking at device-specific content where that's needed
- **How WordPress stores content**—An overview of the main content types and where they are stored in the database
- **Custom post types**—When to use them, how to set them up, and how to get the most from them
- **Post data**—When to use categories, taxonomies, and tags, as well as assigning custom fields and post metadata
- **Media and attachments**—How WordPress stores and displays these, plus how to leverage thumbnails (or featured images)

You'll work through each of these topics in turn, going into each one in detail before moving onto the next, although there will be references to each of them in most of the sections, as the topics are so closely related.

In this chapter I'll be using a dummy e-commerce site to demonstrate some of the learning points—see the Introduction to this book for information on how to download the code.

As you can imagine, there's a lot to cover, but once you have grasped these fundamental aspects of working with content, you'll be able to build rich, complex sites with customized structure and functionality.

Rationalizing Your Content

Chapter 2 covered what you should talk to your client about with respect to what the site needs to achieve, the content it will contain, and how that content will be generated and uploaded. Now you need to identify what content types you'll be using across the site. These could include a selection from the following:

- **Posts**—A type of content most commonly used for blogs or news articles. These create the site feed.
- **Pages**—These live outside the time-based post listings and are used for static content. They can be hierarchical, so one page can be the child or parent of another.
- **Custom post types**—Additional types of content that work similarly to posts but are stored and can be queried separately.
- **Attachments**—Images, video, documents, and other media that can be displayed either in a post or page, in its own attachment page, or using a gallery or slideshow.
- **Links**—Previously called a blogroll, this has been removed from the default admin menu in WordPress 3.5 but it may be useful in some sites or blogs. It's used to store a link to an external site with some associated metadata.
- **Categories**—Categories are used to divide up posts and custom post types so you can list posts by category. They are hierarchical, so one category can be the child or parent of another.
- **Tags**—These are similar to categories but aren't hierarchical. They tend to be used more for tagging content than for sorting it into a structure, as categories are.
- **Custom taxonomies**—Categories and tags are a taxonomy—you can also create your own to which can be hierarchical or not. Commonly these are used in conjunction with custom post types.
- **Widgets**—Areas in a theme which allow users to add in content using a drag and drop interface in the Widgets admin screen. These don't just have to be in the sidebar!
- **Options content**—Site editors can specify this via the theme customizer or a theme options screen (see Chapter 8 for more details on setting this up).
- **Hardcoded content**—Anything coded into your template files that isn't pulled from the database.
- **Content sourced from elsewhere**—This might include mapping, streamed video, social media feeds, or RSS feeds. You can display these in a page or post's content, use a widget, or code them into a template file or an include file.

The following sections look at the different elements of a site and how to identify what content type to use for each.

Considering a Site's Layout and Structure

When designing a theme or a website, it helps to consider the structure of the site as well as its layout. The structure will derive from the content and the different sections and pages needed to display it most logically. The layout will provide you with the visual structure to place the content of each page inside.

Generally, you'll define the layout of each section of the site in the relevant template files, adding headers, footers and sidebars or widget areas as necessary, along with the content as displayed using the loop. The site structure will then be added via the WordPress admin by yourself or sometimes by the client.

Layout Considerations

If you've created wireframes for your site design, they should include the key areas of content on each section of the site. Figure 3-1 shows an example.

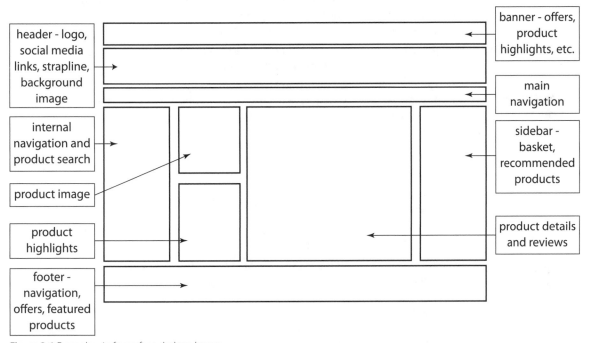

Figure 3-1 Example wireframe for a desktop layout

Of course, your site may include different wireframes for different screen sizes, which may vary in terms of layout or in the way content is displayed. See Chapter 11 for more information about creating different layouts for different devices.

Using the layout shown in Figure 3-1 as an example, the types of content you could use are shown in Table 3-1.

Table 3-1: Options for Populating the Products Pages of an E-commerce Site

Area of Layout	Content	Content Type Options
Top banner	Offers, adverts, product highlights	Widget Coded into `header.php` Link to an external API (e.g., advertising provider) Custom loop (e.g., listing a featured product or displaying a specific post's content) Option on theme options page
Header	Logo, strapline, social media links, background image	Coded into `header.php` (with use of bloginfo tag) Theme options page Custom slideshow (possibly linked to posts)
Main navigation	Navigation menu	Menu (using Menus admin page) Custom menu coded into `header.php`
Internal navigation and product search	Menu and search box, possibly tag or category/taxonomy-based searching	Menu (using Menus admin page) Category listing using wp_dropdown_categories or `wp_category_checklist` Taxonomy listing using `get_the_term_list` Search box using widget or coded into relevant template file (e.g., sidebar-left.php)
Content	Product image, highlights, details, and reviews	Custom post type displayed using the loop Featured image, gallery, or slideshow Post metadata for product highlights List of reviews (using comments, metadata, or related custom post types)
Sidebar	Basket, recommended products	Widgets provided via an e-commerce plugin
Footer	Additional navigation, listings, featured products	Widgets Navigation menu Custom loop

As you can see, plenty of methods are available for displaying content in different areas of the page. The main methods are as follows:

- Running the loop or one or more custom loops in your template files

- Content added by plugins (your own or those you install), via hooks

- Code in template files

- Theme options

- Menus

- Widgets

- External sources (possibly via a widget or a plugin)

In many scenarios you have more than one way to display the same content—for example, you could use a menu, a custom loop, a plugin, or a category listing to list content in your footer. The method you use will depend on the needs of the site and the preferences and capabilities of your team, as well as the extent to which site editors need to be able to edit content.

Structure Considerations

Having looked at each of your wireframes and identified what methods you'll use to display each part of the layout, you need to look at the site's structure. Most sites include several static pages and posts but may also require custom post types as well as categories and taxonomies. Many also use attachments, which you will be displaying in their own attachment pages, within other content, in listings, in galleries, or as slideshows or lightboxes.

Work through your site's structure and identify the different types of content and how they need to be stored in WordPress. Table 3-2 provides a truncated example of this process for an example e-commerce site for a clothing retailer.

Table 3-2: Example Content Types for an E-commerce Site

Content	Content Type	Relevant Taxonomies
Home page, About page, Terms and Conditions, Returns policy, etc.	Static page	N/A
News items (including offers)	Post	Category, Tag
Products	Product custom post type	Tag, Custom taxonomies - Size, Color, Department, Clothing type
Product images	Attachment	N/A
Product highlights	Post metadata in Product custom post type	N/A
Reviews	Comment	N/A

This site will need one custom post type and four custom taxonomies. It will also need post metadata inputs in the `product` custom post type editing screen. In this case I've chosen to display reviews using comments (with nested comments switched off), but another method would be to create a 'Review' meta key for the `product` post type.

Identifying Editing Requirements

When deciding how to store and display content, you need to take into account who will be editing that content and what access they will have to the site. Consider the following:

- Some content may not need to be edited by anyone other than the development team, in which case it can be displayed using PHP or HTML.

- Some content will be provided by site editors or authors, who will have access to the WordPress admin but may not be able to write code, so you need to ensure that is set up in such a way that they can easily add or edit relevant content without writing HTML or PHP. You need to decide whether these users will have access to widgets and menus.

- Some content will be added by site visitors, who won't have access to the WordPress admin—for them you need to provide a method to add content via the front end. In the example site, this is the case for reviews—by choosing to use comments, you can handle this easily.

Widgets and menus are unusual cases because they are designed to be easy for WordPress users to edit, but they could be broken by inexperienced site editors.

You may choose to code menus into the relevant template files, to avoid editors having to change the menu whenever they add a new page. However, this removes the ability to specify exactly where in the menu that new page will appear.

In the case of widgets, I advise against expecting site editors to edit these unless they are experienced with WordPress. For example, suppose you have chosen to use a text widget to display a call to action button in the sidebar—what happens when the e-mail address in that button changes? The site editor may access the widgets screen and edit the button's content but not realize that the link must also be edited from the button as well. For this reason you should avoid using widgets for any content your editors will need to change, and instead make use of one of the following:

- A content options screen (built in a similar way to a theme options screen but using a plugin instead so the content isn't theme-specific).

- A custom post type for longer pieces of content, which the editor can update and which are then displayed in the sidebar using a custom loop.

You'll learn how to implement these in Chapter 4.

Displaying Device-Specific Content

With an increasingly large number of people accessing content from mobile devices, it is likely that you will sometimes be asked to create a site that needs to display different content according to the device on which it is accessed. This may be because the design makes use of capabilities available on specific devices or because specific content only needs to be displayed on specific devices.

In most cases a responsive design will be the most appropriate approach, but sometimes you may need to create a mobile-specific site or theme. You can learn more about this in Chapter 11.

A Design Making Use of Device Capabilities

For example, in the hypothetical e-commerce site described in the preceding section, the wireframe for tablet devices looks quite different from the one for desktop, as shown in Figure 3-2.

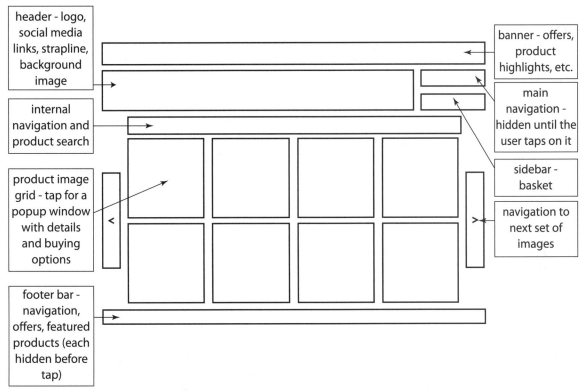

Figure 3-2 The example site's wireframe for tablet devices

This wireframe doesn't just use a different layout, which could be achieved with media queries. It has very different navigation, most of which is hidden until the user taps on it; and instead of displaying each product in a page containing detailed information and reviews, it uses a swipeable grid displaying the featured image for each product. When the user taps on an image, a pop-up window appears with full information. Typically, this window features tabs for product description, images, and reviews.

This type of display is sufficiently different to warrant the use of a separate theme for tablet devices, combined with a theme switcher plugin to display the correct theme on the correct device. This is covered in more detail in Chapter 11.

Different Devices, Different Content

There is currently a debate running among web designers about whether it's appropriate to send completely different content to different device types. On the one hand is the argument that content on mobile devices should be shorter and easier to access quickly for usability reasons (as put forward by Jakob Nielsen at `http://www.useit.com/alertbox/mobile-vs-full-sites.html`). On the other hand is the "one web" argument, which posits that website content should be independent of device and that mobile users shouldn't be denied access to content that's visible to desktop users (as put forward by Bruce Lawson on Smashing Magazine at `http://mobile.smashingmagazine.com/2012/04/19/why-we-shouldnt-make-separate-mobile-websites/`, among others).

I'm firmly of the latter view. As more and more people access the Internet primarily through mobile devices, they expect all the same content that users on desktops can access. The challenge is to optimize the layout, the design, and the user experience on mobile devices so that the experience of browsing your site on a smartphone is as easy as on a desktop. In short, it is hoped that the expectation of a smaller amount of content for a smaller screen will eventually go the way of the "above the fold" concept of ensuring all the important page content can be viewed without scrolling—it will become obsolete.

Space and size limitations aside, you might sometimes need to display some content differently on mobile devices than you would on desktop screens. Examples include the following:

- **Navigation**—You may want to structure the navigation differently, move it, or make it accessible via a button on small screens.
- **Images**—Sending smaller image files to devices with smaller screens improves performance and is a good practice.
- **Maps and other content using geolocation**—This is easier on mobile browsers, which are more likely to have geolocation enabled.

For scenarios in which you need to send different content to different devices, you can detect the browser, device, or screen size using a variety of methods, and then send the correct content accordingly. Alternatively, you can use a separate mobile theme. Again, all this is covered in much more detail in Chapter 11.

However, notwithstanding my opinion on this issue, your client may think differently and want to display a different version of a page or post on different devices. How would you go about this? I don't recommend creating multiple posts or pages, as this will have a negative impact on SEO and mean that anyone sharing a link with someone on a different device could be sending them the wrong link.

Instead, I recommend adding an additional editing area to the post editing screen for the relevant post type. Depending on the extent of the differences, this could be a custom field or a completely new editing pane to add additional post metadata.

Examining How WordPress Stores Content

If you're going to customize the way your site's content is uploaded, stored, and displayed, it helps to understand how content is actually stored in WordPress. You've already learned about the different types of content used by WordPress, but you also need to know where that content is stored in the WordPress database. This will help you ensure that data is stored and retrieved correctly when you're adding post metadata or plugin settings, for example. It also helps you to understand how categories, tags and other taxonomies are stored and how these interact with posts and pages.

I'll cover how the different content types work in detail in the next section, but first I'll explain the core database structure, as used in a standard WordPress installation.

The Core Database Structure

A standard WordPress installation's database consists of the 11 tables shown in Figure 3-3, which is taken from the WordPress codex at `http://codex.wordpress.org/Database_Description`.

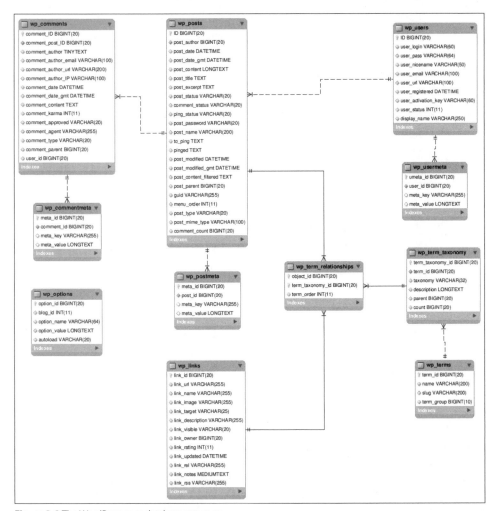

Figure 3-3 The WordPress core database structure

As you can see, each table is related to at least one other table, except for one—the `wp_options` table.

Table 3-3 summarizes these tables and their relationships.

Table 3-3: The WordPress Database TablesTable

	Data Stored	*Linked to*
`wp_posts`	Posts, pages, attachments, revisions, and navigation menu items	`wp_postmeta` (via `post_id`)
		`wp_term_relationships` (via `post_id`)
`wp_postmeta`	Metadata for each post	`wp_posts` (via `post_id`)
`wp_comments`	Comments	`wp_posts` (via `post_id`)
`wp_commentmeta`	Metadata for each comment	`wp_comments` (via `comment_id`)
`wp_term_relationships`	Relationships between posts and taxonomies	`wp_posts` (via `post_id`)
		`wp_term_taxonomy` (via `term_taxonomy_id`)
`wp_term_taxonomy`	Taxonomies—category, tag, and your custom taxonomies	`wp_term_relationships` (via `term_taxonomy_id`)
`wp_terms`	Your categories and tags and the categories within each custom taxonomy	`wp_term_taxonomy` (via `term_id`)
`wp_links`	The links in your blogroll	`wp_term_relationships` (via `link_id`)
`wp_users`	Your site's registered users	`wp_posts` (via `post_author`)
`wp_user_meta`	Metadata for each user	`wp_users` (via `user_id`)
`wp_options`	The options set in the Settings admin screen	n/a (these relate to the site, not to any other data)

The relationships between the tables are one-to-many—i.e., one record in one table can have many related records in the other table. For example, each comment applies to only one post, but each post can have multiple comments.

The relationship between the `wp_posts` and `wp_terms` tables are different—the fact that they are related via the `wp_term_relationships` table, which exists purely to make this link, creates a many-to-many relationship. In other words, a post type (including standard posts as well as custom posts) can have many taxonomies assigned to it, and a taxonomy can apply to many post types. The `wp_term_relationships` table includes just three fields to make this work:

- `post_id` to link to `wp_posts`
- `term_taxonomy_id` to link to `wp_term_taxonomy`
- `object_id` (which is the unique ID of each record in `wp_term_relationships`)

Understanding how the database is structured can help you understand how the content works. In particular, seeing the way that metadata is stored can be useful. It would be logical to expect tables such as `wp_posts` to have fields for each item of metadata, but this would result in a lot of (mostly empty) fields and make calls to the database less efficient. Instead, the `wp_postmeta` table includes a record for each item of metadata, with a key (`meta_key`) and a value (`meta_value`). Different records may have the same key.

It's worth mentioning that while taxonomies have their own table, post types do not. When you register a custom post type, it's not actually stored in the database as a post type, but the name of the post type is stored in the `post_type` column of the `wp_posts` table against any posts it applies to.

> **WordPress Multisite has additional tables. These include global tables relating to the entire network, and site-specific tables created when a site is set up. The global tables store metadata relating to the network. The site-specific tables are the same as those for a standard installation and have the blog ID as part of the table name. Therefore, for example,** `wp_posts` **for a site with the blog ID of 3 would be** `wp_3_posts`. **For a site with the blog ID of 1, the number isn't appended and the tables would simply be called** `wp_posts`. **For more on the Multisite database structure see** `http://codex.wordpress.org/Database_Description#Multisite_Table_Overview`.

The WordPress Options Table

The only table that isn't related in some way to another table is the `wp_options` table. That's because this table stores data about the site as a whole, as specified in the Settings screens and elsewhere.

As well as Settings values such as the site title and description, it includes data relating to the plugins being used and the site's management, including the list of recent comments and more. A complete list of everything that can be stored in the `wp_options` table is beyond the scope of this chapter, but if you want to understand it better I suggest taking a look at your database using phpMyAdmin or similar.

You'll want to interact with the options table when you need to store values that are site-specific rather than content-specific. This includes theme options screens, customizations to the theme customizer, and other settings that can be added by plugins you develop.

> **Options screens and settings are covered in more detail in Chapter 4, and you'll see how they can be used to create a custom CMS interface for your clients.**

Building Custom Post Types

Custom post types were introduced with version 2.9, with a lot more support added for them in 3.0, and they marked a huge leap forward in WordPress's development. They enable you to create your own types of content in addition to those WordPress already provides, which are:

- Post
- Page

- Attachment
- Link
- Revision
- Navigation Menu

Each custom post type you create works in a similar way to each of the six default content types. The terminology can be misleading—custom post types are *not* posts. It might be easier to think of them as custom content types.

Custom post types greatly helped to advance WordPress from being a blogging platform to a content management system (CMS). They enable you to store and display data however you need for your project, especially when combined with custom taxonomies. You can use custom post types to separate the different kinds of content in your site, and you can query them in exactly the way you want using custom loops or the relevant template file.

Custom post types are displayed using one of the following template files, in order of precedence. For example, for a single post of the post type `product`, the hierarchy would be as follows:

1. `single-product.php`
2. `single.php`
3. `index.php`

For that post type's archive listing, this would be the hierarchy:

1. `archive-product.php`
2. `archive.php`
3. `index.php`

> The template hierarchy is covered in more detail in Chapter 8. To see how different template files apply to each content type, see `http://codex.wordpress.org/Template_Hierarchy`.

This means you have more control over how your custom post types are displayed, such as displaying additional metadata or filtering the query before running the loop in a specific template file (for example, to display posts in an archive in ascending order instead of descending order).

Registering a custom post type is simple, and can be done with a single function. I recommend creating a plugin to register your custom post types instead of adding them to your theme's functions file, as you don't want all your post types to be lost if the theme is changed.

For the example post type of `product`, the function would be as follows:

To create a custom post type, you use the `register_post_type()` function, which has the following parameters:

```php
<?php register_post_type( $post_type, $args ) ?>
```

- `$post_type`—the name of the new post type
- `$args`—an array of arguments relating to the post type, which will include the labels applied to it in the WordPress admin, the taxonomies it supports and more, as I'll demonstrate next

So to register a products custom post type, I add the following to my plugin or functions file:

```php
<?php
// register custom post type for products
function wpptl_create_post_type() {
 $labels = array(
   'name' => __( 'Products', 'wpptl' ),
   'singular_name' => __( 'product', 'wpptl' ),
   'add_new' => __( 'New product', 'wpptl' ),
   'add_new_item' => __( 'Add New product', 'wpptl' ),
   'edit_item' => __( 'Edit product', 'wpptl' ),
   'new_item' => __( 'New product', 'wpptl' ),
   'view_item' => __( 'View product', 'wpptl' ),
   'search_items' => __( 'Search products', 'wpptl' ),
   'not_found' =>  __( 'No products Found', 'wpptl' ),
   'not_found_in_trash' =>
      __( 'No products found in Trash', 'wpptl' ),
 );
 $args = array(
  'labels' => $labels,
  'public' => true,
  'supports' => array(
   'title',
   'editor',
   'excerpt',
   'thumbnail',
  ),
  'taxonomies' => array( 'post_tag', 'category'),
 );
 register_post_type( 'product', $args );
}
add_action( 'init', 'wpptl_create_post_type' );
?>
```

The `wpptl_create_post_type()` function includes a number of elements:

- `$labels`—an array of labels which will appear in the WordPress admin when editors are working with the post type

- `$args`—the arguments applying to the post type, including its labels (the `$labels` variable I've already defined) and more

I'll explain each of the arguments and labels in detail in the next section, on "Specifying Post Type Parameters."

Finally, I attach the function to the 'init' action hook, ensuring that it runs when WordPress is initialized.

This function creates a post type that looks like what is shown in Figure 3-4 in the WordPress admin.

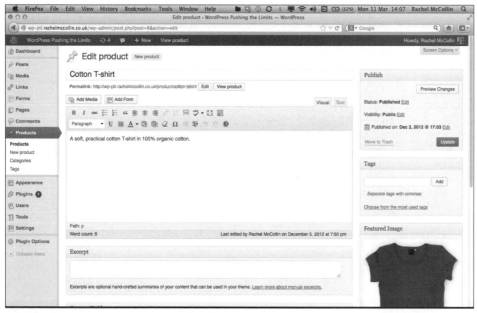

Figure 3-4 The editing page for my custom post type

Having registered your post types, you can then customize their editing pages and the way they're displayed. For example, the example products post type would have some additional meta keys and taxonomies assigned, which would be output in `single-product.php`. Taxonomies are covered in more detail later in this chapter, in the "Working with Taxonomies" section.

Manipulating Post Type Parameters

Post types give you a lot of flexibility in terms of how they work and interact with other content. The parameters in Table 3-4 describe how the custom post type works. More are listed at `http://codex.wordpress.org/Function_Reference/register_post_type`, and Chapter 4 takes a look at some others related to the admin screens and their customization.

Table 3-4: Custom Post Type Parameters

Parameter	Description	Example
`id`	The post type's ID, which should be a meaningful term. You use this in exactly the same way as you would `'post'` or `'page'`. This isn't usually visible to users, as they will see your labels instead. It's good practice to make this unique by adding a prefix.	`'product'`

`labels`	The labels visible to site editors when adding a new object of this post type	`'labels' => array(`
		`  'name' => __( 'Products' ),`
		`  'singular_name' => __( Product'),`
		`  'add_new' => __( 'New product' ),`
		`  // etc`
		`),`

`description`	Description of your custom post type	
`public`	Specifies whether the post type's queries and its admin screens are shown	`'public' => true,`
`exclude_from_search`	A Boolean value defaulting to the opposite of your `'public'` argument. Specifies whether the custom post type will be excluded from site search.	`'exclude_from_search'=>true;`
`hierarchical`	A Boolean value specifying whether the post type is hierarchical; the default is `false`	`'hierarchical' => true,`
`capability_type`	A string used to create custom capabilities for the post type. You can then use these when assigning capabilities to specific user roles. The default is `'post'`.	`'capability_type'=>'product'`

`capabilities`	An array of the post type's capabilities. The default is taken from the capability type but you can use the `capabilities` argument to provide finer control.	`capabilities => array(`
		`  edit_posts => 'edit_products',`
		`  publish_posts => 'edit_products'`
		`)`

(continued)

Table 3-4 *(continued)*

Parameter	Description	Example
supports	Specifies which items in the editing page the post type supports—some of these are essential to be able to edit the post, others will depend on your editors' needs.	`'supports' => array( 'title', 'editor', 'excerpt', 'thumbnail', 'page-attributes' ),`
rewrite	An array that lets you specify the permalink structure of posts in this post type. The array has five arguments—`'slug'` enables you to specify a custom slug, the others alter the display of the permalinks.	If your permalinks were set up to use /blog as a post prefix: `'rewrite' => array( 'slug' => 'fashion', 'with_front' => false ),` results in an URL such as http://example.com/fashion/post-slug. `'rewrite' => array( 'slug' => 'fashion', 'with_front' => true, pages'=>true ),` results in http://example.com/blog/fashion/post-slug with pagination turned on.
taxonomies	The taxonomies available to the post type. Defaults to none. If you include custom taxonomies, you must register those before adding them to the custom post type, or you can register them later and specify the post types they apply to at that stage, as you'll learn in the section in this chapter on "Working with Taxonomies."	`'taxonomies' => array( 'post_tag', 'category '),`
has_archive	A Boolean value specifying whether archives are automatically handled by WordPress for the post type. The default is `false`.	`'has_archive'=>true,`

These are just a selection of the post type parameters available. Now we'll look at an example from the hypothetical e-commerce site. The `products` post type is already registered but you want to add a few finer controls:

- It shouldn't be visible in site searches, as the products section will have its own search box (yes, I know this may not be best practice, but let's roll with it).

- You want to add a string for capability types, as you'll be assigning the capabilities for products to specific user roles in Chapter 4.

- You want to be able to generate archives for the post type.

- You also want to specify the permalink slug for this post type for SEO purposes.

The function to use with these parameters added would be as follows:

```php
<?php
// register custom post type for products
function wpptl_create_post_type() {
$labels = array(
  'name' => __( 'Products', 'wpptl'  ),
  'singular_name' => __( 'product', 'wpptl'  ),
  'add_new' => __( 'New product', 'wpptl'  ),
  'add_new_item' => __( 'Add New product', 'wpptl'  ),
  'edit_item' => __( 'Edit product', 'wpptl'  ),
  'new_item' => __( 'New product', 'wpptl'  ),
  'view_item' => __( 'View product', 'wpptl'  ),
  'search_items' => __( 'Search products', 'wpptl'  ),
  'not_found' =>  __( 'No products Found', 'wpptl'  ),
  'not_found_in_trash' =>
     __( 'No products found in Trash', 'wpptl'  ),
 );
 $args = array(
  'labels' => $labels,
  'public' => true,
  'has_archive' => true,
  'supports' => array(
   'title',
   'editor',
   'excerpt',
   'thumbnail',
   'page-attributes'
  ),
  'taxonomies' => array( 'post_tag', 'category'),
  'exclude_from_search' => true,
  'capability_type' => 'product',
  'rewrite' => array( 'slug' => 'hot-new-trends', )
  );
 register_post_type( 'product', $args )
}
add_action( 'init', 'wpptl_create_post_type' );
?>
```

A note on capability_type

Adding the `capability_type` parameter means that you need to set up user roles with the capability to edit this post in order to be able to access the post editing screen. If you don't do this, you'll be faced with a blank screen when you try to add a new product. For more on specifying user roles and capabilities, see Chapter 4.

The possibilities with custom post types are as great as your imagination—and you don't have to limit yourself to just one. I've developed sites that are dependent on custom post types and don't make use of posts. When combined with custom taxonomies, custom post types can be even more powerful, as you shall see shortly. In addition, you can take them even further with custom editing screens, as demonstrated in Chapter 4.

Building Relationships Between Content

As you have seen, WordPress uses relationships between tables to manage content. In the vast majority of sites, the existing relationships are fine; but what if you wanted to establish other relationships, such as between custom posts, for example?

To create parent-child relationships between your posts of custom post types, you can set the relevant custom posts to be hierarchical when you register them, using `'hierarchical' => true`. The function would look as follows:

```php
<?php
// register custom post type for products
function wpptl_create_post_type() {
// $labels defined here
 $args = array(
   'labels' => $labels,
   'has_archive' => true,
   'public' => true,
   'hierarchical' => true,
   'supports' => array(
     'title',
     'editor',
     'excerpt',
     'thumbnail',
     'page-attributes'
   ),
   'taxonomies' => array( 'post_tag', 'category'),
   );
 register_post_type( 'product', $args );
}
add_action( 'init', 'wpptl_create_post_type' );
?>
```

The two important arguments here are:

- `'supports'`, which must include `'page-attributes'` in its array in order for the page attributes box to be displayed on the page editing screen—this is where you select the post parent (see Figure 3-5).

- `'hierarchical' => 'true'`, which ensures the custom post type is hierarchical.

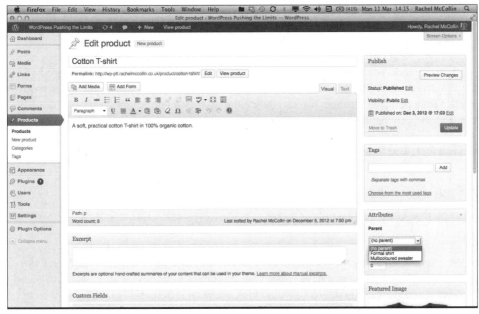

Figure 3-5 This custom post type is hierarchical, so each post can have a parent.

Adding Extra Data to Content

As you saw earlier when looking at the database structure, each post (by which I mean all content types) has metadata attached to it.

Metadata can include the following:

- **Custom fields or post metadata**—The key and value for each, stored in the `wp_postmeta` table
- **Specific categories, tags, and terms from your custom taxonomies relating to the post**—Held in the `wp_terms` table, accessed via the `wp_term_relationships` table
- **Comments attached to the post**—Stored in `wp_comments`
- **Post author**—Stored in `wp_users`
- **Post parent**—Stored using the `post_parent` field in `wp_posts`
- **Post metadata unique to each post, such as publication date, status, and visibility**—Held in `wp_posts`

WordPress provides a number of template tags which you can use to display post metadata. For example, the `the_category()` tag displays links to all of the categories for a post:

```
<p><?php the_category('|'); ?></p>
```

The preceding snippet displays link to all the categories relating to the current post, with a separator between them.

You can do much more with metadata. You can create your own taxonomies, which work in the same way as categories and tags, and you can add your own fields, customizing them to add data in the way your project requires. You can customize the post editing page to make it easier for users to edit the metadata for each post and strip out any metadata they don't need to see. You can define metadata values programmatically based on a condition you specify, and you can display your metadata in a variety of ways on your site.

To do all that, however, you first need to understand exactly how taxonomies work and when to use them.

Working with Taxonomies

It's important to understand that a taxonomy is not the same as a category—instead, a category is a type of taxonomy.

For instance, suppose the example e-commerce site introduced earlier will need three taxonomies: Size, Color, Department, and Clothing Type. Assume that you have already set up some categories for your news posts and some tags as well. The current site's taxonomy structure would look like what is described in Table 3-5, which shows the labels for each post type and term

Table 3-5: Taxonomies for the E-commerce Site

Taxonomy	Terms	Applicable Post Type(s)
Category	Fashion, Stores, Featured, Offers	Post, Product
Tag	Oxford Street, Skinny Jeans, Aran Wool, Biker Boots	Post, Product
Size	XS, Small, Medium, Large, XL	Product
Color	Black, White, Red, Blue, Orange, Navy, Charcoal, Silver, Hot Pink, Teal	Product
Department	Men, Women, Children	Product
Clothing Type	Tops, Jeans, Trousers, Sweaters, Coats, Jackets, Boots, Shoes	Product

You can see from this example that the taxonomies for products will need to be queried and listed separately from the categories for the news items. In the left sidebar in this layout, you need to be able to list each taxonomy separately and enable users to select a term from each, in order to narrow down the list of products displayed.

If taxonomies weren't available, you might have tried to use a hierarchical category structure to achieve this, using a parent category in place of a new taxonomy. It is possible to list the child categories of a given parent category, but using taxonomies gives you much more control (and makes the necessary queries easier to write and more efficient).

When deciding whether to use hierarchical categories or register custom taxonomies instead, consider two things:

- Will your taxonomy relate to one or more specific post types, which are different from those to which categories relate?

- Are the terms you need to use significantly different in structure and use from each other? As you can see, the taxonomies I've identified are quite distinct, and it doesn't make sense to include them all together as categories.

Taxonomies vs. Post Metadata

For some data, using metadata will be more appropriate than setting up a taxonomy. This will depend on the type of metadata you need to store against your posts. For example on a jobs listing site, you would use a taxonomy to store data about the country a vacancy is in as there will be a limited list of countries and you may want to add continents as parent terms. However, for the individual city it will be better to use post metadata as this could be different for every job on the site. When you're deciding how to structure your data, keep in mind the database relationships described earlier—taxonomies are used to group posts, while post metadata is used to store extra data about a post.

A key advantage of taxonomies is that they are easier to display in an archive, as you can make use of the relevant template file. If you wanted to display a lit of posts with a given custom field, you would have to write a custom query, which wouldn't be an ideal solution.

To clarify this with an example, suppose each product in the online shop is available in several sizes. You could set this scenario up in one of two ways:

- Register a taxonomy of `size`, then use the post editing screen to add terms to that taxonomy for each size available and select the available sizes for each product.

- Create a metadata form for the `product` post type that includes tick boxes, one for each size available. You could also edit this information in the post editing screen, but using the custom field meta box, not the taxonomy box.

If you wanted to display a list of available sizes on a product page, you could do so using either of these methods. In the first case you would use the following in the loop:

```php
<?php the_terms( $post->ID, 'size', 'Available sizes: ' , ', ' ' ); ?>
```

In the second case you would use a completely different function:

```php
<?php get_post_meta($post->ID, 'size' ); ?>
```

The real advantage of using taxonomies, however, can be seen when you want to display the data the other way around. Let's say you want to display all medium-size clothes in stock. If you were using post metadata, you would have to write a custom query to fetch all instances of the custom field with the key of size and a value of medium.

If you instead use a custom taxonomy, you wouldn't have to write a query at all—you would just display the relevant archive page. In addition, it would be easier to control how that archive page is displayed via the relevant template file and its generated CSS classes and IDs.

Registering Taxonomies

To register a taxonomy, you add the `register_taxonomy()` function to your theme's functions file or to a plugin—I recommend the latter as you don't want to lose your taxonomy if you switch themes.

The `register_taxonomy()` function has the following variables:

```php
<?php register_taxonomy( $taxonomy, $object_type, $args ); ?>
```

- `$taxonomy`—The taxonomy name as a slug, e.g., `'size'`
- `$object_type`—The object type it applies to, in this case the custom post type `'product'`. This avoids the need to add it to the function registering the post type.
- `$args`—An array of arguments, which will include the following:
    - `'hierarchical'`—Two of the example taxonomies have this set to `true`, while the other two are set to `false`. For example, Departments will be hierarchical, as they may have other departments as parents.
    - `'labels'`—The labels displayed in the WordPress admin, set as an array in a similar way as for custom post types.
    - `'query_var'`—Setting this to `true` enables you to run queries on this taxonomy through `WP_Query`.
    - `'rewrite'`—Setting this to `true` enables the use of attractive permalinks for your taxonomies.

To add a `size` taxonomy to the plugin you add the following code:

```php
<?php
//register custom taxonomies
function wpptl_create_taxonomies() {
 //define labels for the taxonomy
 $labels = array(
   'name' => __( 'Size', 'wpptl' ),
   'singular_name' => __( 'Size', 'wpptl' ),
   'search_items' => __( 'Search Sizes', 'wpptl' ),
   'all_items' => __( 'All Sizes', 'wpptl' ),
   'parent_item' => __( 'Parent Size', 'wpptl' ),
   'parent_item_colon' => __( 'Parent Size:', 'wpptl' ),
   'edit_item'  => __( 'Edit Size', 'wpptl' ),
   'update_item' => __( 'Update Size', 'wpptl' ),
   'add_new_item' => __( 'Add New Size', 'wpptl' ),
   'new_item_name' => __( 'New Size', 'wpptl' ),
   'separate_items_with_commas' =>
      __( 'Separate sizes with commas', 'wpptl' ),
   'menu_name' => __( 'Size' ),
 );
```

```
register_taxonomy( 'size', 'product', array(
 'hierarchical' => false,
 'labels' => $labels,
 'query_var' => true,
 'rewrite' => true,
 'show_admin_column' => true
 )
 );
}
add_action( 'init', 'wpptl_create_taxonomies', 0 );
?>
```

This adds the custom taxonomy with the relevant labels and parameters. The `show_admin_column` parameter is new for version 3.5—by setting it to `true`, you're adding a column for this taxonomy to the products listing screen in the WordPress admin.

Now when you're editing a product, you have a metabox for adding terms to the new taxonomy, as shown in Figure 3-6.

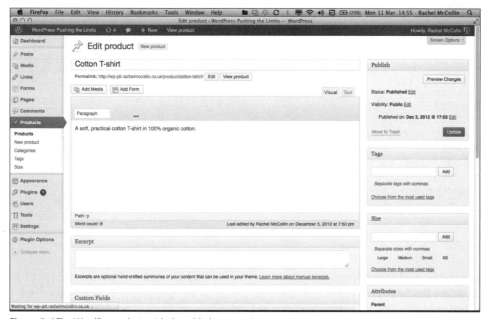

Figure 3-6 The WordPress admin with the added taxonomies

You can now add more terms as needed for each product, enabling you to display an archive for each taxonomy if you wish or to list your taxonomies in a sidebar so that visitors can see all the available sizes, departments, and so on. In the plugin I'll add three more taxonomies: `color`, `department`, and `clothingtype`. These are similar to the `size` taxonomy, except the `department` and `clothingtype` taxonomies have `hierarchical` set to `true`, which means they will behave like categories rather than tags. You don't need to use the separate_items_with_commas label with hierarchical taxonomies as it won't be used. You can download the code for the full plugin from `www.wiley.com/go/ptl/wordpress`.

WordPress Functions for Working with Taxonomies

You can manipulate your main loop to output taxonomy data as needed or add additional queries to a page.

The design for a single Product page on the e-commerce site has a section listing the taxonomies that apply to the product so users know the sizes, colors, and so on in which it is available. To create this, you add a function to your `single-product.php` template file listing the taxonomies. The function to use to list the terms against each taxonomy is `get_the_term_list()`:

```php
<?php get_the_term_list( $id, $taxonomy, $before, $sep, $after ) ?>
```

This function takes the following parameters:

- `id`—The post ID
- `taxonomy`—The taxonomy whose terms you want to retrieve
- `before`—The text before the list
- `sep`—The separator between terms
- `after`—The text after the list

The code you insert is as follows:

```php
<?php
$args = array(
 'public'   => true,
 '_builtin' => false,
 );
$taxonomies = get_taxonomies( $args, 'objects', 'and' );
if ($taxonomies) {
 foreach ($taxonomies as $taxonomy) {
 echo '<p><strong>' . $taxonomy->labels->name . '</strong>:  ';
 echo get_the_term_list( '' , $taxonomy->name, '', ', ', '' );
 echo '</p>';
 }
}
?>
```

This calls the `get_taxonomies()` function passing arguments to only retrieve public taxonomies but not the built-in ones, and assigns the result (an array) to `$taxonomies`. Then it loops through the array echoing the taxonomy name wrapped in some HTML and the result from `get_the_term_list()` for each taxonomy.

Finally, it loops through each taxonomy output by that function, echoing some HTML, the taxonomy name, and the list of terms for each.

The result is displayed on the product page, as shown in Figure 3-7.

Figure 3-7 A list of terms for each taxonomy

Custom Fields and Post Metadata

As well as assigning categories, tags, and taxonomy terms to your posts and custom post types, you can also use custom fields or post metadata to store more data. Custom fields are one way of storing post metadata, but you have more control if you interact with the Metadata API (`http://codex.wordpress.org/Metadata_API`). Post metadata is stored in the `wp_postmeta` table, using the `meta_key` and `meta_value` fields. Unless you specify otherwise, you can use `meta_key` more than once, both within each post and across posts—so a given post could have a number of metadata values with the same key, and that same key can be used for multiple posts.

For example, if you were using a meta field to store ratings for a product, there could be more than one rating for each product with different values, and there could also be ratings for multiple products.

I won't go into the process of setting up a custom field in the WordPress admin here, as I'm assuming readers are familiar with that (if not, it's covered in the codex at `http://codex.wordpress.org/Custom_Fields`). Instead, this section demonstrates how to create custom meta boxes, which give you a lot more control and make life easier for your site's editors. For example you can create a more intuitive user interface and add text which will help users to understand how to use the meta box.

Creating Post Metadata Controls Using Meta Boxes

In the example e-commerce site, you use post metadata to store data about each product: the fabric, the washing instructions, and the country of origin. However, you only want these fields to be available on the editing page for products, not for pages and posts; and you want editors to be able to select from some predefined options in some cases.

Instead of simply adding a custom field, you can have more control over the data entered and create a more intuitive user interface. To do this, you create a custom meta box, which will be displayed on your post editing screen for products and save the data input to the `wp_postmeta` table for the relevant product. Custom meta boxes are a useful tool in WordPress. They are used by the plugins that provide you with controls on your post or page editing pages—for example, SEO plugins use post meta boxes.

To add your own metabox, you use the function `add_meta_box()`. It has several available parameters as follows:

```php
<?php
add_meta_box( $id, $title, $callback, $post-type, $context, $priority,
$callback_args );
?>
```

- `$id`—Adds a CSS ID to the div containing your meta box
- `$title`—The name of the meta box as displayed on the post editing page
- `$callback`—The name of the function containing the HTML for your meta box
- `$post-type`—The type of content for which this meta box will be available (leave it blank for all)
- `$context`—Where in the editing page the meta box should be displayed—`'normal'`, `'advanced'` or `'side'`
- `$priority`—The priority level for displaying your meta box— `'high'`, `'core'`, `'default'` or `'low'`. The default is (unsurprisingly) `'default'`; use `'high'` to move it above other meta boxes.
- `$callback_args`—Arguments to pass into your callback function. This is needed if your function requires arguments other than $post, which is automatically passed to the callback function.

You want to create a custom metabox for the `'Fabric'` meta_key. You do this by adding the following function to your plugin or functions file, activating it via the `add_meta_boxes` action hook:

```php
<?php
function wpptl_create_fabric_meta_box() {
 add_meta_box( 'wpptl_fabric_metabox','Fabric this garment is made
from:','wpptl_create_fabric_metabox','product','normal','high' );
}
function wpptl_fabric_metabox($post) {
 echo 'This is where the fabric type will be input';
}
add_action( 'add_meta_boxes','wpptl_create_fabric_meta_box' );
?>
```

This creates the meta box and displays it immediately below the main editing pane, as shown at the bottom of Figure 3-8.

Figure 3-8 The newly created meta box

Now define the `wpptl_create_fabric_metabox` callback function to add the HTML for the meta box:

```
function wpptl_create_fabric_metabox( $post ) { ?>
 <form action="" method="post">
  <?php // add nonce for security
  wp_nonce_field( 'wpptl_metabox_nonce', 'wpptl_nonce' );
  //retrieve the metadata values if they exist
  $wpptl_fabric = get_post_meta( $post->ID, 'Fabric', true ); ?>
  <label for "wpptl_fabric">What fabric is this garment made from?</label>
  <input type="text" name="wpptl_fabric" value="
    <?php echo esc_attr( $wpptl_fabric ); ?>" />
 </form>
<?php }
```

Note a few things about this function:

▢ It passes the `$post object` as a parameter to the function, which gives the function access to all data for the current post.

▢ It uses `get_post_meta()` to retrieve any existing value for this meta key for the current post (`$post->ID`), so that this will be used in your input field. The meta key is the name of the metadata element.

▢ It then adds the HTML to display the input field, using the `$wpptl_fabric` variable defined using `get_post_meta()` as the value of the input field.

Figure 3-9 shows that your meta box now includes an input field.

Figure 3-9 Now the meta box includes an input field.

Next, save any data added to the meta box, using the `save_post` hook:

```
// save the meta box data
add_action( 'save_post','wpptl_save_fabric_meta' );
function wpptl_save_fabric_meta( $post_id ) {
 if ( isset( $_POST['wpptl_fabric'] ) ) {
  $new_fabric_value = ( $_POST['wpptl_fabric'] );
  update_post_meta( $post_id ,'Fabric' , $new_fabric_value );
 }
}
```

This accomplishes the following:

▨ It adds an action to `save_post` to run the `wpptl_save_fabric_meta` function.

▨ It then defines that function, using $post_ID as the ID of the post to which the data should be saved.

▨ It checks whether the $wpptl_fabric variable has been set—i.e., whether the editor has added a fabric.

▨ If so, it updates the `meta_value` for this key with the new value, using the variable $new_fabric_value.

> In Chapter 4 you examine how to customize the WordPress admin in more depth and create more meta boxes for different types of content.

Adding a Nonce for Security

At the moment this field doesn't include any validation to check that the data has been input via this screen. To add this you need to do two things: Add a nonce field to the form and then check that nonce when saving the data.

> **For more on nonces and security, see Chapter 6.**

Firstly, use the `wp_nonce_field()` function to create a hidden field with a nonce in the form. Edit the callback function to create the field as follows:

```
function wpptl_create_fabric_metabox( $post ) { ?>
 <form action="" method="post">
  <?php // add nonce for security
  wp_nonce_field( 'wpptl_metabox_nonce', 'wpptl_nonce' );
  //retrieve the metadata values if they exist
  $wpptl_fabric = get_post_meta( $post->ID, 'Fabric', true ); ?>
  <label for "wpptl_fabric">What fabric is this garment made from?</label>
  <input type="text" name="wpptl_fabric" value="
    <?php echo esc_attr( $wpptl_fabric ); ?>" />
 </form>
<?php }
```

Next, add a check for the nonce in the function you wrote to save the data:

```
// save the meta box data
add_action( 'save_post','wpptl_save_fabric_meta' );
function wpptl_save_fabric_meta( $post_id ) {
 // if the nonce isn't verified, prevent saving
 if( !isset( $_POST['wpptl_nonce'] ) ||
     !wp_verify_nonce( $_POST['wpptl_nonce'],
     'wpptl_metabox_nonce' ) ) return;
 if ( isset( $_POST['wpptl_fabric'] ) ) {
  $new_fabric_value = ( $_POST['wpptl_fabric'] );
  update_post_meta( $post_id ,'Fabric' , $new_fabric_value );
 }
}
```

This creates a nonce and checks it's present before saving data, which adds security to your form.

Listing a Post's Metadata Values

Having set up a number of meta keys in your site, you'll want to display them somewhere. The most obvious place is on the page for each post or custom post type. In this case it's the `product` custom post type.

The template tag used to list metadata values is as follows:

```
<?php get_post_meta($post_id, $key, $single); ?>
```

The parameters are as follows:

- `post_id`—The ID of the post whose values you want to list (use `$post->ID` for the current post)
- `key`—The `meta_key` being listed. Leave this blank to list values for all meta keys
- `single`—If this is set to `true`, the function will return the first value of the key; if set to `false` or not passed, it will return all values against the key.

For the example site you want to display all the values against each key separately, and you don't want to display anything if the key has no values set. To do this, you will use the `get_post_meta()` function to define some variables and then check whether they are empty, displaying their values if they are not. Add the following in the relevant place in the template file:

```php
<?php
 $fabric_list = get_post_meta( $post->ID, 'Fabric', true );
 $washing_instructions = get_post_meta( $post->ID, 'Washing
   Instructions', true );
 $origin_country = get_post_meta( $post->ID, 'Country of origin',
   true );
 if( !empty( $fabric_list ) ){ ?>
  <p><strong>This garment is made from </strong><span class =
    "metalist fabric"><?php echo $fabric_list; ?> . </span></p><?php
 }
 if( !empty ( $washing_instructions ) ){ ?>
  <p><strong>Washing instructions:</strong><span class = "metalist
    washing"><?php echo $washing_instructions; ?> . </span></p><?php
 }
 if( !empty( $origin_country ) ){ ?>
  <p><strong>Country of origin:</strong><span class = "metalist
    country"><?php echo $origin_country; ?> . </span></p><?php
 }
 ?>
```

As you can see, this process consists of two main steps, which are repeated for each meta key:

1. A variable is assigned based on the results of the `get_post_meta()` function.
2. The variable is checked to confirm that it's not empty. If so, it outputs some HTML to display the metadata value in a span within a paragraph.

> Another way to do this would be to assign use `get_post_meta()`, **looping through the returned meta keys using** `foreach` **and retrieving each value, using a similar method to the one used with** `get_the_term_list()` **to display taxonomy terms. However you have no control over the order of the keys returned using this method .**

As shown in Figure 3-10, this now displays only meta keys containing values.

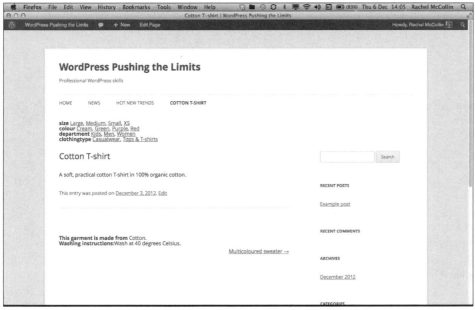

Figure 3-10 The single product page now displays any meta key values that are set.

Of course, you would need to style this and display it in the right place, according to the design chosen for the site—an exercise you can save for later.

Listing Posts by Meta Key Value

At this point, you have your metadata listed on single product pages, but what about listing products with a given meta key value? Suppose, for example, on each product page you want to display all other products made from the same fabric. You'll need to do this outside the main loop, so you define a new query using `WP_query`, and use the `$fabric_list` variable you've already set as one of the arguments for your query, as follows:

```php
<?php
if ( !empty ( $fabric_list ) ) { ?>
 <?php
 //display other products with the same meta key value
 $the_query = new WP_query(
  array(
   'post__not_in' => array($post->ID),
   'post_type' => 'product',
   'meta_key' => 'Fabric',
   'meta_value' => $fabric_list,
  ) );
if ( $the_query->have_posts() ) { ?>
<h3>Other products made from this fabric:</h3>
 <?php while ( $the_query->have_posts() ) : $the_query->the_post();
   ?>
```

(continued)

```
    <div class="common-fabric-listing">
     <a href="<?php the_permalink(); ?>">
        <?php the_post_thumbnail( 'thumbnail' ); ?></a>
     <a href="<?php the_permalink(); ?>"><?php the_title(); ?></a>
    </div>
  <?php endwhile;
  }
  wp_reset_postdata();
  }
  ?>
```

This creates a new query object passing arguments to retrieve posts of `post_type` product with a meta value equal to `$fabric_list` (populated in the earlier code) for the "Fabric" meta key. It excludes the current post being displayed.

After running a loop based on this query, it then uses `wp_reset_postdata` to reset the query (which you should always do when running a custom query).

This code uses conditional tags in two places:

1. It checks if the current product has a value assigned to the 'Fabric' meta key using `if ( !empty ( $fabric_list ) )`.

2. Before displaying other products, it checks that the query does actually have posts in it using `if ( $the_query->have_posts() )`.

If neither of these is the case, nothing will be displayed.

The result, shown in Figure 3-11, is a display of other products with the same fabric type.

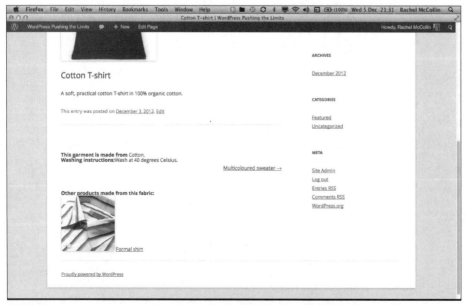

Figure 3-11 Other garments with the same meta key value are now displayed beneath the selected garment

You can see by looking at the query defined here that you could do similar things with your taxonomies, running queries to show products in the same color, for example. Simply define a new variable using `get_the_term_list` to identify terms associated with the current product and then use `foreach` to run a query for each term listed. Because taxonomies are likely to have a number of terms, this would take more effort than doing the same thing for meta keys.

Adding Media to Content

The final content type in WordPress is attachments (or media). This includes images, video, and documents. Four file types are supported by WordPress:

- **Images**—`.jpg, .jpeg, .png, .gif`
- **Documents**—`.pdf, .doc, .docx, .ppt, .pptx, .pps, .ppsx, .odt, .xls, .xlsx`
- **Audio**—`.mp3, .m4a, .ogg, .wav`
- **Video**—`.mp4, .m4v, .mov, .wmv, .avi, .mpg, .ogv, .3gp, .3g2`

How Post Attachments Work

Media can be uploaded in one of three ways:

- In a post or page
- Via the Media screen
- Via a plugin or options screen

All media are known as attachments, regardless of whether they are attached to a post or not. Attachments are stored in the `wp_posts` table, with metadata stored in `wp_postmeta`. Attachment data stored in the `wp_posts` table includes the following:

- `ID`—A unique numeric ID
- `post_author`—The author of the post
- `post_date`—Date of the upload
- `post_title`—The post's title
- `post_status`—Generally inherit as attachments the status of their parent content
- `comment_status` and `ping_status`—Inherited but specified as open or closed in `wp_posts`
- `post_name`—The post's slug
- `post_modified`—Last modification date
- `guid`—"Globally Unique Identifier"
- `post_type`—Always `attachment`
- `post_mime_type`—MIME type; for example, `image/jpeg` or `image/png`
- `comment_count`—Number of comments made about it via its attachments page

Two fields are particularly important, as they link to other content—`post_parent` links to another post in the same table and specifies which post or page the attachment is attached to (if any), while `ID` links to `wp_postmeta`, where additional data on the attachment is stored.

An example `wp_posts` table with `post_parent` highlighted is shown in Figure 3-12.

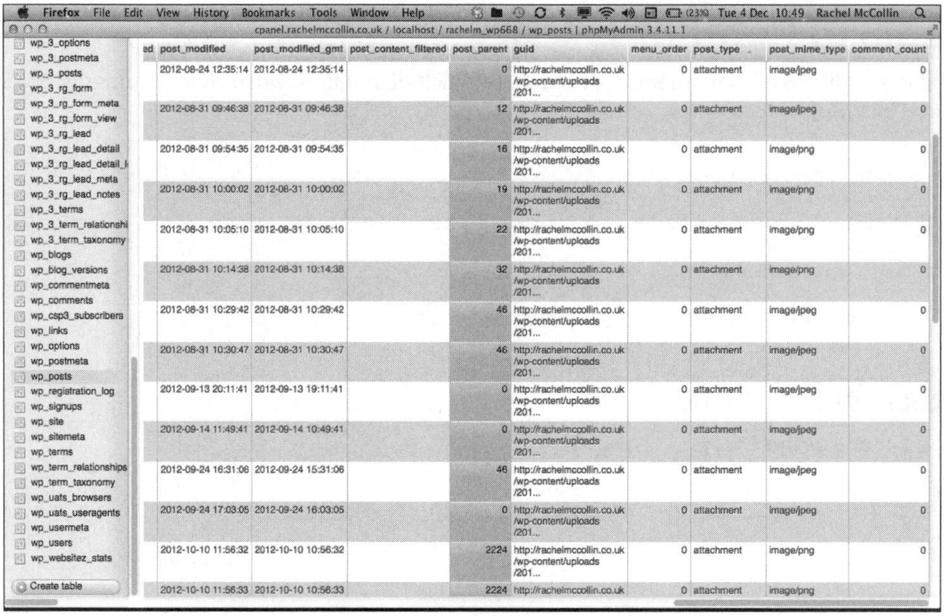

Figure 3-12 The wp_posts table with post_parent data for attachments highlighted

The `wp_postmeta` table stores additional metadata, using the following keys in the `meta_key` field:

- `_wp_attachment_metadata`—A serialized string of data, including the size of an image's different files, for example

- `_wp_attachment_backup_sizes`—A serialized string of data containing the sizes stored for an image

- `_wp_attachment_image_alt`—The `alt` attribute for images

- `_wp_attached_file`—The URL of the original attached file

- `_thumbnail_id`—The ID of any image attached as a thumbnail (or featured image). You can use this with `get_post_thumbnail_id` to get the ID of the thumbnail attached to a given post and then output that thumbnail, or to output all attachments to a post *except* the thumbnail.

Each of these has a `post_id` record corresponding to a `post_id` in the `wp_posts` table, and a `meta_value` record containing the value for that meta key.

It may seem simpler to store this data in `wp_posts` instead of `wp_postmeta`, but keep in mind that not only attachments have keys in `wp_postmeta`—if the `wp_posts` table included a unique field for every `meta_key` used in `wp_postmeta` (by posts, attachments, and menu items), it would be a very large table indeed, with a lot of empty cells.

Adding Metadata to Your Attachments

A major feature of WordPress 3.5 is the enhancements to media upload. The interface for uploading media has been overhauled, and the interface in the media editing screen is clearer, as shown in Figure 3-13.

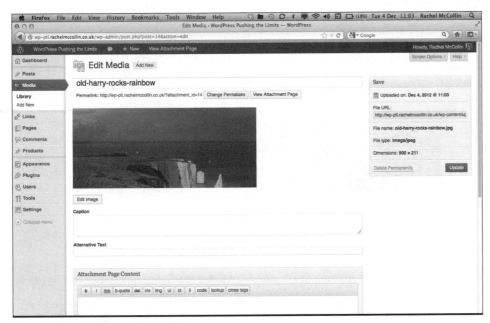

Figure 3-13 The WordPress 3.5 Media Editing page

This screen lets you add metadata such as the caption and `alt` attribute. The 'Attachment Page Content' metabox holds the same metadata as the old 'Description' meta box, but has been enhanced with the addiiton of a TinyMCE-enabled editor, giving you much more control over what's displayed on attachment pages.

The Edit Media screen also gives you the option of enabling or disabling comments for an attachment and the ability to edit the slug, all of which makes it possible to work with attachment display in a similar way to posts and pages. For me, this capability turns attachment pages from being a bit of a nuisance that do little more than add an extra click to the process of viewing an attachment into something really useful.

Figure 3-14 shows the attachment viewed in its own attachment page.

The content is below the image and doesn't have any styling applied yet, but you could easily customize the loop on the `attachment.php` template file to display the content and any metadata as desired. The Twenty Twelve theme uses an image attachment template called `image.php`, which uses `the_content()` to display content added to the image editing screen in the standard way:

```
<div class="entry-description">
 <?php the_content(); ?>
</div><!-- .entry-description -->
```

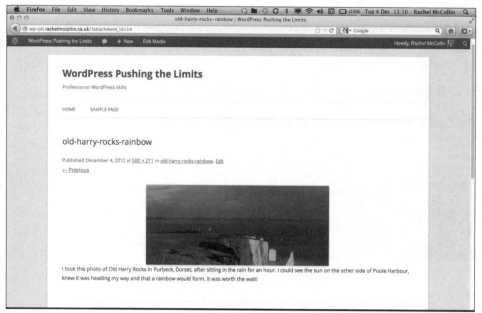

Figure 3-14 An image displayed in its attachment page

It's as easy as that! The content added in the editing page is simply added to the field `post_content` in the `wp_posts` table, and it can be output in the same way that it would be for any content type.

Displaying Galleries Outside the Post Content

Another feature of WordPress that most developers have worked with at one time or another is galleries. Many of us use plugins such as NextGEN Gallery (`http://wordpress.org/extend/plugins/nextgen-gallery/`) to create custom galleries, but WordPress enables you to create galleries using post attachments out of the box.

Adding a Gallery Outside the Main Loop

Adding a gallery within a post's content is a straightforward job of uploading images via the new image uploader, which features a Create Gallery screen, shown in Figure 3-15.

What if you want to set up this gallery in your template file? For example, you might want to add a gallery in the sidebar or elsewhere outside the loop. The single product page currently displays the featured image in the content—you want to add a gallery in the sidebar. However, because the featured image is already displayed, you want to omit that from the sidebar display.

To do this, you use the `wp_get_attachment_image` function and pass arguments to it specifying exactly which images to display—specifically, to omit the featured image.

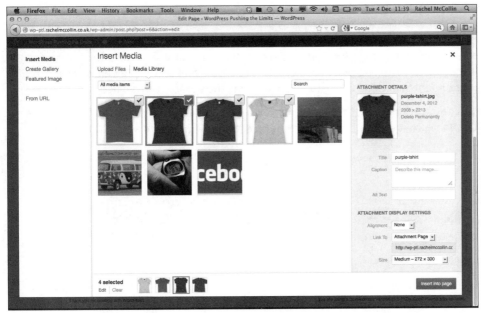

Figure 3-15 Creating a T-shirt gallery

Add a gallery to the sidebar just for the `product` post type, using a conditional tag:

```php
<?php if (is_singular( 'product' )) {} ?>
```

Then add the code for the attachments inside the conditional tag's braces:

```php
<?php if (is_singular( 'product' )) {
  $current_featured_image_id = get_post_thumbnail_id( $post->ID );
  $attachment_image_args = array(
    'post_parent' => get_the_ID(),
    'post_type' => 'attachment',
    'post_mime_type' => 'image',
    'exclude' => $current_featured_image_id,
    ) ;
  $attachments = get_posts($attachment_image_args);
  if ($attachments) {
  foreach ($attachments as $attachment) {
    echo wp_get_attachment_image( $attachment->ID, 'thumbnail' );
  }
 }
}
?>
```

That code does two main things:

- It defines two variables—the ID of the featured image using `get_post_thumbnail_id`, and then an array of arguments that you pass to `wp_get_attachment_image()`. These include the post parent as the current post, the `post_type` and `post_mime_type` to ensure that only images are retrieved, and the `'exclude'` argument to exclude the featured image using the variable you defined.

- Then it defines `$attachments` using the arguments you've just defined; and as long as attachments are found, it loops through each one, using `wp_get_attachment_image()` to display the actual image.

The result is a gallery in the sidebar, as shown in Figure 3-16.

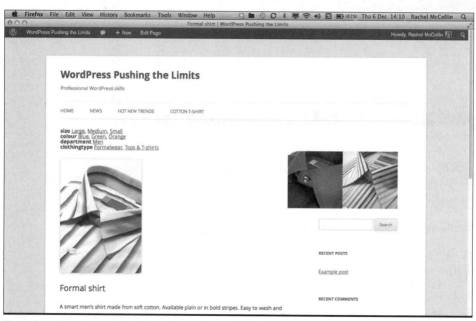

Figure 3-16 The gallery is displayed in the sidebar; the featured image is in the main content.

It still needs some styling, but you have all the images in the right place now.

An alternative method if you want to display a gallery with a list of images you define is to use the `[gallery]` shortcode and add the image IDs.

In your template file, you add the following:

```php
<?php echo do_shortcode( '[gallery ids="19,20,21,22"]' ); ?>
```

This creates a gallery to display the images with those IDs, as shown in Figure 3-17. This gallery doesn't just display on the page those images have been uploaded to.

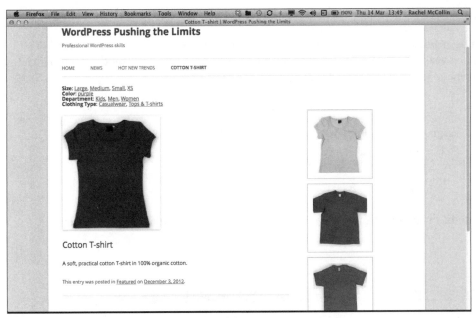

Figure 3-17 The alternative gallery displayed in the sidebar

You could do more with this gallery—display it as a slideshow, customize the links from each image, or add a lightbox to it. For now, however, we'll leave it as it is.

Featured Images

Featured images are great. Introduced with WordPress 2.9, they provide functionality that a lot of developers were already achieving using metadata, but they make it much easier. Working with featured images is so straightforward that it isn't necessary to devote a lot of space to it here, so this section briefly explains how they work and clarifies a few possible points of confusion:

- *Featured image* is the term used in the WordPress admin for an image attached to a post as its main image.

- The WordPress back end calls this the *thumbnail*. It stores the attachment itself in `wp_posts` but creates a record for its parent post in `wp_postmeta` with the key of `thumbnail_ID` and a value equal to the `post_id` of the attachment. This means that images can be used as the featured image for multiple posts, but each post can only have one featured image.

- Finally, `'thumbnail'` is the term used for a specific size of image as displayed using `the_post_thumbnail( 'thumbnail' )`. This use of `thumbnail` can apply to any image, and has no relationship whatever to the featured image. If you find this confusing, you could simply write a function renaming the `'thumbnail'` size and calling it something else—`'teeny_weeny'`, for example. Or you could just live with it like most developers!

Terminology aside, the following example uses an archive page to display featured images with each post title.

In the site you have been creating in this chapter, you have a template file called `archive-product.php`, which lists the products available. Instead of having it list the titles and extracts for each product, you want it to display the featured image. Inside the loop, add the following:

```
<div id="product-image-grid post-<?php the_ID(); ?>"
    <?php post_class(); ?>>
  <a class="image-link" href="<?php the_permalink(); ?>">
      <?php the_post_thumbnail( 'thumbnail' ); ?></a>
  <a class="product-link" href="<?php the_permalink(); ?>">
      <?php the_title(); ?></a>
</div><!-- #product-image-grid -->
```

This displays the featured image and the title of each product on the products listing page, as shown in Figure 3-18.

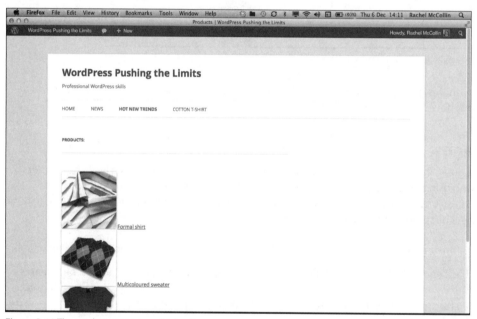

Figure 3-18 The products page now displays images.

The next step would be to style this as a grid and maybe give the titles absolute positioning so they're overlaid over the images, but that's outside the scope of this book.

Summary

In this chapter you learned how WordPress stores data in the database tables, and how relationships are defined between those tables so that you can associate images with posts, for example. You also learned how to register custom post types and taxonomies and create custom queries to output data using those taxonomies.

You learned about creating custom meta boxes and adding security to these. You'll work more on this in Chapter 4, where you'll learn how to further customize the admin and create admin pages, and in Chapter 6, which goes into more detail on security.

Understanding how WordPress manages, stores, retrieves, and outputs data is key to creating your own bespoke pages and sites, and hopefully what you've learned here has given you food for thought for your own and your client's projects.

Further Resources
Device-Specific Content

Jakob Nielsen on why sites should have different content for different devices
`http://www.useit.com/alertbox/mobile-vs-full-sites.html`

Bruce Lawson on why not to send different content to different devices
`http://mobile.smashingmagazine.com/2012/04/19/why-we-shouldnt-make-separate-mobile-websites/`

How WordPress Stores Content

The WordPress database structure
`http://codex.wordpress.org/Database_Description`

The WordPress Multisite database structure
`http://codex.wordpress.org/Database_Description#Multisite_Table_Overview`

Custom Post Types

Registering post types
`http://codex.wordpress.org/Function_Reference/register_post_type`

Justin Tadlock on custom post types
`http://justintadlock.com/archives/2010/04/29/custom-post-types-in-wordpress`

Showing post types on your blog's home page
`http://justintadlock.com/archives/2010/02/02/showing-custom-post-types-on-your-home-blog-page`

Taxonomies

Codex documentation on taxonomies
`http://codex.wordpress.org/Taxonomies`

How to create custom taxonomies in WordPress
`http://wp.smashingmagazine.com/2012/01/04/create-custom-taxonomies-wordpress/`

Detailed overview of custom taxonomies

http://justintadlock.com/archives/2010/06/10/a-refresher-on-custom-taxonomies

The get_taxonomies function

http://codex.wordpress.org/Function_Reference/get_taxonomies

The get_the_term_list function

http://codex.wordpress.org/Function_Reference/get_the_term_list

Custom Fields and Post Metadata

The WordPress Metadata API

http://codex.wordpress.org/Metadata_API

Custom field tips, tricks, and hacks

http://www.wpbeginner.com/wp-tutorials/wordpress-custom-fields-101-tips-tricks-and-hacks/

Jeff Starr's custom field tutorial

http://perishablepress.com/wordpress-custom-fields-tutorial/

The add_meta_box function

http://codex.wordpress.org/Function_Reference/add_meta_box

Chapter 4

Customizing the WordPress Admin

If you're developing sites, themes, or plugins for others, it may be necessary to customize the admin screens in WordPress in order to include additional options or settings for your users to control or to make things simpler for them. In this chapter you'll learn how to do that. In particular, you'll learn about the following:

- **Roles and capabilities**—How they work and how to customize and add to them
- **Admin screens**—Customizing the existing screens (including the Dashboard) and adding new ones
- **Theme options**—Adding options to your theme and integrating the Theme Customizer
- **Data sanitization**—Why it's necessary and how to do it
- **Content and editing**—How to customize administration to make it easier for your clients to edit their sites and minimize the risk of errors

> As the chapter progresses, you'll find the code for a series of plugins that you can download from `www.wiley.com/go/ptl/wordpress`. **This includes code for theme options screens, although you would normally place these in the theme's functions file, not a plugin. For more on functions and plugins, see Chapter 9.**

When to Customize the WordPress Admin

For users and developers familiar with WordPress, the admin screens are very straightforward to use. For complete novices, however, especially those with a nontechnical bent, working with these screens can be a little daunting. This is one reason why it's a good idea to customize the WordPress administration for nontechnical clients.

In addition, your theme or plugin may have options that your users need to be able to configure—in which case you need to add options screens to enable this.

Client Sites

Customizations you might make to client sites include the following:

- Adding branding to the login screen and/or admin screens—either your own or your client's. This will be particularly relevant if your client requires users to log in via the login screen.

▓ Adding tips and help to the Dashboard and the admin screens, to provide instructions on editing and managing the site

▓ Creating admin screens so that users can edit non-post content (such as contact details or copyright information) and make changes to the theme where relevant

▓ Making it possible for editors to add and edit content other than posts and pages—for example, the content of the header, sidebar and footer

You'll learn how to do each of these as you work through this chapter.

Themes and Plugins

Customizing the WordPress admin screens is relevant if you're developing for clients or if you're releasing themes or plugins to the public:

▓ Clients may never have used WordPress before, so your customizations should have the objective of making things simpler for them.

▓ Publicly released themes may require theme options screens that enable users to add content such as banner or background images or make changes to the CSS, for example.

▓ Publicly released themes will also benefit from Theme Customizer support.

▓ Your plugins may need settings screens, either a single screen within an existing section of the menu or in a new menu section that you create.

You'll learn how to do each of these in this chapter.

In all cases, the quality and validity of data input via the screens you're customizing or adding is important, as you will see in the section "Sanitizing Data," later in the chapter, and in Chapter 9.

WordPress Roles and Capabilities

WordPress uses roles and capabilities to control the level of access users have to core options, settings, and functions, and you can use these to control access to your own functions and screens too.

Each role has a number of capabilities assigned to it, which determine what users with that role can do. This means that you can change the capabilities assigned to a role, or you can add new roles or capabilities yourself.

Roles

WordPress has six default roles:

▓ **Super Admin**—Only relevant to Multisite networks, users with this role can make changes to the network, to the sites in it, and to installed themes and plugins.

▓ **Administrator**—In a non-Multisite installation, this role has access to all the administration features. In the case of Multisite, users with this role will have restrictions, such as not being able to install plugins or themes.

- **Editor**—Users can publish and manage posts and pages as well as manage other users' posts, etc.
- **Author**—Users can publish and manage their own posts.
- **Contributor**—Users can write and manage their own posts but not publish them.
- **Subscriber**—Users can only manage their profile; they cannot write, edit, or manage posts.

Each of these roles has a different set of capabilities and provides a different admin screen that users can access.

Roles and the WordPress Admin

When users are logged in to the WordPress admin, the menu they see varies according to the role they hold, as shown in Table 4-1. Screens that admin users can't access in a Multisite installation are marked with an asterisk.

Table 4-1: Admin Screens Available to WordPress Roles

Menu Item	Super Admin	Admin	Editor	Author	Contributor	Subscriber
Dashboard	X	X	X	X	X	X
Sites—all sites, add new	X					
Posts—all posts, add new	X	X	X	X	X	
Posts—categories, tags	X	X	X			
Media—library, add new	X	X	X	X	X	
Pages—all pages, add new	X	X	X			
Comments	X	X	X	X	X	
Appearance—themes, widgets, menus, editor	X	X				
Plugins—installed plugins	X	X				
Plugins—add new, editor	X	X*				
Users—all users, add new	X	X				
Users—your profile (called Profile for non-admin users)	X	X	X	X	X	X
Tools—available tools (called Tools) to non-admin users)	X	X	X	X		
Tools—import, export	X	X				
Settings—general, writing, reading, discussion, media, permalinks	X	X				

Figure 4-1 and Figure 4-2 illustrate how the appearance of the WordPress admin differs according to user role—in this case, the administrator role and the contributor role, respectively. Not that the Sites menu item is not shown here as this is only available on a multisite installation.

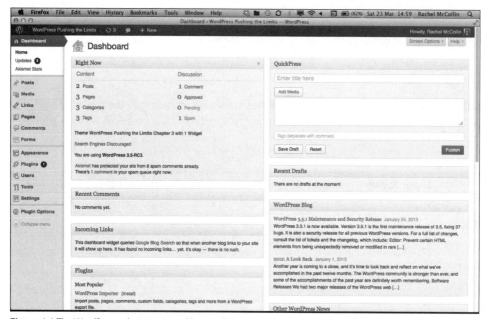

Figure 4-1 The WordPress admin as viewed by an administrator (on a standard installation)

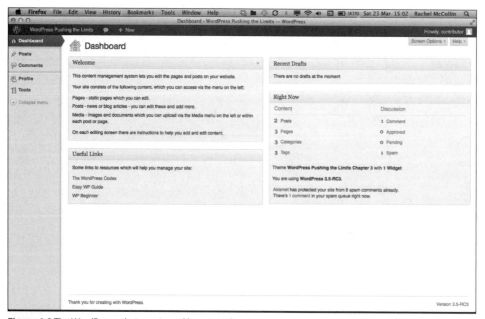

Figure 4-2 The WordPress admin as viewed by a contributor

Capabilities

Capabilities are what allow users to carry out actions in WordPress. WordPress 3.5 includes a set of capabilities that relate to actions a user might take when viewing, editing, or working on a site or installation. These capabilities are then assigned to each of the roles.

The capabilities are defined, or named, in terms of the actions they allow and the content to which they are related, as shown in the following examples:

- Management capabilities begin with `manage_`, such as `manage_others_posts` and `manage_links`.
- Editing capabilities include `edit_private_posts` and `edit_published_pages`.
- Capabilities relating to plugins end with `_plugins`, such as `update_plugins` and `delete_plugins`.

Table 4-2 provides a list of default capabilities, grouped by the actions and content type to which they are related.

Table 4-2: WordPress Capabilities By Activity and Content Type

	Management	Content Creation	Editing	Deletion	Reading
Site	manage_ network, manage_site				
Users	manage_ network_users, list_users, promote_users , create_users		edit_users	delete_ users, remove_ users	
Themes	install_ themes, manage_ network_ themes, switch_themes, update_themes		edit_themes	delete_ themes	
Plugins	install_ plugins, activate_ plugins, update_plugins		edit_ plugins	delete_ plugins	

(continued)

Table 4-2 *(continued)*

	Management	Content Creation	Editing	Deletion	Reading
Posts		publish_ posts	edit_posts, edit_ others_ posts, edit_ published_ posts	delete_ posts, delete_ others_ posts, delete_ private_ posts, delete_ published_ posts	read_ private_ posts
Pages		publish_ pages	edit_pages, edit_ others_ pages, edit_ published_ pages, edit_ private_ pages	delete_ pages, delete_ others_ pages, delete_ published_ pages, delete_ private_ pages	read_ private_ pages
Categories and tags	manage_ categories				
Comments	moderate_ comments				
Links	manage_links				
Options	manage_ network_ options, manage_options		edit_theme_ options		
Other	unfiltered_ html, update_ core, edit_ dashboard, export, import	unfiltered_ upload, upload, upload_ files	edit_files		read

For a full list of WordPress capabilities by role, see `http://codex.wordpress.org/Roles_and_Capabilities`.

Custom Roles and Capabilities

Sometimes you may need to give users access to a capability without upgrading their role. For example, you might want users with the Editor role (who I'll refer to in this chapter as Editors) to be able to manage options without giving them access to all the other capabilities assigned to administrators. There are three ways you can go about this:

- Assign the capability to an existing role using `add_cap()`.

- Create a new role with that capability plus any others you want users with that role to have, using `add_role()`.

- Create a new capability relevant to your theme or plugin, and define which role(s) it applies to, using `add_cap()`.

Each of these options has its place. The first option is the simplest, and it is useful if you want to add one or two capabilities to an existing role. If you want to make more changes, I recommend setting up a new role with the relevant capabilities. Creating your own capability gives you finer control over exactly what users with that capability can do—for example, you might want some users to only be able to edit posts from a certain post type.

Understanding How Roles and Capabilities Are Stored

Before adding custom roles and/or capabilities, you should understand how they are stored so you can add them correctly. Roles and capabilities are stored in the `wp_options` table, in the `user_roles` field. This means that if you're adding them in your theme or plugin and that theme or plugin is deactivated, the information is still held in the database. How roles and capabilities are stored has two consequences:

- When adding new roles and/or capabilities, it's best to do so upon activation of your theme or plugin—using the `register_activation_hook()` action hook, which runs when a plugin is activated.

- You need to clean up after yourself if your theme or plugin is deleted, removing any data added to the `wp_options` table; see Chapter 9 for more information on using an uninstall function to do this.

Assigning Capabilities to Roles

To create a new capability, you use the `add_cap()` function, which creates a capability (or fetches an existing one) and adds it to a role you define in your function:

```php
<?php
function wpptl_add_cap() {
 $role = get_role( $role_name );
 $role->add_cap( $cap );
}
add_action( 'register_activation_hook', 'wpptl_add_cap' );
?>
```

The `add_cap()` function takes two parameters:

- `$role`—The role you are assigning the capability to; if it's not an existing role, you need to define your new role separately.

- `$cap`—The name of the capability you're assigning to the role, which could be an existing capability or a new one you're creating, in which case be sure you give it a unique name with a prefix.

Therefore, to add `manage_options` to the editor role, you would add the following to your plugin or functions file:

```php
<?php
function wpptl_add_cap2() {
 $role = get_role( 'editor' );
 $role->add_cap( 'edit_theme_options' );
}
add_action( 'register_activation_hook' , 'wpptl_add_cap2' );
?>
```

This would give users with the editor role access to theme options screens, for example.

Creating Your Own Capabilities

To add a new capability to the editor role, you would use the same function:

```php
<?php
function wpptl_add_cap3() {
 $role = get_role( 'editor' );
 $role->add_cap( 'wpptl_new_capability' );
}
add_action( 'admin_init', 'wpptl_add_cap3' );
?>
```

To use this new capability, you would check for it when creating an admin screen for your theme or plugin, as described shortly.

The next example extends the editor role in my plugin by adding a brand-new capability to it. The following code first sets up the plugin:

```php
<?php
/*
Plugin Name: WordPress Pushing the Limits Customize Admin
Plugin URI: http://rachelmccollin.co.uk/wpptl/chapter4
Description: Plugin containing the functions from chapter 4 of the book
 'WordPress Pushing the Limits' on user roles and capabilities and
 customising the WordPress admin.
Version: 1.0
Author: Rachel McCollin
Author URI: http://rachelmccollin.com
License: GPLv2
*/
?>
```

Below this I add my function to fetch the role and assign my new capability to it:

```php
<?php
function wpptl_add_editor_capability() {
 $role = get_role( 'editor' );
 $role->add_cap( 'wpptl_editor_cap' );
}
add_action('register_activation_hook', 'wpptl_add_editor_capability' );
?>
```

This adds a new `wpptl_editor_cap` capability, which I can now use in my plugin to define screens that users with that capability can access.

Creating Your Own Roles

Creating a new role uses the `add_role()` function:

```php
<?php
add_role( $role, $display_name, $capabilities );
?>
```

The `add_role()` function has the following parameters:

- `$role`—The name of the new role; make this unique, memorable, and use a prefix
- `$display_name`—The name of the role as displayed in the admin; again, choose something unique and logical
- `$capabilities`—An array of capabilities assigned to the role

As you can see, this gives you two ways to add capabilities to your role: You can add them when creating your role in the array, or you can add them after the role has been defined using `add_cap()`. The first method is the easiest, but the second can be useful when you want to add a capability to a role you've defined in a plugin or a function for which you want to keep all the functionality together in your functions file or an include.

The next example sets up a new plugin to add a new role called "Photo Uploader," with the capability to upload files but nothing else:

```php
<?php
/*
Plugin Name: WordPress Pushing the Limits Add Role
Plugin URI: http://rachelmccollin.co.uk/wpptl/chapter4
Description: Plugin demonstrating the process of adding a user role, as
 covered in Chapter 4 of 'WordPress Pushing the Limits'
Version: 1.0
Author: Rachel McCollin
Author URI: http://rachelmccollin.com
```

(continued)

```
License: GPLv2
*/

function wpptl_add_photo_uploader_role() {
 add_role( 'wpptl_photo_uploader', 'Photo Uploader',
  array( 'upload_files', true ) );
}
add_action( 'register_activation_hook',
  'wpptl_add_photo_uploader_role' );
?>
```

This adds a new role to the list of available roles when assigning roles to a user, as shown in Figure 4-3.

Figure 4-3 The new user role

Assigning Roles and Capabilities to Users

As well as assigning capabilities to roles, it's also possible to assign them to individual users. This can be useful when you have a group of users, such as editors, for example, but you want to give just one of them access to additional capabilities.

Use this method with caution. If you have one user who needs a different capability but the identity of the user or the number of users with that role will change over time, it may be better to set up a new user role and assign it to that user.

Assigning a Capability to an Individual User

To assign a capability to a user, you use the `WP_user` class (`http://codex.wordpress.org/Class_Reference/WP_User`) with the user ID to get the User Object for the user you want and then add (or remove) roles and capabilities for that user.

First, you identify the user using either their ID or their username. Here is the code to use the ID:

```php
<?php
$user = new WP_User( $id );
?>
```

Here is the code to use the username:

```php
<?php
$user = new WP_User( null, $name );
?>
```

The next step is to define the capability you're adding:

```php
<?php
$user->add_cap( $cap_name );
?>
```

This lets you add the defined capability (`$cap_name`) to that user without altering the capabilities they already have, as you're not changing their role.

Assigning a Role to an Individual User

Assigning a role to a user is done in the same way as assigning a capability:

```php
<?php
$user->add_role( $role_name );
?>
```

This lets you add the defined role to that user without altering the role that's already been assigned to them, meaning a user can have multiple roles.

> While WordPress supports multiple roles per user, there are currently issues with the reliability of this. Plans are afoot to make things better. See `https://core.trac.wordpress.org/changeset/22686` for more information.

For example, the following adds the Photo Uploader role to an existing user but preserves the capabilities they already have via the role to which they are currently assigned:

```php
<?php
function wpptl_add_role_to_user() {
  $user = new WP_User( null, 'madonna' );
  $user->add_role( 'wpptl_photo_uploader' );
}
add_action( 'admin_init', 'wpptl_add_role_to_user' );
?>
```

To override any existing roles assigned to the user, use `set_role()` instead of `add_role`.

You can also add or remove a user's capability. This can be useful when you have multiple users with the same role but you want just one of them to have a given capability, or you want to remove a capability (or capabilities), such as from the admin account you've set up for a client.

For example, if you have an administrator with the user ID of 3, and you want to remove the `install_plugins` capability from that user, you would use the following:

```php
<?php
function wpptl_remove_cap_from_user() {
  $user = new WP_User( '3' );
  $user->remove_cap( 'install_plugins' );
}
add_action( 'admin_init', 'wpptl_remove_cap_from_user' );
?>
```

You can do this to set up an individual user with more or fewer capabilities than other users with that role. If you need to add a lot of capabilities, I recommend creating a role with those capabilities and then assigning that role to the user.

Assigning a Role to Users with an Existing Role or Capability

You can take this further by using a conditional statement to identify users with given capabilities, and then adding a capability or role to that user. WordPress doesn't let you use `WP_user` to check the current user's role directly, but you can use it to check whether the user has a given capability that only applies to users with the role you're targeting.

For example, to add the Photo Uploader role to all administrators, you would check for the `manage_options` capability, which only admins have:

```php
<?php
function wpptl_add_role_to_administrators() {
  $user = new WP_User( $id );
  if $user->has_cap( 'manage_options' ); {
    $user->add_role( 'wpptl_photo_uploader' );
  }
}
add_action( 'admin_init', 'wpptl_add_role_to_administrators );
?>
```

This is one reason why it's a good idea to create new roles if you want to move capabilities around; if another plugin is checking for a capability in order to identify administrators and you've assigned that capability to another role, it will cause problems. This can be a useful way to separate the capabilities associated with different roles, instead of simply adding those capabilities to the existing role. It also means you can easily remove those capabilities from users with that role without having to list all the capabilities—you can just use `remove_role()`, which is covered next.

Removing Roles and Capabilities

As mentioned earlier, adding roles and capabilities adds data to the database, in the `wp_options` table. If your theme or plugin adds this data, you want to ensure that the data is deleted when the theme or plugin is deleted.

> You should only do this when the plugin or theme is deleted, *not* when it's deactivated. For more details about this, see Chapter 9.

To remove capabilities, you use `remove_cap()`; and to remove roles, you use `remove_role()`. Each of these has just one parameter—the name of the role or capability you're removing.

Returning to the plugin with the added Photo Uploader role—suppose you want to ensure that when the plugin is deleted (i.e. uninstalled), the role is removed from the database. You can do this either in the main plugin file or in an include called `uninstall.php`.

In this case you are adding the code in the main plugin file, so you use the uninstall hook as follows:

```php
<?php
// uninstall function to remove the role
function wpptl_remove_role_data() {
 remove_role( 'wpptl_photo_uploader' );
}
// activation function to register the uninstall hook
function wpptl_activate_plugin() {
 register_uninstall_hook( __FILE__,  'wpptl_remove_role_data' );
}
register_activation_hook (__FILE__, 'wpptl_activate_plugin' );
?>
```

Working through this code:

- The first part is the uninstall function `wpptl_remove_role_data()`, which includes `remove_role()`.

- Next is an activation function, which attaches the `wpptl_remove_data()` function to `register_unistall_hook()`, ensuring it fires when the plugin is uninstalled.

- Finally, the `wpptl_activate_plugin()` function is attached to `register_activation_hook`, ensuring it fires when the plugin is initially activated.

Now when you delete the plugin altogether (but not when you deactivate it), the Photo Uploader role is removed from the list of available roles, as shown by its absence in Figure 4-4.

Figure 4-4 The list of roles has returned to its default values

> **Warning:** If you have added roles or capabilities that are critical to the functioning of a site, removing them will likely cause problems. Therefore, you may need to assign alternative default roles or capabilities to users or roles as part of your deactivation function. Carefully consider the possible consequences of deleting the given roles and/or capabilities when deciding on your approach.

Checking User Capabilities

After you have set up user capabilities, you'll need to use these elsewhere. For example, you might have a function that is activated only if the current user has a certain capability. To do this, you use the `current_user_can()` function (http://codex.wordpress.org/Function_Reference/current_user_can).

To determine whether the current user has a given role, you need to identify the user and then check if they have a given capability:

```php
<?php
if ( current_user_can( $cap ) ) {
 // do something
    }
?>
```

Therefore, to check the plugin to which the `wpptl_editor_cap` capability was added, you would use the following:

```php
<?php
if ( current_user_can( 'wpptl_editor_cap' ) ) {
 // do something
    }
?>
```

I return to this process of checking later in this chapter, in the "Populating the Admin Screen" section, where you see how you can determine whether the user has this capability, making the admin screen you create visible to them if so.

Creating Admin Screens

If you're developing themes, either for clients or for other WordPress users and developers, you might need to include an options page or a series of them. Theme options pages can incorporate just about any options you wish to add. Common uses include the following:

- **Layout**—Number of sidebars used, settings for a grid system if that's used for layout, page width, etc.
- **Styling**—Changes to colors, fonts, and other styling; custom CSS
- **Images**—Header or background images, logos, etc.
- **Content**—Content to be inserted into the theme, such as contact details or copyright information

In addition to options pages, beginning with WordPress 3.4 you also have the option to add support for the Theme Customizer (`https://codex.wordpress.org/Theme_Customisation_API`). You'll learn how to do this later in this chapter.

For plugins, the range of uses for your settings pages will be related to the plugin itself and the functionality it contains. Many plugins include settings pages, which range from a simple single page to turn the plugin off and on and maybe make some simple tweaks, to a range of settings pages such as those provided by the larger form and SEO plugins.

> Theme options pages and plugin settings pages are essentially the same thing—admin screens. The only difference is where you add the code for them.

In this section you'll learn how to edit and add admin screens for plugins and themes. You'll also learn how to integrate the Theme Customizer and how to customize the Dashboard and login screens.

Customizing the Dashboard

If you're developing for clients, customizing the Dashboard enables you to provide an interface that is cleaner and more user-friendly, and that provides specific information to site editors about how to manage their site. The default Dashboard page is shown in Figure 4-5. For the purposes of this example, the following widgets are removed from the editor user role:

- Recent Comments
- Incoming Links
- Plugins
- QuickPress
- WordPress Blog
- Other WordPress News

Added are two new widgets: one for welcome text and one for useful links.

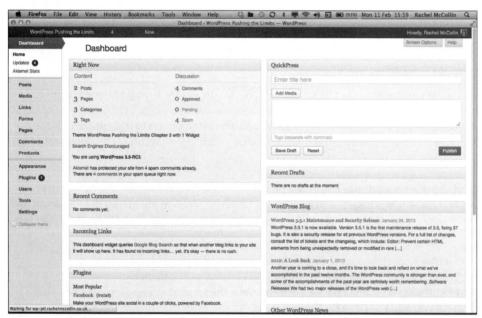

Figure 4-5 The default WordPress dashboard

Dashboard widgets are controlled via the (you guessed it) Dashboard Widgets API, which includes functions to add and remove widgets.

Removing Widgets from the Dashboard

To remove the unwanted widgets for users with a role other than administrator, you use the `remove_meta_box()` function:

```php
<?php
remove_meta_box( $id, , 'dashboard', $position );
?>
```

The parameters are as follows:

- `$id`—The unique ID of the widget. The following are the IDs of the default widgets:
  - `dashboard_browser_nag`—The reminder to update your browser if it's out of date
  - `dashboard_right_now`
  - `dashboard_recent_comments`
  - `dashboard_incoming_links`
  - `dashboard_plugins`
  - `dashboard_quick_press`
  - `dashboard_recent_drafts`
  - `dashboard_primary`—The WordPress Blog widget
  - `dashboard_secondary`—The Other WordPress News widget
- `'dashboard'`—This tells WordPress that you're removing the widget from the Dashboard, which is necessary because `remove_meta_box` isn't specific to the Dashboard (indeed, you can use it anywhere you like in the admin).
- `$position`— The position of the widget, which is `'normal'` for widgets on the left side and `'side'` for right-hand side widgets

You should hook your function to call `remove_meta_box()` into the `wp_dashboard_setup` action hook, which sets up the Dashboard widgets.

The following code removes unwanted widgets from the customized admin plugin created earlier:

```php
<?php
// remove unwanted dashboard widgets for relevant users
function wpptl_remove_dashboard_widgets() {
 if ( ! current_user_can( 'manage_options' ) ) {
  remove_meta_box( 'dashboard_recent_comments', 'dashboard', 'normal' );
  remove_meta_box( 'dashboard_incoming_links', 'dashboard', 'normal' );
  remove_meta_box( 'dashboard_plugins', 'dashboard', 'normal' );
  remove_meta_box( 'dashboard_quick_press', 'dashboard', 'side' );
```

(continued)

```
remove_meta_box( 'dashboard_primary', 'dashboard', 'side' );
remove_meta_box( 'dashboard_secondary', 'dashboard', 'side' );
    }
  }
add_action( 'wp_dashboard_setup', 'wpptl_remove_dashboard_widgets' );
?>
```

This does the following:

1. It first gets the current user with `wp_get_current_user`.

2. It checks whether the current user does *not* have the `manage_options` capability, which will be the case for all roles except administrator.

3. If so, it removes the unwanted meta boxes.

4. It attaches the function to do all this to the `wp_dashboard_setup hook`.

Now, when the relevant users log in, they see the Dashboard shown in Figure 4-6.

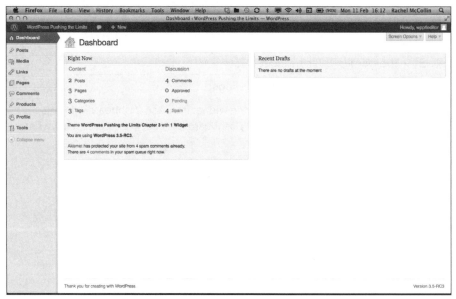

Figure 4-6 The Dashboard after the unwanted widgets are removed

Because subscribers can't see the last two dashboard widgets, when they log in they will see two empty areas surrounded by dotted lines. If your site has subscribers who will be using the admin, you will need to separate the `remove_meta_box()` functions for the last two widgets into a separate function which doesn't apply to subscribers. You would do this by checking that the user doesn't have the `manage_options` capability but does have the `edit_posts` capabilty, which all roles except the Subscriber role have.

Moving Dashboard Widgets

The next example moves the two widgets to the right side, enabling the new widgets to be added on the left. You can do this using the $wp_meta_boxes global variable, adding the following to the plugin:

```php
<?php
// Move the 'Right Now' dashboard widget to the right hand side
function wpptl_move_dashboard_widget() {
 if ( ! current_user_can( 'manage_options' ) ) {
  global $wp_meta_boxes;
  $widget =
  $wp_meta_boxes['dashboard']['normal']['core']['dashboard_right_now'];
  unset( $wp_meta_boxes['dashboard']['normal']['core']
       ['dashboard_right_now'] );
  $wp_meta_boxes['dashboard']['side']['core']['dashboard_right_now'] =
  $widget;
 }
}
add_action( 'wp_dashboard_setup', 'wpptl_move_dashboard_widget' );
?>
```

This does the following:

1. It confirms that the current user does not have the manage_options capability.

2. It accesses the $wp_meta_boxes global variable.

3. It defines a new variable called $widget as the Dashboard widget you want to move, using $wp_meta_boxes.

4. It removes the Dashboard widget using unset.

5. It adds the Dashboard widget back to the correct place by defining the $wp_meta_boxes variable's value as the $widget variable's value.

6. It attaches the function to the wp_dashboard_setup hook.

Now the Dashboard looks like Figure 4-7.

Adding Dashboard Widgets

The final step is to add the new Dashboard widgets: Welcome and Useful Links. Both of these need HTML to define what they will display, and are added using the wp_add_dashboard_widget() function with callback functions:

```php
<?php
wp_add_dashboard_widget( $widget_id, $widget_name, $callback,
  $control_callback = null );
?>
```

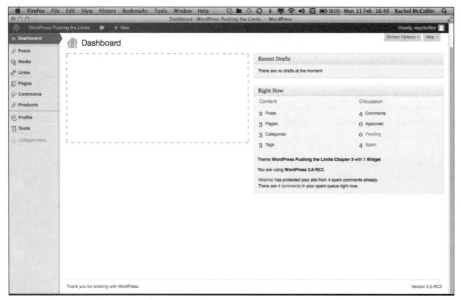

Figure 4-7 The Dashboard with the Right Now widget on the right

The parameters are as follows:

- `$widget_id`—A unique ID for the widget; use a prefix to ensure this doesn't clash with any widgets added by other plugins

- `$widget_name`—The name of the widget as displayed on the Dashboard screen

- `$callback`—The name of the function that will display the widget's contents; this must be unique

- `$control_callback`—An optional parameter that specifies the name of a second function to handle submission of forms contained in the widget

To add the new Dashboard widgets, you begin by defining the `wp_add_dashboard_widget()` function in your plugin:

```php
<?php
// add new dashboard widgets
function wpptl_add_dashboard_widgets() {
 wp_add_dashboard_widget( 'wpptl_dashboard_welcome', 'Welcome',
   'wpptl_add_welcome_widget' );
 wp_add_dashboard_widget( 'wpptl_dashboard_links', 'Useful Links',
   'wpptl_add_links_widget' );
}
function wpptl_add_welcome_widget(){
}
function wpptl_add_links_widget() {
}
add_action( 'wp_dashboard_setup', 'wpptl_add_dashboard_widgets' );
?>
```

This adds three new functions:

- `wppt1_add_dashboard_widgets()`—Adds the new widgets using the `wp_add_dashboard_widget()` function

- `wppt1_add_welcome_widget()`—Defines the contents of the Welcome widget

- `wppt1_add_links_widget()`—Defines the contents of the Useful Links widget You now have two empty widgets in the Dashboard, as shown in Figure 4-8.

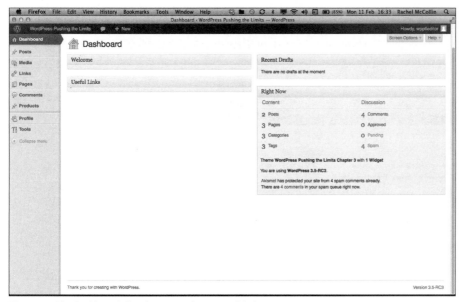

Figure 4-8 The Dashboard after the new widgets are added

The final step is to add content to each of the widgets.

First the Welcome widget:

```php
<?php
function wppt1_add_welcome_widget(){ ?>
 <p>This content management system lets you edit the pages and posts on
  your website.</p>
 <p>Your site consists of the following content, which you can access via
  the menu on the left:</p>
 <ul>
  <li>Pages - static pages which you can edit.</li>
  <li>Posts - news or blog articles - you can edit these and add more.</li>
  <li>Media - images and documents which you can upload via the Media menu
  on the left or within each post or page.</li>
 </ul>
 <p>On each editing screen there are instructions to help you add and edit
  content.</p>
<?php }
?>
```

Then the Useful Links widget:

```php
<?php
function wpptl_add_links_widget() { ?>
 <p>Some links to resources which will help you manage your site:</p>
 <ul>
  <li><a href="http://wordpress.org">The WordPress Codex</a></li>
  <li><a href="http://easywpguide.com">Easy WP Guide</a></li>
  <li><a href="http://www.wpbeginner.com">WP Beginner</a></li>
 </ul>
<?php }
?>
```

Each of these adds the markup required to populate the widget. They now look like what is shown in Figure 4-9.

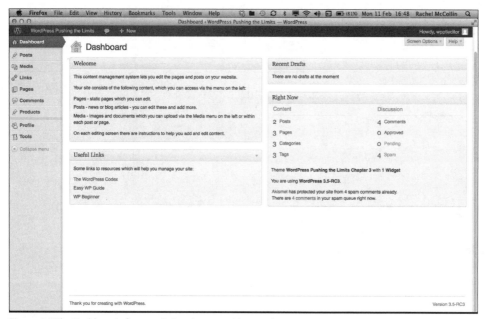

Figure 4-9 The Dashboard after populating the new widgets with content

Customizing the Login Screen

For some of your projects, you will want to customize the login screen by replacing the WordPress logo with another logo—typically the client's logo or your own depending on who will be using the screen.

WordPress uses a background image to display a logo on the login screen, so all you need to do to alter this is add some new CSS. First you need to create a logo with the desired dimensions, but it shouldn't be bigger than 323 pixels wide by 67 pixels high in order to fit in the login screen. This example changes the logo to that of my framework theme, Compass Framework.

First create the image and save it to the `/media` directory within your plugin's directory, in this case `wp-content/plugins/wpptl-media-admin/media/`. The next step is to add the code to your plugin to display it:

```php
<?php
// add a new logo to the login page
function wpptl_login_logo() { ?>
 <style type="text/css">
  body.login #login h1 a {
  background-image: url( <?php echo plugins_url( 'media/compass-
  framework.png' , __FILE__ ); ?> );
  }
 </style>
<?php }
add_action( 'login_enqueue_scripts', 'wpptl_login_logo' );
?>
```

This adds CSS inside `<style>` tags to display the new background image, and then attaches your function to the `login_enqueue_scripts` hook, which fires when the login page is loaded. Note that `plugins_url` is used to identify the file path for the image file—if you were doing this in a theme, you would use `get_bloginfo ( 'stylesheet_directory' )`. When users log in, they now see the new logo, as shown in Figure 4-10.

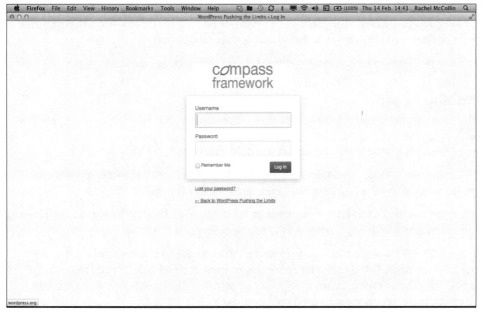

Figure 4-10 The login screen displaying the new logo

Creating Admin Sections and Screens

To create admin screens, you need to use the Settings API to define settings for those screens, and one or more functions for adding the screens themselves.

The WordPress Settings API

The Settings API includes all the functions needed to create admin pages with settings fields. This API, which was introduced with WordPress 2.7, makes the process of creating admin pages semi-automatic, enabling WordPress to handle some of the work for you. The following functions are included in the Settings API:

- `register_setting()`—Registers a setting and its sanitization callback

- `unregister_setting()`—Removes settings groups (e.g. the built-in ones) while your plugin is active

- `add_settings_field()`—Registers a settings field to a defined settings page and section

- `add_settings_section()`—Registers a section to an existing settings page, creating a list of sections in the page

- `settings_fields()`—Outputs nonce, action, and option_page fields for a settings page

- `do_settings_sections()`—Prints all settings sections added to a defined settings page. When you use this, it automatically calls `do_settings_fields()` and `get_settings_errors()` for the fields n your settings section

- `do_settings_fields()`—Prints the settings fields for a defined settings section

- `add_settings_error()`—Registers an error to be displayed to users when a settings field is incorrectly populated as part of the sanitization process

- `get_settings_errors()`—Checks the $wp_settings_errors array for any errors that occurred during the current pageload and returns them, also as part of data sanitization

- `settings_errors()`—Displays settings errors added by `add_settings_error()`

Functions for Adding Pages

Functions to create the pages to contain your settings include the following:

- `add_menu_page()`—Adds a page to the menu that you define with the function

- `add_object_page()`—Adds a top-level menu page at the object level, creating a new top-level menu section in the group that contains the Posts, Media, Pages, and Comments pages

- `add_utility_page()`—Adds a top-level menu page at the utility level, creating a new top-level menu section in the group that contains the Appearance, Plugins, Users, Tools, and Settings pages

- `remove_menu_page()`—Removes a menu page from the Dashboard, either one you've created or (more commonly) a default page. This is useful for hiding pages from users who don't need them, but it also needs to be backed up by ensuring those pages aren't accessible to users without the appropriate permissions, as they could still access the pages via their permalink.

- `add_submenu_page()`—Adds a submenu page below the top-level page you specify, which may be your own page or an existing one. WordPress also includes specific functions for adding submenu pages to the default menus, such as `add_posts_page()`, which adds a submenu page below the Posts page. See http://codex.wordpress.org/Administration_Menus for a list of these.

- `remove_submenu_page()`—Removes a submenu page, in a similar way to `remove_menu_page()`

Creating an Admin Screen

The first step in creating a new admin screen with settings for users to interact with is to create the admin screen itself and a menu item for it. To do this, you create two functions—one to create the menu item, and the other (which will be referenced by the first) to populate the new screen.

In your plugin, you're going to create a new submenu item in the Appearance menu, and call it Theme Options. Where you add your screen and what you call it will depend on the nature of the screen—in this case I'm creating something similar to a theme options screen, although I'm adding it to my plugin so I can activate it on any theme I want.

> Note that WordPress uses `page` **within many of the functions to set up admin screens. Throughout this chapter I will refer to admin screens, not pages, in order to differentiate between these and pages as a content type in WordPress.**

To do this, you use the `add_submenu_page()` function:

```php
<?php
add_submenu_page( $parent_slug, $page_title, $menu_title, $capability,
  $menu_slug, $function );
?>
```

The `add_submenu_page()` function takes the following parameters:

- `$parent_slug`—The slug of the parent screen in the menu, i.e., the top-level screen
- `$page_title`—The title of the screen
- `$menu_title`—The title to be used in the menu
- `$capability`—The capability required in order for a user to access the screen and see the menu item
- `$menu_slug`—The unique slug for the new menu item
- `$function`—The function to output the screen content. The parent slugs for the default top-level screens are as follows:
  - Dashboard—`index.php`
  - Posts—`edit.php`
  - Media—`upload.php`
  - Links—`link-manager.php`
  - Pages—`edit.php?post_type=page`
  - Comments—`edit-comments.php`
  - Appearance—`themes.php`
  - Plugins—`plugins.php`
  - Users—`users.php`
  - Tools—`tools.php`
- Settings—`options-general.php`

The code to add the menu item is as follows:

```php
<?php
// add menu item
function wpptl_setup_theme_options_page() {
 add_submenu_page( 'themes.php', 'Theme Options', 'Theme Options',
   'manage_options', 'theme-options-page',
   'wpptl_theme_options_page_content');
}
add_action('admin_menu', 'wpptl_setup_theme_options_page');
// function to define content of new admin screen
function wpptl_theme_options_page_content() {
}
?>
```

A couple of things to note:

- You use the `manage_options` capability, as only administrators will have access to this screen.

- You hook the function to the `admin_menu` action hook, which is fired just before the admin menu is displayed.

- You add the function to define the new screen's content but not populated it yet—if you didn't add this function, an error would occur if I clicked the menu item.

Figure 4-11 shows how the menu item and new screen look now.

Figure 4-11 The new menu item and empty page

Populating the Admin Screen

The next step is to define the contents of the page. In this case I'm going to add a few input fields so that users can add contact details that will be displayed in the site header. First, however, I'll add a heading and a function to prevent users without the necessary permissions from accessing the page via its permalink. I'll also enclose my content in <div class="wrap">, which will keep the UI consistent with other WordPress admin pages:

```php
<?php
function wpptl_theme_options_page_content() {
 // Check that the user has permission to access the page
 if ( !current_user_can( 'manage_options' ) ) {
  wp_die('Sorry, you do not have sufficient permissions to access this
  page.');
 }
 // Page content
 echo '<div class="wrap">';
 screen_icon();
 echo '<h2 >' . __('Theme Options', 'wpptl' ) . '</h2>';
 echo '</div>';
}
?>
```

Now the options page, shown in Figure 4-12, is looking a little better.

Figure 4-12 The options page has a heading and looks good.

Registering Settings Sections and Fields

You can create form fields using three functions, which you pass to a new function attached to the `admin_menu` hook:

- `add_settings_section()`—Adds a section to the page for settings fields

- `add_settings_field()`—Adds each field in turn

- `register_setting()`—Tells WordPress that you're using the Settings API for these settings sections and fields

Creating a Settings Section

Use `add_settings_section()` to create the section for your fields:

```php
<?php
add_settings_section( $id, $title, $callback, $page );
?>
```

This function takes the following parameters:

- `$id`—The unique ID of the settings section

- `$title`—The title of the settings sections as displayed onscreen

- `$callback`—The callback function to fill the section with content

- `$page`—The slug of the page where the settings section is located

Adding Settings Fields

Each settings section is populated by fields, each of which is created using `add_settings_field()`:

```php
<?php
add_settings_field( $id, $title, $callback, $page, $section, $args );
?>
```

This function takes the following parameters:

- `$id`—A unique ID for the field

- `$title`—The title of the field as displayed onscreen

- `$callback`—The callback function that fills the field with inputs and echoes its output

- `$page`—The slug of the page on which the field appears

- `$section`—The ID of the section where the field appears (optional; you only need this if you have created sections)

- `$args`—An optional array of arguments passed to the `$callback` function. For accessibility purposes, it's good practice to specify the label for each field here using the `'label_for'` argument.

Registering Settings

As well as defining your sections and fields, you need to register the settings with WordPress so that it knows you are using the Settings API. WordPress will "whitelist" the request variables in your settings so they will be processed. Any request variables not in the whitelist are stripped for security. You do this with `register_setting()`:

```php
<?php
register_setting( $option_group, $option_name, $sanitize_callback );
?>
```

The `register_setting()` function takes the following parameters:

- `$option_group`—The unique name of the option group; it must be the same as that set in `settings_fields()`. You'll use it later when getting the value of these options using `get_option()` and `update_option()`.
- `$option_name`—The name of the option, which will be sanitized and saved
- `$sanitize_callback`—A callback function to sanitize data added by users. For details of how to add this, see the "Callback Functions to Sanitize Data" section later in this chapter.

Pulling all these together into a function called `wpptl_theme_options_resgiter_setting()`, I add the following to my plugin:

```php
<?php
function wpptl_theme_options_register_setting() {
 add_settings_section( 'wpptl_contact_settings', 'Contact Details',
  'wpptl_contact_settings_cb', 'theme-options' );
 add_settings_field( 'wpptl_contact_tel', 'Contact Telephone',
  'wpptl_contact_tel_cb', 'theme-options', 'wpptl_contact_settings',
  array( 'label_for' => 'Contact Telephone Number' ) );
 add_settings_field( 'wpptl_contact_address', 'Address',
  'wpptl_contact_address_cb', 'theme-options', 'wpptl_contact_settings',
array( 'label_for' => 'Address' ) );
 add_settings_field( 'wpptl_contact_email', 'Email Address',
  'wpptl_contact_email_cb', 'theme-options', 'wpptl_contact_settings',
array( 'label_for' => 'Email address' ) );
 register_setting( 'wpptl_theme_options_group', 'wpptl_theme_options_tel'
  );
 register_setting( 'wpptl_theme_options_group',
  'wpptl_theme_options_address' );
 register_setting( 'wpptl_theme_options_group',
  'wpptl_theme_options_email' );
}
add_action( 'admin_init', 'wpptl_theme_options_register_setting' );
?>
```

Outputting Settings Sections and Fields to the Screen

Registering your settings sections and fields sets them up but it doesn't output them to the page. To do that, you have to add some more functions:

- Callback functions required by the `add_setting_section()` and `add_settings_field()` functions

- The `settings_fields()` and `do_settings_sections()` functions, which are placed inside the `wpptl_theme_options_page_content()` function, which defines the content of your settings page

The `settings_fields()` function must be placed inside a `<form>` element and has just one parameter:

```php
<?php
settings_fields( $option_group );
?>
```

The value of this parameter for each field is then passed to the `register_settings()` function, which I've already defined.

The `do_settings_sections()` function enables the settings sections to render in the page, and it also has one parameter:

```php
<?php
do_settings_sections( $page );
?>
```

The `$page` parameter is the slug of the page in which the sections appear.

First, here are the callback functions:

```php
<?php
// callback function for the wpptl_contact_settings section
function wpptl_contact_settings_cb () {
 echo __('<p>Enter your contact details as you want them to appear on the
  site</p>', 'wpptl');
}
// callback function for the wpptl_contact_tel field
function wpptl_contact_tel_cb () {
 $setting = esc_attr( get_option( 'wpptl_theme_options_tel' ) );
 echo "<input type='text' name='wpptl_theme_options_tel' value='$setting'
  />";
}
// callback function for the wpptl_contact_address field
function wpptl_contact_address_cb () {
 $setting = esc_attr( get_option( 'wpptl_theme_options_address' ) );
 echo "<input type='text' name='wpptl_theme_options_address'
  value='$setting' />";
}
```

```php
// callback function for the wpptl_contact_email field
function wpptl_contact_email_cb () {
 $setting = esc_attr( get_option( 'wpptl_theme_options_email' ) );
 echo "<input type='text' name='wpptl_theme_options_email'
  value='$setting' />";
}
?>
```

To make these appear on the page, expand the `wpptl_theme_option_page_content()` function, which defines the contents of the page:

```php
<?php
function wpptl_theme_options_page_content() {
// Check that the user has permission to access the page
 if (!current_user_can( 'manage_options' ) ) {
 wp_die('Sorry, you do not have sufficient permissions to access this
page.');
 }
// Page content
echo '<div class="wrap">';
 screen_icon();
 echo '<h2 >' . __('Theme Options', 'wpptl' ) . '</h2>';
 echo '<form method="post" action="options.php">';
  do_settings_sections( 'theme-options' );
  settings_fields( 'wpptl_theme_options_group' );
  submit_button();
 echo '</form></div>';
}
?>
```

This has added the `do_settings_sections()` and `settings_fields()` functions inside the `<form>` element.

As shown in Figure 4-13, the page is now populated with the section and fields.

Now that the admin screen allows users to enter data, which is saved to the `wp_options` table, it can be used in your theme.

Using Settings in Your Theme

Adding the settings screen enables site administrators to update the contact details for the site, but this is only helpful if that is then displayed somewhere. Because the data has been saved as options in the `wp_options` table, you need to use the Options API.

Figure 4-13 The options page with its fields in place

The Options API

The Options API (`http://codex.wordpress.org/Options_API`) includes a number of functions that enable you to interact with options saved in the database:

- `add_option()`—Enables you to add an option/value pair to the database
- `delete_option()`—Enables you to delete an option from the database; you would use this when uninstalling a plugin or theme that added the option
- `get_option()`—Fetches an option from the database
- `update_option()`—Updates the value of the option

For Multisite installations, there are corresponding functions that are global to the whole network installation: `add_site_option`, `delete_site_option()`, `get_site_option` and `update_site_option()`. If you use the functions without `_site_` in a Multisite installation, then they will apply only to a single site, not the whole network.

Outputting an Option's Value in the Theme

The `register_setting()` functions added in the previous section created options in the `wp_options` table with the following IDs:

- `wpptl_theme_options_tel`
- `wpptl_theme_options_address`
- `wpptl_theme_options_email`

You can therefore use `get_option()` with each of these to output their values. It is used with `echo`:

```php
<?php
echo get_option( $option, $default );
?>
```

The `get_option()` function takes two parameters:

- `$option`—The name of the option to retrieve
- `$default`—An optional default value to return if no option is found

Therefore, to add the values of the three options to your theme, you add them where you want them to appear in `header.php`, which is below the site name and description:

```php
<address>
 <p class="address"><?php echo get_option( 'wpptl_theme_options_address'
   ); ?></p>
 <p class="tel"><?php echo get_option( 'wpptl_theme_options_tel' ); ?></p>
 <p class="email"><a href="mailto:<?php echo get_option( 'wpptl_theme_
options_email' ); ?>"><?php echo get_option(
   'wpptl_theme_options_email' ); ?></p>
</address>
```

Note that in the case of the `email` option, `get_option()` is used twice—once for the link and once for the output text.

Now the option values are displayed in the header, as shown in Figure 4-14.

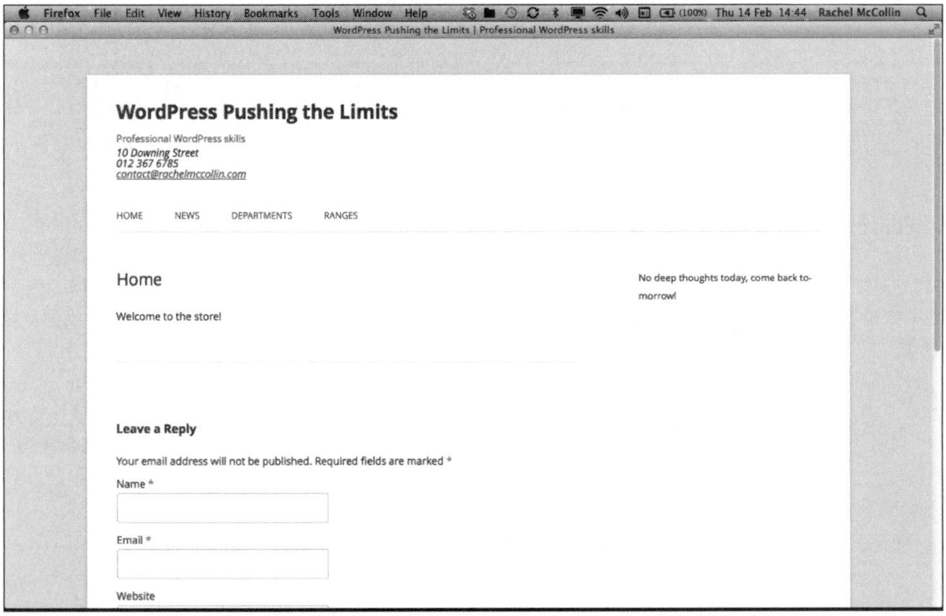

Figure 4-14 The options are output in the theme.

This provides an easy way for site administrators to update content that needs to be displayed on the site but isn't added via a post or a page, without having to hack the template files.

Multiple Options Screens and Menu Items

You've learned how to create a new admin screen and a submenu item for it. Creating a menu section is very similar, but instead of using the `add_submenu_page()` function to add a top-level page, you use `add_menu_page`, and then add submenu pages to that:

```php
<?php
add_menu_page( $page_title, $menu_title, $capability, $menu_slug,
  $function, $icon_url, $position );
?>
```

The `add_menu_page()` function has the following parameters:

- `$page_title`—The title of the page

- `$menu_title`—The title to be used in the menu

- `$capability`—The capability required in order for a user to access the screen and see the menu item

- `$menu_slug`—The unique slug for the new menu item

- `$function`—The function to output the page content

- `$icon_url`—An optional URL for the icon to be displayed next to the menu item's title. Leave this blank for the default icon.

- `$position`—Where in the menu the new item should appear. The higher the number, the higher it will appear. If you leave it blank, it will appear at the bottom. If two menu items have the same position, one will overwrite the other; you can avoid this by using decimals for the position.

> For more on default values and positions for new menu items, see `http://codex.wordpress.org/add_menu_page#Parameters`.

For example, the following creates a new Plugin Options section in a plugin menu:

```php
<?php
function wpptl_create_menu_section(){
 add_menu_page( 'Plugin Options', 'Plugin Options', 'manage_options',
  'wpptl-plugin-options', 'wpptl_plugin_options_screen' );
}
add_action( 'admin_menu', 'wpptl_create_menu_section' );
?>
```

As shown in Figure 4-15, this creates a new top-level menu item at the bottom of the left navigation menu.

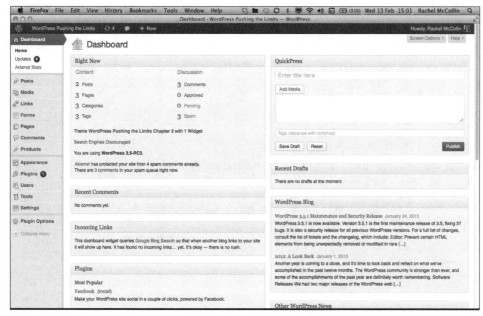

Figure 4-15 The new menu item appears at the bottom of the left navigation menu.

The next steps are to create a screen using the `wpptl_plugin_options_screen()` function and then create submenu items and corresponding pages, which was covered earlier in this chapter.

> Sometimes you may want to enable users to move between options screens more easily than by creating a menu, or you may have numerous screens and not want to clutter up the menu with all of them. In this case you can create tabbed screens. The method to do this is exactly the same as you would use when designing a tabbed effect in a theme—you write the markup for the admin screen with content for all the tabs, and then use CSS or JavaScript to create the tabbed effect.

The Theme Customizer

For many themes, the Theme Customizer will be all you need to enable users to tweak settings in your theme. The Theme Customizer, introduced in WordPress 3.4, provides you with a quick way to enable users to make changes—one that doesn't require the trouble of creating a theme options page.

Adding Theme Customizer Support

To add Theme Customizer support, you define a function in `functions.php` with `$wp_customize` as the object, and then attach that to the `customize_register` action hook. The function contains all the code required to enable various options in the Theme Customizer:

```php
<?php
function wpptl_customize_register( $wp_customize )}
{
  // Add sections, settings, and controls here
}
add_action( 'customize_register', 'wpptl_customize_register' );
?>
```

This function activates the Theme Customizer and displays the default settings, as shown in Figure 4-16.

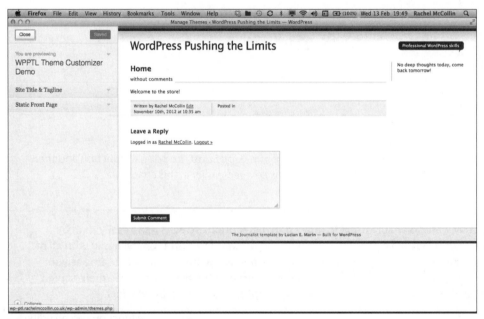

Figure 4-16 The Theme Customizer, with default settings

Adding Sections, Settings, and Controls

Inside the function, you need to define three things:

▧ Sections for the Theme Customizer, which structure its contents

▧ Settings, which are the things users will be able to change

▧ Controls, which provide the interface that enables users to change the settings

The settings added by default are Site Title & Tagline and Static Front Page, which mirror the settings in the Settings and Readings screens. If the theme supports menus, that's added automatically too.

The next step is to add some settings and controls. To do this, you use the `WP_Customize_manager` class with two controls: `add_setting()` and `add_control`. Each of these uses and can only be accessed via the `wp_customize` object, which is the parameter of the `wp_customize_register()` function.

First, to add a setting you use `add_setting()`:

```php
<?php
$wp_customise->add_setting($id, $args);
?>
```

The `add_setting()` parameters are as follows:

- `$id`—The unique ID of the setting
- `$args`—An array containing arguments for the setting. The following arguments are available:
  - `default`—A default value for the setting
  - `type`—The type of setting; the default is `'theme_mod'`, and the other option is `'option'`
  - `capability`—Defines the capability a user must have to modify this setting (optional)
- `transport`—Also optional, use this when you're using custom JavaScript to control the Theme Customizer's live preview.

Second, add a control for your setting using `add_control()`:

```php
<?php
$wp_customise->add_control($id, $args);
?>
```

The parameters are a unique ID for the control, and an array of arguments:

- `label`—The label for the control as displayed onscreen
- `section`—The section of the Theme Customizer in which the control is placed, where relevant
- `settings`—The ID of the setting to which the control refers

All of these are required. Therefore, to add a control for content text and link colors, the function can be edited as follows:

```php
<?php
function wpptl_customize_register( $wp_customize ) {
 $colors = array();
 $colors[] = array(
  'slug'=>'content_text_color',
  'default' => '#333',
  'label' => __( 'Content Text Color', 'Ari' )
  );
```

(continued)

```
$colors[] = array(
 'slug'=>'content_link_color',
 'default' => '#047',
 'label' => __( 'Content Link Color', 'Ari' )
 );
foreach( $colors as $color ) {
 // SETTINGS
 $wp_customize->add_setting( $color['slug'], array(
  'default' => $color['default'],
  'type' => 'option',
  'capability' => 'edit_theme_options' )
 );
 // CONTROLS
 $wp_customise->add_control( new WP_Customize_Color_Control(
  $wp_customize, $color['slug'], array(
  'label' => $color['label'],
  'section' => 'colors',
  'settings' => $color['slug'] )
 ) );
 }
}
?>
```

Stepping through the code, this is what's happening:

1. First, the $colors variable is defined for each color option being added, using an array that includes the default color and its label.

2. Next, settings are added for each color (using foreach($colors as $color)). This uses the add_ setting function, with the arguments defined in the array.

3. Finally, a control is added for the settings, still in the foreach statement. This uses the new WP_ Customize_Color_Control() function, which creates a color control.

> In this case, you don't have to add a section for your colors settings, as this is built in to WordPress. To add extra sections for your settings, you use the $wp_customize->add_section() method. For more information and a list of built-in sections, see https://codex.wordpress.org/Class_ Reference/WP_Customize_Manager/add_section.

Now when the site is previewed in the Theme Customizer, the colors section is added, as shown in Figure 4-17.

Activating Theme Customizer Settings in Your Theme

At this point, if the user makes any changes in the Theme Customizer it won't have any effect in the theme, as nothing has been added to the relevant theme files. You need to call your options in the <head> section of the page, again using get_option().

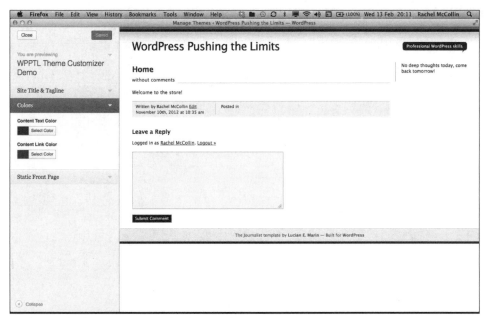

Figure 4-17 The Theme Customizer with color controls

To do this, you can either insert the relevant code into the `<head>` section of your theme's `header.php` file, or you can use the `wp_head` hook to hook into your theme. The second is better practice as it means you can still work in your functions file.

Add the following to your `functions.php` file:

```php
<?php
add_action( 'wp_head', 'wpptl_custom_colors' );
function wpptl_custom_colors() { ?>
 <style type="text/css">
  #content { color:  <?php echo get_option('content_text_color', '#333'
  ); ?>;}
  #content a { color:  <?php echo get_option('content_link_color', '#047'
  ) ?>;}
 </style>
<?php }
?>
```

This defines two variables, `$content_text_color` and `$content_link_color`, using `get_option()`, and then adds styling defining the color in each case as the value of the variable. Now if you make tweaks—to the text color, for example—you can see the effect in the Theme Customizer, as shown in Figure 4-18.

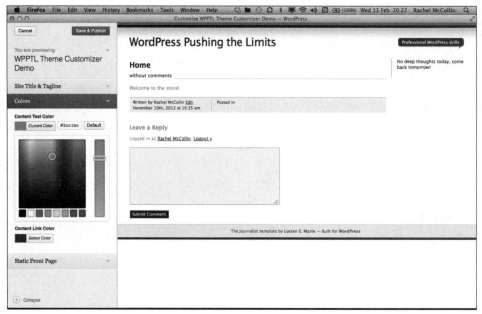

Figure 4-18 Theme Customizer settings taking effect

This is just one possibility with the Theme Customizer. You can add any theme settings to the customizer, just as you might add them to a theme options screen. In fact it's good practice to add them to both.

Content and Editing

So far in this chapter you've learned how to manage and create user roles and capabilities, customize the Dashboard, create settings screens, and add Theme Customizer support. These are core activities for customizing the WordPress admin that will be useful in most cases as you're developing sites for clients, or themes for users. However, I have found that clients often need a little bit more—some clients have no experience editing a website or using WordPress, and even with training they find the process daunting. This section describes how you can make their lives easier by making some additional customizations to the admin.

The first customization amends listing screens to remove unwanted columns and add new ones. Then you'll learn a method for adding help text to admin screens, such as the page and post editing screens, as well as customizing listing screens.

Customizing Listing Screens

To customize listings screens, you have to hook into the relevant action filters for each screen:

- For the posts listing screen, `manage_posts_columns`

- For the page listings screen, `manage_pages_columns`

- For a custom post type listings screen, `manage_$post_type_posts_columns`, where `$post_type` is the slug of the post type

To demonstrate this, we'll work with the Posts listing screen, which by default looks like what is shown in Figure 4-19.

Figure 4-19 The default Posts listing screen

Removing Columns

In Figure 4-19, no tags are shown for the posts, because this site isn't using tags. I want to remove the tags column, and I also want to hide the comments column because the site design doesn't include comments.

To remove columns, you define a new function to hook into the `manage_posts_columns` filter. This function has `$columns` as its object. You then use the `unset` function and the `$columns` variable as follows:

```php
<?php
// customise the posts listing screen
function wpptl_remove_pages_column( $columns ) {
  unset($columns['tags']);
  unset($columns['comments']);
  return $columns;
}
add_filter( 'manage_posts_columns', 'wpptl_remove_pages_column' );
?>
```

This removes the columns from the Posts page, as shown in Figure 4-20.

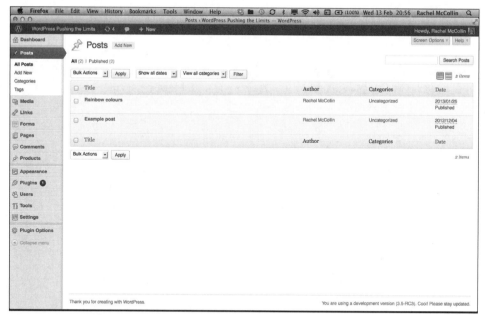

Figure 4-20 The Posts listing screen with columns removed

Having defined the function to remove these columns, you can also use it with other types of content, such as the products post type, which is registered on the example site. All you need to do is repeat the `add_filter` function using the appropriate filter hook:

```php
<?php
add_filter( 'manage_product_posts_columns', 'wpptl_remove_pages_column'
   );
?>
```

Adding Columns

In some cases you might want to add columns—for example, where you want to list the terms from a custom taxonomy you've registered. The method for doing this used to be by hooking into the same filter but define an array of new columns to add these to the existing columns.

However since WordPress 3.5, this is much simpler, as you can add support for columns when you register your taxonomies, using `'show_admin_column' => true`.

> For more on registering taxonomies, see Chapter 3.

Providing Help for Editors

Earlier in this chapter you learned how to add widgets to the Dashboard, which can be useful for helping editors to familiarize themselves with WordPress and their site. In addition, help text on editing screens provides extra support.

Adding Tips to Editing Screens

Adding tips to an editing screen is a simple process of creating a meta box and assigning it to the relevant screen. You use the `add_meta_box()` function:

```php
<?php
add_meta_box( $id, $title, $callback, $post_type, $context, $priority,
  $callback_args );
?>
```

The `add_meta_box()` function takes the following parameters:

- `$id`—The unique ID of the meta box

- `$callback`—The callback function defining the meta box's content

- `$post_type`—The editing screen to which the meta box will be added, such as `'post'`, `'page'` or `'$custom_post_type'`, i.e., the slug of a custom post type

- `$context`—The part of the screen where the meta box should be displayed (`'normal'`, `'advanced'` or `side'`)

- `$priority`—How high up the meta box should be (`'high'`, `'core'`, `'default'` or `'low'`)

- `$callback_args`—Arguments for the callback function

The `add_meta_box` function is then attached to the `add_meta_boxes` action hook.

Therefore, to add a meta box with some help text in the post editing screen, you define a function to create the meta box itself and then a callback function with the meta box content:

```php
<?php
// add meta box to post editing screen with help text
function wpptl_add_posts_help_text() {
 add_meta_box( 'wpptl_posts_help_text', 'Using this screen',
   'wpptl_posts_help_text', 'post', 'normal' );
}
add_action( 'add_meta_boxes', 'wpptl_add_posts_help_text' );
// callback function defining content of meta box
function wpptl_posts_help_text() { ?>
 <p>Use this screen to create new posts and edit existing ones. Some
 tips:</p>
 <ul>
  <li>After creating your post, you can preview how it will look before
  saving it by clicking the 'Preview' button</li>
  <li>To save your post, click 'Publish'</li>
  <li>After editing an existing post, click 'Update' to save your
  changes</li>
 </ul>
<?php }
?>
```

This creates a meta box on the post editing screen with the tips, as shown in Figure 4-21.

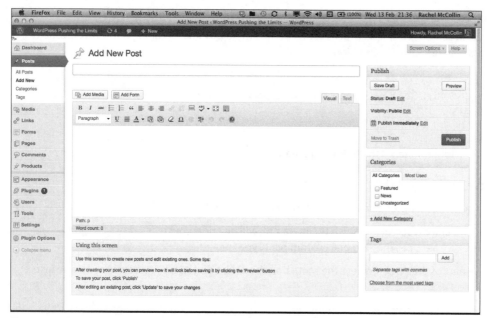

Figure 4-21 The Add New Post screen with the meta box added

Sanitizing Data

So far in this chapter you've learned how to create settings and controls or input fields for users to make changes or input data to those settings.

It's very important when doing this to ensure that you sanitize any data before saving it to the database—this will avoid any problems with incorrectly entered data or extraneous tags.

Chapter 9 covers sanitization and validation of data in detail, so I won't repeat that information here. However, you may recall that earlier in this chapter, when defining settings for the settings page, I referred to sanitization functions but didn't actually add any.

Callback Functions to Sanitize Data

Earlier in this chapter, in the section "Creating Admin Screens," the `register_settings()` function was used to register the settings for the admin screen:

```php
<?php
register_setting( $option_group, $option_name, $sanitize_callback );
?>
```

The final parameter of this function is `$sanitize_callback`, which is a sanitization function that is run when the settings are saved to the database.

You can choose from a number of methods to sanitize your data, including the following:

- Checking that it is using the correct data type, such as a number
- Checking that it is in the correct format, such as an e-mail address
- Stripping tags

Stripping tags is covered in detail in Chapter 9; in the following example, we'll add a function to verify that data input to the email field validates as an email address.

> **Note the use of validation instead of sanitization. The difference is that sanitized data is cleaned and then passed to the database, whereas validated data isn't accepted if it is invalid.**

To do this you use two functions: `is_email()` and `add_settings_error()`. The `is_email()` function checks whether the input is indeed an e-mail, and `add_settings_error` throws an error if that isn't the case:

```php
<?php
add_settings_error( $setting, $code, $message, $type );
?>
```

The `add_settings_error` function takes the following parameters:

- `$setting`—The unique slug of the setting as defined by `register_setting()`
- `$code`—The slug of the error message, used in the output HTML
- `$message`—The error message
- `$type`—An optional parameter that specifies the type of error message Your sanitization function must have the input as its object, so that this can be checked:

```php
<?php
//callback function to sanitize the email field
function wpptl_email_option_sanitize( $input ) {
  $output = get_option( 'wpptl_theme_options_email' );
  if( is_email( $input ) ) :
  $output = $input;
  else;
  add_settings_error( 'wpptl_theme_options_email', 'invalid-email', 'The
    text you have entered is not a valid email address. Please try again. '
    );
  return $output;
}
?>
```

This does the following:

- It defines the `wpptl_email_option_sanitize()` function named as the sanitization function in `register_setting()`, with `$input` as its object.
- It checks whether `$input` is a valid e-mail address.
- If not, it adds the settings error.

If a user types in a valid e-mail address, it will be accepted and saved; if not, the previous input (if there was any) is retained and the error message is displayed.

Summary

Customizing the admin screens is an important part of creating a personalized CMS for your clients using WordPress, and important for any plugin and theme developers who need to allow their users to changes settings.

In this chapter, you learned how to do all the following:

- Manage roles and capabilities, including adding new ones
- Customize the Dashboard
- Add admin screens and create fields in them using the Settings API
- Customize the listings pages
- Add meta boxes to admin screens to help users
- Sanitize any data input to your admin screens

The examples demonstrated in this chapter give you just a taste of what can be done—if you're prepared to experiment and push the limits, you can create a truly customized admin for your clients that need not look anything like the default WordPress admin.

Further Resources
Roles and Capabilities

Codex guide to roles and capabilities
`http://codex.wordpress.org/Roles_and_Capabilities`

Codex page on the admin panels and screens
`http://codex.wordpress.org/Administration_Panels`

Ultimate guide to roles and capabilities
`http://www.garyc40.com/2010/04/ultimate-guide-to-roles-and-capabilities/`

The `admin_init()` action hook
`http://codex.wordpress.org/Plugin_API/Action_Reference/admin_init`

Adding capabilities with `add_cap()`
http://codex.wordpress.org/Function_Reference/add_cap

The `WP_User` class
http://codex.wordpress.org/Class_Reference/WP_User

The `wp_get_current_user()` function
http://codex.wordpress.org/Function_Reference/wp_get_current_user

Admin Screens and the Settings API

Codex page on the Settings API
http://codex.wordpress.org/Settings_API

Administration menus functions
http://codex.wordpress.org/Administration_Menus

Dashboard widgets API
http://codex.wordpress.org/Dashboard_Widgets_API

Customizing the login form
http://codex.wordpress.org/Customizing_the_Login_Form

Complete guide to the Settings API
http://wp.tutsplus.com/series/the-complete-guide-to-the-wordpress-settings-api/

Settings API tutorial
http://ottopress.com/2009/wordpress-settings-api-tutorial/

Guide to the Settings API
http://kovshenin.com/2012/the-wordpress-settings-api/

The Options API
http://codex.wordpress.org/Options_API

The Theme Customizer

Theme Customization API
https://codex.wordpress.org/Theme_Customisation_API

The `WP_Customise_Manager` class
http://codex.wordpress.org/Class_Reference/WP_Customise_Manager

The `add_setting()` method
http://codex.wordpress.org/Class_Reference/WP_Customise_Manager/add_setting

The `add_control()` method
http://codex.wordpress.org/Class_Reference/WP_Customise_Manager/add_control

Theme customization tutorial

`http://ottopress.com/2012/how-to-leverage-the-theme-customiser-in-your-own-themes/`

Digging into the Theme Customizer

`http://wp.tutsplus.com/tutorials/theme-development/digging-into-the-theme-customiser-overview/`

A developer's guide to the Theme Customizer

`http://wp.smashingmagazine.com/2013/03/05/the-wordpress-theme-customizer-a-developers-guide/`

Listings Screens

Managing listings screen columns

`http://codex.wordpress.org/Plugin_API/Filter_Reference/manage_edit-post_type_columns`

The `manage_posts_columns` filter

`http://codex.wordpress.org/Plugin_API/Filter_Reference/manage_posts_columns`

Adding Meta Boxes

The `add_meta_box()` function

`http://codex.wordpress.org/Function_Reference/add_meta_box`

Data Sanitization

The `add_settings_error()` function

`http://codex.wordpress.org/Function_Reference/add_settings_error`

Chapter 5

Development and Hosting Environments

If you're making the move from being a freelancer or working in an agency or large organization, one of the most unfamiliar aspects of running a web design business can be setting up hosting and development environments. Regardless of whether this was always taken care of in the past by someone else or you were the person who took care of it, this is an area in which you'll need to make some decisions—namely, the following:

- What development environment will you work with? The solution you choose will depend on your experience and preferences, but it will also depend on the needs of the client, each project, and the rest of your team.

- Will you offer or set up hosting for your clients? You could provide reseller hosting, or you could just set up sites on your clients' hosting for them—or you could do neither and hand sites over to clients for them to upload to their hosting environment. The latter option is unlikely for most projects, unless all of your clients have their own web team that can handle this process.

This chapter covers development and hosting environments in detail. By the end of it you'll have learned the following:

- How to identify the most appropriate development environment for each project
- How to set up your development environment, whether locally or remotely
- How to prepare for launch of a site and migrate a WordPress site
- How to decide what hosting to offer and identify the best hosting provider for you (either for your own hosting or for resale)

Creating a Robust Development Environment

Whether you're developing on your own or as part of a team, you need to set up a robust development environment for each project. The exact criteria for this varies from project to project but includes the following:

- **Security**—Your development environment must be private and secure from potential attack.
- **Parity with the live environment**—Your development environment should be as similar as possible to the environment on which the site will eventually be hosted in terms of space, bandwidth, software, and languages supported.
- **Your client**—The extent to which your client needs access to your development environment will affect where you have it and how you set it up. This consideration is important, for example, if the client is adding content as you develop the site.
- **Your team**—This includes all the people involved in development, with respect to their roles and locations. If your team is all in one place, developing locally will be easier than if they're dispersed.

In Chapter 2 you looked at the pros and cons of different development environments—these are summarized again in Table 5-1.

Table 5-1: Development Options

Option	Pros	Cons
Local installation	This option is the fastest and easiest to work with and won't require an Internet connection. It's also the most secure—bar your machine getting lost or stolen, no one will see your work until you're ready to put it online.	If multiple team members are working on the site and can't access the same local installation, there could be versioning problems. Clients won't be able to see progress as you work on the site.
Remote installation on client's server	Some clients may require this because they are more comfortable with the security or accessibility of their server than yours. Makes migration easier, as the site is being developed in the same environment it will be hosted on at launch (assuming it will be hosted on the client's server). It's easy for clients to see progress (although this does run the risk that they could look at the site when you don't want them to, e.g., if it's temporarily broken).	You have no control over access to the server. You may need to jump through some access or security hoops with the client to be able to set up a development installation of WordPress (although you may have to do this later anyway). You must ensure that security measures are in place so members of the pubic don't accidentally land on the development site when browsing the client's existing live site.
Remote installation on your server	You have control over the environment in which the site is installed. All members of the team can access the site and so can the client. You can control the client's access to the site. Useful if the client doesn't have an existing site or server and you are in the process of setting this up for them.	You have to put in place security measures to ensure that members of the public don't inadvertently access the site. The client may be less comfortable with the security or privacy of the site.

As you can see, there isn't a one-size-fits-all approach that is suitable for every team and every project. Most developers do prefer to work locally, however, at least in the early stages of a project, so the following section begins by examining why that is so.

The Advantages of Local Development

Not all local development environments opr processes are the same. Local development can take one of three forms:

- **Develop locally and show the local site to the client by taking your development machine to a presentation meeting.** This gives you maximum control and removes any risk associated with version control, as the site is only in one place. It also means you have access to your work if you don't have an Internet connection, such as when traveling. However, it won't be viable if you're working as part of a team or the client will be adding content as you develop the site—or if you want to test using devices that don't have access to your local server.

- **Develop locally, migrating to a remote server at key stages in the project for client review.** This is a common approach because a small number of remote migrations minimizes the risk of losing data. If you do take this approach, I recommend using a version control system and saving a version of your site at each stage rather than overwriting an earlier stage—at the very least, make a separate version of the site's theme and plugins.

- **Develop locally, migrating to a remote server on a daily basis for client review or for other team members to work on.** This option involves the most risk and effort, as you need a very well defined system in place to ensure that data is not lost from one day to the next. You can mitigate this risk by having a version control system in place and ensuring everyone in the team is using the system consistently. You'll look at how you can do this later in this chapter, and compare it to its closest alternative—developing remotely.

Each of these options has its advantages and disadvantages. My own practices have changed over time, as I'm now more likely to work with a dispersed team than I was in the early days of my agency—so 100% local development is rare. I also want to be able to test my development sites on multiple devices, which isn't possible with local development either. Therefore, I typically adopt the second or third of the preceding approaches, or develop remotely.

Local development does have its advantages. If you lose your Internet connection, you can continue working; you can pick up your laptop (if that's what you're developing on) and continue working if you're traveling; and you have complete control over the site's security.

Setting Up a Local Development Environment

Setting up a development environment on your local machine is fairly straightforward, so this section doesn't provide detailed instructions on how to do it. Instead, it offers an overview of the process and links to more detailed resources if this is something you haven't done before.

If you're developing locally, you'll need to install one of the following:

- MAMP if you're on a Mac (`http://www.mamp.info`)

- WAMP if you're on a Windows PC (`http://www.wampserver.com`)

- XAMPP, which is cross-platform and has versions for Windows, Mac, and Linux (`http://www.apachefriends.org`)

Each of these does the same job: It enables you to run MySQL and PHP so you can set up a database and run WordPress on your local machine. The download site for each contains instructions on how to install and run the software.

Another option is to have a virtual machine running locally with the same version of Linux as the live server, which will replaicate the live environment as closely as possible.

You also need a database for your content. As you now have MySQL on your machine, you can set one up using SQLite Manager or phpMyAdmin. Simply create the database with a username and a secure password, and make a note of the username, password database name, and host name for use when you install WordPress.

After your server environment is up and running, you need to install WordPress—you can download the latest version at `http://wordpress.org/download/`. This is also a straightforward task and therefore not covered here, but you can find detailed instructions on the WordPress site at `http://codex.wordpress.org/Installing_WordPress`. When prompted, simply enter the username, password, database name, and server (localhost) from your database and you're good to go!

Backing Up a Local WordPress Installation

Although working locally means that you have more control over the security of your development environment, and your site is less likely to be attacked or stop working because of server problems, mistakes and other issues can arise. Therefore, it pays to make backups.

As you would with all of your important files, make sure you take backups of your local site's files on a daily basis, using whichever backup software you prefer—this might be a product such as Time Machine (for Mac), cloud-based file storage such as Dropbox, or something else. Your local site is unlikely to be in the same location on your machine as your other work files—so it may be missed by any backup process you already have in place.

To help you with backup, Table 5-2 summarizes the default location of your site's components for each server application.

Table 5-2: What to Back Up When Working Locally

Application	Database Location	WordPress Location (including themes, plugins, etc.)
MAMP	`Applications/MAMP/db`	`Applications/MAMP/htdocs/sitename`
WAMP	`c:/wamp/bin/mysql/mysql5.x.x/data/`	`c:/wamp/www/`
XAMPP	`c:/xampp/mysql/data/ (or Applications/xampp/mysql/data/)`	`c:/xampp/htdocs (or Applications/xampp/htdocs/)`

Make sure you back up these files regularly so that if anything happens to your machine, you won't lose your work.

Working Collaboratively on Large Projects

If you're working as part of a team, simple local development may not be practical. Example scenarios include the following:

▪ **Co-located team.** If your team is in one location, you might use a shared server to store the development site, or network your machines so you all have access to the machine on which the site is hosted. You might want to sometimes work on a local copy of the site on your own machine to avoid breaking the shared copy, in which case syncing data and code will be as much of an issue as for a dispersed team.

You need to ensure your server can handle multiple users and traffic, and put processes in place to ensure that no one overwrites someone else's code—see the "Team Development Best Practices" section later in this chapter.

- **Dispersed team.** If your team is based in multiple locations, you won't be able to do all your work locally. You might adopt a mix of local and remote development, with individuals developing locally and uploading their work to a shared server regularly. Alternatively, you might decide to do all your development on a remote site, in which case security is important.

- **Client needs access to the development site.** If the client is part of the team and needs to add content to the development site or have access to it for other reasons (for example, if client staff are working on the development with you), you need to either set up a remote development environment or have the main development on the client's server, and then work with the client to find the best way for you and your team to access that server or upload work to it. You may also have to set up temporary user privileges for client staff during development, for example to give specific individuals access to the relevant areas of the WordPress admin.

Whatever your situation and whichever approach you adopt, two things are important: ensuring that work isn't duplicated or overwritten, either in the database or in theme files or plugins; and ensuring that the site is secure and robust (including restricting access and backing up).

Keeping Your Code and Content in Sync

When more than one team member is working on a site build at the same time, and you're not all working on the same networked or remote installation, different versions of your database or your code reside in different places. Adopting the best practices outlined in the next section will help you to manage this, but you need a system in place first. Following are some options you can consider.

GitHub

GitHub (`http://github.com`) is a web-based service built around the open source Git version control software. You can't host your development site on it (not that you would want to, given that the world would see your code when it's not at its best!), but you can use it as a repository for files you create during the site build. GitHub will automatically store each file added to it as a new version and provide team members with information about it, as provided by the person who created it. GitHub has one major drawback when developing client sites, though—because it is open source, your code will be public, which your client might not be happy about. However, if you're working on an open-source project, GitHub could solve your versioning problems.

If you want to store your code privately on GitHub you can set up a paid account, for more information see `https://github.com/plans`.

> You can't use GitHub to manage version control in your database, only for theme files, uploads, and plugins.

Subversion

WordPress itself uses subversion for version control of themes and plugins, which you can learn more about in Chapter 12. However you can also set up your own subversion repository for your projects, letting you check files in and out as needed. A free and open source subversion control system is Apache Subversion, available at `http://subversion.apache.org`.

WordPress

WordPress itself saves versions of your content in the `wp_posts` table. You can access these via the admin, in the relevant post's editing screen. The WordPress admin not only provides access to versions of your content, it also gives you an overview of the differences between versions, so it can help you identify which one should be used.

Dropbox

As mentioned earlier, you can't use Dropbox (`http://dropbox.com`) to host your site, but you can use it to store copies of your template files, plugins, and other working documents. I always use Dropbox when working collaboratively on a project—I use it to share source files and project documentation with my team, as well as to share files with clients. Combined with robust file management and naming conventions, you can use Dropbox to store different versions of files you're developing. It won't make version control as easy as GitHub but it will be private.

Code Comparison Software

Some code editors include the capability to compare the content of two files, and other applications are specifically designed for that purpose. This capability can help you quickly identify the differences between versions of your files (but not your database).

Applications that have this feature include the following:

- **Diffuse (free)**—`http://diffuse.sourceforge.net`
- **BBEdit (paid)**—`http://www.barebones.com/products/bbedit`
- **Dreamweaver (paid)**—Enables you to compare local and remote versions of the same file: `http://www.adobe.com/products/dreamweaver.html`
- **UltraCompare (paid)**—`http://www.ultraedit.com`

> If you use Git or Subversion as detailed previously, these include the facility to compare your code between versions without using separate code comparison software.

Team Development Best Practices

Setting up software and/or systems to manage versions is an effective way to control your project, but it won't work unless you and your team use it correctly and agree to to some ground rules and practices to minimize the risk of losing code or data. Such best practices include the following:

- Each team member should have clearly defined responsibilities and know which part of the build they're responsible for. This includes understanding any overlaps to ensure that effective collaboration is maintained, which proactively guards against potential problems.
- All team members should check in before working on the site to tell other team members what they'll be working on and to confirm that no other team member is already working on the same piece of functionality. If two team members are collaborating on an aspect of the site's functionality, they need to establish their roles and communicate regularly to avoid duplication of effort, clashes, or loss of work.

- Use commenting in your code to ensure that other team members understand how it might interact with theirs.

- Hold regular meetings, either physically or virtually, to check in, identify any changes to planned activities and responsibilities, and update one another on progress. Depending on the size and pace of the project, this might be daily or weekly.

- Only one person should be working on the database at any time. Any changes to a local version of the database should be uploaded to the shared database as often as possible (with a backup of the shared version being taken first).

- Before migrating the site, warn other team members to confirm that they're not working on any unsaved files or data.

All team members must agree upon exactly how they will communicate with each other when they're making changes to files or the database—this could be directly (the easiest option if you're in the same place) or via an online collaboration tool, which is the best practice even if you're co-located, as it ensures that you have a record of what happens for everyone who may not have been involved in all the conversations.

Project Collaboration Tools

Dozens of online collaboration tools are available. Selecting one is typically a question of your needs, preferences, and experience, as well as who needs access to it—in particular the client. Some popular tools include the following:

Basecamp

Basecamp (`http://basecamp.com/`) uses a social media-like interface for project communication, including lists, notifications, schedules, file labeling and storage, and more. Its clean, professional interface means it is also suitable when you need clients to be in on the conversation.

The P2 Theme

The WordPress P2 theme (`http://p2theme.com`) was developed by Automattic for collaboration on their own projects, and it provides an interface for project updates. It's based mainly on tagging but you can use categories. I also use P2 Reloaded (`http://p2reloaded.com`), which is based on P2 but enables you to select team members for e-mail notification when you post an update. The best thing about these themes is that they're free and built into WordPress, so if they don't do exactly what you need you can always customize them.

Zoho Projects

Zoho Projects (`http://www.zoho.com/projects/`) is compatible with Google apps and has different pricing structures that vary according to number of users (starting at free). It can integrate with other Zoho products for CRM, invoicing support, and more.

Google Docs and Google Drive

Google Docs (`http://docs.google.com`) provides basic file sharing but it is free and easy to set up. If you need to share just a couple of files with an extended team or with team members who can't access files in your Dropbox for some reason, Google Docs can be a quick and useful tool.

If you want more advanced file management capability, Google Drive (`https://drive.google.com`) goes further than Google Docs. It lets you access your files in a similar way to Dropbox and edit them using Google Docs.

Virtual Machines and Browser Testing

Cross-platform and cross-browser testing is something you'll have to do whether you're developing alone or with a team, but developer teams will need to know which browsers should be accommodated, the devices you're supporting, and whose responsibility browser testing is.

Identifying which browsers you're supporting and ensuring that everyone takes this into account from the beginning will prevent a lot of headaches, instead of testing at the end and having to add browser hacks too. Best practice is to use progressive enhancement, where the important content, design, and functionality of your site works across all supported browsers and any extras that only work on more modern browsers aren't essentail for user experience (UX) but are just added enhancements. Supported browsers should be established in the contract you have with your client.

Ensure that all team members have access to the tools they need for cross-browser testing, or allocate responsibilities for testing in different browsers to those team members who have access to them. You'll need to decide the following:

- Which browsers you'll support

- How you'll test for them (i.e., using real machines, virtual machines, or browser emulation software)

- How the different aspects of your site's design will work in different browsers (i.e., what's essential and what's not)

- Any polyfills, shims, or libraries you're going to use. These are external scripts or codebases which will power specific aspects of your site or add support for browsers which don't natively support all of the code you're using.

Browser Testing and Support Tools

Some browser testing and cross-browser support tools I've used include the following:

- Adobe BrowserLab (`https://browserlab.adobe.com`) simulates all the major browsers, although it only takes a snapshot of each page so it won't help you test how any interactions or animations are working cross-browser.

- Boot Camp for Mac (`http://www.apple.com/support/bootcamp/`) is preinstalled on Macs and enables you to run a virtual machine from a different, virtual boot drive. You can then configure this as a Windows machine for testing.

- Parallels for Mac (`http://www.parallels.com`) enables you to run OSX and Windows on your Mac without setting up separate drives, meaning you can easily switch from one to the other.

- Crossover for Mac (`http://www.codeweavers.com/products/`) enables you to run Windows applications on a Mac without setting up a virtual machine or buying multiple copies of Windows.

- Modernizr (`http://modernizr.com`) is a JavaScript-based feature-detection library that enables you to identify browsers that don't support the HTML and CSS you're using, and then adds classes to target these browsers specifically. Instead of relying on browser detection, this method uses feature detection, which can be more efficient and reliable. However, it can clutter up your stylesheet if you make extensive use of it.

- CSSPie (`http://css3pie.com`) adds support for CSS3 features such as border-radius and box-shadow to older versions of IE.

- HTML5shiv (`http://code.google.com/p/html5shiv/`) adds support for HTML5 to older versions of IE.

> You should list all the browsers you'll support in the project contract. That way, if your site breaks in an older browser you're not supporting, the client can't demand you fix it without paying extra (or being talked out of the idea instead, I hope!)

Testing on Other Devices

In addition to testing on alternative browsers, you'll probably need to test your client sites and your themes across a range of devices and mobile browsers. This is especially true given the current demand for responsive apps that service the needs of mobile device users.

Because of the myriad devices available, which vary in terms of both capabilities and screen size, it's unlikely you'll be able to test every possibility. I therefore recommend the following approach:

- Test on one or two real devices, preferably of different size and operating systems (e.g., an iPhone and an Android tablet). This will help you test user interaction with the site and how intuitive and ergonomic these are.

- Use browser simulators or emulators to test for additional devices—I list some you can use shortly.

- To test how your layout is displayed at different screen sizes, use an extension for your browser to resize the browser window—although I recommend always doing this manually as well, to see what your layout looks like at widths other than those of the main mobile devices. This will become increasingly relevant as new devices are released with a wider range of screen dimensions.

Mobile Device Testing Tools

Some useful device testing tools include the following:

- Firefox includes a tool for testing responsive sites via Tools⇨Web developer⇨Responsive Design. You can also find a range of mobile developer tools on the Firefox developer community at `https://developer.mozilla.org/en-US/mobile`.

- Opera Mobile Emulator (`http://www.opera.com/developer/tools/mobile/`) emulates Opera Mobile running on a variety of mobile devices.

- Opera Mini Simulator (`http://www.opera.com/developer/tools/mini/`) simulates Opera Mini in the browser.

- Safari Web Inspector (`https://developer.apple.com/technologies/safari/developer-tools.html`) enables you to test code running on your iOS device using desktop Safari. You can also use desktop Safari to test mobile sites by switching the user agent via Develop ⇨ User Agent.

- The Android SDK (`http://developer.android.com/sdk/index.html`) includes a mobile browser emulator.

- The Windows Phone emulator (`http://msdn.microsoft.com/en-us/library/windowsphone/develop/ff402563(v=vs.92).aspx`) includes an emulator for mobile IE.

- RIM provide a range of BlackBerry simulators at `http://us.blackberry.com/sites/developers/resources/simulators.html`.

Development Software and Tools

When working collaboratively on web design and development projects, you need to use a range of tools at various stages of the project. The list of tools available is always changing, and what you use will vary according to your preference, experience, and budget, so the following sections outline the general categories of tools you'll need in addition to the tools already mentioned.

Wireframing

Wireframing tools help you build layouts for your themes or sites without getting bogged down in the details of the design. If you don't need to work online, your tools can be anything from pencil and paper to Photoshop. Personally, I start with pencil and paper sketches and then work them up in Adobe Fireworks. For collaborative designing, consider the following online tools:

- Balsamiq Mockups (`http://www.balsamiq.com/products/mockups`) is a collaborative wireframing tool that enables you to build wireframes to which other team members (and the client) can add comments and make changes. Everything is tracked and it's all online, so you have access to it wherever you are. It has nice ready-to-use components for wireframes, such as buttons and forms, so you can focus on your layout, not on your drawing.

- Justinmind (`http://www.justinmind.com`) is another popular wireframing tool, with a slant toward responsive and cross-device prototyping. You can sign up for it on an annual or monthly basis—annual is cheaper.

Mood Boards and Color Palettes

If you're producing mood boards, color palettes, or other visual design concepts, you might want to work offline in a graphics program or use an online tool for collaborative working. Online tools include the following:

- MyDeco (`http://mydeco.com/rooms/moodboard/`) enables you to create online mood boards and share them with colleagues and clients.

- Pinterest (`http://pinterest.com`) enables you to upload, pin, sort, and browse images, which can be useful for both you and clients as you seek a design that inspires you and reflects the client's requirements.

- Evernote (`http://evernote.com`) can be used to help create mood boards—tips on how to do this are at `http://blog.evernote.com/2010/08/10/creating-a-mood-board-with-evernote-part-of-evernotes-creative-series/`.

- Image Spark (`http://www.imgspark.com/image/listing/all`) enables you to create your own online mood boards and view the boards of others.

- Pictaculous (`http://pictaculous.com`) generates color schemes from images you upload.

- COLOURlovers (`http://www.colourlovers.com`) enables you to create and share color palettes as well as download palettes created by other users.

Design Comps and Mockups

As mentioned earlier, choosing mockup software varies according to your preferences, your team's experience, and your client's requirements; but some developers forego creating full mockups in programs like Photoshop or Fireworks and go straight from wireframing and moodboarding to creating mockups in the browser using static HTML and CSS. The only tool you need for this is a code editor and a standards-compliant browser. If your team includes designers who don't have coding experience, Dreamweaver can be a useful tool, although be careful about importing the code it generates into your eventual WordPress theme—generally it isn't as tidy as what you would code by hand.

Code Editors

Of course, all web developers have their favorite code editor, and you're probably no exception. If you're developing in a team, however, you may need to rethink your preferences to find something that meets everyone's needs. If you're working remotely, you need an editor with FTP built in; and if you have a large team and a tight budget, you'll want a free code editor. I tend to use one of the following depending on the needs of the project:

- Text Wrangler (`http://www.barebones.com/products/textwrangler/`) includes FTP, syntax color-coding for multiple languages, and fast searching. I find it very fast.

- Kompozer (`http://www.kompozer.net`) is a free WYSIWYG code editor that I use in place of Dreamweaver. It features design and code views, support for creating WYSIWIG forms and tables, and it runs on Mac, Windows, or Linux. Its design interface isn't as smart as Dreamweaver's, but it's free—hard to argue with that.

Many other text editors are available, and an exhaustive list of the benefits of each is beyond the scope of this chapter. As long as you determine exactly what your team needs from your text editor(s), you should be able to find a suitable candidate.

Creating a Client Approval Site

After you have done the development work, you need your client to approve it. This won't just be at the launch stage—you should have interim stages built into your project plan, and your contract should specify at which stage the client will sign off the work. This is important for communication, to help things keep on track, and to provide clear milestones at which you are paid.

The Approval Process

The client approval process I use in my agency and recommend is as follows:

1. Have an initial meeting with the client to identify their requirements and outline the site's content and objectives, as well as any other needs such as graphic design, SEO, or social media support.

2. Prepare a proposal for the site, including a summary of what has been discussed, proposals for improvements over the existing site if applicable, and other work that will be done to make the site as effective, SEO-friendly, and accessible as possible. This is also when you provide a quote for the work, which is normally itemized.

3. Assuming the proposal is accepted, this becomes the brief that you pass to your team. You (or your team) then prepare mood boards and wireframes, along with an overview of the proposed site's structure. The site structure document should include notes describing how content will be generated for each part of the site and what WordPress content types will be used.

4. After the preceding items have been accepted, prepare a mockup using static HTML and CSS for the client to review, comment on, and approve with any agreed changes. This replaces the use of static mockups. For small projects with a very well defined brief, you might skip this stage and go straight to building a WordPress theme.

5. The static HTML and CSS is then imported into a WordPress theme, at my company built on an in-house framework we use for all site builds. Any content is added to the site either by the development team or the client. Once this is complete, the site is considered to be at the alpha stage and is presented to the client for approval.

6. The next stage is the beta stage, which is developed following agreement about any changes to the alpha. Any outstanding content is also added at this stage. The site is tested and presented to the client again for approval. This beta version is intended to be very close to the final site—any changes made to this will be minor. I have a clause in my contracts stating that significant changes at this stage can incur extra costs.

7. After the beta has been signed off, the site is launched. The WordPress admin is customized (unless this has been done already), client users and roles are created, and the site is moved to its live location. Give it a final test and provide the client with training in how to use WordPress to manage it (unless you will be doing this). The training is either via online videos or face to face.

Some of the preceding stages are linked to payment stages. I charge a deposit on acceptance of the proposal and before doing any design or development work. I then invoice the remaining fee for the project in two stages—at the point where the alpha is presented to the client and at launch. I highly recommend adding clauses in your contracts that state payment terms if a project is delayed by the client—for example, this might mean payment for all work completed to date is invoiced when a delay exceeds two weeks, sometimes longer for large projects.

On a larger project, you can add an extra invoice stage, possibly on acceptance of moodboards, wireframes, and site structure. This reflects the additional work involved but also covers some of the work still to be done on the alpha version of the site.

Controlling Access and Search Engine Visibility

Your client will need access to a working version of the site in order to review and approve your work. While it's good practice to present your work to clients face to face or via a video conference, clients will also want a version of the site they can "play with" at their leisure so they can show it to colleagues and explore its content and functionality. Obviously, it is important that this site is private. There are a few ways of tackling this:

- Install the site locally on the client's network, so only users with access to that network can access it.

- Install the site on a local machine at the client's premises—this was common some years ago when clients didn't always have network servers that could run WordPress, but I don't advise it now because it severely restricts access to the site.

- Make the site available remotely with password protection. You could create one client user account or individual accounts for client staff, depending on the needs of the project and your client.

Hiding Your Development Site from Search Engines

If your development and/or approval site is hosted remotely, you need to ensure that it isn't indexed by search engines, first by changing the privacy settings in the WordPress admin (now on the general Settings page in the admin since version 3.5).

If your site is in the root directory, WordPress will automatically generate a `robots.txt` file reflecting this privacy setting. If you're working on static HTML and CSS as part of your development process, you'll need to create your own `robots.txt` file to block crawler access and then use Google Webmaster tools (following the instructions at `http://support.google.com/webmasters/bin/answer.py?hl=enanswer=1663427`) to request that the site not be crawled.

A `robots.txt` file blocking access to the entire site for all search engines should include the following code:

```
User-agent: *
Disallow: /
```

Simply create a file with this content, name it `robots.txt`, and save it to your site's root directory.

Client Approval Access and Privileges

If you are hosting the approval site remotely, you need to set up user privileges for your client. This may include creating various roles in line with the roles the live site will use, if your client wants to test these. You'll also need to set up passwords for access to the site.

Setting Up Client Access

You could take one of two approaches to client access:

- Create password protection for the site in CPanel, with one or more usernames to access relevant directories.
- Configure user access in WordPress, either using a single client user account for access or creating individual user accounts with the relevant roles. Block access to the site for anyone other than logged-in users.

There are a number of plugins that you can use to restrict access to logged in users. Creating user roles and access privileges is also covered in depth in Chapter 4.

Setting Up User Roles

You may also need to set up multiple user roles (with corresponding accounts) for testing. If your site includes multiple roles, you will have done this already for use by the development team, but you may also have to create roles for the client to use when reviewing the site.

The user roles you set up at this stage should relate to the front end of the site, not the admin. Therefore, it's unlikely you will need to set up different editing roles, but you may need to set up roles that make certain content accessible. At the beta stage your client may want to test the admin, at which point you would need to set up accounts for all roles the client needs. For example, if the client has a number of staff members who will be contributing content and one who will be editing that content, you'll need to set up user accounts with the relevant roles so your client can see how things will work.

Tracking and Responding to Amendments

The method you use to track and handle bugs and changes is important, as it will help you and your team to be more efficient and to ensure that all changes are made before the site goes live.

Choosing a system depends on who needs access to it. Will clients be requesting amendments or reporting bugs using your tracking system or will someone in your team be transferring these to the system, maybe from the content of e-mail messages?

Some of the capabilities to look for in your bug tracking system include the following:

- Pinging the relevant developer when a change is requested, so changes can be actioned
- Ease of use and the capability to quickly add content
- Allowing the creation of tasks or to-do items, which can be tracked and marked as complete
- Accessibility from team and/or client locations—which means you may need an online system

My team uses the P2 Reloaded theme internally (`http://p2reloaded.com`) to track bugs, with clients contacting us via e-mail, as I have found that clients don't like being forced to use systems with which they are unfamiliar. However, some clients may have their own preferred system or may be happy to use an online system to report bugs or request changes.

The project collaboration tools I've already listed previously might meet your needs—Zoho Projects and Basecamp, for example, include bug tracking. Alternatively, you might want to use one of the following dedicated bug tracking tools:

- TheBugTrack (`http://www.thebugtrack.com`) is an online bug tracking tool designed to integrate with Google apps.
- Bugzilla (`http://www.bugzilla.org`) is a free and open-source online bug tracking tool.
- BontQ (`http://www.bontq.com`) has a more user-friendly interface than the free tools but it does require a subscription.

Migrating a Site for Launch

So, it's finally happened. Your client has approved the beta version of your site, the development work is done, and you're ready for launch. Not so fast, though: You can't just move the site and assume you're finished. Before you migrate the site, take time to prepare first so that you get it right.

Preparing to Go Live

It's important to involve the client in the launch process. Make sure you get their sign-off approval for the site in writing; and if you intend to make any final minor changes, ensure that the client is aware of these and has approved them.

If your client will be managing the site, provide instructions or training to help them to do this. It could take the form of face-to-face training with client staff, it could be online videos that you create yourself or include in the site's admin via a plugin, or it could be via user documentation. The latter is especially useful if the site uses nonstandard editing processes that the client needs to follow. Make sure your user documentation is easy to understand for the layperson and written in plain English—for advice on doing this see `http://wp.smashingmagazine.com/2012/07/04/writing-effective-wordpress-documentation/`.

If necessary, get a signature from your client before going live. This could be useful for high-stakes sites, major site rebuilds, projects that underwent significant changes compared to the original brief, or projects for which disagreements had to be overcome along the way.

Identify the best time to launch the site. Your client may have a launch date linked to a business or product launch, or you may choose to launch the site at a time when traffic will be slow and any problems would cause minimal disruption. You could also decide to migrate the site but restrict access to it for a day or so, hiding it behind a teaser page while you carry out final tests. The bottom line is to choose a time that is aligned with your client's expectations and needs to the extent that is possible; and if technical reasons constrain the launch time in any way, be sure your client understands why.

Going Live Site Checklist

Before you launch any site, use a final checklist to ensure that everything is done. Some of the following actions need to be completed before migrating the site, some during migration, and some afterward.

Pre-migration checklist:

- Confirm that any changes requested are made and that bugs are fixed.
- Test applicable browsers and devices (checking especially that no recent changes break in legacy browsers).
- Confirm that the print stylesheet works following any recent changes.
- Check any photo credits.
- Confirm that no pages contain dummy text or missing content.
- Confirm that customizations to the admin are working correctly, including any links to WordPress training or embedded videos.
- Check the Dashboard welcome message and any other messages or customizations you've added to the admin.
- Back up theme files, plugins, content, and database.

Post-migration checklist:

- Confirm that links and navigation work.
- Confirm that attachments are displayed and link correctly.
- Configure the client's hosting package and CPanel if provided.
- Remove any restrictions to site access that aren't needed in the live site.
- Run some tests on the live site using the different user roles your client will be using to work on the site if necessary.
- Remove any search engine restrictions.
- Register the site with Google Webmaster Tools (`https://www.google.com/webmasters/tools`).

- Add the site to Google Analytics if it hasn't been done already.

- Tell the client the site is live, provide them with any information or resources they need to support it, and invoice them!

Your checklist might include additional checks specific to the project, or it may omit some of the preceding items, but it serves as a useful starting point. Regardless of the checklist's specific items, it ensures that in the excitement of a site launch nothing is forgotten.

Moving WordPress Sites

Moving WordPress can seem daunting at first, but it needn't be. The important thing to be aware of is that a WordPress site consists of three things: the WordPress installation itself, your `wp-content` folder, and the database. Generally you'll only have to move the last two of these items, as you'll simply install a fresh installation of WordPress in the new location.

The following sections walk through the steps needed to move WordPress, first from a subdirectory to the root directory and then between locations.

Before Moving WordPress

Before you move a WordPress site, you *must* take a backup. Make sure your backup includes the following:

- The database, which you can make a copy of using the Export functionality in phpMyAdmin or using a backup plugin such as WP-DB-Backup (`http://wordpress.org/extend/plugins/wp-db-backup/`)

- The contents of the `wp-content` folder, especially your themes and uploads. You could omit the plugins and reinstall those on the new site, but I find it quicker to copy them across with everything else.

Moving WordPress from a Subdirectory to the Root Directory

This is very simple and should only take a few minutes, as you are moving only one or two files:

1. Back up and remove any existing site in the root directory. It may be another WordPress installation or it may be a static site. If it's a WordPress site, make a backup of the database and `wp-content` directory. If it's a static site, back up the files.

2. Turn off permalinks in your development site.

3. Select Settings ➪ General, and change the address of your site but not the address of WordPress as follows:

   - WordPress address (URL): `http://example.com/subdirectoryname`

   - Site Address (URL): `http://example.com`

4. Using FTP, copy (don't move) the following files from your WordPress directory to the root directory:

   - `index.php`

   - `.htaccess` (If you don't have this file, just skip this step.)

   Edit the `index.php` file that you copied by finding the line

   `require (./wp-blog-header.php)`

and changing it to the following:

```
require (./subdirectoryname/wp-blog-header.php)
```

For example if you have been developing in `example.com/development`, you would change it to the following:

```
require (./development/wp-blog-header.php)
```

5. Save the new `index.php` file.

6. Back in the WordPress admin, enable permalinks again, with whatever setting you need for your site. Visit the root domain of your site in the browser and it will display the site that's stored in the subdirectory, but it won't display this in the URL, which will be displayed as the root URL. You're done!

> You need to be aware that if your site is in a subdirectory, this will be visible in the URL when users are accessing attachment files, although not when they're viewing pages. So make sure you don't use a directory name that might cause confusion or get you into trouble!

Uploading WordPress to a Remote Host

Moving WordPress to a new location is more complicated. The following process applies if you're uploading a site from a local installation to a remote host or if you're moving between hosts or servers. As described earlier, don't forget to make a backup.

1. Turn off pretty permalinks in the Permalinks screen in the Settings menu.

2. Install WordPress in the new location and upload content. Using your preferred method, install WordPress on the server to which you want to move your site. Using FTP, copy the files from your local `wp-content` directory to the remote `wp-content` directory, using the same folder structure as your local install.

3. Make a copy of the database file and give it a name that will help you remember it's a new version. Using your preferred text editor, replace the old, local URL for the site with the new, remote URL in the database file. For example, if your local URL were `http://localhost/example`, you would change it to `http://example.com`.

   Using the replace command in your text editor will speed this up—there could be thousands of instances. Save your new database.

4. Still in phpMyAdmin, upload the database you have edited:

   a. Click the Import tab.

   b. Click the Choose file button.

   c. Select the database you saved in step 3 and click Choose or OK.

   d. Click the Go button.

   After a while (depending on the size of your database), you will see a message indicating that the upload has successfully finished.

5. Clear your browser's cache before accessing the site or testing. This avoids any problems you may have if the browser has cached content from the old version of the remote database.

6. Update permalinks and test. Everything should be working fine, but you may want to use the aforementioned going live checklist to be absolutely sure.

Hosting Options for Clients

Whether you provide hosting for your clients is a decision only you can make. You should understand exactly what this involves, the pros and cons, and what you need to consider when selecting a hosting provider. All web developers need a hosting provider for their own site and personal projects, so even if you don't intend to offer reseller hosting, this information could be beneficial to you.

What You Need to Know

The following list describes the main types of hosting available. The package you choose will depend on whether you intend to sell hosting to your clients and offer them their own CPanel or similar.

- **Shared hosting**—This involves buying space on a shared server on which you can then store files. Normally you would have access to CPanel or an alternative such as Plesk, which you can use to configure your sites, set up e-mail accounts, manage databases, and more. Only one account is included, which means you can't give your clients access to CPanel. You can still manage multiple domains via shared hosting, but you can't give clients their own hosting account.

- **Reseller hosting**—This provides you with a hosting account plus a Web Host Manager (WHM), which enables you to set up multiple accounts on your hosting server. You can create an account for each client (or for each member of your team if you wish) and configure CPanel for them so that they only have access to the tools they need. Reseller hosting makes it much easier to manage multiple domains.

- **Virtual Private Server (VPS) hosting**—This is like reseller hosting but provides a virtual server for your account within a server that is physically shared. This means that you are protected from any problems caused by other server users—for example, if another user's site were hacked and the server blacklisted, you wouldn't be affected.

- **Dedicated server hosting**—This provides your own dedicated server, giving you potentially more storage space, a tailored server configuration, and no risk of problems caused by other users—but it can be very expensive.

- **Managed hosting**—This handles everything for you. The hosting provider not only provides you with hosting space, but also looks after your WordPress installation, optimizes your site(s) for performance, makes regular backups, and installs any updates. You could buy this or you could provide something similar to your clients with your own reseller or VPS account.

As you might guess, shared hosting is the cheapest option, whereas managed hosting is the most expensive. Which you choose will depend on your budget, your business model, and the income you can expect to make from selling hosting to your clients.

Table 5-3 summarizes how each option meets different needs.

Table 5-3: Characteristics of Different Hosting Options

Requirement	Shared Hosting	Reseller Hosting	VPS Hosting	Dedicated Server Hosting	Managed Hosting
Client accounts	Clients don't have their own hosting accounts or CPanel access. If all they need is website maintenance access, you can provide this via their WordPress user account.	Clients have their own hosting accounts with CPanel access.	Clients have their own hosting accounts with CPanel access.	Clients have their own hosting accounts with CPanel access.	Available with or without additional accounts.
E-mail accounts	You can create and configure client e-mail accounts.	You and the client can create and configure client e-mail accounts.	You and the client can create and configure client e-mail accounts.	You and the client can create and configure client e-mail accounts.	Available with or without additional accounts.
Security	Your hosting is on a shared server so there is some vulnerability to attack or server failure.	Your hosting is on a shared server so there is some vulnerability to attack or server failure.	Vulnerability to attack is reduced. If your server should fail, you may be entitled to speedier service to get it up and running again.	Vulnerability to attack is further reduced. If your server should fail you should be entitled to speedier service to get it up and running again.	Your hosting provider handles your site's security, so you don't need to worry about it.
Performance	Performance should be good (but depends on your provider and your configuration).	Performance should be good (but depends on your provider and your configuration).	Performance should be enhanced.	Performance should be further enhanced.	Performance will be optimized by your provider.
Software and updates	Server software (such as PHP) will automatically be updated but WordPress won't, so you (or the client) will have to do this yourself.	Server software (such as PHP) will automatically be updated but WordPress won't, so you (or the client) will have to do this yourself.	Server software (such as PHP) will automatically be updated but WordPress won't, so you (or the client) will have to do this yourself.	Server software (such as PHP) will automatically be updated but WordPress won't, so you (or the client) will have to do this yourself.	All updates will be automatic.

(continued)

Table 5-3: *(continued)*

Requirement	Shared Hosting	Reseller Hosting	VPS Hosting	Dedicated Server Hosting	Managed Hosting
Storage space	The amount of storage you get depends on your package.	The amount of storage you get depends on your package.	The amount of storage you get depends on your package and can be changed easily.	Potentially, your server can cope with greater traffic (although VPS hosting can be more flexible here—for example, if you need more than the physical size of your server).	Your provider automatically configures your storage to handle changes to your site(s).

As you can see, there are some huge advantages to the higher-end packages. These come at a price, however. When identifying what sort of provision you need, consider the following:

▨ The income you can make from selling hosting to your clients

▨ Whether not offering hosting will put some clients off (e.g., startups or nontechnical clients)

▨ The fact that working with your own hosting is more efficient than working with different account types and providers held by your clients

▨ The time you will spend managing your hosting and your sites

▨ The time you could spend dealing with any downtime

Most agencies start off with reseller hosting and expand as the need arises. However, in some cases you may only need shared hosting—for example, if you're using WordPress Multisite to manage your client sites and they don't need access to hosting or e-mail configuration. Alternatively, you may opt for managed hosting to minimize the amount of time you have to spend looking after your own hosting.

If you don't want to sell hosting but you want the benefit of dealing with only one provider and one interface, you could offer to set up your clients with the same hosting provider but with each having their own account that they manage themselves—but be aware that some clients may still expect you to manage this anyway.

Finding and Getting the Most from a Hosting Provider

Finding a good hosting provider isn't easy. The marketplace is full of companies competing for your business and if you end up with the wrong one, migrating your site(s) to another provider could be a lengthy and costly process.

Most web developers choose a hosting provider based on personal recommendation; but if you don't have this information, following are some of the criteria I recommend considering when choosing your provider:

▨ **Software**—Do they include the software you need to run WordPress? The current requirements are PHP version 5.2.4 or greater and MySQL version 5.0 or greater.

- **CPanel access**—Is CPanel or an alternative provided? CPanel is recognized as the leading interface for managing hosting, and I always recommend finding a provider that includes it with their hosting packages.

- **Cost**—Can you afford the package you need? As with most things, you get what you pay for. If it's very inexpensive, make sure that it's still good quality and offers the services you require—cheap hosting providers tend to be less reliable or have poorer service.

- **Location**—Where are their servers located? Your clients may require their servers to be located in a specific country. If a hosting provider's operations and servers are on opposite sides of the world, this may have implications for their support and service levels.

- **Support**—How easy is it to raise a support ticket? How quick is the response?

- **Service**—When you first contact the provider, how helpful are they? If you're migrating from an old provider, will they help you with that process? Do they have 24/7 coverage? Do they have a phone number you can call to speak to someone if a support ticket isn't enough?

- **Reviews**—Check online for reviews of your chosen provider, and look for positive references to them on Twitter.

- **Scalability**—When your requirements increase, can the provider scale up to demand easily and quickly? How fast can they respond to spikes in traffic?

After finding a hosting provider, stay in contact with them. Tell them if you're not happy with the service you're getting; ask them questions about how they can meet your needs; and if they do well, recommend them to others. Hosting is a very crowded market, so your provider should work hard to retain your business, and not rely on the fact that moving can be difficult.

I've deliberately not gone into a huge amount of detail on hosting here because it may not be something you offer; and if you do, your setup could consist of many different alternatives. For readers who want more information, the "Further Resources" section contains some links to useful resources for setting up and maximizing your hosting.

Summary

This chapter has covered a range of topics that will be important to you if you're establishing a WordPress business and working with clients. Understanding what development environment you need and being able to make that work for a development team will make you more efficient and streamlined, while having the right tools and software in place enables you to focus on getting the work done. Having a solid process for client approvals and launching sites will avoid potential problems, and if you decide to offer hosting to your clients, you'll need to do your homework before getting started. The following section will help you learn more about these topics.

Further Resources

Setting Up a Local Development Environment

MAMP

```
http://www.mamp.info
```

WAMP

```
http://www.wampserver.com
```

XAMPP
http://www.apachefriends.org

Download WordPress
http://wordpress.org/download

Guide to installing WordPress
http://codex.wordpress.org/Installing_WordPress

Guide to installing WordPress locally with MAMP
http://codex.wordpress.org/Installing_WordPress_Locally_on_Your_Mac_With_MAMP

Tools for Collaborative Working

Version control with Git
http://net.tutsplus.com/tutorials/other/easy-version-control-with-git/

Compare local and remote files with Dreamweaver
http://help.adobe.com/en_US/dreamweaver/cs/using/WSc78c5058ca073340dcda911
0b1f693f21-7edda.html

Dropbox
http://dropbox.com

Diffuse
http://diffuse.sourceforge.net

BBEdit
http://www.barebones.com/products/bbedit

Dreamweaver
http://www.adobe.com/products/dreamweaver.html

UltraCompare
http://www.ultraedit.com

Basecamp
http://basecamp.com

The WordPress P2 theme
http://p2theme.com

P2 Reloaded
http://p2reloaded.com

Zoho Projects
http://www.zoho.com/projects

Google Docs
http://docs.google.com

Google Drive
https://drive.google.com

Balsamiq
http://www.balsamiq.com/products/mockups

Justinmind
http://www.justinmind.com

Browser Testing Tools

Adobe BrowserLab
`https://browserlab.adobe.com`

Boot Camp for Mac
`http://www.apple.com/support/bootcamp/`

Parallels for Mac
`http://www.parallels.com`

Crossover for Mac
`http://www.codeweavers.com/products/`

Browser Support Tools

Modernizer
`http://modernizr.com`

CSSPie
`http://css3pie.com`

HTML5shiv
`http://code.google.com/p/html5shiv/`

Mobile Testing Tools

Firefox mobile developer community
`https://developer.mozilla.org/en-US/mobile`

Opera Mobile Emulator
`http://www.opera.com/developer/tools/mobile/`

Opera Mini Simulator
`http://www.opera.com/developer/tools/mini/`

Safari Web Inspector
`https://developer.apple.com/technologies/safari/developer-tools.html`

Android SDK
`http://developer.android.com/sdk/index.html`

Windows Phone emulator
`http://msdn.microsoft.com/en-us/library/windowsphone/develop/ff402563(v=vs.92).aspx`

Blackberry simulators
`http://us.blackberry.com/sites/developers/resources/simulators.html`

Moodboard and Color Palette Tools

MyDeco
`http://mydeco.com/rooms/moodboard`

Pinterest
`http://pinterest.com`

Evernote
```
http://blog.evernote.com/2010/08/10/creating-a-mood-board-with-evernote-
part-of-evernotes-creative-series
```

Image Spark
```
http://www.imgspark.com/image/listing/all
```

Pictaculous
```
http://pictaculous.com
```

COLORlovers
```
http://www.colourlovers.com
```

Bug Tracking Tools

TheBugTrack
```
http://www.thebugtrack.com
```

Bugzilla
```
http://www.bugzilla.org
```

BontQ
```
http://www.bontq.com
```

Moving a WordPress Site

Codex documentation on moving WordPress
```
http://codex.wordpress.org/Moving_WordPress
```

Giving WordPress its own directory
```
http://codex.wordpress.org/Giving_WordPress_Its_Own_Directory
```

Installing WordPress
```
http://codex.wordpress.org/Installing_WordPress
```

Documentation on phpMyAdmin
```
http://www.phpmyadmin.net/documentation/
```

Hosting

Codex documentation on hosting WordPress
```
http://codex.wordpress.org/Hosting_WordPress
```

Choosing a WordPress hosting provider
```
http://www.wpbeginner.com/wordpress-hosting/#hostneeds-slidetoggle
```

Yoast on WordPress hosting
```
http://yoast.com/articles/wordpress-hosting/
```

Recommended WordPress hosting providers
```
http://wordpress.org/hosting/
```

Tips for a healthy relationship with your hosting provider
```
http://www.smashingmagazine.com/2009/03/29/9-steps-to-a-happy-
relationship-with-your-hosting-provider/
```

Chapter 6

Avoiding and Dealing with Disaster

The biggest headaches you experience when working for clients are likely to be caused by unanticipated problems. You can plan for the site build itself, including launch and addition of content, but many developers fail to plan for problems that might arise after a site goes live.

All experienced developers have tales of disasters that have struck their sites, and each one provides a learning experience. My own worst experience occurred when my hosting provider moved its servers and lost all of my and my clients' data. Luckily I had an automated backup system in place and was therefore able to restore every site using a backup that was just a few days old (with a new hosting provider, needless to say). However, the impact on my time and my ability to take on work while this was being fixed was huge.

Fortunately, by learning from my experience and those of other developers, you can avoid the same disasters! Problems aren't always avoidable, but there's a lot you can do to minimize the chances of them occurring. This chapter describes some common causes of downtime and failure of WordPress sites, and identifies ways you can avoid them where possible, as well as how to deal with problems when they do arise.

What Could Go Wrong and the Consequences

A variety of issues can lead to problems, which could be caused by changes to the site itself, to the pattern of visits to the site, or by external factors such as hacking or server problems. Some of the most common problems include the following:

- **Bandwidth or storage issues**—If these are exceeded due to an increase in the size of the site or a spike in demand, a site could experience downtime or a dip in performance just when its owner most needs it to be up and running smoothly.

- **Server failure**—This could have a variety of causes depending on the hosting environment you're using. For example, if you're using shared hosting and another user on your server's site is hacked in a way that affects it use of bandwidth (for example, the server is being used to send spam emails), it could affect server performance or even result in the server being blacklisted. See Chapter 5 for more information on hosting environments.

- **Loss of data**—Due to server failure or human error (or possibly following an update), some or all of a site's data could be lost. You'll learn more about backup regimes in detail in this chapter, as well as processes to minimize the risk of human error.

- **Updates**—An update to WordPress or to a plugin or theme may cause conflicts within your WordPress installation. In my experience, well-coded sites, plugins, and themes are unlikely to experience problems following WordPress updates, but sometimes a plugin update can cause a conflict with another plugin.
- **Malicious attacks**—As WordPress has gained in popularity, it has also become the target for an increasing number of hackers. There are a variety of ways you can protect a WordPress site from attack, which include keeping it updated, password security, and changes you can make to the configuration.

Avoiding Problems

The consequences of any of the problems listed earlier will vary from downtime to disaster for a site. The better you proactively anticipate and prepare for problems, by putting into place measures to avoid them, the better your chances of avoiding disaster.

There are measures you can put in place to avoid many potential problems, or minimize risk at the very least. In this section you'll learn methods to anticipate and avoid the following:

- Site performance problems
- Data loss
- Problems arising when you update WordPress
- Security breaches

Site Performance Problems

A site could experience performance problems due to one of three factors:

- Changes to the site itself
- Changes to site usage
- Changes to the server or hosting environment

Hosting environments are covered in detail in Chapter 5, so the following sections look at the first two factors, which can be closely linked—for example, a site that has undergone a significant upgrade or redesign and is then launched, causing a spike in usage.

Anticipating Site Performance Requirements

You can sometimes anticipate changes to the site or its usage, and therefore create a plan to handle those changes. For example, some years ago I worked on a political party's website, which saw huge surges in demand during election campaigns, meaning we had to buy additional server capacity during those times.

Before you launch a site, it's a good idea to have a conversation with the client to determine what their future plans are and to understand any changes in demand that they expect. If you will be managing the site's performance on an ongoing basis, this early conversation provides you with information that can help you do so effectively; if the client will be handling such changes, you can help them to plan.

Find out the following, either by asking your client or by examining historical site data where relevant:

▪ Anticipated usage levels for the site and whether there is a pattern for these (e.g., at different times of the day, days of the month, or times of the year). This includes demand due to product launches, media campaigns or reports, or processes supported by the site that users will want to complete at given times.

▪ How does the client plan to launch the site and do they anticipate high demand on launch?

▪ Any specific events or campaigns that will lead to spikes in demand for a short period of time.

▪ Any planned additions to the site that will affect storage or bandwidth requirements.

▪ How fast the site is likely to grow—will the client be adding new content on a continuous basis or only sporadically?

Create a plan for a relevant time period (this could be annually, quarterly, monthly, weekly, or even daily depending on the site's requirements), with anticipated storage, bandwidth, and usage changes. This needn't be exact, only an approximation of the fluctuations. Table 6-1 shows an example plan with some very approximate estimations.

Table 6-1: Example Site Performance Plan

Month	Anticipated Changes	Storage Requirement	Bandwidth Requirement
January	Site launch	3,000MB	10,000MB – spike to 20,000MB on 10th of month
February	Site content to grow by 20%; average visitor numbers to rise by 20%	3,600MB	15,000MB
March	Site content to grow by 10%; develop new interactive purchasing tool for site	3,400MB	17,000MB
April	Major advertising campaign to launch interactive tool	3,400MB	22,000MB
May	Some continuing demand from advertising campaign; other site content to grow by 10%	3,750MB	20,000MB
June	Site content to grow by 10%	4,150MB	20,000MB
July	Site content to grow by 10%	4,600MB	20,000MB
August	Quiet period; site content continues to grow for rest of the year	4,800MB	17,000MB
September	New product launch	5,000MB	23,000MB
October	Continuing demand following new product launch	5,000MB	21,000MB
November	Christmas advertising campaign begins	5,300MB	23,000MB
December	Christmas advertising continues, increased demand all month	5,300MB	25,000MB

In the preceding example, both storage and bandwidth requirements grow over the year, but bandwidth has some ups and downs. Of course, the figures used here are overly simplistic and not based on a complex understanding of exactly how visitors engage with the site—for example, not only the number of visitors have an impact, but also the pages they interact with, the length of time they spend on the site, and the transactions they carry out.

After you determine this information, you can identify what storage and bandwidth requirements the site is likely to have at given times. This can help you identify when you will need to make changes to the server or hosting environment, whether these are incremental or temporary. For large sites with a lot of seasonal traffic (e.g., retail sites with a big surge prior to Christmas), try to negotiate increases to your server space or bandwidth with your hosting provider well in advance, as your site won't be the only one with such requirements. Hosting plans vary in terms of how easy it is to dynamically add and subtract space as needed.

Monitoring Server and Site Performance

After your site is live, you will have access to much more reliable data on performance requirements than anything you can attempt to predict. Depending on the nature of a site, you may need to monitor performance continually, or just every now and again. For smaller sites, where changes are infrequent, the alerts provided by your hosting provider may be sufficient; but for high-traffic sites where downtime or reduced performance is a potential risk and will have increased negative consequences, you need to use monitoring tools—both to track current and past performance and to anticipate future performance.

Tools for Performance Testing and Monitoring

You can use the monitoring tools which come with a control panel, but these have limitations. Monitoring tools available with control panels (such as CPanel) can include the following:

- **Bandwidth monitor**—Monitors bandwidth usage over set periods of time.

- **Webalizer**—Monitors usage statistics and can output raw statistics for use in spreadsheets, and provides stats on usage and trends.

- **Analog Stats**—Provides stats on server requests, data transferred, page views, and more. It can also give you a useful indication of trends in your website's usage, as it provides numerous charts and graphs documenting the statistics it generates.

- **Awstats**—Generates similar statistics to Analog Stats, but displays them in a different format and gives you more options for viewing data.

In addition, many third party CPanel monitoring apps are available—for a full list, see `http://applications.cpanel.net/tag/monitoring/`.

A variety of hosted tools and WordPress plugins are available that provide additional tools. Enhancements they offer may include how the data is presented, methods for exporting it, queries you can run, or the capability to be notified when a problem occurs.

Plugins include the following:

- **Verelo Blog Monitoring** (`http://wordpress.org/extend/plugins/verelo-blog-monitoring/`)—Monitors your site and notifies you if there is downtime or malicious code is present, when linked to an account with Verelo.

- **Hosting Monitor** (`http://wordpress.org/extend/plugins/hosting-monitor/`)—Monitors storage levels and alerts you when these are close to being exceeded.

- **JetPack** (`http://wordpress.org/extend/plugins/jetpack/`)—Includes a variety of features, including website stats in the Dashboard. It also includes other features which you can activate as required, including widgets, spell checking, and more.

Third party tools include:

- **Monitor.us** (`http://www.monitor.us/website-monitoring`)—Monitors server performance, website response times, page load times, and more. It's free and open source, with its own API. It also has an associated WordPress plugin (`http://wordpress.org/extend/plugins/wp-monitorus/`).

- **SiteUpTime** (`http://www.siteuptime.com`)—A premium service with a variety of optional services and pricing plans. It monitors your server and alerts you of problems, and has its own API.

- **OSSEC** (`http://www.ossec.net`)—This open-source system was specifically designed to monitor a site for intrusions, so it will alert you if your site is hacked. It won't fix any problems it finds, however—see the section "Dealing with Disaster" later in this chapter for advice about that.

- **Sucuri** (`http://sucuri.net`)—A premium service that includes monitoring your site for attacks and malware and fixing any problems it finds.

Avoiding Data Loss

Losing data or files from a site is another serious risk to avoid. Lost data can include any of the following:

- Database content (posts, pages, etc.)
- Uploads (e.g., media)
- Theme files (or versions of them if these are edited)
- Plugin files

To prevent such loss, it's important to back up all of these on a regular basis, and to have an automated system in place to handle it; otherwise, you run the risk of either forgetting to do it or putting it off until it's too late. In addition, you don't want to spend all your time making backups.

WordPress stores versions of posts added to a site, which can be incredibly useful if you need to roll back a post to a previous autosaved version. However, it doesn't store backups of the database or keep snapshots of it at given points in time—you need to use another tool to do that. It also doesn't store backups of your uploads.

Effective Backups and Version Control

How often a site needs to be backed up varies according to the nature of the site and how frequently it's updated. Generally the following guidelines will apply:

- **Database**—Back this up daily for frequently updated sites, weekly for less frequently updated sites. In some cases you may need hourly backups, particularly for news sites or e-commerce sites with heavy traffic and frequent updates.

- **Uploads**—These should be backed up as frequently as the database itself, as any posts containing media won't restore correctly if the attached media is lost.

- **Theme files**—If you are backing up manually, do this before and after making any changes to the theme files. You should also add a new version number to the theme whenever you make changes. This is covered in more detail in the next section. If you are backing up automatically, a weekly backup will normally suffice, although you may opt to back up theme files every time the database is backed up.

- **Plugin files**—You can always reinstall third-party plugins from the WordPress repository or the original plugin files if needed; but if for some reason you need to use an older version of a plugin, you'll need to keep your own backup. Some plugins include customizations you've made, in which case you need to keep your own backup—I recommend doing this weekly for most sites. For plugins you have developed yourself, you'll need to make backups whenever you edit the plugin, and of course use version control as you would for themes.

The frequency of backups should be specified in your client contract—if they later need more frequent backups, this must be agreed upon, including any additional costs. You also need to agree on the retention period for backups—it's a good idea to keep a number of backups in case the most recent one is corrupted, but of course keeping too many will consume a lot of storage space wherever the backups are kept (which should be separate from where the site is hosted). You'll also need to determine with the client who will store the backups, and who has responsibility for restoring the site from backups—both of these factors affect costs.

Version Control Best Practice

For version control you can use subversion tools such as Github to manage your files and keep on top of things. Alternatively you can set up your own directory structure on your local machine or network to keep backups. This is covered in more detail in Chapter 5.

Whenever you edit a theme you should save it as a new version in the correct directory structure and amend the version number in the stylesheet accordingly. For example, the current version number for the theme powering my blog is 1.1, as reflected in the stylesheet comments:

```
/*
Theme Name: Rachel McCollin
Theme URI: http://rachelmccollin.co.uk/
Description: Theme for Rachel McCollin site. Version 1.1 with changes to
    styling. Based on Compass Framework 4.0.
Author: Rachel McCollin
Template: compassframework4.0
Version: 1.1
Tags: two-columns, fluid, responsive, mobile, threaded-comments,
  sticky-post, translation-ready, widgets
*/
```

How you number your versions is, of course, up to you; but use a consistent system throughout your team. Generally, small changes merit a 0.1 increment, whereas significant changes to the theme (such as a redesign or the addition of new template files) increment the version to the next whole number. In the preceding example, I've added a note about the changes in this version, which is visible in the Themes selection screen, as shown in Figure 6-1.

Figure 6-1 The version number displayed in the Manage Themes screen

Themes released to the public *must* be named with a new version number whenever you make a new version available.

Plugins are given version numbers in a similar way. For example, the plugin I wrote to accompany Chapter 3 of this book is currently at version 1:

```php
<?php
/*
Plugin Name: WordPress Pushing the Limits Chapter 3
Plugin URI: http://rachelmccollin.co.uk/wpptl/chapter3
Description: Plugin containing all of the functions from chapter 3 of the
    book 'WordPress Pushing the Limits' including registering custom post
    types and taxonomies and setting up custom fields and meta boxes.
Version: 1.0
Author: Rachel McCollin
Author URI: http://rachelmccollin.com
License: GPLv2
*/
?>
```

Again, minor changes need a 0.1 version increment, whereas significant changes or additions to the plugin's functionality are incremented to the next whole number. Using versioning correctly for publicly available plugins is also vital—this is covered in more detail in Chapter 12.

Backup Tools

Numerous tools are available to automate the backup process, including both free and premium tools—the premium versions typically handle more of the work for you, whereas the free versions typically mean you need to use more than one solution or do some of the backup manually.

A full list of free backup plugins is available at `http://wordpress.org/extend/plugins/tags/backup`. Some plugins include automation tools; and some just back up the database, whereas others back up your files. Backing up files is important, as it backs up not only plugin and theme files, which you control, but also uploads. A popular plugin for this purpose is Online Backup for WordPress (`http://wordpress.org/extend/plugins/wponlinebackup/`).

If you want a tool you can set and forget, you might decide to invest in a premium tool. When you consider the potential time such a tool can save you in the long run and the impact on your clients and your business in terms of downtime and extra work fixing problems, it's often a worthwhile investment; and if you are charging your clients for website support (which I recommend!), you can recoup the cost there.

Premium tools include the following:

- **BackupBuddy** (`http://ithemes.com/purchase/backupbuddy/`)—This popular tool is a "set it and forget it" tool that enables you to back up all the database's content and files associated with a WordPress site and easily restore them when needed. You can then store them on Dropbox, Amazon S3, or your own server, or have them emailed to you (don't store them on the same server as the site you're backing up!). It also has facilities for easily moving WordPress from one place to another.

- **VaultPress** (`http://vaultpress.com`)—Developed by Automattic, this service claims to be the world's best WordPress backup solution. It's expensive, so it is best suited to large-scale operations. In addition to backup and restore features, it has a dashboard that enables you to drill down into changes over time and restore exactly what you need—so for large sites that are frequently updated, this could save a lot of time.

- **blogVault** (`http://blogvault.net`)—This backup and restore service, which also includes migration, enables you to test a restored site on their servers before actually doing the restore.

Educating Clients and Users

As part of the handoff of a site, it's worthwhile to provide training in the use of WordPress to any staff in your client's organization who will be working with the site. This could be face to face or via video or written documentation. Part of this training should include guidance on version control and backups, which is particularly important for anyone who will have access to the theme files. Training advice should include the following:

- Instructions on using the version control built into WordPress posts and pages (including restoring a post from an autosave)

- Guidance on uploads and media—it's good practice for users to keep a copy of uploaded files locally in case they need to edit them or restore them. Your client may have a network where these will be stored. This won't replace any automated backups you put in place for uploads in case of file loss.

- Guidance on version control for theme files where relevant, including where backups need to be saved whenever a theme file is edited

- Guidance regarding the frequency with which different elements of the site will be automatically backed up and where these will be stored

Updating WordPress and Installed Plugins Safely

When you develop or install plugins and themes you will test that these are compatible with the version of WordPress running on the site—but when you upgrade WordPress, a plugin or theme may become incompatible in some way. This generally shouldn't affect the database but may lead to conflicts in the code.

Updating WordPress

Updating WordPress itself is the first weapon in the security arsenal of any WordPress site, but it is a good idea to take care when updating. That means, before updating ensure that you make a full backup, or that you have an automated backup that is more recent than any changes made to the site or the theme.

For a conservative approach, some developers also recommend deactivating all plugins before upgrading, and reactivating them one by one afterward to test for any incompatibilities.

If you do experience problems when updating WordPress, you should restore your backup, including a backup of the version of WordPress itself that you were previously running. It's important to identify the problem so you can update to the latest version, though, as that will improve security.

Updating Plugins

If you are updating a plugin, it's sensible to make a backup of the previous version beforehand in case any conflicts occur. In my experience of trawling the WordPress support forums, one of the most common causes of problems that I've seen is conflicts between plugins. If a new version of a plugin conflicts with another critical plugin installed on your site, you will want to be able to restore the old version quickly while you look for a more long-term solution.

Try to identify any conflicts if possible and raise them with the plugin developers, so that eventually you can ensure that all of your plugins are up to date. In extreme cases, you may need to use a new plugin to do the same job, edit the one you've been using, or write your own. While you're doing this work, you need the site to continue operating correctly, of course.

Minimizing Risks Associated with Updates

In addition to observing the preceding precautions when installing updates, there are measures you can take to minimize potential risks associated with updates. These include the following:

- **Adhere to the WordPress coding standards.** When writing themes and plugins, use the WordPress coding standards (`http://codex.wordpress.org/WordPress_Coding_Standards`).

- **Use robust naming conventions.** Use unique names for plugins, themes, and functions, avoiding `wp_` at the beginning of any function and instead using a unique prefix—many developers use their own initials or the initials of the theme or site.

- **Only use themes and plugins from trusted sources.** The WordPress plugin and theme repositories are a good place to start, but if you're buying premium themes or plugins, make sure they are recommended by other developers. This best practice also increases site security, as well-written themes and plugins are more secure.

- **Comment your own code well.** This will help you identify the source of any conflicts between themes and plugins you've developed. If your theme or plugin is incompatible with an upgrade of WordPress a year or more down the line, you want to make it as esay as possible to skim code you may long since have forgotten about and identify any problems.

Improving Security

Despite its popularity, WordPress has been criticized for poor security—therefore, you might occasionally find that a client raises objections to using it for this reason. In recent years, however, as WordPress has become more widely adopted, the development team behind it has worked hard to address its vulnerabilities, and it takes security very seriously. If a client objects to the use of WordPress on these grounds, you need only refer them to the list of WordPress-powered sites at `http://wordpress.org/showcase/`. This list includes some high-profile sites, including media and government organizations for whom site security is critical.

Of course, you must still take some responsibility for hardening your client's WordPress site to make it more secure. A good risk reduction process includes improving server security and the security of the site and the WordPress installation itself.

Server Security

You won't always have control over the server, particularly if your client wants to use their own server or hosting provider. If you are using your own provider, make sure it meets the minimum requirements for hosting WordPress (you can find these at `http://wordpress.org/about/requirements/`) and that processes are in place to increase security and deal with attacks. If your client has their own hosting, educate them about necessary requirements so they get the best from their hosting provider.

All files on your server should be owned by your user acocunt and writable by you. Any file that needs write access from WordPress needs to be writable by the web server, while others should be writable only from your account. You should ensure the folders are set up as follows:

- `/`—the root WordPress directory: All files should be writable only by your user account, except `.htaccess`, if you want WordPress to automatically generate rewrite rules for you.

- `/wp-admin/`—the WordPress administration area: All files should be writable only by your user account.

- `/wp-includes/`—the bulk of WordPress application logic: All files should be writable only by your user account.

- `/wp-content/`—user-supplied content: Intended to be writable by your user account and the web server process. Within this folder, the `/plugins/` folder should only be writable by your account and the `/themes/` folder will need to be writable by the server if you want access to the theme editor in the WordPress admin.

> **For more information on file permissions, see** `http://codex.wordpress.org/Hardening_WordPress#File_Permissions.`

WordPress Security

Improving the security of a WordPress installation starts with some quick easy fixes you can put in place in moments, but also includes some more in-depth alterations to key files and configurations to further enhance security. How far you need to go will depend on the degree of risk to which the site is subject—and will, of course, need to be agreed upon with your client as part of the contract.

Some simple steps that all WordPress site owners should take include the following:

▣ **Update WordPress each time a new version is released.** This is the single most important step you can take to improve security. New releases will have security patches that address security issues which hackers are aware of and have been using to attack sites—so by installing the update, you reduce the risk of hacking.

▣ **Only download WordPress updates from the official WordPress site at** http://wordpress.org/download/. There's absolutely no reason to download an update from anywhere else.

▣ **Only download plugins and themes from trusted sources.** The official plugin repository (http://wordpress.org/extend/plugins/) and theme repository (http://wordpress.org/extend/themes/) are the only places from which I would consider downloading free themes or plugins. If you're buying premium themes and plugins, make sure they have a GPL license and that they are recommended by other developers. It's also wise to inspect the code before activating any plugins or themes.

▣ **Use SFTP instead of FTP when uploading and downloading or editing site files.** SFTP stands for Secure FTP and uses Secure Shell (SSH) to transfer files, encrypting both commands and data and making the file transfer process much more secure than straight FTP.

▣ **Use strong passwords.** This is something you should particularly be encouraging your clients to do. You may even want to write it into your site support contract, stating that the client must use secure passwords in order to receive help for any malicious attacks without incurring additional costs. For a strong password generator, see http://strongpasswordgenerator.com.

▣ **Use security keys.** These are keys added to the config.php file, which you don't need to remember but they will ensure better encryption of information stored in cookies. Security keys look like the following code (taken from the Codex at http://codex.wordpress.org/Editing_wp-config. php#Security_Keys—*do not* use these!)

```
define('AUTH_KEY', 't`DK%X:>xy|e-Z(BXb/f(Ur`8#~UzUQG-^_Cs_GHs5U-
  &Wb?pgn^p8(2@}IcnCa|');
define('SECURE_AUTH_KEY',
  'D&ovlU#|CvJ##uNq}bel+^MFtT&.b9{UvR]g%ixsXhGlRJ7q!h}XWdEC[BOKXssj');
define('LOGGED_IN_KEY', 'MGKi8Br(&{H*~&0s;{k0<S(O:+f#WM+q|npJ-
  +P;RDKT:~jrmgj#/-,[hOBk!ry^');
define('NONCE_KEY', 'FIsAsXJKL5ZlQo)iD-pt??eUbdc{_Cn<4!d~yqz))&B
  D?AwK%)+)F2aNwI|siOe');
define('AUTH_SALT', '7T-
  !^i!0,w)L#JK@pc2{8XE[DenYI^BVf{L:jvF,hf}zBf883td6D;Vcy8,S)-&G');
define('SECURE_AUTH_SALT', 'I6`V|mDZq21-J|ihb u^q0F
  }F_NUcy`1,=obGtq*p#Ybe4a31R,r=|n#=]@]c #');
define('LOGGED_IN_SALT',
  'w<$4c$Hmd%/*]`Oom>(hdXW|0M=X={we6;Mpvtg+V.o<$|#_}qG(GaVDEsn,~*4i');
define('NONCE_SALT', 'a|#h{c5|P
  &xWs4IZ20c2&%4!c(/uG}W:mAvy<I44`jAbup]t=]V<`}.py(wTP%%');
```

You can generate your own keys at https://api.wordpress.org/secret-key/1.1/salt/. Copy them into config.php and then forget about them.

In addition to the preceding steps, you can lockdown or secure parts of your WordPress installation:

- **Restrict access by IP address.** In your `.htaccess` file you can specify IP addresses from which users are permitted to edit the site. This may not be ideal for a client site (after all, the client may want to edit their site from another IP address while traveling), but it can make your own site very secure. To do this, add the following to your `.htaccess` file, replacing `xxx.xxx.xxx.xxx` with your IP address:

```
order deny,allow
deny from all
#IP address to Whitelist
allow from xxx.xxx.xxx.xxx
```

- **Password-protect the wp-admin directory.** It's fairly simple to add a server-side password to the wp-admin directory using CPanel and it adds an additional layer of security to this directory, meaning any hacker that manages to get in via a username and password will also have to get through this password (which you will of course make very strong). For a guide on doing this, see `http://www.wpbeginner.com/wp-tutorials/how-to-password-protect-your-wordpress-admin-wp-admin-directory/`.

  Note that this approach could break any properly coded AJAX functionality on your site, including the use of plugins like BuddyPress—so use it with caution and test throughly afterwards.

- **Disallow file editing via the Dashboard.** This can also help prevent problems due to user error—and editing files via the Dashboard is not a good practice anyway compared to using a text editor with FTP, as there is no means of undoing changes. To disallow file editing in this way, add the following to `wp-config.php`:

```
define('DISALLOW_FILE_EDIT', true);
```

> For more on WordPress security measures, see `http://codex.wordpress.org/Hardening_WordPress#Resources`.

The following steps are what is referred to as "security by obscurity"—that is, making your installation appear different from standard ones, so that hackers looking for directories, user accounts or database tables with "standard" names will be less likely to get access to your site. It can have some use, but it doesn't actually make your site secure, just a bit harder to attack:

- **Don't use default accounts.** If an admin account is created when you install WordPress, remove it. Create an administrator account with a unique username instead. This will protect you from opportunistic hackers looking for a backdoor via the admin account (something that hasn't happened for several years now which is one reason why secuirty by obscurity shouldn't be your only line of defense).

- **Change the WordPress table prefix.** By default this is `wp_`, but you can change it while installing WordPress by changing the `$table_prefix` value in your `wp-config.php` file or by specifying a different prefix when installing WordPress. If your installation is attacked by an exploitable SQL injection bug, nonstandard table names prevent the SQL injection attempt from succeeding.

Planning for the Future

Future-proofing any site is going to have an impact on its stability and resistance to attack. You've learned about planning for changes to storage and bandwidth requirements in the preceding sections, but it's worth taking some time to consider how you can plan for future WordPress releases. The best way to avoid any problems when installing WordPress updates is to test prior to the update being released.

This will be particularly pertinent if you're developing themes and plugins for release to the public—your product will be more highly trusted by users if it's compatible with the latest version of WordPress, and it will get more downloads. It's sensible to maintain backward compatibility with the previous version as well, to accommodate any users who haven't upgraded—but you don't typically need to maintain compatibility with earlier versions of WordPress.

WordPress Upgrades Overview

Most WordPress upgrades are released in order to fix bugs and add new features, but they often also fix security issues, which is why it's so important to keep your sites up to date. Updates will also include other improvements, in response to tickets raised by the WordPress community and addressed by the core development team, which includes a small army of volunteer developers.

Upgrades and WordPress development are documented on the WordPress trac site at `http://core.trac.wordpress.org` and the Make WordPress site at `http://make.wordpress.org`. Beware, however, as once you start reading both of these sites you can be sucked in for hours. For advance notification of upgrades, make sure you subscribe to the RSS feed at `http://wordpress.org/news/`.

If you will be testing with WordPress versions before they are released, you need to install beta releases or nightly builds, which are covered shortly.

Using the WordPress Trac Site

The WordPress trac site incorporates a huge amount of information about the development of WordPress. It's a good idea to get to know its structure and what information you need, as it's easy to spend hours browsing interesting updates that may not be immediately relevant to you—at least I've found time can be swallowed up that way!

The trac site (`http://core.trac.wordpress.org`) is structured around *tickets*, which are issues submitted by users and developers at `http://core.trac.wordpress.org/newticket` and then addressed by other developers, which could include you. The trac site has a handbook at `http://make.wordpress.org/core/handbook/trac/` that provides information on the site itself as well as how the ticket system works.

A ticket can be related to anything that needs attention, large or small. Existing tickets are listed in the Tickets section of the trac site. A list of keywords (i.e., tags) for tickets is at `http://core.trac.wordpress.org/report`. These include keywords relating to the area of development (e.g., mobile), the status of the ticket (e.g., Active Tickets) or to WordPress releases (e.g., Next Minor Release), as well as keywords added by users submitting tickets. You can search and view tickets by keyword, which enables you to quickly find issues currently being addressed or issues already handled relating to a specific aspect of WordPress. If you want to raise a ticket, first check that a ticket doesn't already exist relating to your issue, and then use the reporting page at `http://core.trac.wordpress.org/report` to raise your ticket. You'll need to provide information about the issue to be addressed, including whether it's a bug, an enhancement, or a feature request, and to which part of WordPress it is related. You also assign one or more keywords to the ticket, which enables easy searching. I won't list all the options here—the form for submitting tickets is self-explanatory.

If you want to know what is currently being developed for future WordPress releases, the most useful section of the trac site is the Roadmap at `http://core.trac.wordpress.org/roadmap`. This shows you the tickets applicable to each upcoming release of WordPress, as shown in Figure 6-2.

Figure 6-2 The Roadmap page on the WordPress trac site

This helps you identify changes that will be implemented for each upcoming release. If you're a plugin developer, this is useful for knowing which of these might affect your plugin, enabling you to focus your testing.

Testing with Pre-release WordPress Versions

Although the trac site helps you stay informed about what's coming up in future WordPress releases, you still need to get your hands on code to use for testing. Fortunately, there's a plugin that enables you to do just that: WordPress Beta Tester (`http://wordpress.org/extend/plugins/wordpress-beta-tester/`). Using this plugin, you can install the latest nightly builds of future WordPress releases on a test site. Don't use it on a live site, however, as the WordPress versions it installs are pre-release and may not be stable.

After installing the plugin, you access its settings via the Tools menu and select one of two options—Point release nightlies (more stable) or Bleeding edge nightlies (the very latest code, possibly less stable). As you can see in Figure 6-3, you are warned to take care when installing updates with this plugin—I advise only ever using it on a test site, and never migrating that test site back to the live site afterward.

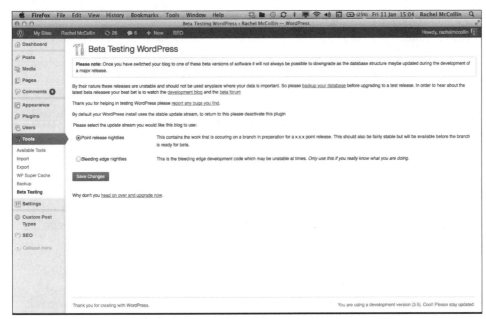

Figure 6-3 The WordPress Beta Tester plugin

After selecting your preferred option and clicking Save Changes, you complete an update in the same way you normally would.

> **Warning:** Before installing a pre-release version of WordPress, *always* make a backup of your database and files first.

Once you have completed the installation, you need to test all aspects of a site or a plugin's operation to ensure that nothing breaks. Exactly what you need to test depends on your site, theme, or plugin—and on the changes made to the relevant version of WordPress—but a good starting point is the list in the following section.

Pre-release Testing Checklist

Front end:

- Confirm that each page in the site loads correctly, particularly those based on different template files—for a large site you may not be able to test everything, but you should test each content type (pages, posts, custom post types, archives, etc.).

- Test any content or actions generated by plugins (e.g., widgets, SEO, custom content generated by your own plugins) or by custom functions in your theme.

- Confirm that custom content (post types and fields) is working correctly.

- Confirm that all user interactions work as they should when accessed via all user roles that will be using them (especially if you have defined custom user roles).

- Test any aspects of the site that you have identified as being potentially affected by changes to WordPress as documented in the trac site.

- Repeat your testing for all major browsers and devices supported by the site.

Back end:

- Test any customizations to the WordPress Dashboard, switching user roles to test for each role set up on the site.

- Test any items you have identified from the trac site that might affect customizations.

If you're testing a plugin with a pre-release version, you need to install it on a number of test sites with different configurations. This is similar to the testing detailed in Chapter 12. You might find that other WordPress users are happy to help you test it on their own sites, but be sure you point out to them that this is a test version that shouldn't be used on a live site.

Make sure you test up to the final release date—the nightly build released immediately before release will mirror the final release, so you can be confident that your site or plugin will work after release. Don't leave it until the last minute to test, however—earlier builds won't be as close to the final release, but using them will give you time to iron out any bugs, and to report them by raising a ticket on the WordPress trac site at `http://core.trac.wordpress.org/newticket`.

Testing and Debugging Plugins and Themes

You can also test beta versions of plugins you have installed on your site, so that you're ready when a new version is released. This will be less of an immediate issue than testing future WordPress releases, but if your site relies on a third-party plugin that is expecting a major update, it means you can take advantage of that update as quickly as possible.

The Plugin Beta Tester plugin (`http://wordpress.org/extend/plugins/plugin-beta-tester/`) enables you to install beta versions of plugins you have on your site and test them. As with beta versions of WordPress itself, you should only use this on test sites.

After installing and activating the plugin, you will have access to beta versions of plugins from the Plugins admin screen, shown in Figure 6-4.

Note that this plugin gives you access only to beta versions of plugins made available via the WordPress plugin repository—for premium plugins you have to download any beta releases from the vendor's website.

Detecting and Supporting Multiple Versions of WordPress

As mentioned earlier, it's a good practice to ensure that a plugin supports both the current and previous versions of WordPress. If your plugin doesn't work (or worse, creates problems) with an earlier version of WordPress, you can prevent users with that version from activating the plugin.

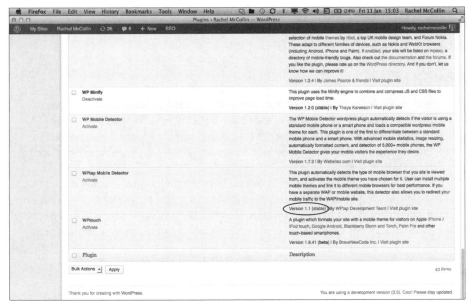

Figure 6-4 The Plugin Beta Tester plugin gives you access to beta versions of plugins

To do this, you use the WordPress plugin activation function, `register_activation_hook()` combined with the `version_compare()` and `deactivate_plugins()` functions.

The plugin activation function accepts two parameters, both of which are required:

- The path to the main plugin file in the plugins directory. If you're using this function within the main plugin file itself, you can use __FILE__ to refer to the current file.
- The function that will execute when the plugin is activated—in this case, a function that checks the WordPress version, deactivating the plugin if it's a version incompatible with the plugin.

The `version_compare()` function takes three parameters:

- `$wp_version`, which retrieves the number of the WordPress version installed on the site
- The version you are checking for
- An operator, either =, <, >, <= or >=, depending on the check you need to make

For example, to deactivate a plugin if a WordPress version earlier than 3.0 is in use, you would add the following to your main plugin file:

```php
<?php register_activation_hook( __FILE__, 'wpptl_pluginactivate' ); ?>
function wpptl_pluginactivate () {
 global $wp_version;
 if ( version_compare( $wp_version, '3.0', '<' ) ) {
  deactivate_plugins( plugin_basename( __FILE__ ) );
 }
}
?>
```

This function checks the WordPress version installed on the site and if it's earlier than version 3.0, the plugin simply won't be activated.

When Disaster Strikes

Despite all your best efforts, disaster will occasionally strike. If you're building sites for clients, a site could be hacked or data could be lost due to a corrupt file, a conflict, or user error. If you're providing hosting, server problems could arise leading to downtime or data loss. If you're a theme or plugin developer, a vulnerability in your code could lead to users' sites being attacked or to incompatibilities with other plugins or WordPress updates.

If this happens, the first thing to remember is to keep calm. You need to take a methodical approach to identifying and dealing with the problem, and you need to demonstrate that you're in control of the situation to your clients. Therefore, take a deep breath, sit back, and work systematically instead of diving in and possibly causing more problems. The following sections outline an approach for tackling problems when they occur.

Communicating with Clients or Users

The first thing you want to do is ensure that your clients or users know that you're aware of the problem and that you're dealing with it. If you become aware of an issue before the client or users, it can be tempting to remain silent, hoping that they don't notice anything amiss; but in my experience, clients appreciate being warned of potential problems or being told that an issue has been resolved—even if they would never have spotted the problem in the first place.

This kind of communication increases trust in you and in the solution you put in place. This is important for clients, with whom you need to maintain an ongoing relationship, and with plugin or theme users, who you don't want to lose—or even worse, to have tweeting or blogging about any problems your theme or plugin has caused. Therefore, before going into detail about the problem, communicate with your clients or users in the most appropriate way to let them know the following:

- You are aware there is a problem.
- You're sorry for any difficulty it might be causing them.
- You are working on the solution to fix it.
- You will tell them when it's fixed.

If relevant, also tell them if you need to take down a site while you fix it, or if any third parties need to be involved to solve the problem (e.g., your hosting provider). They may also be able to give you useful information to help you fix the problem.

You might want to email clients directly, using social media or a support forum—whatever is most efficient for reaching as many people as possible, as quickly as possible. Of course, if the problem is related to hosting, don't attempt to contact them via an email address associated with an account you host. Instead, make sure you have an alternative email address on file.

Identifying the Problem

Having reassured your clients that you're dealing with the problem, you can now focus on identifying what's causing it. Obviously, the source of the problem will vary depending on what's happening, but many issues will stem from the symptoms described in the following sections.

A Website Isn't Accessible

If a site has gone down or you can't access it, there could be one of a number of causes. Visit the site's URL from a variety of browsers and IP addresses or network connections. The problem could be as simple as your network connection—on one occasion my Wi-Fi provider wasn't displaying any U.K.-based sites; and because the only U.K.-based sites I was checking were my own, I mistakenly assumed it was my server. If you're unable to do this manually, you can use Just Ping (`http://www.just-ping.com`) to ping a site from a variety of locations around the world.

When you try to access the site, check the error message you receive. Common messages include the following:

- A 500 error (internal server), shown in Figure 6-5, is a generic message indicating a problem with the server. It means "Internal server error," which can have one of a number of causes, inlcuding a configuration error, a PHP syntax error (including duplicate function names), or sometimes another system error like out of memory.

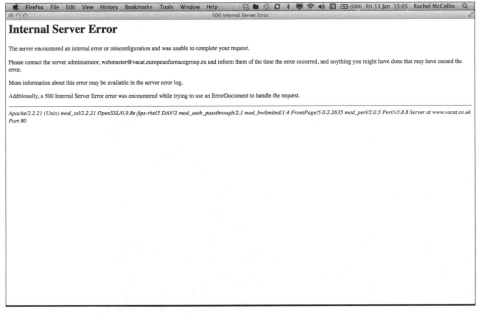

Figure 6-5 500 internal server error

▓ If your DNS settings aren't working, you may see the CPanel default web page, shown in Figure 6-6. This is displayed for a domain that exists but whose DNS settings or IP address haven't been configured correctly.

▓ If the site has been hacked, you'll see a warning screen, shown in Figure 6-7.

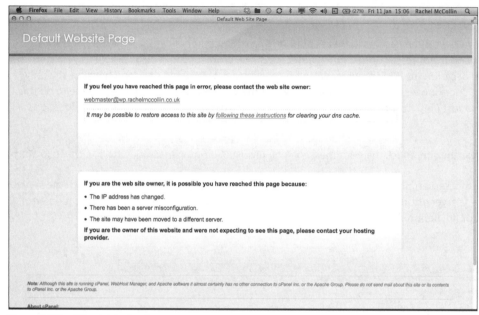

Figure 6-6 The CPanel default web page

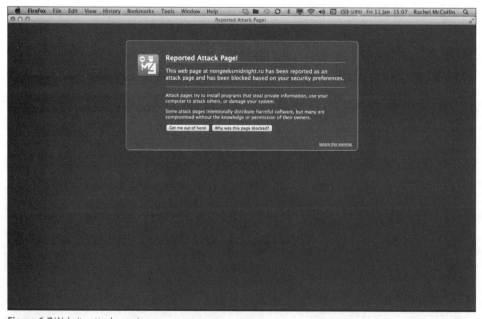

Figure 6-7 Website attack warning

Data Has Been Lost

If the site produces 404 errors for pages or posts that were previously valid, or media is missing, then it is likely that data has been lost. This could be due to human error, server failure, or (more rarely) an update.

A Website Has Been Hacked

If a sit is hacked, anything could appear. A site I managed once had a very unpleasant-looking hack that overwrote the `index.php` file in the active theme with text and music. Fortunately, it was very simple to fix, but you might not be so lucky.

It's possible that the first thing you'll see is a warning dialog indicating that the site may harm your computer, as shown in Figure 6-8. However you may not see such a warning at all, depending on the nature of the hack—many hacks add hidden links to a site or run spam scripts from the server, which won't be detected in this way.

Figure 6-8 Warning that a site may have been hacked

If this is the case, the best thing to do is perform a security check on it using the tools in the "Website Hacks" section later in this chapter.

Alternatively, the hack may only be visible via search engine results. The WordPress Pharma hack inserts title tags and spammy links that are only visible to search engines, not to visitors. Therefore, you won't know you have it unless you check your site's listing in Google or someone alerts you to the problem. If your site has this hack, your search engine listing will include references to pharmaceuticals, so you can't miss it (unless the site contains valid references to pharmaceuticals, in which case it may be harder to spot).

A Theme or Plugin Has Been Hacked

If a user of your theme or plugin reports that it has been hacked, you need to take this very seriously. These hacks could take any of the same forms as those for a hacked site, but obviously you are responsible for ensuring that your theme or plugin works correctly. Therefore, you need to fix the problem and release a safe version of your theme or plugin as quickly as possible. You'll learn what to do if this happens in the next section.

Fixing the Problem

Having identified the cause of the problem, you need to fix it. How you do this will depend on the nature of the problem.

Hosting Problems

If the server isn't responding (which could be affecting websites and email), you need to contact your hosting provider. Check whether they have added an update to their website or Twitter account about the issue or whether you have received an email from them first. Occasionally a server will experience short periods of anticipated downtime, which your provider will warn you about. If they don't warn you about this, I suggest changing providers!

The server could be experiencing problems for a variety of reasons. Another user's account could have been compromised, or it could be a physical problem. Occasionally a server can be blacklisted, which can happen if part of that server is sending out spam, for example. If you're on a shared hosting plan and this happens frequently, you might want to switch to VPS hosting. For more information on different hosting options, see Chapter 5, "Development and Hosting Environments."

In the worst-case scenario, your hosting provider may not be able to retrieve data lost due to server problems. In that case, you'll need to restore the site from a backup—and you keep regular backups, of course.

DNS Problems

If the DNS for a site isn't resolving correctly, it may just be a case of waiting a day or two for DNS settings to resolve themselves (assuming they've been changed recently); but you should always confirm that any NS, MX, A, or CNAME records are correct. These relate to the following:

- **NS**—NS stands for nameserver. The nameservers registered for the domain will map to the hosting server on which the site is stored.

- **MX**—MX stands for Mail Exchange, which directs email to the correct server. If your client is using a different server for email and their website and experiences email problems, confirm that the MX record is configured correctly for the domain. You can do this via the domain registrar's account pages or in CPanel.

- **A**—An A record is the fundamental record used in DNS. It directs a domain name to an IP address. If your hosting provider changes the server's IP address, you may need to update the A record to reflect this (although a good hosting provider will do this for you).

- **CNAME**—CNAME stands for Canonical name and it's used to direct to a domain name rather than an IP address. It can be used to direct a www address to one without www (or vice versa) or to direct to a subdomain. If you're having problems with domains resolving correctly, confirm that you don't need to add a CNAME record or edit one.

For a guide to DNS, see `http://support.google.com/a/bin/answer.py?hl=en&hlrm=en&answer=48090`.

Website Hacks

If a site you manage has been hacked, the best starting point is to do a website check. The checker at `http://sucuri.net` is free and will check for a variety of hacks. Figure 6-9 shows what the checker looks for (thankfully this example is clean, as it's my own blog).

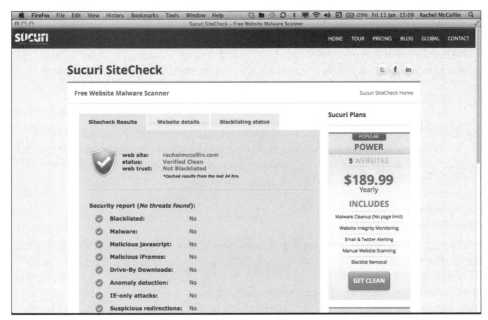

© 2012 Sucuri LLC

Figure 6-9 A site check at sucuri.net

It's not possible to provide a finite list of how to resolve hacks here, as the list of hacks is always changing. The most common types of hacks include the following:

- **Overwriting or uploading of files or code**—For example, a new `index.php` may be added to the site or php files may be added to plugin folders. If this is the case, deleting or replacing the malicious files might fix the problem.

- **Script injections**—In this case the malicious code takes the form of a script that is executed when a page loads or a user clicks a link. This script may download software onto a user's machine or it may redirect the user to a malicious site.

- **Drive-by downloads**—These cause the site to download malicious software to users' machines, and can take the form of SQL injections, scripts, or link injections. Cleaning these can be tricky—for detailed instructions see `http://wp.smashingmagazine.com/2012/10/09/four-malware-infections-wordpress/#drive-by-downloads`.

- **Malicious iFrames**—These are iFrames injected into your site's content, which will display content from another site. You can normally find them by querying your database for iFrames, or it may be easier to restore your site from a clean backup.

- **Malicious redirects**—These redirect users to a malicious site, either when a page or the site is loaded or when a link is clicked. The malicious site could be a harmless spam site or it could download software to the user's machine. They are normally found in the `.htaccess` file—check this and edit or replace it with a clean version.

Specific WordPress Hacks

Two specific WordPress hacks have been well documented online. The first, the TimThumb hack, exploited a vulnerability in the TimThumb plugin that allowed files to be written to the server without secure access. The hack added additional php files or changed their filenames. For a guide on detecting and dealing with TimThumb, see `http://www.wpbeginner.com/wp-tutorials/how-to-fix-and-cleanup-the-timthumb-hack-in-wordpress/`.

The second is the previously mentioned Pharma hack. This one is sneaky, as it injects title tags and links that are visible only to search engines, meaning your search engine listings will be full of pharmaceutical references but your site's visible content won't be affected. You can find out how to diagnose and clean it up at `http://www.pearsonified.com/2010/04/wordpress-pharma-hack.php`.

Preventing Hacks from Happening Again

After you have removed a hack or restored your site from a clean backup, you *must* take steps to ensure that the site doesn't remain vulnerable to the attack—otherwise, you will be subject to the same attack again.

Follow the steps outlined earlier in the chapter on WordPress security to make your site more secure, and educate the site's editors and users to use secure passwords. Following a malicious attack, every password (for the site and for FTP/SFTP) should be changed to reduce the risk of future attack. You can manually change every user's old password to a secure one via the Users screen—for a strong password generator, see http://strongpasswordgenerator.com.

Finally, if the hack was executed via a third-party plugin or theme, update to the latest version, and verify that it has been fixed to prevent the hack. If not, you'll need to alert the developer of the problem and use an alternative until it is fixed. Alternatively, if you've managed to fix the problems yourself, you might be able to help the developer update the plugin or theme.

Data Loss

If data has been lost on a site, either through server error or human error, you have two options for retrieving it: via the WordPress versioning system or by restoring from a backup. It's not uncommon for users to lose data when editing a post—if they're not aware of the fact that WordPress creates autosaves and versions that they can switch to, they may contact you for help restoring data. Find out what data has been lost and check any saved versions to see if it can be restored—or educate your client about how to do it themselves.

If the data lost is in the form of files, due to either error or an attack, you or your client will need to re-upload the lost files via FTP/SFTP, from a recent backup. If the file is so recent that it hasn't been backed up, then hopefully your client has a copy of it on their system (in the case of image files, for example).

For more serious or widespread cases of data loss, the only solution may be a full restore from the database, which is where your regular backups will come in handy.

Summary

Having worked through this chapter, it is hoped that you're better prepared to deal with any problems that might arise with your sites, plugins, and themes. More important, you know how to reduce the risk of them occurring in the first place, and how to minimize the damage if they do occur. Essential processes you have to put in place as a WordPress professional include making regular automated backups; ensuring all the sites you manage are secure (including development sites); and being able to anticipate and monitor server performance. If disasters do strike, you know how to identify the problem, reassure your clients and/or users, and fix the problem as quickly and calmly as possible.

Further Resources

Server Monitoring

Server monitoring tools
`http://sixrevisions.com/tools/10-free-server-network-monitoring-tools-that-kick-ass/`

CPanel monitoring apps
`http://applications.cpanel.net/tag/monitoring/`

Monitor.us
`http://www.monitor.us/website-monitoring`

Backing Up

Codex page on backing up WordPress
`http://codex.wordpress.org/WordPress_Backups`

List of free WordPress backup plugins
`http://wordpress.org/extend/plugins/tags/backup`

BackupBuddy
`http://ithemes.com/purchase/backupbuddy`

VaultPress
`http://vaultpress.com`

blogVault
`http://blogvault.net`

WordPress Upgrades and Planning for the Future

Overview of WordPress upgrades
`http://codex.wordpress.org/Updating_WordPress`

Downloading previous versions of WordPress
`http://wordpress.org/download/release-archive/`

WordPress trac site
http://core.trac.wordpress.org

WordPress trac site handbook
http://make.wordpress.org/core/handbook/trac/

WordPress Beta Tester plugin
http://wordpress.org/extend/plugins/wordpress-beta-tester/

Plugin Beta Tester plugin
http://wordpress.org/extend/plugins/plugin-beta-tester/

The plugin activation function
http://codex.wordpress.org/Function_Reference/register_activation_hook

WordPress Security

WordPress hosting requirements
http://wordpress.org/about/requirements/

Five top WordPress security tips
http://www.wptavern.com/top-5-wordpress-security-tips-you-most-likely-dont-follow

Strong password generator
http://strongpasswordgenerator.com

Security key generator
https://api.wordpress.org/secret-key/1.1/salt

Password-protecting the wp-admin directory
http://www.wpbeginner.com/wp-tutorials/how-to-password-protect-your-wordpress-admin-wp-admin-directory/

Dealing with Disaster

Just Ping
http://www.just-ping.com

HTTP status codes
http://en.wikipedia.org/wiki/List_of_HTTP_status_codes

Basic guide to DNS
http://support.google.com/a/bin/answer.py?hl=en&hlrm=en&answer=48090

Common WordPress malware infections
http://wp.smashingmagazine.com/2012/10/09/four-malware-infections-wordpress/

Removing the TimThumb hack
http://www.wpbeginner.com/wp-tutorials/how-to-fix-and-cleanup-the-timthumb-hack-in-wordpress/

How to diagnose and remove the WordPress Pharma hack
http://www.pearsonified.com/2010/04/wordpress-pharma-hack.php

Part IV

Pushing the Limits: The Best Tools for Site Development

Chapter 7

Theme Building: Frameworks, Standalone Themes, or Child Themes?

Theme Building is at the heart of WordPress development—if you can't build or customize themes, it's impossible to develop a personalized WordPress site. As a WordPress professional, however, it's important that you develop a theme-building process that is efficient and works for your team.

In this chapter you'll learn about the different approaches to theme development and how to identify the right one for your team and your project. Some developers and agencies choose to use the same approach for every project they work on, while others adopt different methods depending on the project's needs. Although choosing a development style is ultimately your decision, understanding how the approaches vary will enable you to the select the most appropriate one, rather than just choose the path of least resistance.

Theme-Building Principles

If you're developing a theme for a client site, you need to work with your team (if you have one) and with the client to identify what that theme needs to incorporate and how to best achieve that, as well as ensure that it is future-proofed. If you're developing a theme for release to other developers and users, your theme should meet an identified need if it's to be useful to people. You'll learn more about this in detail in Chapter 12.

When identifying which approach to take to theme building, consider the following criteria:

- **Time**—Which theme-building approach will be most time-efficient for your team?
- **Theme functionality**—Which approach gives you the functionality you need for your project?
- **Consistency**—A consistent approach to theme building will make your team more efficient and help them to work together.
- **Future-proofing**—You should develop themes in a way that makes it as easy as possible for you to update and develop them in the future.
- **Quality and robustness**—Your clients will expect the themes powering their sites to not only deliver the site you've designed for them, but also to run quickly and efficiently with minimal risk of problems. Your code also needs to be accessible and standards-compliant. If you're developing themes for release to the public, the robustness of your code is particularly important, as some users may edit it.

In the long run, you'll find it easier to plan your approach to theme building before diving into projects, and to take a view that encompasses not just the next project on the books, but future projects too. Anything you can do that will make projects easier to get off the ground will make you more efficient and more profitable.

Approaches to Theme Building

There are a few different approaches to building themes, each of which has its merits. As you might guess, there is no one-size-fits-all solution, so this section examines the pros and cons of each approach and looks at the kinds of projects or teams to which each lends itself. With this information, and the information you already have about your project, your clients or users, and your team, you should be able to make a considered decision as to which route to take.

The most commonly used approaches to theme building are as follows:

- Build a theme either from scratch or by importing static HTML to WordPress.

- Adapt an existing theme to meet your needs.

- Create a child theme from an existing theme (the parent), using the child to make customizations.

- Use a theme framework to build themes using child themes, or develop your own framework.

You'll see how each of these approaches works in detail later in the chapter, but first it is useful to understand the pros and cons of each.

Choosing the Right Approach for Your Project

Table 7-1 shows some of the pros and cons of each approach to theme building.

Table 7-1: Theme Development Approaches: Pros and Cons of Each

Theme-Building Approach	Pros	Cons	When It Might Be Suitable
Develop from scratch (or from existing static HTML).	It provides a good way to start if you're experienced in building static sites. It helps you understand how WordPress themes work. It's helpful if the design is done in the browser using static HTML and CSS.	Can be very inefficient and repetitive.	When the design needs to be done in the browser (e.g., to prototype responsive site layouts) and a static HTML template has been written to avoid repetition and ease the transfer into WordPress.
Adapt an existing theme.	It's quick and easy if you just want to make minor changes to a theme. It gives you a starting point if you want to build your own theme without starting from scratch.	It's risky—changes you make may conflict with each other or break the theme. Any changes you made will be lost if you update the theme. Any faults in the starter theme will be carried through to your theme.	When the changes you need to make are permanent and you won't need to update the starting theme. When you want to use a robust theme as a starting point for your own customized development (e.g., many developers use the default WordPress themes in this way).

Theme-Building Approach	Pros	Cons	When It Might Be Suitable
Build a child of an existing theme.	The parent theme can be updated without your changes being lost. It's easy to identify what code is from the starting theme and what code is your own. It enables you to use a starting theme for basic functionality and/or layout and then add only what's needed in child themes for each project.	It's more time-consuming than adapting an existing theme. It requires an understanding of how parent and child themes work.	When the starting theme is designed for use as a parent theme or is likely to be updated in the future, or it is a basic theme with the layout you need but not all of the content and/or styling.
Work with an off-the-shelf framework.	It's very quick to get started, especially if you work with specially designed child themes. You can avoid coding all the functionality or layout yourself. Some frameworks let you make your own customizations to your site without having to write code.	To get the most from a framework, you'll need to spend time getting to know it well. The framework may well include code that you don't need in your site. Theme frameworks can have complex structures that are easily broken if you try to make manual customizations.	When you'll be developing a lot of sites using a framework and can spend time understanding it, so you can use it efficiently and get the most from it.
Build your own framework or parent theme.	It gives you a starting point for all new projects without having to repeat yourself. It offers more flexibility than off-the-shelf frameworks—just include what you need.	It takes work to develop a robust framework that will work for all your sites. You need to ensure your framework is updated and maintained, particularly in line with WordPress updates.	When you will be developing a lot of sites and want to have complete control over how they work, with a robust framework as a starting point to kick off each project.

Rapid Theme Development for Teams

If you're working with a team, it is particularly important to have a well-defined process for building and editing themes so that everyone knows what's expected of them. This will maximize efficiency and reduce the risk of errors or repetition.

Identifying the Best Approach

To identify which of the approaches presented in Table 7-1 will be best for your team, consult with the team members who will be involved in theme building. This includes front-end developers coding the theme's layout and styling, and back-end developers coding its functionality. Of course, you need to take into account the needs of your clients and projects as well as your long-term development plans, but it pays to find out a few things from your team:

- What approaches to theme building have they used in the past?

- What skills do they have that you can use? Can they pass these skills on to other team members?

- Have they developed any code that the rest of the team can use? For example, in one case a member of my team was working on an open-source theme framework of his own and we were able to combine elements of that with elements of work I had done to build our own theme framework together.

- How can the team work together to make your chosen approach(es) work on a long-term basis?

Ensuring Efficiency and Robustness

Whatever approach you adopt, you need to ensure that the team is using it effectively. The following are some tips to make it work:

- Ensure that everyone understands the approach you're using and what's expected of them.

- If you're developing a starter theme, parent theme, or theme framework for the team to use, add a lot of comments to the code so everyone understands how it works and how the different parts of the theme interact with each other. This is particularly the case for includes and custom function files called from the theme functions file.

- When developing new themes for projects, all team members should comment their code so others working with it understand how it operates, how it interacts with the core theme functionality, and how it may differ from your usual approach if relevant.

- Keep copies of your theme files in a location everyone can access, and use robust version controls.

- Document the approach you use for each project, versions of themes, frameworks, or parent themes, and any custom functionality added.

These guidelines may seem contrary to the idea of "rapid theme development," but over time they will make your team quicker and more efficient. Although it is tempting to dive in and start coding a new theme for your first project, when you're on the tenth project and either repeating yourself or working with code that's difficult to understand, you'll be glad you took the time to be thorough.

Of course, the preceding advice also applies if you're working on your own—having a robust, consistent process will make you more efficient and less repetitive, and commenting your own code will prove useful when you have to work with it again a year later and can't remember exactly what you did. Moreover, if you're developing themes for release to others, clear and consistent use of code and comments will help other developers working with your themes.

Building Themes from Scratch

It's rare for any WordPress developer to sit down in front of a blank HTML or PHP file and code a theme entirely from scratch—it's both time-consuming and repetitive.

Instead, many theme developers (particularly if they have experience building static sites) begin with some existing HTML, importing that to WordPress, splitting it into template files and includes, and adding the relevant template tags. This is one of the beauties of WordPress—it's relatively easy to convert a static site to WordPress in this way.

Making It Work

This approach can be useful if you want to design and prototype in the browser (as an increasing number of web designers are doing), but you don't want to build a whole theme until the design is finalized and agreed upon by the client. In order to make this work, you need to take a more efficient approach than coding each new design from scratch. It also pays to ensure that any static HTML files you're importing are set up to make the transition to WordPress as quick as possible—for example, by including commented-out template tags and using the same classes that will be generated by WordPress in your CSS.

Tips for Importing Static HTML to WordPress

One of the great things about WordPress is that it's relatively straightforward to import static HTML into it, but it's important to take care when doing so. The following are some tips for importing HTML to WordPress:

- Create a template for your prototypes to use as a starting point for all projects.

- In the template, include the common elements, IDs, and classes you'll be using in WordPress sites. These might include the following:

  - `<header>`

  - `<div class="main">` for the main part of the site

  - `<div id="content">` for page content

  - `<aside class="sidebar">` for widget areas

  - `<footer>`

  Note that I've used classes here instead of IDs, as that's the way I work—what you do will depend on the way you work. The one exception is `<div id="content">` – here I've used an ID as I use that as an anchor for screen readers to skip the navigation menu in the header.

- Use semantic HTML, making use of HTML5 semantic elements where possible.

- Ensure that your template is accessible and standards-compliant.

- Include template tags that you'll need to activate when importing your HTML into WordPress. You can comment these out for the time being but it helps to have them there, as it saves repeating yourself.

- Include code to run the loop (commented out) and use an `<article>` tag around any dummy content you insert into the prototype site, applying the same classes you would apply to posts by WordPress.

- Add classes and IDs that WordPress will generate. These will include the following:

  - Classes for the body tag, generated by the `body_class($class)` template tag

  - Classes and IDs for individual posts and post types, generated by `post_class()` and `the_ID()`

  - Classes for widget areas, generated by `register_sidebar()` in `functions.php`

  - Classes for menus, generated by the `register_nav_menus()` function in `functions.php`

- Add include template tags, in addition to dummy static code for prototyping. Comment out the template tags and use comments to identify what will stay and what will be deleted in the final theme.

- Add widget areas, commented out. Alternatively, you might want to keep a starting `sidebar.php` and `footer.php` file.

For example, the code for your sidebar might look like this:

```
<-- prototype sidebar - delete all code between this and the next comment
    in the final theme -->
<aside id="sidebar" class="widget-area">
 <div class="widget container">
  <h3 class="widget-title">Widget area title</h3>
  <div class="textwidget">
   <p>Widget area content (text widget)</p>
  </div>
 </div>
</aside>
<-- end of prototype sidebar -->
<--<?php get_sidebar() ?> sidebar call - uncomment this in the final
    theme-->
<-- sidebar - copy all of the code between this and the next comment into
    the sidebar.php file
<?php if ( is_active_sidebar( 'sidebar-widget-area' ) ) : ?>
 <aside class="sidebar">
  <?php dynamic_sidebar( 'sidebar-widget-area' ); ?>
 </aside> -- end of sidebar -->
<?php endif; ?>
```

You would then use the classes and IDs in the prototype and those generated by WordPress in your prototype's stylesheet, meaning that it can be imported straight into WordPress without any significant changes.

It takes time to set up a template that includes the relevant code you'll need once the design is imported into WordPress, but it will enhance the robustness of your code; and over time it be much more efficient.

Customizing an Existing Theme

Another approach often used by new theme developers is to edit an existing theme to achieve the desired functionality. This approach has its place, but I certainly don't recommend doing this for every WordPress theme you build. You'll find yourself repeating a lot of work, it won't help you truly learn how WordPress themes work, and in the end you'll reach a point where you wish you had started from scratch because it's taking longer to customize the existing theme!

This approach can be useful, however, in some scenarios. For example, you may want to create your own starter theme or parent theme, using a robust existing theme as a starting point. This can save you a lot of work by injecting the right code in the right places, and it ensures that your starter or parent theme includes everything necessary for future projects. If you decide to do this, make sure you use a high-quality theme that doesn't include a lot of functionality your project doesn't need. A lot of developers use the WordPress default theme to create their own theme (currently Twenty Twelve—`http://wordpress.org/extend/themes/twentytwelve`) or the underscores theme (`http://underscores.me`), which has been developed for precisely this purpose.

Making It Work

If you're going to customize an existing theme, there are a few things you need to consider to make it work, including the theme you'll start with and the nature of the changes you need to make.

Choosing the Right Starter Theme

The starter theme you use depends on your needs and that of the project. Consider the following:

- **Time**—How much time do you have available to develop your theme? For themes needed quickly, you can likely tweak the default theme to create a new site that's up and running in a matter of minutes. For a more complex project, you may need to make several customizations to the theme—but never so many that you would have been better off starting from scratch.

- **Budget**—Do you have the budget for a premium theme with configurable options? How much are you being paid for your time?

- **Future needs**—Will you need to update the starter theme in the future? If so, it's best to use a child theme instead. Do you anticipate making a lot of changes to the site over time? You'll need to ensure that any changes you make are easy to work with.

- **Project requirements**—Ensure that the starter theme is as close as possible to the theme ultimately needed for your project, or you'll be making a lot of changes. This won't apply if you're using a minimalist starter theme such as underscores.

- **Skills**—Adapting an existing theme isn't as simple as it may first seem. This isn't a job to give to an inexperienced team member, assuming he or she will find it easy. Depending on the extent of customization, working with an existing theme can sometimes be trickier than rolling your own.

Identifying Necessary Changes

Before you start (and as part of identifying the right starter theme), you need a good understanding of any changes the theme requires. Make two lists—one for your project and one for the starter theme, with details regarding layout, content, and functionality. Then compare the two. Confirm that where differences exist, you can make the required changes to the starter theme without things getting too complicated.

Take the time to dig into the theme's code and understand what you'll need to change. It's tempting to simply look at a theme on the theme repository, maybe run it on a test site, and check what it does in the browser; but unless you understand how that's achieved through code, you won't be able to customize the theme.

Making Changes Efficiently

When adapting an existing theme, you want to make as few changes as possible to achieve what your project needs. This will help when you have to revisit the code in the future, in terms of both speed and efficiency.

The following tips will help you achieve both those goals:

- After you have identified the changes needed, identify the relevant code. This might not be limited to one part of the theme (for example, a function may be referenced in a template file but coded in the functions file, or some CSS may apply to more than one area).

- Identify any other parts of the theme that are affected by this code. Will any changes you make cause problems elsewhere?

- Identify any code you can remove, but be sure to test that its removal doesn't have unexpected consequences. Before deleting any code from the starter theme, comment it out and test.

- Use comments to identify where you have made changes.

While it is true that some of these tips will take you longer than simply diving in and hacking the theme, ultimately you will be more efficient if they can minimize repetition and prevent errors that you would need to fix later.

When It's Best to Build Your Own

Having worked through the preceding steps, you'll have a thorough understanding of the changes you need to make to the starter theme and the work involved. Before starting, revisit your plans. If modifying an existing theme means changing more than half of it, it might be better to build your own. Alternatively, you might decide that creating a child theme and using the starter as the parent is a better approach.

Developing with the Underscores Theme

The underscores (or _s) theme has been developed by Automattic for use as a starter theme. It's very minimal, with very little styling except for some sample layouts. Its purpose is to provide you with the template tags and structure needed to build a theme, giving you the flexibility to add to this however necessary. If you are working with the default theme but find that you have to remove a lot of code you don't need, I recommend switching to the underscores theme.

You can find out more about it at `http://underscores.me`.

Using Child Themes

If you want to adapt an existing theme but still want to be able to make updates to that theme without losing your work, creating a child theme will be a better approach than editing the theme itself. You would also use a child theme with a theme framework, or if you've developed your own starter theme or framework you want to use as a basis for all projects, adding custom functionality for that site to the child theme or via plugins as required.

The Parent/Child Theme Relationship

Theoretically, any theme can be used as a parent theme, so you don't have to limit yourself to specially designed parent themes (although some themes, including those powering theme frameworks, are designed as parent themes and wouldn't work on their own).

The relationship between the parent and child themes can be summarized as follows:

- WordPress defaults to using template files contained in the child theme. If both themes have a version of the same template file (e.g., `index.php`), WordPress will use the one from the child theme.

- Where a template file is required and the child theme doesn't have it, WordPress will use the file from the parent theme. Therefore, you wouldn't bother creating a template file for your child theme if it would be identical to that in the parent theme.

- WordPress uses the stylesheet in the child theme. In most cases, it also uses styling from the parent theme's stylesheet, but only if you specify that in the child theme's stylesheet—by adding the `@import` tag.

Figure 7-1 identifies the template files that WordPress would use for an example parent and child theme:

Child Theme template files	Parent Theme template files
style.css	style.css
index.php	index.php
single.php	single.php
single-product.php	page.php
category-widgets.php	archive.php
	category.php
	search.php
	404.php

Figure 7-1 Parent and child themes—example of the template files used where these are duplicated

Therefore, in this example:

- Single posts for the products custom post type would be displayed using `single-product.php` from the child theme.

- Single posts for other post types (including normal posts) would be displayed using `single.php` from the child theme.

- Listings for the widgets category would be displayed using `category-widgets.php` from the child theme.

- Other category listings would be displayed using `category.php` from the parent theme.

- Other archive listings would be displayed using `archive.php` from the parent theme.

- Search results would be displayed using `search.php` from the parent theme.

- 404 pages would be displayed using `404.php` from the parent theme.

- Other pages without a specific template file would be displayed using `index.php` from the child theme.

The Child Theme Stylesheet: Telling WordPress This is a Child Theme

To make a theme operate as a child theme, you add some commented-out code at the top of the theme's stylesheet.

> **Don't make any changes to the parent theme's stylesheet or template files—just the child theme.**

The lines to add are as follows:

```
/*
Theme Name:     WPPTL Child
Theme URI:      http://rachelmccollin.co.uk/wpptl/
Description:    Child theme for the Twenty Twelve theme
Author:         Rachel McCollin
Author URI:     http://rachelmccollin.co.uk/
Template:       twentytwelve
Version:        1.0
*/
```

This example would create a theme that is a child of the Twenty Twelve theme. The crucial line is this one:

```
Template:       twentytwelve
```

This line tells WordPress that the theme is a child of the theme contained in the named directory—it is *not* the title of the parent theme. This avoids any conflict if you have multiple versions of a theme installed on your site—the directory name will be unique because WordPress doesn't let you create duplicate directories for themes. Apart from this line, the header is the same as for any normal standalone theme.

In addition to this code, which enables the theme to operate as a child theme, you should add an `@include` tag to access styling from the parent theme. This goes immediately below the preceding code and before any styling in the child theme's stylesheet.

```
@import url("../twentytwelve/style.css");
```

This imports the parent theme's stylesheet at the beginning of the child theme's stylesheet, meaning that the child theme's styles will override the parent theme where rules exist in both themes' stylesheets for the same element, class, or ID. If you don't add this line, the parent theme's stylesheet won't be used at all.

Importing the parent theme's stylesheet is useful for a few reasons:

- Using a parent theme whose styling is close to what you need for your project avoids duplication.
- If the parent theme includes reset styling, you don't need to add that again.
- Styling for the parent theme's template files will be carried through to your child theme.

Choosing Your Parent Theme

Choosing the right parent theme is similar to choosing the right starter theme if you're adapting an existing one for your own use, but there are some additional considerations:

- How closely does the theme's layout, styling, and functionality match that required by your project?
- Is the theme a stripped-down one that you can use as a starting point?
- Does the theme have clean, efficient code that will respond well to the changes made by your child theme?
- Is the theme accessible and standards-compliant?
- If you plan to develop a lot of sites using this theme, will it meet the needs of multiple projects or can you adapt it so it does?

In some cases you may decide to develop a parent theme for use on a project for which you will be developing a number of similar sites with common requirements. For example, I developed a set of sites for a client with five subsidiaries. Each subsidiary needed its own site but a consistent layout and functionality was wanted across all the sites in the group. To meet that requirement, I built a parent theme for the group as a whole and then used a child theme for each subsidiary to apply the relevant styling and add the necessary template files. Two of these sites are shown in Figures 7-2 and 7-3, each using a child theme of the same basic parent theme.

Source: http://www.supersystemsuk.co.uk
Figure 7-2 The SuperSystems UK website

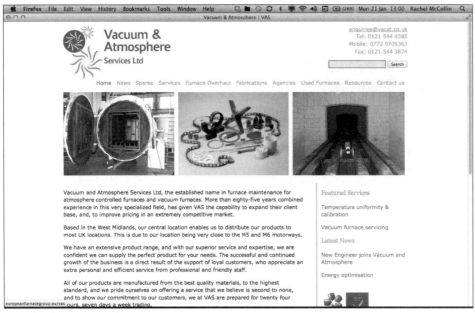

Source: http://www.vacat.co.uk

Figure 7-3 The Vacuum & Atmosphere Services website uses the same parent theme as SuperSystems because it's part of the same group of companies.

A Note on Child Themes and Responsiveness

Parent and child themes can become complicated when you are trying to build a responsive site. If your parent theme uses media queries for responsiveness and you add desktop styling in the child theme that overrides these media queries, the responsive design may break. There are three ways around this issue:

- Don't change the layout in your child theme—check what elements are styled in the parent theme's media queries and avoid adding layout styling for these. This will only work if your project requires the same layout as the parent theme.

- Add media queries to your child theme's stylesheet and include all the responsive styling there (some of which will be copied from the parent theme).

- Adopt a *mobile first* approach, styling your small device screen layout first in the child theme and then adding media queries for larger screens. The media queries for larger screens will override any styling specified earlier in your child theme's stylesheet for small screens, as well as styling for the same elements in the parent theme's stylesheet. Using the mobile first approach, you can use the mobile layout from the parent theme without copying this across.

This means if you plan to code media queries in your child theme, you needn't look for a responsive parent theme.

Developing with Theme Frameworks

The number of available theme frameworks is growing with the popularity of WordPress itself. Frameworks include premium and free versions, and some that incorporate both free and paid content (such as premium child themes or subscription-based support).

This section describes some of the most popular available frameworks and what they offer, enabling you to choose the right framework for your project, get to grips with your chosen framework, and get more out of it using features such as hooks and filters.

So Many Frameworks!

Most developers who work with frameworks tend to find one (or maybe two) that meet their needs and then stick with them. This enables you to develop a deeper understanding of, and familiarity with, the framework—and ultimately get more from it. Learning a framework can take some time, so it's worthwhile to carefully consider which framework will work not only for your current project, but also for future projects.

With all the frameworks you will be able to delve into the code and make your own modifications (using child themes). They may also come with their own APIs in addition to those provided by WordPress, and will make extensive use of WordPress APIs.

Whether you choose a premium or free framework depends on your budget, skills, and requirements. Free frameworks are not necessarily inferior to premium frameworks, but they can require more coding experience to adapt and customize, as they are less likely to offer multiple options screens or configurable layouts, meaning you'll have to add customizations with code. Many developers choose to use free frameworks because they prefer to code customizations themselves and don't want the bloat that may be associated with a framework aimed at a less technical market.

There are a few different pricing models for theme frameworks:

- **Premium frameworks**—You pay for the framework files and for child themes. Examples include Genesis (`http://www.studiopress.com`) and Thesis (`http://diythemes.com`).

- **Free frameworks**—You don't pay for the framework, for support, or for child themes. Examples include Wonderflux (`http://wonderflux.com`) and Thematic (`http://themeshaper.com/thematic/`).

- **Free frameworks with paid support**—You can download the framework for free but must subscribe to receive support. An example is Hybrid (`http://themehybrid.com`).

In addition to these models, there are plugins that operate in a way which is comparable to a framework, providing functionality that can be extended with the use of hooks, theme options, and specially designed parent or child themes. These include e-commerce plugins such as Jigoshop (`http://jigoshop.com`) and the social networking plugin BuddyPress (`http://buddypress.org`).

Frameworks vs. Parent Themes

It's worth exploring the difference between a theme framework and a parent theme. After all, some of the theme frameworks could simply be used as a parent theme without taking advantage of their advanced functionality.

In general, a theme framework has some or all of the following features, which a regular theme won't have:

- Configurable layout options, which may be accessible via a theme options or settings screen. For example, the Wonderflux theme is grid-based and enables you to specify how you will use the grid on your layout; and the Hybrid theme has multiple template files, enabling you to choose one in the page editing screen to specify your layout.

- Preconfigured widget areas into which you can simply drop widgets. The Hybrid theme has multiple widget areas in places other than the sidebar and footer (for example, in the header, and above and below the content), as well as a template file that consists purely of widget areas.

- WYSIWYG design customizations, over and above what's offered by the WordPress Theme Customizer. Thesis includes a visual design template editor as well as what it calls *skins*, which change the colors and styling of a site without requiring you to write your own CSS.

- Additional off-the-shelf functionality. Many frameworks include additional functionality that you would normally use a plugin for, such as the *boxes* included in Thesis, which you drag and drop into your theme in a similar way as you would widgets.

- Child themes, which you can use off the shelf and may come bundled with the framework or have a cost attached. For example, Genesis works only with Genesis-enabled child themes, of which many are available on the StudioPress website (or you can build your own, of course).

- Plugins designed specifically to work with the theme (for example, in the case of Genesis).

- Additional hooks and filters over and above those provided by WordPress. As a developer, these are the features you are likely to be most interested in, and you'll learn more details about them in the section ""Getting More from Frameworks."

> **For more on the differences between frameworks and parent themes, see** `http://justintadlock.com/archives/2010/08/16/frameworks-parent-child-and-grandchild-themes.`

Some of the Most Popular Frameworks

I've already listed some of the most popular frameworks in the "So Many Frameworks!" section—here I'll describe what they offer in more detail. Of course, features change over time, so you'll need to do your own research when deciding which to choose.

Genesis

The Genesis framework is designed for both users with no coding skills as well as developers, who can use it to achieve advanced customization. It includes the following:

- A large (and growing) number of predesigned child themes (`http://my.studiopress.com/themes/`) that can be customized if needed. These have to be purchased individually and are shown in Figure 7-4.

- Built-in SEO

- Online support

- Automatic WordPress updates

- Six default layout options

- A long list of free plugins (`http://www.studiopress.com/plugins`)

- More than 50 hooks in addition to the core WordPress hooks (`http://my.studiopress.com/docs/hook-reference/`)

- More than 60 filters (`http://my.studiopress.com/docs/filter-reference/`)

- Tutorials and documentation at `http://my.studiopress.com/tutorials/`

© 2013 Copyblogger Media LLC

Figure 7-4 The Genesis child themes page

Genesis is robust and easy to use, although it can take some time to learn. For users who want to set up and tweak one of its child themes, it can provide a very quick solution. It's a premium framework, with pricing for individual themes (with the framework included) or the Pro-Plus package, which includes the framework and all current and future themes for a onetime payment.

Thesis

Thesis uses its own highly individualized system to build sites, shown in Figure 7-5. This is based around three main concepts—boxes, skins, and packages:

- **Boxes**—These are basically widgets that can be dragged and dropped into several places in your layout using the Visual Design Template Editor. This effectively drops pre-packaged widgets into one or more of a number of defined widget areas in the framework.

- **Skins**—These are child themes developed for the framework, not by Thesis developers (DIYThemes) but by third-party developers, which makes finding a skin harder than finding a child theme for Genesis or Hybrid, for example. Skins can be customized via the Skin Editor.

- **Packages**—These are CSS customizations that are set using the Packages settings pages, which work in the same way as a theme options page.

© 2012 DIYthemes, LLC

Figure 7-5 The Thesis methodology

In addition to this core methodology, Thesis includes the following:

- SEO functionality, including title tags, meta descriptions and Google Analytics
- Documentation at `http://diythemes.com/thesis/rtfm/`
- Advanced capability for creating and editing theme files from the WordPress Dashboard (with all the risks that entails)
- More than 40 hooks (`http://diythemes.com/thesis/rtfm/hooks/`) and more than 20 filters (`http://diythemes.com/thesis/rtfm/filters/`)

Thesis is also a premium framework, with basic, professional, and plus options—the latter two providing child themes (skins) from independent developers. Because Thesis has such a unique structure, including its own terminology (such as boxes and skins instead of widgets and child themes), it's a framework I recommend using only if you're going to be developing with it full time for a lot of sites, as switching between it and a "standard" WordPress site may prove confusing.

Hybrid

Hybrid is a free theme framework with free child themes, all available at `http://themehybrid.com`. The only thing you'll have to pay for is support, which requires a paid subscription to the Hybrid website.

Hybrid works in a different way from the premium themes. It's a stripped-down framework with template files, widget areas, hooks, and filters, but limited Dashboard functionality—much of that is added via plugins. Figure 7-6 shows Hybrid's theme page.

Hybrid includes the following:

- More than 20 free child themes (`http://themehybrid.com/themes`), shown in Figure 7-6

- Multiple widget areas in a variety of locations in the layout, including one template file that consists entirely of widget areas

- More than 20 plugins (`http://themehybrid.com/plugins`), many of which don't require Hybrid to work

- A range of hooks and filters

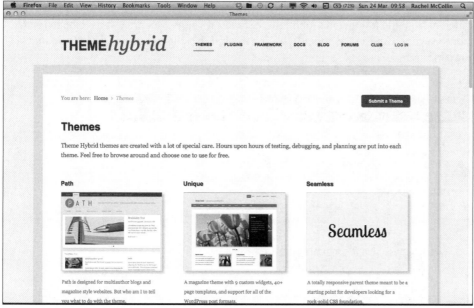

Source: http://themehybrid.com/themes
Figure 7-6 Hybrid child themes

Non-developers can use Hybrid with a child theme to get a website up and running very quickly, but its main strength lies in its code. It's a popular framework with developers, who value its hooks and filters to create customized sites that couldn't be done with the Dashboard alone. However, in order to get the most from it, you need to subscribe to the support forums—for example, without a subscription, it's not even possible to get documentation on the filters and hooks.

Wonderflux

Wonderflux is a completely free, open-source theme framework that requires no charge for support. Although it includes functionality aimed at non-coders, such as layout options configured via the Dashboard, it is really aimed at developers.

Features include the following:

- A dynamic grid-based layout that can be configured via the Dashboard
- Additional CSS classes generated on the body and post, allowing for custom styling
- More than a dozen hooks and a smaller number of functions and filters, all documented
- The capability to filter, remove, or replace every core function
- A comprehensive user guide at `http://wonderflux.com/guide/`
- A free child theme called WFX Girder (`http://code.google.com/p/wonderflux-girder-theme/`) that demonstrates how to use Wonderflux

Wonderflux is quite different from the frameworks mentioned already. It's aimed squarely at developers, with most customization done via code, not the Dashboard. The one exception is the layout, which is configured via the Stylelab page, shown in Figure 7-7.

Figure 7-7 Configuring layout via the Wonderflux Stylelab page

Its files are stored on Google Code, which makes it seem more daunting for inexperienced WordPress users than the other frameworks. However, it is fully open source and hugely customizable; and if you have the time and skill to stretch what it can do, it has a lot of potential.

Thematic

Thematic, developed by Automattic, is completely free and open source. The framework itself is really an advanced parent theme, with a stripped-down design and a number of widget areas, hooks, filters, and more for customization via child themes. It has minimal theme options and is aimed at developers. Figure 7-8 shows a simple Thematic-powered blog.

Thematic includes the following:

- 13 widget areas, including additional sidebars and widget areas in specific template files (the `index.php`, `single.php` and `page.php` files)
- Free and premium themes created by third-party developers
- 22 template files and 8 include files (for template file–specific sidebars)
- Documentation at `http://docs.thematictheme.com`
- A limited number of hooks, filters, and overrides

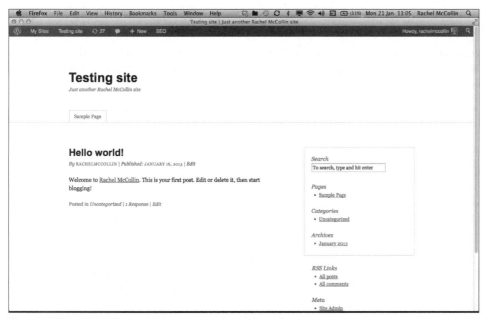

Figure 7-8 Thematic can be used on its own as a stripped-down theme.

As with other Automattic projects, Thematic is open source and not designed to be developed in a vacuum. The documentation is community-editable, and development of the framework itself is done in a similarly collaborative way to WordPress core development. Support is available via the developer community at `http://thematictheme.com/forums/forum/the-lounge/`.

Choosing the Framework for Your Project

Selecting the best framework for your project and your team isn't always easy. Many developers spend time experimenting with more than one of them before hitting on the one they'll use. Obviously, if you're looking at the premium frameworks, experimentation could be costly.

Factors to consider include the following:

- **Budget**—Do you or your client have the budget for a premium framework?

- **Time**—For a project with a short schedule, you need a framework that helps you get a site up and running quickly; whereas a longer schedule gives you time to build your own child theme and to make full use of the framework's APIs to achieve the desired result.

- **APIs**—What does the framework offer over and above a core WordPress installation? Look at the hooks, filters, and functions provided by your chosen framework and consider how you might use these in your project(s).

- **Layout**—Consider the CSS and the way layout is driven—does the framework (or its child themes) support responsiveness, for example? Are multiple layouts achieved using different template files or with a grid system?

- **The future**—Do you envisage yourself developing multiple projects with this framework? If so, then the investment in a premium framework with advanced features will be more justifiable.

- **Support**—Will you or your team require support? How quick do you need turnaround times to be? This is likely to be better with paid themes or paid support.

- **Skills**—Will development be done by people who have little experience with coding or WordPress development? The Dashboard functionality of the premium themes may help inexperienced users, whereas for coders it may just get in the way.

- **Efficiency and size**—How many files are included with the framework? How much functionality won't be needed? And if there's a lot, how easy is it to switch it off?

- **Learning curve**—How steep is the learning curve for each framework? If you're an experienced WordPress developer, you'll probably want to use a framework whose functions and terminology are consistent with WordPress, but if you're new to WordPress that might not be an issue.

- **Updates and security**—Is the framework updated regularly to remain in sync with WordPress updates? Is security a priority? Is the framework updated to incorporate support for new WordPress features as they are released? Like developers, framework vendors have access to the WordPress trac site, so they should be able to prepare updates for release very soon after new WordPress releases.

- **Recommendations**—Ask developers you respect what they use and why. Their choices may not be appropriate for you, so it's important to understand how a particular framework benefits them before you can apply a recommendation to your own requirements.

Spend some time with your team and client identifying your criteria, both for the project and for the team long-term if relevant, and draw up a short list of potential frameworks. If possible, spend some time getting to grips with the frameworks on your list to determine which one works for you. Choosing the framework you'll develop with can be as important as choosing the CMS you'll use, so it's worth being thorough.

Getting More from Frameworks

You could buy or download a framework, use its core functionality, child themes, and Dashboard settings, and build some great sites. However, if you want to push the limits of your chosen framework, you need to gain a deeper understanding of it and what it offers.

This section looks at some of the developer features commonly offered by frameworks and describes how to get the most from them in your projects.

A Quick Guide to Functions, Filters, and Hooks

Understanding functions, filters, and hooks is key to getting the most from theme frameworks (and indeed from pushing WordPress further). Here's a quick overview of what each of these does:

- **Functions** specify how something will happen. You code a function to query data, to output content, or to perform many other tasks. You can call (execute) functions from your own code, from your template files, or by hooking them into WordPress using an *action hook* (often referred to as a *hook*), or a *filter hook* (often referred to as a *filter*). Functions can also include template tags, and strictly speaking, hooks and filters are types of functions. For more information, see `http://codex.wordpress.org/Function_Reference`.

- **Action hooks** (sometimes referred to be developers simply as hooks) are triggered when something takes place, such as loading a page, a user logging in, or a custom action that you define. You can add your own action hooks within template files using `do_action()` and they will make your functions run if you have assigned functions to that action, using the following code:

  `<?php add_action ( 'name_of_action_hook', 'name_of_function' ); ?>`

- **Filter hooks** (sometimes referred to by developers as filters) enable you to control how data is output or input. For example, you can use a filter to output metadata in a specific format (e.g., date formats) or to prevent something from being displayed at all.

You'll learn how to add your own hooks and filters in the section "Building Your Own Framework" and in Chapter 9. Actions and filters are most commonly used in plugins (although they can be coded into a theme's functions file). The Codex guide to them is located in the Plugin AI documentation at `http://codex.wordpress.org/Plugin_API`.

Building with Theme Functions

To give you extra functionality, many frameworks include additional functions on top of those provided by WordPress. Details about the functions offered by some of the frameworks previously described are available in the following locations:

- Hybrid: `http://themehybrid.com/docs/functions`

- Wonderflux: `http://wonderflux.com/guide/function/`

- Thematic: `http://docs.thematictheme.com/type/function/`

- Genesis doesn't have a functions list in its documentation, but details about some useful ones can be found at `http://shaynesanderson.com/2011/05/24/handy-genesis-functions/`.

These functions can save you time coding your own or provide more flexibility when developing your own child themes or sites. An example is the `breadcrumb_trail()` function included with Hybrid. It's a simple template tag that lets you insert a breadcrumb trail into your template files, and it works in exactly the same way as the Breadcrumb Trail plugin (`http://themehybrid.com/plugins/breadcrumb-trail`). You can see the breadcrumb trail it outputs in Figure 7-9.

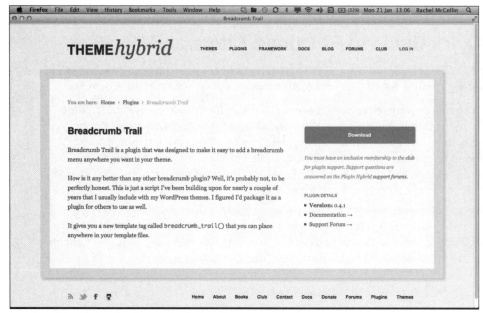

Source: http://themehybrid.com/plugins/breadcrumb-trail

Figure 7-9 The breadcrumb trail output by Hybrid's breadcrumb trail function

The Wonderflux framework includes two functions designed to help you change the output of other functions and filters by outputting either Y or N within a filter:

- The `wfx__N()` function (`http://wonderflux.com/guide/function/wfx__n/`) outputs the text string `N`.

- The `wfx__Y()` function (`http://wonderflux.com/guide/function/wfx__y/`) outputs the text string `Y`.

You can use this in a filter to switch off existing framework functionality, for example:

```php
<?php
 //In your child theme functions.php file:
 //Hide sidebar globally
 add_filter( 'wflux_sidebar_1_display', 'wfx__N' );
?>
```

This would prevent the sidebar from displaying across the site, and overrides any settings you've made via the Dashboard. It effectively switches off the `wflux_sidebar_1_display()` filter (`http://wonderflux.com/guide/filter/wflux_sidebar_1_display/`), which displays the primary sidebar.

Thematic has just one function, `thematic_doctitle` (`http://docs.thematictheme.com/thematic-doctitle-function/`), that echoes the title tag for the page. It would be used in the `<head>` section of the page as follows:

```php
<title><?php bloginfo('name'); ?> <?php thematic_doctitle(); ?></title>
```

Adding Content with Hooks

Most frameworks come with additional action hooks over and above those provided by WordPress. These let you add content in specific places in your theme or make functions fire when a certain action takes place, such as the Genesis `genesis_pre()` hook, which executes when Genesis is started, meaning any function you attach to it will fire as soon as the framework is loaded.

A list of hooks for the major frameworks can be found at the following locations:

- Genesis: `http://my.studiopress.com/docs/hook-reference/`
- Thesis: `http://diythemes.com/thesis/rtfm/hooks/`
- Hybrid: `http://themehybrid.com/docs/hooks`
- Wonderflux: `http://wonderflux.com/guide/hook/`
- Thematic: `http://docs.thematictheme.com/type/actions/`

The Genesis framework, for example, includes more than 50 hooks, many of which relate to locations in a theme's layout or structure. You can use these to output content at a specific place in your theme without coding it into template files. For example, using the `genesis_after_content()` hook you can output content after the content on each page as follows:

```php
<?php
function wpptl_call_to_action() { ?>
 <div class="CTA">
  <h1>Call us to find out more</h1>
  <p>Call 000-00000 or <a href="mailto:mail@example.com">email us</a> to
speak to one of our friendly advisors</p>
 </div><!--.CTA-->
<?php }
add_action ('genesis_after_content', 'wpptl_call_to_action');
?>
```

This simple example would enable you to output a Call to Action box after the content of each page on the site without having to code this into the relevant template files.

Alternatively, you could use this hook to output a list of posts in the same category as the current one when on a single post page:

```php
<?php
function wpptl_list_category_posts () {
 global $post;
 if ( is_single () ) {
  $categories = get_the_category( $post->ID );
  foreach ( $categories as $category ) {
   echo '<h3>' . $category->name . '</h3>';
   $args = array(
   'category_name' => $category->slug,
   'post_status' => 'publish',
   'post_count' => '10',
   );
```

(continued)

```
$the_query = new WP_Query( $args );
echo '<ul>';
while ( $the_query->have_posts() ) {
 $the_query->the_post();
 echo '<li><a href="' . get_permalink() . '">' . get_the_title() .
 '</a></li>';
}
echo '</ul>';
}
}
}
add_action( 'genesis_after_content', 'wpptl_list_category_posts' );
?>
```

The preceding snippet of code does the following:

▨ Checks if you are on a single page

▨ Fetches the list of categories for the current post using `$categories = get_the_category($post->ID)`

▨ For each category, runs the loop, first outputting the category name in a `<h3>` tag

▨ Defines the arguments for the posts to be displayed for each category so that only published posts are displayed with a link to the post's permalink, and no more than ten

▨ Lists all the posts according to the arguments inside a link to the posts' permalink

▨ Hooks the `wpptl_list_category_posts()` function to the `genesis_after_content` action hook to fire the function

This adds a list of up to ten other posts in the categories assigned to an individual post after its content on its own page. Alternatively, instead of using the `is_single()` conditional tag as shown in the preceding example, you could add your own hook to the `single.php` template file in your child theme. This is covered in the section "Building Your Own Theme Framework."

Thesis also includes a large number of hooks, all of which are related to locations in the theme and let you add content wherever you want in the same manner already outlined. Thesis has two hooks for adding content after the content area:

▨ `thesis_hook_after_content` (http://diythemes.com/thesis/rtfm/hooks/thesis_hook_after_content/), which is located after the content but immediately before the closing `</div>` tag for the content area

▨ `thesis_hook_after_content_area` (http://diythemes.com/thesis/rtfm/hooks/thesis_hook_after_content_area/), which is located immediately after the closing `</div>` tag for the content area

These two hooks give you more flexibility, in that you can choose to place additional content inside or outside the content's containing `div`—something that could be very useful for layout or structure.

Hybrid has a quite different set of hooks, which are not related to locations in a theme but to breadcrumb trails and grid columns. Some of the hooks listed in its hook documentation are actions, while others are filters.

Wonderflux has hooks relating to locations but fewer of them than Thesis and Genesis, while Thematic has three main hooks:

- `thematic_before` (http://docs.thematictheme.com/thematic_before/) is located between the opening `<body>` tag and the opening `<div id="wrapper">` tag, meaning you can use it to insert functions or scripts that need to run at the beginning of a page.

- `thematic_aboveheader` (http://docs.thematictheme.com/thematic_aboveheader/) is located in `header.php` just before the opening of `<div id="header">` (at the time of writing, thematic hasn't been updated to include HTML5 semantic elements).

- `thematic_header` (http://docs.thematictheme.com/thematic_header/) builds the content of the header and includes five additional action hooks relating to the header contents.

Using Filters to Change Styling and Output

Even though you are using a framework for development, there will be times when you don't want it to output layout areas or content in the default manner. Most of the frameworks have filters that you can use to alter the way data is output or to prevent it from being output altogether. This is a very powerful capability, as it gives you much more control over your site.

You can find a list of filters for the frameworks at the following locations:

- Genesis: `http://my.studiopress.com/docs/filter-reference/`
- Thesis: `http://diythemes.com/thesis/rtfm/filters/`
- Hybrid: `http://themehybrid.com/docs/hooks`
- Wonderflux: `http://wonderflux.com/guide/filter/`
- Thematic: `http://docs.thematictheme.com/type/filters/`

These perform a wide array of tasks, and the selection varies for each framework. Some enable you to specify whether elements of the framework will be displayed or not or how it will be displayed, such as the Thesis framework's `thesis_show_footer`, which lets you specify whether the footer will be displayed. For example, if you wanted to display the footer on most of your site but not on the home page, you would use the following:

```php
<?php
function wpptl_no_home_footer() {
 if ( is_front_page())
  return false;
 else
  return true;
}
add_filter('thesis_show_footer', 'wpptl_no_home_footer');
?>
```

This uses the conditional tag `is_front_page()` to check if you're on the home page, returning `false` if so and `true` if not. It then hooks this function to the `thesis_show_footer` filter, which if given a `true` value outputs the footer, and if given a `false` value does not. You can see how filters like this (as well as action hooks) can be used to make conditional tags much simpler by avoiding the need to create your own function to run if the condition is met.

Another example of using a filter to alter styling is provided by Wonderflux, whose `wflux_css_theme_path` filter enables you to change the stylesheet used when the site is loaded. You could use this to load an alternative stylesheet based on a condition you set, such as for a specific page template or for logged-in users:

```php
<?php
add_filter('wflux_css_theme_path', 'wpptl_new_stylesheet');
function wpptl_new_stylesheet( $path ) {
 if ( in_category( 'amazing-design' ) ) {
  return WF_THEME_URL.'/style-alternative.css';
 }
 return $path;
}
add_filter('wflux_css_theme_path', 'wpptl_new_stylesheet');
?>
```

You can also use filters to replace the default content that the framework adds to certain areas of the site or theme. For example, the `genesis_title_comments` filter in Genesis enables you to alter what is output in the title above comments on a page or post. The default is `__( '<h3>Comments</h3>', 'genesis')` but you could amend this to use a title of your own:

```php
<?php
function wpptl_comments_title( $title ) {
  __return __( '<h3>Your comments:</h3>', 'genesis' );
}
add_filter( 'genesis_title_comments', 'wpptl_comments_title' );
?>
```

Alternatively, you could make things more interesting by adding the post title to the comments heading:

```php
<?php
function wpptl_postname_comments_title( $title ) {
 return __('<h3>Your comments on ' . get_the_title( $post->ID ) .
  ':</h3>');
}
add_filter( 'genesis_title_comments', 'wpptl_postname_comments_title' );
?>
```

This means that without having to create template files in your child theme for every scenario in which comments are listed, you can quickly change the way their title is output. By using the range of available filters like this, you can create a site that looks nothing like a "default" framework site.

Building Your Own Theme Framework

You might decide that none of the available theme frameworks offer quite what you need, or that one of them comes close but needs some modification to meet the needs of your team and your projects. Or you might prefer to have more control over, and familiarity with, exactly how the framework you're using works. You may even be ambitious enough to develop a framework for release to the public (no easy task).

For any or all of these reasons, you might decide to build your own theme framework. Your framework need not be a full framework like some of the larger publicly available ones—for example, you might not need much in the way of options pages and WYSIWYG layout control. Your framework may well just start out as an advanced parent theme, with content, layout, and functionality that you'll need for the majority of your projects.

In the long run, coding your own framework can save you time and make life easier for you and your team, but in the short term it will be a lot of work. Depending on the complexity of what you have planned, it could require much more work than a site build, or it could require the same amount of time as developing a theme. You might decide to start out with something simple and build on it over time, or use a stripped-down parent theme with hooks and filters added to help you with development projects.

> Even if you don't decide to build your own theme framework, much of the content in this section will help you when building parent themes or advanced standalone themes.

Identifying Framework Requirements

Before you start building your own framework, it's important to take some time to identify what you need from it. To the extent possible, you need to consider future requirements of your clients and projects, as well as the approaches you'll take to building your framework. Your decisions will depend on you and your team and your preferred working style, but some of the things you'll need to consider are as follows:

- **Scaled down or all-inclusive**—Will your framework be a bare-bones starting point for you to build on with child themes or will it include full-featured content and functionality that you can remove in child themes, either manually or using hooks or filters? Alternatively, will you develop a set of plugins that you can activate alongside your framework as needed?

- **Template files**—What template files will you include in your framework? Will you take a minimalist approach, adding additional files in child themes, or start with a multitude of them for all occasions?

- **Include files**—To what extent will you use include files (in addition to the standard `header.php`, `sidebar.php` and `footer.php` files). Files such as `loop.php` and `page-content.php`, for example, mean that if you're working with multiple template files, you only need to code specific content once, which can make it much easier to push updates and debug problems.

- **Child themes**—Will you develop "starter" child themes to work with your framework? I use an advanced parent theme as my framework, and have developed a number of starter themes to go with it. These have minimal styling but vary in terms of markup, whether comments are included, and whether they're responsive. These starter themes enable a quick start to every new project—and it's easier to use them with the framework parent theme than to code each of them from scratch.

- **Hooks and filters**—What hooks and filters do you think you'll need for future projects? You can always add more to future versions of your framework, but it makes sense to take a logical, planned approach from the beginning.

- **Widget areas**—Will you include widget areas in locations other than the sidebar and footer? These can be useful if you're working with clients or team members who have enough WordPress knowledge to add widgets but not enough to code. However, if you expect clients to edit widget content and they have little or no technical capability, another approach may be needed (as covered in Chapter 4).

- **Menus**—How many menus will your framework support and where will they be located? My framework supports two menus, one in the header and one below it, either of which can be switched off for projects for which only one menu is needed, or (occasionally) both can be kept for more complex site builds that need more than one menu. You might also want to include a menu in the sidebar, possibly in a specific template file that is activated only where this is needed, or using a filter to change how it is output.

- **Theme options**—To what extent will you include theme options in your framework? My framework includes a simple options page for clients to edit their contact details and social media links, but more can be added if needed.

- **Admin customization**—If you want to customize the admin for certain user roles, it makes sense to add this to your framework. See Chapter 4 for more information on how to do this.

- **Layout**—Will you incorporate layout in your framework's styling or will you add this in child themes? If you incorporate it in the framework, how will you make changes possible—you could use either template files with different layouts or a grid-based layout. Will you make the framework responsive or mobile first? You might add mobile-specific themes to your list of child themes if you have clients who will need this.

- **Libraries**—Will your framework include any scripts or libraries not already included with WordPress? For a list of included scripts, see `http://codex.wordpress.org/Function_Reference/wp_enqueue_script#Default_scripts_included_with_WordPress`.

- **Browser compatibility**—It makes a lot of sense to build browser compatibility into your framework, targeting those browsers you'll be supporting for clients. My framework supports IE7 and later and all the other major browsers, and so do my starter child themes. Using an approach like this means that when you develop with these themes, any tweaks you have to make for browser support will be minimal.

- **Development approach**—How will you approach the development of your framework? You could take a theme you've already developed and extend that, or use a publicly available, open-source theme or framework and customize and build on those. Revisit the earlier sections of this chapter to determine which approach suits you best.

- **Future projects**—What might the projects you accept in two years' time look like and how can you ensure that your framework can adapt and/or scale to meet their requirements?

This is a long list and you may well have other items to add to it, but building your own framework could be an important piece of work in the establishment of your business. Getting it right from the start will help you be more efficient and tackle site builds in a way that's quick and consistent, so taking your time now will pay dividends in the long run.

What to Include Where

Having identified what you'll need to include in your framework, the next consideration is where to include it. Possible locations include the following:

- **Template files**—You might develop a simple theme with a small number of template files, maybe using conditional comments within those for location-specific content. Alternatively, you might create a range of template files with all the options coded in. If you do go down this path, it's a good idea to use template parts (sometimes referred to as includes) such as `loop.php` to avoid repeating yourself.

- **The functions file**—Your framework will require some functions to give it the functionality needed for your projects, and you may choose to use functions in place of code within the template files in many cases. If so, be aware that less experienced developers may find it harder to work with content generated via functions than content coded into the template files. However, using functions does give you the flexibility to use hooks and filters more extensively.

- **Plugins**—You might decide to include only very limited functionality in your functions file, making the rest of your functionality modular by developing plugins for different features your projects may need. This gives you the benefit of not having code you don't need in every site you build using the framework, and in some cases it may be useful because the functionality provided shouldn't be theme-dependent. For more details about identifying when to use plugins and when to use functions, see Chapter 9.

- **Child themes**—You might choose to make your framework very minimal and code more into your child themes. As mentioned earlier, this avoids the risk of having more code than you need for each project, but it risks repetition—after all, the whole point of developing your framework is to speed up the development process and ensure that you don't have to do things more than once. Even if you use starter child themes, it's going to be more time-consuming to update all of these in the future than it would be to update your framework theme or plugins.

What you choose to do will depend on your anticipated projects and your team's preferred way of working, but it should be agreed upon by everyone concerned.

Adding Action Hooks and Filter Hooks

So, you have set up your framework, and you have a parent theme that either has a lot of options or is very minimal and designed to be complemented by child themes. This in itself could be useful as an approach to developing sites using child themes; but you can get more from your framework (just as you saw how to get more from the publicly available frameworks) by adding action hooks and filter hooks for use in your child themes.

Adding Action Hooks

Action hooks use two basic functions, `do_action()` and `add_action()`:

- `do_action()` creates an action hook in a given place in your theme, meaning you can then use `add_action` to fire functions at that point in your theme or framework. This is the function you use to add your own action hooks in your framework.

▨ `add_action()` specifies a function that will run when a predefined action hook (such as one you've created using `do_action()`) is fired. You've already seen how to use this in conjunction with hooks provided by the publicly available themes and in various places elsewhere in this book, using action hooks provided by WordPress. For more details on `add_action()`, see `http://codex.wordpress.org/Function_Reference/add_action`; and for a list of WordPress action hooks, see `http://codex.wordpress.org/Plugin_API/Action_Reference`.

The `do_action()` function takes one tag and as many arguments as needed:

```php
<?php
do_action( $tag, $arg1, $arg2, etc…);
?>
```

`$tag` is the name you give to your action—it's a good idea to make this self-explanatory based on where it's located, and obviously to add a prefix to avoid conflicts with any other actions. The arguments are additional (optional) parameters. For the purposes of developing your own framework, this is less likely to be the case than it might be if you were building a plugin, for example (see Chapter 9 for more information about this).

For example, to add an action hook immediately after the opening `<body>` tag, you would use the following:

```php
<body>
<?php do_action( 'wpptl_body_open');
// rest of code within the body tag
?>
```

You could then use this hook to insert content, display data, or add markup. For example, suppose your framework has one hook immediately after the opening `<body>` tag and one immediately before the closing `</body>` tag. For the sake of simplicity and standards compliance, you've kept the markup in your framework's template files as simple as possible with the minimum number of elements required. However, for a particular project you need to insert a container `div` inside the `<body>` tag for styling. You could code this into the `header.php` and `footer.php` files manually, or alternatively you could add it via a couple of functions. This means you could write a small plugin to add that containing `div` and activate it only in those sites that need the extra markup. Activating a plugin for a couple of lines of markup is probably a bit excessive, but it illustrates how you can add content to themes without having to repeat the code in different child themes.

In the `header.php` file of your framework, you would add the following code:

```php
<body>
<?php do_action( 'wpptl_body_open');
// rest of code within the body tag
?>
```

In your framework's `footer.php` file, you would add this:

```php
// rest of code for footer
<?php do_action( 'wpptl_body_close' );
?>
</body>
```

In the functions file of your child theme, or in your plugin, you would add the following:

```php
<?php
// add opening of container div immediately after opening of body tag
function wpptl_add_container_opening() { ?>
 <div class="container">
 <?php }
add_action( 'wpptl_body_open', 'wpptl_add_container_opening' );
// add close of container div immediately before close of body tag
function wpptl_add_container_closing() {; ?>
 </div><!-- .container -->
 <?php }
add_action( 'wpptl_body_close', 'wpptl_add_container_closing' );
?>
```

This would add an extra `div` to the child theme's markup without actually adding any code to the template file, which could save you having to create a template file and therefore be more efficient. However, if you're releasing child themes to the public, it may be risky, as users won't be able to see how that `div` is generated by looking at the template files.

As well as adding content with an action hook, you can also remove it using the `remove_action()` function, which takes four parameters:

```php
<?php
remove_action( $tag, $function_to_remove, $priority,  $accepted_args );
?>
```

- `$tag`—The name of the action hook you want to work with

- `$function_to_remove`—The name of the function attached to this hook that you want to remove

- `$priority`—The priority given to the function in the `add_action()` function already coded in your framework (if this has been specified, otherwise it defaults to a value of 10)

- `$accepted_args`—The number of arguments the function you're removing contains

> For this to work, the `$tag`, `$function_to_remove`, and `$priority` **parameters must be an exact match to the parameters specified in the original function.**

For example, if your framework used the function `wpptl_display_comments()` to display comments on a page, by attaching it to the `wpptl_after_content` action that is located after the content, you could turn this off and prevent comments from being displayed using `remove_action()` as follows. First, the function in the theme's functions file might be something like this:

```php
<?php
function wpptl_display_comments() {
 //code for comments display
}
add_action( 'wpptl_after_content', 'wpptl_display_comments', 5 );
?>
```

The function you would use to remove the comments display would be as follows:

```php
<?php
remove_action( 'wpptl_after_content', 'wpptl_display_comments', 5 );
?>
```

Notice that I've also included the $priority argument here—without it, remove_action() wouldn't work and the function would continue to run. You could also use remove_action() in this way to prevent a function from running in specific circumstances using a conditional tag—for example, on the home page or for admin users.

There are several functions related to action hooks that you can use to perform functions, such as checking whether a hook has a function associated with it, removing all functions attached to a hook, and more. For a full list, see http://codex.wordpress.org/Function_Reference/add_action#Related.

You can add as many action hooks as you like to your framework—how many you use depends on the degree of flexibility you anticipate needing for child themes in the future. They are a great way to enable the addition of extra code or functions at a later date without having to anticipate everything and code it into your framework—indeed, with the right hooks (and filters), you could theoretically build child themes with just a stylesheet and functions file and no other template files, simply using functions in functions.php or your plugins to add extra content as required.

> Before adding your own hooks, check the list of those offered by WordPress so you don't duplicate functionality already provided. A full list is at http://codex.wordpress.org/Plugin_API/ Action_Reference.

Adding Filter Hooks

Adding filter hooks as well as action hooks gives you even more flexibility, as they enable you to alter the way data is queried and displayed by the framework. This also enables you to avoid hard-coding alterations into template files in the child theme. A good example of this is the loop—if you wanted posts to display differently in different parts of your site but didn't want to add an additional include file or template file.

Filter hooks use two basic functions, which are similar (but not as similar as you might think) to those for action hooks:

- add_filter() adds a function you specify to a pre-existing filter so it will execute when that filter fires.

- apply_filters() calls the functions hooked by calls to add_filter()—it uses the plural form because more than one filter can be attached to one filter hook.

The apply_filters() function has three parameters:

```php
<?php
apply_filters( $tag, $value, $var ... );
?>
```

- $tag—The name of the filter hook being created

- $value—The parameters passed to any filters added to the hook

- $var—One or more additional variables passed to the filter. These are optional and vary according to the kind of filter you're adding.

For example, suppose you wanted to amend the way post and page titles were displayed in each child theme without having to code this into every relevant template file.

In your framework's `loop.php` file, you would have the following:

```
<h2 id="post-<?php the_ID(); ?>">
 <a href="<?php the_permalink() ?>" rel="bookmark" title="Permanent Link
  to <?php echo the_title_attribute( 'echo=0' ); ?>">
  <?php echo apply_filters( 'wpptl_page_title', get_the_title() ); ?>
 </a>
</h2>
```

This adds a filter called `wpptl_page_title` to the display of the page or post title, giving it the value of `the_title()` as a default.

In a child theme, you might want to change this for single posts only, perhaps displaying some static text before the post name. You would add the following to your child theme's functions file:

```
<?php
function childtheme_post_title_display( $title ) {
 if ( is_single() ) {
  return 'Read about: ' . $title;
 }
 return $title;
}
add_filter( 'wpptl_page_title', 'childtheme_post_title_display' );
?>
```

You might have noticed that the filter added to the framework with `apply_filters()` includes data, which is then amended (filtered) by the filter function hooked by `add_filter()`. This is different from `do_action()`, which doesn't specify any data to be included in the action hook but merely creates it for you; then you can hook functions to it using `add_action()` in the child theme.

As with action hooks, filters have a few functions associated with them, such as `remove_filter()`, which works very similarly to `remove_action()`. For a full list, see `http://codex.wordpress.org/Function_Reference/add_filter#Related`.

> Before adding filters to your framework, check the ones offered by WordPress—you may well find that what you need is already covered, as many of the pre-existing filters work with data that you're likely to be manipulating in your framework. There's more information about WordPress filters in Chapter 9, and you can find a list of WordPress filters at `http://codex.wordpress.org/Plugin_API/Filter_Reference`.

Widgets, Menus, and More

As well as hooks and filters in your framework, you'll also need to think about content areas that can be manipulated from the WordPress Dashboard. These will be particularly useful if your users have enough knowledge of WordPress to use all aspects of the Dashboard but not enough to add functions to hook to your actions and filters. All of these are also useful if you're developing themes for release to the public, as they'll give users the capability to adapt your theme using code or the Dashboard.

The functionality you'll most likely need to add to your framework includes the following:

- **Widget areas**—You may want to include just the standard ones in the sidebar and footer, or perhaps add others to different areas of the layout or in different template files. Chapter 8 describes a case study using different widget areas in different template files.

- **Menus**—Your theme could have support for one primary menu or for multiple menus, perhaps if a menu will be needed in the sidebar for some child themes, or you want to add a mobile-specific menu or more than one location for the main menu.

- **Theme options pages**—These enable users to add data or configure options that aren't included in the database content, such as header content, color options, or layout configuration.

- **Theme Customizer compatibility**—In addition to (or sometimes instead of) one or more theme options pages, you might want to make aspects of your framework compatible with the Theme Customizer, giving users the capability to edit them and preview the results before saving.

Options pages and the Theme Customizer are covered in detail in Chapter 4, so here I'll outline the code required to add widget areas and menus to your framework (or to your themes if you're building standalone themes).

Adding Widget Areas

To add a widget area, you use the `register_sidebar()` function in your `functions.php` file. For example, the theme powering my blog at `http://rachelmccollin.com` has nine widget areas, which are provided by my compass framework parent theme. The code for the first two is similar to the following:

```
function compass_widgets_init() {
  // Area 0, located above the header.
  register_sidebar( array(
    'name' => __( 'Before Header Widget Area', 'compass' ),
    'id' => 'before-header-widget-area',
    'description' => __( 'The header widget area', 'compass'),
    'before_widget' => '<div id="%1$s" class="widget-container %2$s">',
    'after_widget' => '</div>',
    'before_title' => '<h3 class="widget-title">',
    'after_title' => '</h3>',
  )
);
```

```
// Area 1, located at the top of the sidebar.
register_sidebar( array(
  'name' => __( 'Primary Widget Area', 'compass'),
  'id' => 'primary-widget-area',
  'description' => __( 'The primary widget area', 'compass'),
  'before_widget' => '<div id="%1$s" class="widget-container %2$s">',
  'after_widget' => '</div>',
  'before_title' => '<h3 class="widget-title">',
  'after_title' => '</h3>',
  )
 );
}
add_action( 'widgets_init', 'compass_widgets_init' );
?>
```

The code for the remaining seven widget areas is very similar to the preceding, and inserted inside the braces of the `wpptl_widgets_init()` function. Each instance of `register_sidebar()` has an array of parameters, including the following:

- `name`—The name of the widget area as seen in the Widgets Dashboard screen

- `id`—The unique ID of the widget area, as referenced in the relevant template file to display its contents

- `description`—A description of the widget area as displayed in the Widgets Dashboard screen—particularly useful if your theme or framework will be used by clients or other developers, or released to the public

- `before_widget`—The markup to add before the widget, a `div` in this case, which will have a unique numbered ID generated by `%1$s` and a class of `widget-container` plus a unique number generated by `%2$s`.

- `after_widget`—Markup to place after the widget, in this case the closing `</div>` tag

- `before_title` and `after_tiltle`—Similar to `before_widget` and `after_widget`, these add markup around the widget titles and are useful for styling.

After the function to register the sidebars is the `add_action` function, ensuring that the `compass_widgets_init()` function is run when the `widgets_init()` action is fired.

The code in the functions file on its own won't make the widgets work—to ensure that each widget area's contents are displayed in the theme, you need to add some code to the relevant template file in the location where you want the widget. In my theme, the first widget is above other header content and is added to the theme's `header.php` file with the following:

```
<!-- widget area above the header -->
<aside class="before-header widget-area" role="complementary">
 <?php if ( is_active_sidebar( 'before-header-widget-area' ) ) {
 dynamic_sidebar( 'before-header-widget-area' );
 } ?>
</aside><!-- end of widget area -->
```

This does the following:

- Opens the widget area with an opening `<aside>` tag

- Checks whether the `before-header-widget-area` sidebar is active—i.e., whether it contains any widgets

- If so, it outputs its contents.

The other widget areas are coded into their relevant template files. The Widgets Dashboard page, shown in Figure 7-10, shows them all on the right, ready for widgets.

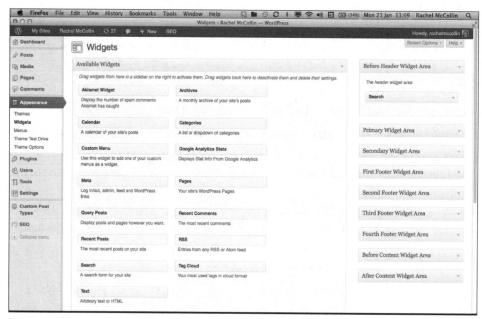

Figure 7-10 The nine widget areas in the WordPress Dashboard

Adding Menus

You can also add menus by registering them in the functions file and then adding theme support in the relevant template file(s). To register a single menu, you use the `register_nav_menu()` function as follows:

```php
<?php
register_nav_menu( $location, $description );
?>
```

The parameters are as follows:

- `$location`—The unique location or name of the menu

- `$description`—The description of the menu as displayed in the Menus admin screen

You can also register multiple menus at the same time using `register_nav_menus()`. This takes an array of locations and descriptions as follows:

```php
<?php
register_nav_menus( array(
 $location1 => $description1,
 $location2 => $description2,
 )
);
?>
```

For example, my compass framework parent theme has code for two menus:

```php
<?php
function compass_setup() {
 register_nav_menus( array(
   'primary' => __( 'Primary Navigation', 'twentyten' ),
   'sidebar' => __( 'Sidebar Menu', 'twentyten' ),
   )
 );
}
add_action( 'after_setup_theme', 'compass_setup' );
?>
```

This uses the function `compass_setup()` (which also includes some other elements, such as adding support for thumbnails) to register two sidebars: one primary menu and one in the sidebar. It then hooks this function to the `after_setup_theme()` action, using `add_action()`.

As with widgets, this alone won't make the menus work—they also need to be coded into the theme's template files using `wp_nav_menu()`:

```html
<nav class="menu main">
 <?php wp_nav_menu( array(
   'container_class' => 'main',
   'theme_location' => 'primary'
   )
 );
 ?>
</nav><!-- .main -->
```

This adds the menu with the primary location from the functions file, adds a class of `.main` to its containing element, and wraps it in `<nav class="main">`.

As shown in Figure 7-11, the Dashboard now shows two menus, to which links can be added for display in the relevant place.

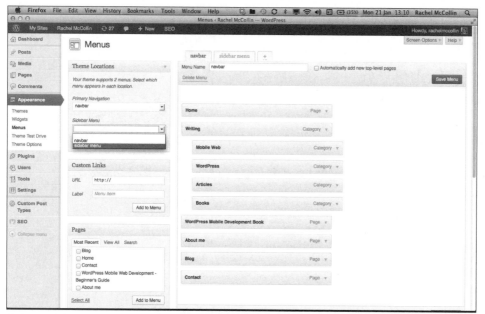

Figure 7-11 The two menus in the WordPress Dashboard

Managing and Updating Your Framework

After you have built your framework, your work doesn't stop there. As your projects evolve, as WordPress itself changes, and as your experience and that of your team grows, you need to adapt and update your framework. Some points to bear in mind include the following:

- **WordPress compatibility**—Ensure that your framework remains compatible with WordPress over time. Test it against new releases to confirm that it doesn't use deprecated code or have any conflicts. See Chapter 6 for more information on responding to WordPress updates.

- **Bug fixes**—If you or your users spot bugs in the framework, you'll need to create a new version. Don't be tempted to edit the framework files used in one site without creating a new documented version—that's a recipe for chaos and confusion.

- **Rolling changes out to client sites**—It's up to you whether you update sites you've already built with the new version of your framework each time. Doing so means having a consistent code base across all the sites you manage and it will simplify WordPress updates, but it runs the risk of conflicts with code in the relevant child themes.

- **Version control**—Make sure you use strict version control, documenting changes in each version, both in the theme's stylesheet and in a separate readme file. If you're releasing your code to the public, you should also document this on a website supporting the framework. Currently, providing documentation on a dedicated site or page of your own site is advised for themes in the WordPress theme repository, but there's a good chance that in the future it will become mandatory.

- **Simplifying updates**—If you decide to roll updates out to all your client sites, you need to find a simple way to do this. If you also manage and host those sites, you might find it simplest to host them all in WordPress Multisite, meaning you only need to update the framework theme once. WordPress Multisite is the subject of the next section.

Theme Building for Networks

There are a few reasons you might want to build a WordPress network using Multisite:

- You're building a set of sites for a single client and want to simplify their administration.
- You use your own network of sites for testing or you want to host a range of sites you own.
- You can easily update all the client sites you host.
- You run a network of hosted sites to which people can subscribe, effectively buying their own site.

Whatever your reason, Multisite will make things a lot simpler for you. A complete discussion of Multisite is beyond the scope of this chapter (I've listed some useful resources at the end if you want to know more), but this section provides an overview of some considerations for theme building and site management.

Differences Between Single and Multisite

The main Multisite features that differ from single sites are as follows:

- Only one WordPress installation is used for multiple sites.
- Creating a new site is done by the network admin and is a very quick and straightforward process compared to creating a new single site.
- An additional role is created—that of Network Administrator. This role allows editing and administration of all sites in the network and is the only role allowed to add and edit themes and plugins.
- Themes and plugins can be activated across the network or for individual sites (the network administrator must specify which).
- There is only one database for the entire network, with each site having its own set of tables (identified by a unique ID number).
- Themes and plugins for all of the sites are held in the same place in the `wp-content` directory, while uploads are held in a separate directory called `wp-content/uploads/sites/`, with a subdirectory for each site. Versions of Multisite from 3.0 to 3.4.2 (i.e., prior to 3.5) used the `wp-content/blogs.dir/` directory.
- Site administrators for each individual site have restricted capabilities and cannot install themes or plugins—only the network admin can do this.

Planning How to Use Network Themes

Multisite can be useful when you are managing a number of sites that all use the same theme, or child themes of a given parent theme. This way, you only need update that theme each time it changes, and all of the sites in the network will also be updated.

To achieve the required degree of difference between each site, you can use one of the following approaches to theming:

- **Child themes**—Use a child theme for each site if you want the sites to be quite different and individually customizable, perhaps making use of different template files and functions.

- **Theme options or the Theme Customizer**—You can achieve some difference between sites by allowing users to customize their sites via a theme options screen or the Theme Customizer. This gives users the power to alter their own sites without relying on you to code any differences into a child theme.

- **Custom CSS**—You could allow site owners to write and edit CSS using an options screen, which gives them more control than the Theme Customizer. This will only be relevant if the users have sufficient understanding of CSS. For more information about customizing the admin, see Chapter 4.

Multisite can be extremely useful if you're managing a number of sites for yourself or your clients or users; but as with most things, you need to take a considered approach and understand what's needed before diving in. For a good guide to Multisite network administration, see `http://wpmu.org/wordpress-multisite-guide/`.

BuddyPress and Beyond

If your themes will require advanced interactivity between users, and support a community of users, then you'll need the BuddyPress plugin (`http://wordpress.org/extend/plugins/buddypress/`). BuddyPress has become more than a simple plugin—it has its own community of developers and extends WordPress in significant ways. It has its own dedicated codex at `http://codex.buddypress.org`.

BuddyPress adds a lot of functionality to a WordPress site, so it's important to understand what it includes when deciding whether it is what you need or whether a simpler approach would suffice. Main features of BuddyPress include the following:

- Activity streams
- Front-end user profiles
- Options to add user profile fields and sections
- Avatar uploads
- Groups
- Group discussion forums
- Events
- Friend system
- Messaging
- Custom themes
- Individual blogs for each user

As well as all this, you can add much more with BuddyPress-specific plugins—for a list, see `http://buddypress.org/extend/plugins/`.

You might find that you only want one or two of these features, in which case you can specify in the BuddyPress interface which aspects to switch on and off. However if you're switching almost everything off, BuddyPress might not be what you need. Some alternatives to BuddyPress include the following:

- The P2 theme (`http://wordpress.org/extend/themes/p2` and `http://p2theme.com`) enables the use of activity streams using posts, post formats, and comments. It's used by Automattic for communication related to WordPress development, and it is a good way to enable discussion between site users.

- BBPress (`http://wordpress.org/extend/plugins/bbpress/`) is a plugin that creates forum or bulletin board functionality. Like BuddyPress, it has its own website, with a codex and more, at `http://bbpress.org`.

BuddyPress and Themes

Depending on the kind of development you'll be doing, you may choose to write all your themes (or your framework) to be BuddyPress-compatible. Alternatively, if you are developing a one-off BuddyPress site, you may prefer to customize an existing BuddyPress theme. In my experience, BuddyPress can be added to well-coded themes without too much tweaking needed, so if your themes or framework have functionality you want to make use of in addition to BuddyPress, this is probably the route to take. If you're going to be developing a lot of BuddyPress sites, though, it makes sense to create a BuddyPress-enabled framework, parent theme, or starter theme of your own, to avoid the extra work adding the required additional template files.

How BuddyPress Themes Differ from Standard Themes

BuddyPress themes need some additional template files to help make BuddyPress work. These enhance the styling of your BuddyPress-enabled theme (for example, adding padding and changing text sizes and layouts). The additional files are as follows:

- `header-buddypress.php`
- `sidebar-buddypress.php`
- `footer-buddypress.php`
- `/activity/index.php`
- `/blogs/create.php`
- `/blogs/index.php`
- `/forums/index.php`
- `/groups/index.php`
- `/groups/create.php`
- `/groups/single/home.php`
- `/groups/single/plugins.php`
- `/members/index.php`
- `/members/single/home.php`

- /members/single/plugins.php
- /members/single/settings/delete-account.php
- /members/single/settings/general.php
- /members/single/settings/notifications.php
- /registration/activate.php
- /registration/register.php.

You'll see how you can add these to an existing theme shortly.

BuddyPress template files use a default markup structure that you might need to edit to provide compatibility with your existing theme or with your project's requirements:

```php
<?php get_header( 'buddypress' ); ?>
<div id="content">
 <div class="padder">
  <!-- content goes here using the loop -->
 </div><!-- .padder -->
</div><!-- #content -->
<?php get_sidebar( 'buddypress' ); ?>
<?php get_footer( 'buddypress' ); ?>
```

As you can see, the important elements here are `<div id="content">` and `<div id="padder">` as well as the includes. You can either edit this core structure in a pre-existing BuddyPress theme or add it to your own to make your theme BuddyPress-compatible.

Adapting a BuddyPress Theme

The main benefit of editing an existing BuddyPress theme is that it will include all the necessary template files pre-installed. The downside is that it won't include custom functionality you are already using in your themes; and if you want to make significant changes, you'll have a lot of template files to edit.

Several pre-existing themes with BuddyPress compatibility are included, so if you're starting from scratch, want to get a project off the ground quickly, or prefer to work with an existing theme, using one of these may be the best approach. You can find a list of BuddyPress-compatible themes at http://wordpress.org/extend/themes/tags/buddypress.

Whether you choose to edit the theme itself or create a child theme depends on your project's needs and your approach to theme building. The considerations are very similar to those mentioned earlier in the sections on adapting existing themes and creating child themes.

Adding BuddyPress to Your Own Theme

Adding BuddyPress to your own theme can take longer but it's worth it if you need to add BuddyPress compatibility to an existing theme or you have a parent theme or framework with functionality you want to be able to use.

The main adaptation you'll need to make to your theme is adding the additional template files. To add these to an existing theme, you use the BuddyPress Template Pack plugin (http://wordpress.org/extend/plugins/bp-template-pack/).

Changes to BuddyPress Theming

At the time of writing, BuddyPress 1.7 is due out at any time, and it will significantly change the way that you build BuddyPress themes. BuddyPress 1.7 will make it possible to add BuddyPress to an existing theme without having to either adapt an existing BuddyPress-ready theme or add a lot of extra theme files. The BuddyPress team is describing it as BuddyPress's "most revolutionary release to date." To find out more, see `http://buddypress.org/2013/02/buddypress-1-7-beta-1/` and `http://buddypress.org/2013/03/buddypress-1-7-beta-2/`.

You'll then need to edit the extra template files so they're in line with your theme's existing template files. You can do this in one of two ways:

- Edit the extra BuddyPress template files to add code from your theme's `index.php` or `page.php` file.

- Make copies of your theme's template files and rename them to the names of the extra BuddyPress files, adding the BuddyPress structural markup as required.

Which option you choose depends on your personal preference; but whatever you do, make a backup first and note which files you've edited or created as you go along to ensure you have all the files you need with the correct content.

Summary

Theme building is a fundamental aspect of WordPress development, and something that many WordPress developers spend a significant proportion of their time doing. If your business is based around theme building (for example, if you're developing client sites or building publicly available themes), you need to adopt a development process that's efficient and consistent—and one that enables you to build fast, standards-compliant, and future-proof themes. Taking some time to decide on the approach you'll use is well worth it in the long run. The approaches you've learned about here include the following:

- Building themes from scratch or from static HTML and CSS
- Customizing an existing theme
- Creating child themes
- Using a theme framework
- Developing your own theme framework
- Using Multisite for theme management
- Adding BuddyPress functionality to themes

All of these approaches have their place and you may find you need to use a few of them on different occasions.

Further Resources

Theme Building

Codex page on theme development
`http://codex.wordpress.org/Theme_Development`

WordPress template files
`http://codex.wordpress.org/Stepping_Into_Templates`

The template hierarchy
`http://codex.wordpress.org/Template_Hierarchy`

Adapting an Existing Theme

The Twenty Twelve theme
`http://wordpress.org/extend/themes/twentytwelve`

The underscores theme
`http://underscores.me`

Parent and Child Themes

Codex page on child themes
`http://codex.wordpress.org/Child_Themes`

Tutorial on creating child themes
`http://wp.tutsplus.com/tutorials/theme-development/child-themes-basics-and-creating-child-themes-in-wordpress/`

Theme Frameworks

Genesis
`http://www.studiopress.com`

Thesis
`http://diythemes.com`

Wonderflux
`http://wonderflux.com`

Thematic
`http://themeshaper.com/thematic`

Carrington
`http://carringtontheme.com`

Hybrid
`http://themehybrid.com`

A roundup of popular theme frameworks
`http://wp.smashingmagazine.com/2009/05/27/wordpress-theme-development-frameworks/`

Differences between frameworks and parent themes
`http://justintadlock.com/archives/2010/08/16/frameworks-parent-child-and-grandchild-themes`

Framework Functions

Hybrid
`http://themehybrid.com/docs/functions`

Wonderflux
`http://wonderflux.com/guide/function/`

Thematic
`http://docs.thematictheme.com/type/function/`

Framework Action Hooks

Genesis
`http://my.studiopress.com/docs/hook-reference/`

Thesis
`http://diythemes.com/thesis/rtfm/hooks/`

Hybrid
`http://themehybrid.com/docs/hooks`

Wonderflux
`http://wonderflux.com/guide/hook/`

Thematic
`http://docs.thematictheme.com/type/actions/`

Framework Filter Hooks

Genesis
`http://my.studiopress.com/docs/filter-reference/`

Thesis
`http://diythemes.com/thesis/rtfm/filters/`

Hybrid
`http://themehybrid.com/docs/hooks`

Wonderflux
`http://wonderflux.com/guide/filter/`

Thematic
`http://docs.thematictheme.com/type/filters/`

Building Your Own Framework

The template hierarchy
http://codex.wordpress.org/Template_Hierarchy

Inside actions and filters
http://wp.smashingmagazine.com/2012/02/16/inside-wordpress-actions-
filters/

Actions and filters are not the same thing
http://ottopress.com/2011/actions-and-filters-are-not-the-same-thing/

Action Hooks

Action hooks reference
http://codex.wordpress.org/Plugin_API/Action_Reference

The do_action() function
http://codex.wordpress.org/Function_Reference/do_action

The add_action function
http://codex.wordpress.org/Function_Reference/add_action

The remove_action() function
http://codex.wordpress.org/Function_Reference/remove_action

List of functions related to action hooks
http://codex.wordpress.org/Function_Reference/add_action#Related

Filter Hooks

Filter hooks reference
http://codex.wordpress.org/Plugin_API/Filter_Reference

The add_filter() function
http://codex.wordpress.org/Function_Reference/add_filter

The apply_filters() function
http://codex.wordpress.org/Function_Reference/apply_filters

Functions associated with filters
http://codex.wordpress.org/Function_Reference/add_filter#Related

Widgets

The register_sidebars() function
http://codex.wordpress.org/Function_Reference/register_sidebars

The is_active_sidebar() function
http://codex.wordpress.org/Function_Reference/is_active_sidebar

Menus

Navigation menus in the codex
`http://codex.wordpress.org/Navigation_Menus`

WordPress Multisite

Codex page on setting up Multisite
`http://codex.wordpress.org/Create_A_Network`

Multisite network administration
`http://codex.wordpress.org/Multisite_Network_Administration`

Guide to Multisite network administration
`http://wpmu.org/wordpress-multisite-guide/`

BuddyPress

BuddyPress website
`http://buddypress.org`

BuddyPress codex
`http://codex.buddypress.org`

BuddyPress plugin
`http://wordpress.org/extend/plugins/buddypress/`

Plugins to extend BuddyPress
`http://buddypress.org/extend/recommended-plugins/`

P2 theme in the plugins repository
`http://wordpress.org/extend/themes/p2`

P2 theme site
`http://p2theme.com`

bbPress in the plugins repository
`http://wordpress.org/extend/plugins/bbpress/`

bbPress website
`http://bbpress.org`

BuddyPress themes
`http://wordpress.org/extend/themes/tags/buddypress`

Examples of communities using BuddyPress
`http://wp.smashingmagazine.com/2012/09/26/buddypress-one-plugin-five-communities/`

Chapter 8

Conditional Display: Functions, Template Files, and Styling

Small, simple sites will have similar content on every page and post, with the same use of the loop, the same widget areas, and the same template tags and hooks. Larger sites, however, which typically have distinct sections or require customization in different parts of the site, will need conditional content or styling. As with many things WordPress, there is more than one way to deal with this. In some cases conditional tags within template files will be the way to go, in others it might be different template files for different areas of the site, and in some cases, where it is styling that needs to change and not content, CSS targeting specific areas of the site will be needed.

This chapter looks at different scenarios that require conditional code and the options you have to make it work. You'll learn when you might use each of the possible approaches and look at some examples of sites and themes that use conditional content and styling, and the code used to achieve it.

Conditional Content: When It Applies

The following are some scenarios in which you would need to use conditional code in a site:

- Some areas of the site include an element not displayed on the rest of the site, such as a home page banner image, or a widget area used in just one section of the site.

- Sections of the site have their own navigation, either connected to the main navigation or in a sidebar—or even within the main content area.

- Different sections of the site require a different layout or display their content in a different way. You might need to do this on static pages, on single post or custom post type listings, or indeed on archive listings.

- The site requires different widgets or widget areas on different pages or in different sections.

- Some areas of the site need to have different colors applied or different branding elements.

- You want to use the loop differently on different post types or in static pages versus posts and archive pages.

This is just a partial list—in fact, the possibilities for conditional content are limited only by your imagination, the site requirements, and your time and budget!

Generally, I recommend choosing your approach to conditional content using the following guidelines:

- Where the differences between pages or sections of the site are small, some conditional code inserted into the theme's main `index.php` or `page.php` file will probably be sufficient. The most commonly used conditional tags are covered in the next section.

- Where the site has distinct sections based on post types or taxonomies, and these have very different content, use template files relating to those post types and taxonomies to display the correct content. You might use a template file such as `single-post_type.php`; or if the only difference is in the header, sidebar, or footer, you could use an include such as `sidebar-post_type.php`. You'll learn the difference between these and when to use them in the section "Theme Files for Conditional Content" later in the chapter.

- Where the content is the same but only the styling is different, use CSS selectors that target specific pages, post types, or taxonomies (or just about anything else!). The classes you'll need to target to do this are generated by the `body_class` and `post_class` template tags, as described in the "Conditional Styling" section later in this chapter.

Sometimes the best solution isn't readily apparent—and in these cases "best" might mean the solution preferred by you and your team, and one that fits best with the way your theme is built.

Using Conditional Tags

You use conditional tags in a template file to check whether certain conditions are met when the page is being displayed, and then display content accordingly.

The basic syntax for conditional code is as follows:

```
<?php
if ( [condition] )
{
   // code to output when condition is met
}
?>
```

You can also check when a condition is *not* true, using an exclamation mark:

```
<?php
if ( ![condition] )
{
   // code to output when condition is not met
}
?>
```

Or, you can use `else` to add an alternative action if the condition is not met:

```
<?php
if ( [condition] )
{
   // code to output when condition is met
}
```

```
else
{
  // code to output when condition is not met
}
?>
```

The `else` statement is optional and only relevant when there are two alternative sets of code to output. If it's a simple case of outputting code when a condition is met but outputting nothing when it's not met, you omit the `else` statement entirely.

If you want to check for multiple conditions, there are four main methods:

- Use `elseif` as many times as needed to check for each condition in turn—this is relevant when the conditions are mutually exclusive.
- Use `&&` between statements to check whether both conditions are met.
- Use `OR` between statements to check whether either condition is met.
- Alternatively, nest `if` statements inside each other to check whether more than one condition is met. This is useful if you need to define a variable or function after checking the first condition, as demonstrated later in this chapter.

> For a full explanation of the syntax for PHP conditional statements, see `http://php.net/manual/en/control-structures.if.php`.

Conditional tags can be used to check a number of things:

- The page or post being displayed
- The template file being used
- The category or taxonomy of the post being displayed
- The post type being displayed
- Paginated pages, and the page number within paginated pages
- The user role accessing the site
- Whether a child theme is in use
- Whether you are currently in the loop (useful for plugins rather than template files)

This is just a subset of the conditional tags available—for a full list, see `http://codex.wordpress.org/Conditional_Tags`. By passing your own function and checking a condition based on that, you can check for a huge range of conditions, based on just about any function you could create in WordPress.

WordPress Core Location Functions

The most common use of conditional tags is to check which page is being displayed or the type of content being displayed. This means you can output different code depending on the page the user is viewing or the post type displayed, for example. A common example is to only display content such as a banner image on the home page, using the `is_front_page` tag:

```php
<?php
if ( is_front_page() ) { ?>
 <img src="<?php bloginfo( 'stylehseet_directory' ); ?>/images/
   home-page-banner.jpg" alt="front page banner" />
<?php }
?>
```

However, you can do much more by using conditional tags—within the loop, for example.

Conditional Tags in the Loop

You might also use conditional tags in the loop. For example, the loop in the Twenty Eleven theme includes several conditional tags to check for the type of content being displayed and tweak the output accordingly. The theme uses various content includes, calling them using the following function:

```php
<?php get_template_part( 'content', get_post_format() ); ?>
```

This calls the appropriate template file based on the type of content being displayed. The `content.php` is the default file, which includes several conditional tags to output content differently according to the type of content being displayed. It's a large file so we'll break it down into its sections.

First, the header:

```php
<article id="post-<?php the_ID(); ?>" <?php post_class(); ?>>
 <header class="entry-header">
  <?php if ( is_sticky() ) : ?>
   <hgroup>
    <h2 class="entry-title"><a href="<?php the_permalink(); ?>"
    title="<?php printf( esc_attr__( 'Permalink to %s', 'twentyeleven' ),
    the_title_attribute( 'echo=0' ) ); ?>" rel="bookmark"><?php
    the_title(); ?></a></h2>
    <h3 class="entry-format">
     <?php _e( 'Featured', 'twentyeleven' ); ?>
    </h3>
   </hgroup>
  <?php else : ?>
   <h1 class="entry-title">
    <a href="<?php the_permalink(); ?>"
    title="<?php printf( esc_attr__( 'Permalink to %s', 'twentyeleven' ),
    the_title_attribute( 'echo=0' ) ); ?>" rel="bookmark"><?php
    the_title(); ?></a>
   </h1>
  <?php endif; ?>
  <?php if ( 'post' == get_post_type() ) : ?>
   <div class="entry-meta">
    <?php twentyeleven_posted_on(); ?>
```

```
    </div><!-- .entry-meta -->
   <?php endif; ?>
   <?php if ( comments_open() && ! post_password_required() ) : ?>
    <div class="comments-link">
     <?php comments_popup_link( '<span class="leave-reply">' .
     __( 'Reply', 'twentyeleven' ) . '</span>', _x( '1', 'comments
     number', 'twentyeleven' ), _x( '%', 'comments number', 'twentyeleven'
     ) ); ?>
    </div>
   <?php endif; ?>
  </header><!-- .entry-header -->
```

This code uses the following conditional tags:

▮ After opening the `<header>` tag it checks whether a sticky post is being displayed (`if ( is_sticky() )`). If so, it displays the post title in an `<h2>` tag.

▮ If the post isn't sticky (`else`), it displays the post title in an `<h1>` tag, then checks whether the post type is `post`. If so, it displays the metadata with the post date.

▮ Finally, it checks whether comments are enabled for the post and whether the post is password-protected (`if ( comments_open() && ! post_password_required() )`). If so, it displays a link to comments as well as showing the comment count.

Next, the code checks whether a search is being displayed, and if so, only displays the excerpt:

```
<?php if ( is_search() ) : // Only display Excerpts for Search ?>
 <div class="entry-summary">
  <?php the_excerpt(); ?>
 </div><!-- .entry-summary -->
```

If a search isn't being displayed, then it displays the content:

```
<?php else : ?>
 <div class="entry-content">
  <?php the_content( __( 'Continue reading <span class=
  "meta-nav">&rarr;</span>', 'twentyeleven' ) ); ?>
   <?php wp_link_pages( array( 'before' => '<div class=
   "page-link"><span>' . __( 'Pages:', 'twentyeleven' ) . '</span>',
   'after' => '</div>' ) ); ?>
 </div><!-- .entry-content -->
<?php endif; ?>
```

Having displayed the content, it opens a `<footer>`, which uses more conditional tags to display categories:

```
<footer class="entry-meta">
 <?php $show_sep = false; ?>
 <?php if ( 'post' == get_post_type() ) : // Hide category and tag text
   for pages on Search ?>
  <?php
  /* translators: used between list items, there is a space after the
   comma */
```

(continued)

```php
$categories_list = get_the_category_list( __( ', ', 'twentyeleven' ) );
if ( $categories_list ):
?>
<span class="cat-links">
<?php printf( __( '<span class="%1$s">Posted in</span> %2$s',
'twentyeleven' ), 'entry-utility-prep entry-utility-prep-cat-links',
$categories_list );
  $show_sep = true; ?>
</span>
<?php endif; // End if categories ?>
<?php
/* translators: used between list items, there is a space after the
comma */
$tags_list = get_the_tag_list( '', __( ', ', 'twentyeleven' ) );
if ( $tags_list ):
if ( $show_sep ) : ?>
 <span class="sep"> | </span>
  <?php endif; // End if $show_sep ?>
  <span class="tag-links">
   <?php printf( __( '<span class="%1$s">Tagged</span> %2$s',
'twentyeleven' ), 'entry-utility-prep entry-utility-prep-tag-links',
$tags_list );
  $show_sep = true; ?>
  </span>
<?php endif; // End if $tags_list ?>
<?php endif; // End if 'post' == get_post_type() ?>
```

The conditional code used here works as follows:

▪ If the post type is post (if ('post' == get_post_type())), then it runs the code to display the categories and tags; if displaying a page or attachment, it omits this.

▪ It calls the function get_the_category_list() to define the variable $categories_list; and if this isn't empty (if ($categories_list)), then it displays the category list for the post.

▪ It repeats the preceding for the tags list using the variable $tags_list, the function get_the_tag_list(), and the conditional tag if ($tags_list).

▪ It checks if the $show_sep variable is true (set if the category list is not empty), and if so, it displays a separator, providing a break between the category listing and the tags listing.

▪ Finally, it closes the if statement checking for the post type.

The final section of this loop displays comments and shows the edit post link to signed-in users with the appropriate permissions:

```php
<?php if ( comments_open() ) : ?>
 <?php if ( $show_sep ) : ?>
  <span class="sep"> | </span>
  <?php endif; // End if $show_sep ?>
  <span class="comments-link"><?php comments_popup_link( '<span
  class="leave-reply">' . __( 'Leave a reply', 'twentyeleven' ) .
  '</span>', __( '<b>1</b> Reply', 'twentyeleven' ), __( '<b>%</b>
  Replies', 'twentyeleven' ) ); ?></span>
```

```php
<?php endif; // End if comments_open() ?>
<?php edit_post_link( __( 'Edit', 'twentyeleven' ), '<span class=
"edit-link">', '</span>' ); ?>
</footer><!-- #entry-meta -->
</article><!-- #post-<?php the_ID(); ?> -->
```

Working through the code and picking out conditional tags:

- The first check is to determine whether comments are open for that post using `if ( comments_open() )`.

- The `if ( $show_sep )` check is used to determine whether there is any preceding content such as category or tag listings, and to display a separator if so.

- The final `endif` closes the comments being open so that the edit post link can be displayed and the relevant tags closed.

Note that the `edit_post_link()` function is located in `wp-admin/includes/post.php`. and includes its own check to determine whether a user with the correct permissions is logged in, so a conditional tag isn't needed here. For more information about this tag, see `http://codex.wordpress.org/Function_Reference/edit_post`.

This walk-through of one of the loops used by the Twenty Eleven theme gives you an idea of some of the possibilities using conditional tags, especially when combining them with your own functions and variables. What if you don't want to complicate your theme files with a lot of conditional tags? Well, you could always insert them into your functions file instead.

Conditional Tags in functions.php

The preceding section demonstrated some ways you can insert conditional tags into your theme to display conditional content, by placing them in the appropriate template file.

An alternative is to insert them in `functions.php`. This can make things easier if you want to change the theme later—it's much easier to paste content from `functions.php` into your new theme than it is to find and copy all the relevant tags in your template files.

For example, many sites don't need the page title on the home page. You could remove it in a number of ways:

- Using CSS:

  ```css
  .home h2.entry_title {display: none;}
  ```

  This isn't a very good practice, however, as the title is still output; it's just hidden from browsers with CSS turned on.

- Alternatively, you could use a conditional tag in `index.php`:

  ```php
  <?php
  if ( !is_front_page() ) { ?>
   <h2 class="entry-title"><a href="<?php the_permalink(); ?>"><?php
   the_title(); ?></a></h2>
  <?php }
  ?>
  ```

This works well if you're going to stick with the same theme and you have only one header file—but as you'll see in the case study later in this chapter, it might be necessary to have more than one header file.

- Another option is to use a template file for the home page—`front_page.php`—and remove the call for the title from that. You'll look at template files in the next section.

- The fourth option is to add a function to `functions.php`:

```php
<?php
add_filter( 'the_title', 'remove_page_title');
function remove_page_title( $title ) {
 if( is_front_page() ) return '';
    return $title;
} ?>
```

This creates the filter to call the function `remove_page_title` which filters the WordPress function `the_title()` in your template files. It then defines the function, only displaying the title if the user isn't on the home page. If you wanted to hide the title from other pages as the site was developed, you could simply add to the conditions checked using `&&` instead of having to edit multiple template files. In addition, if you were to add multiple header includes, you wouldn't have to add the conditional tag to all of them.

Another example that eliminates the need for multiple template files is to add a function to disable given widgets when a condition is met—for example, to disable the sidebar on the home page:

```php
<?php
add_filter( 'sidebars_widgets', 'disable_sidebar');
function disable_sidebar ( $sidebars_widgets ) {
  if ( is_front_page() )
    $sidebars_widgets['sidebar'] = false;
  return $sidebars_widgets;
  }
?>
```

This creates a filter to use the `disable_sidebar` function to filter the `$sidebars_widgets` function in `wp-includes/widgets.php`. It does this by setting the `$sidebars_widgets parameter` to `FALSE` if the home page is being displayed.

As you can see, there's more than one way to skin this cat! The approach you choose will depend on how widely you need to hide the page or post title (or any other content you're hiding), the complexity of your theme, and whether you anticipate switching to a new theme in the future.

Working with Extra Post Data

In the Twenty Eleven example, you saw how a theme can check for the existence of post metadata such as categories, and output code based on the result. For example:

```php
<?php
  /* translators: used between list items, there is a space after the
  comma */
  $categories_list = get_the_category_list( __( ', ', 'twentyeleven' ) );
  if ( $categories_list ):
  ?>
  <span class="cat-links">
```

```php
<?php printf( __( '<span class="%1$s">Posted in</span> %2$s',
  'twentyeleven' ), 'entry-utility-prep entry-utility-prep-cat-links',
  $categories_list );
    $show_sep = true; ?>
</span>
<?php endif; // End if categories ?>
```

This example simply displays the categories if they exist—it's also used later in the loop to determine whether to display a separator before the tag listing and the comments link.

You can take this further. The majority of WordPress conditional tags relate to the type of content or the page being displayed, but there's no reason why you couldn't write your own function to output something depending on other metadata.

Suppose you wanted to show additional content to logged-in users. The most common way to do this is by creating pages or posts that are restricted by user capability or role; but what if you had content relating to each post that was just for logged-in users, such as discounted prices for loyal customers, for example.

To do this, you could set up a custom field, which would be displayed when the post is viewed by a logged-in user, as shown here:

```php
<?php
if ( is_user_logged_in() ) {
  // assign a variable to the private custom field for current post
  $private_content = get_post_meta($post->ID, 'private', true);
  // check if the custom field has a value
  if($private_content!= '') { ;?>
   <section class="private">
    <?php echo $private_content;?>
   </section>
   <?php }
}
?>
```

The preceding code does the following:

1. It checks whether the site is being viewed by a logged-in user, using `is_user_logged_in()`.

2. If so, it retrieves the meta data for the `'private'` meta key and assigns it to `$private_content`.

3. It confirms that `$private_content` is not empty; and if so, outputs its value inside a `<section>` tag.

The possibilities are limited only by the variables and functions you can pass to PHP and by the requirements of the site.

Theme Files for Conditional Content

When you need to display large amounts of content conditionally, or you want sections of the site or types of content to work very differently, template files will be the best approach. Most themes already use a `page.php` template file at the very least in order to display the loop differently (for example, removing any metadata that might be included in `index.php`); you can harness additional template files to achieve even greater control over what is displayed where.

There are two ways of doing this:

- With template files such as `single.php`, `page-about.php`, `category.php`, etc.
- With includes such as `header-home.php` and `sidebar-category.php`

The second option is useful when the only difference is outside the main content area, as it means you can create an include and use it in more than one template file, reducing the amount of code to maintain. As you'll see, you can do this within the main content area too, with `get_template_part`.

The Template Hierarchy: A Refresher

You looked at the template hierarchy in Chapter 7, but it's worth revisiting here to examine those aspects that are relevant when you want to use conditional content:

- Page templates enable you to display different content on different static pages (for example, if you want to display a sidebar on some pages but not all).

- Templates for specific archive displays, such as category and taxonomy templates, enable you to display different content for different listings—for example, if one post type has metadata you want to display, or you want to display featured images.

- Single post templates, including custom post type templates, enable you to display different content for different post types—for example, if you want to use the loop differently (e.g., displaying different metadata).

- Includes, such as `header.php`, `sidebar.php` and `footer.php`, can be created for different areas of the site, in place of or in addition to a template file, to display different widgets or content in these areas. They are not limited to headers, footers, and sidebars—you can use an include anywhere you want to avoid writing the same piece of code into every template file.

An overview of the template hierarchy is shown in Figure 8-1.

Targeting Different Types of Content

The template hierarchy determines the template files you create to target different types of content.

For static pages:

- `page.php` trumps `index.php` when displaying a static page.

- `page-$slug.php` or `page-$ID.php` trumps `page.php` when a page with the correct slug or ID is being displayed.

- `front_page.php` trumps `index.php` and `page.php` when the home page is viewed, whether that is a static page or a list of posts.

- A custom template page, such as `page-without-sidebar.php`, when selected through the page's admin panel, trumps `page.php`, `home.php`, `page-$slug.php`, and `page-$ID.php`.

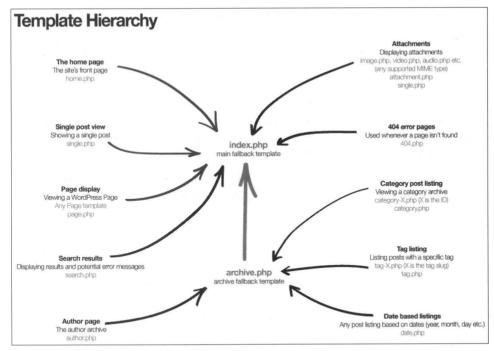

Figure 8-1 The WordPress template hierarchy

For individual posts and attachments:

- `single.php` trumps `index.php` when an individual post or attachment is viewed.

- `single-post.php` trumps `single.php` when a single post is being viewed (as against a single attachment or a single post of a custom post type).

- `single-$posttype.php` trumps `single.php` when displaying a single post of a given custom post type.

- `attachment.php` trumps `single.php` when an attachment is viewed.

- A custom MIME type page (`$mimetype.php`) trumps `attachment.php` when attachments of a given MIME type are viewed. For example, you could use `image.php`, `video.php`, or any accepted MIME type.

For archives:

- `archive.php` trumps `index.php` when a category, tag, date, or author listing is viewed.

- `category.php` trumps `archive.php` when a category listing is viewed. A `category-$slug.php` or `category-$ID` page trumps `category.php` when displaying posts from the relevant category ID or slug.

- `tag.php` trumps `archive.php` when a tag listing is viewed. A `tag-$slug.php` or `tag-$ID.php` file trumps `tag.php`.

- `author.php` trumps `archive.php` when a list of posts by an author is viewed, which in turn is trumped by `author-$ID.php` and `author-$nicename.php`.

- `archive-$posttype.php` trumps `archive.php` when listings for a given post type are being viewed.
- `date.php` trumps `archive.php` when a list of posts for a given date is viewed.

In addition, note the following:

- `search.php` trumps `index.php` when the results from a search are viewed.
- `404.php` trumps everything else when an URL is displayed for which WordPress can find no content. You can use this to display some custom content for 404 pages, such as an error message and search box—or perhaps your own version of the Twitter fail whale!
- `index.php` is essential for the theme to work. No theme will work without an `index.php` file, and WordPress falls back to it when displaying content not accounted for by any of the other templates you've set up.

Include Files

In addition to the template files, WordPress provides several template parts, which are used to specify content that will be part of a template. The most common template parts are `header.php`, `sidebar.php`, and `footer.php`, all of which can have multiple versions, such as `header-home.php`, `sidebar-$posttype.php`, or whatever is needed for your site.

To call the correct template part in a template file, you add its name in brackets:

```
<?php get_header('home'); ?>
```

This would include the `header-home.php` file. You would use this in place of the standard template part in the relevant template file (in this case `home.php`). Alternatively you could use it in a conditional function in `index.php` or another template file, as shown here:

```
<?php
if ( is_home() ) :
 get_header('home');
else :
 get_header();
endif;
?>
```

As demonstrated in the case study at the end of this chapter, you can use this to call one of multiple includes depending on the user's location in the site.

As well as the header, sidebar, and footer includes, WordPress makes use of some other standard includes:

- `get_search_form()` retrieves the `searchform.php` file from your theme—if one doesn't exist, WordPress will generate the search form.
- `comments_template()` retrieves the `comments.php` file from your theme—if there isn't one, it will include `wp-includes/theme-compat/comments.php`.
- `get_template_part` retrieves custom includes, such as `loop.php`, which is covered in more detail next.

Reusing Content with get_template_part

The `get_template_part()` function enables you to display very different content in different areas of the site. You can use it with conditional tags to call different template parts depending on the circumstances; you could include different custom template parts in different template files; or you could use one custom template part but use conditional tags within that to display your content differently depending on what's being displayed.

It's also a great way to minimize the amount of code in your theme. For example, you might have multiple template files because you want to include different sidebars or headers according to post type, or because you have additional markup that's needed for some post types, but you want to run the same version of the loop regardless of post type. Instead of coding the loop into each of your template files, you would code it once, in `loop.php`, and then include it in each of your template files:

```php
<?php get_template_part ('loop'); ?>
```

This would include the file `loop.php`. Note that you can call your template part whatever you want as long as that's reflected in the `get_template_part()` function's parameters—but calling a file with the loop in it `loop.php` is self-explanatory.

You can take this further, creating multiple versions of the loop and including them as needed using the following:

```php
<?php get_template_part( $slug, $name ); ?>
```

The slug is required—in the case of `loop.php`, it's `loop`; but if you wanted to create more than one loop, you would save each as `loop-$name.php`. For example, you could write the following function to include the file `loop-catgeory.php`, which you would use to display category archives:

```php
<?php get_template_part( 'loop', 'category' ); ?>
```

You might have more than one way you want to run the loop for different areas of your site. You could either code all of these into one `loop.php` file (as done in the Twenty Eleven theme), or you could create mutiple template parts for different versions of the loop and use a conditional tag in `index.php` or another template file to include the correct one. For example, in the case of `archive.php` you might have the following:

```php
<?php
if ( is_category() ) :
 get_template_part( 'loop', 'category' );
elseif ( is_tag() ) :
 get_template_part( 'loop', 'tag' );
else get_template_part( 'loop' );
?>
```

This includes `loop-category.php` on a category archive page, `loop-tag.php` on a tag archive page, and `loop.php` on any other archive page.

As you can see, custom template parts can make your life much easier. Nor are they restricted to the loop—in theory, you could use a custom template part for anything you wanted. Just give it an appropriate name that helps you remember what it does, and then include it in your template files as needed. For example, use the following to display data from your theme options in various places in the site, while only writing the code once:

```
<?php get_template_part( 'include', 'options' ); ?>
```

This would include the file `include-options.php`, where you can code everything you need to display the data entered into your theme options screen. Using the slug `include` helps to remind you that the file is indeed an include and not a template file.

Working with Archives: Custom Loops

As demonstrated earlier, the template hierarchy includes a number of alternative template files you can use to display archives. It's when archives are being displayed that you can do some interesting things with the loop to display the content you need in the way that you need it. As you saw with the Twenty Eleven theme, it's possible to display metadata for a post according to what kind of archive listing is being displayed. You can also run multiple loops and run the loop differently depending on what kind of post you're displaying.

Multiple Loops

It's theoretically possible to display as many loops as you need on a page, although it might not always be wise to run many loops, as it means multiple calls to the database.

> **Warning:** Every time you run the loop you are sending a new query to the database. This takes time—sometimes there is a better approach to what you're trying to do than running a lot of loops.

Alternative methods for running more than one loop, or for running a loop in part of the site outside the main loop (e.g., in a sidebar), include the following:

- `query_posts`—This is the simplest method but it isn't recommended, as it overrides the default query that WordPress has already executed against your database, which can cause database load issues, particularly for larger sites. It also breaks pagination. It can sometimes be useful for small sites, though.

- `get_posts`—This is a simple function for creating multiple loops. It uses the `WP_Query` class and needs to have arguments defined for it. It has the advantage over `query_posts` in that it isn't necessary to reset the loop before running it, but it's still not recommended as it doesn't run like a standard WordPress query.

- `WP_Query`—This is the class called by WordPress in the main loop, and the preferred method for defining your own queries. The `have_posts()` call in the loop actually calls `$wp_query->have_posts()`, which is a method call of `WP_Query`. You can use `WP_Query` in many ways, including checking what's being displayed when you're already in the loop.

Another use of multiple loops might be in the main content area if you wanted to display the latest post separately from other posts, or display additional metadata for it. The following code uses `WP_Query` in place of the standard loop:

```php
<?php
$top_post_query = new WP_Query( 'posts_per_page=1' );
while ( $top_post_query->have_posts( )) : $top_post_query->the_post();
$do_not_duplicate = $post->ID; ?>
 <article class="top" id="post-<?php the_ID(); ?>" <?php post_class();
  ?>>
  <h2 class="entry-title"><a href="<?php the_permalink(); ?>"><?php
  the_title(); ?></a></h2>
  <?php the_post_thumbnail('large'); ?>
  <div class="entry-content">
   <?php the_content(); ?>
  </div><!-- .entry-content -->
 </article>
<?php endwhile;
if ( have_posts() ) : while ( have_posts() ) : the_post();
 if( $post->ID==$do_not_duplicate ) continue; ?>
<article class="normal" id="post-<?php the_ID(); ?>" <?php post_class();
  ?>>
  <h2 class="entry-title"><a href="<?php the_permalink(); ?>"><?php
  the_title(); ?></a></h2>
  <div class="entry-content">
   <?php the_content(); ?>
  </div><!-- .entry-content -->
 </article>
<?php endwhile; endif; ?>
```

This runs the loop twice and does the following:

1. It defines a query called `$top-post-query` based on `WP_Query`, with the parameter of `posts_per_page` set at 1.

2. It defines a variable of `$do_not_duplicate` for the post ID of the post output.

3. It runs the loop for that query, outputting the first post.

4. It displays that post in an `<article>` tag, with a class of `.top`, and outputs the post thumbnail between the title and the content in its large size.

5. It stops the first query.

6. It runs the standard loop, checking whether the post ID is the same as the variable `$do_not_duplicate`—that is, whether it's the same as the post that has already been output.

7. It outputs the remaining posts in an `<article>`, with a class of `.normal` and without the featured image.

Different Content, Different Loop

Another thing you can do is vary how the loop is run depending on what type of content is being displayed. In an example shown earlier in the chapter, the Twenty Eleven theme uses the loop to check what type of content is being displayed and then outputs different metadata accordingly—but what if you wanted to run a different query depending on the type of content? For example, suppose that you wanted to display normal posts in descending order, but the "products" post type in alphabetical order.

You could do this in one of four ways:

- Using a separate template file
- With a separate loop include file for each scenario, using `get_template_part` as shown earlier
- Creating a function in `functions.php` that defines how the loop is run for each content type
- Using conditional tags within a single loop

The following example demonstrates the code for separate loops. The default loop would be the standard loop—nothing tricky there. To amend the loop in certain circumstances, you define a function hooked to `pre_get_posts`, a filter hook giving you access to the query. This code would be in the `functions.php` file, while the loop remains the same in all other files:

```php
<?php
function wpptl_archive_order( $query ) {
 if (! is_main_query()|| is_admin())
 return;
 if ( is_post_type_archive( 'product' ) ) {
  $query->set( 'order', ASC );
  return;
 }
}
add_action( 'pre_get_posts', 'wpptl_archive_order' ); ?>
```

This code does the following:

1. It defines a function called `archive_order` based on the `$query` object.
2. If the main query is not being run or the WordPress admin screens are being displayed, nothing is changed.
3. If an archive of posts of the 'products' post type is being displayed, it sets the order of the query to `ASC`, i.e. ascending.
4. It hooks the `wpptl_archive_order` function to the `pre_get_posts` filter to amend the query.

Working with Custom Page Templates

The most basic and commonly used custom template file is for static pages. When you wrote your first WordPress theme, you probably started off with an `index.php` file, maybe divided it into template parts, and added a stylesheet. There's a good chance that in your first basic theme you also added a `page.php` file so you could run the loop differently on static pages—for example, removing metadata.

I won't go into page templates in detail here, as it's a fairly basic topic covered in depth elsewhere, but it's worth noting that you can use a combination of static page templates, template parts, and conditional tags to get custom page templates working for you.

By creating custom page templates (e.g., `page-custom.php`), you can define different markup in different pages, add different classes and IDs for styling, run the loop in different ways, and define which template parts are called. Here are some examples:

- Add additional markup to a custom page template, which may contain static content or content pulled from the database, or elements used just for styling.

- Define custom template parts in custom page templates or remove them. It's common to use a custom page template for full-width pages without a sidebar, for example, which omit the `get_sidebar()` include.

- Run the loop in custom ways—for example, to display metadata on some pages but not others.

- Use the classes generated for custom page templates on the `<body>` tag to style custom page templates in different ways. For example, you would amend the width of the content container in a page template with no sidebar, or you could use different colors, layouts, or fonts for different page templates. I'll cover this in more detail in the next section, "Conditional Styling."

For more on styling the `<body>` tag, see the next section.

> Obviously, your custom page templates will only be applied if site editors or authors select the correct one in the admin screen for each page. If you think users might have problems dong this correctly, you might need to use conditional tags within your default `page.php` file instead, or maybe add styling to target specific pages instead of a page template.

Conditional Styling

WordPress has some great functionality for web designers and developers who want to style different areas of a site or different types of content in a different way. If you're creating a magazine-type site with sections for different topics, or a community site that you want to liven up with the use of color, WordPress is your friend.

As well as making use of all the best semantic HTML5 elements (which you should be doing with your themes these days), WordPress can generate additional classes and IDs that you can use to style your content in whatever way you need. Examples of where these classes and IDs apply include the following:

- The `<body>` tag for any page, post, or archive, which is given one or more classes depending on what type of content is being displayed and what template is being used to display it.

- Classes for targeting post types, added to the `<article>` element within which a post is displayed. This works very similarly to the `<body>` tag.

- The ID of a post being displayed, either in a single post or an archive listing, meaning you can target specific posts and style them in unique ways.

Using and Extending the Body and Post Classes

There are two main areas whose content you can target to add styling: the `<body>` tag on the page, and the ID and class for each post. The first is useful for applying styling to the whole page (or elements within it) in each section of the site, while the second is great for distinguishing different kinds of content, such as within archive listings, for example.

The body_class Tag

To have WordPress automatically generate classes for the `<body>` tag based on a variety of conditions, simply add the following template tag to `<body>` in header.php:

```
<body <?php body_class($class); ?>>
```

This generates a number of classes, related to the following:

- The page type—single, page, search, attachment, archive, or 404, for example
- The page or post ID
- The template file being used
- For archive listings, the category, tag, taxonomy, or post type being displayed
- When users are logged in, the class `.logged-in`
- The parent of the current page if it has one
- The page number, for paginated pages

This just skims the surface of the classes available—for a full list see `http://codex.wordpress.org/Function_Reference/body_class`.

For example, if the user were viewing a page that listed the archive of posts of the "products" post type in the category "sale," the output markup for the `<body>` tag would look something like this:

```
<body class="archive category category-sale">
```

If the home page (a static page in this case) were being displayed using, for example, a `page-without-sidebar.php` page template, the HTML output would be as follows:

```
<body class="home page page-ID page-template page-template-without-sidebar-php">
```

Notice that as well as the class `.page-template-without-sidebar-php`, the class `.page-template` is also generated, as is the case for any page using a custom page template (meaning you can use it to target any page not using `page.php`).

Therefore, let's say that you wanted to style a given page template differently from the others, perhaps with a different color site title. The CSS you would use to achieve this is as follows:

```
h1.site-title, p.site-title {
  color: #333;
}
.page-template-special h1.site-title,
.page-template-special p.site-title {
  color: #b22400;
}
```

That's a very simple example but it gives you an idea of what you can achieve. You could do more with layouts, fonts, pseudo-elements, and any CSS you wanted to play with.

CSS to Target Posts Themselves

In addition to targeting pages of different kinds, you can also use CSS to target individual posts, either by using their post ID or by targeting the kind of post. You do this using two tags: `the_ID` and `post_class`. Within the loop, you assign these to the `<article>` tag:

```
<article id="post-<?php the_ID(); ?>" <?php post_class(); ?>>
```

The first of these is very targeted—`the_ID` adds an ID to the `<article>` equivalent to the post ID. Whatever the kind of content, this will be a unique numeric ID (prefixed by `post-`) that you can use to home in on one specific post and style it uniquely. For example, suppose you are particularly proud of a blog post and want to highlight it separately from all the sticky posts you already have in your blog. Let's say you're already adding some emphasis to sticky posts with the following CSS:

```
.sticky {
  border: 1px solid #b22400;
}
```

I'll show you how the `.sticky` class is generated in just a moment. Alternatively you can style a specific post by using its ID. Imagine that you have one fantastic post (even better than just sticky!) that you want everyone to spot could be styled differently:

```
article#post-43 {
  background: #b2b300;
  border: 2px solid #b22400;
  padding: 5px;
}
```

OK, maybe this wouldn't look too pretty but it would certainly make the post stand out, with a vivid lime green background!

The second available tag is the `post_class` tag, which is a bit more interesting. It works very similarly to the `body_class` tag you've already looked at. It outputs one or more of a smaller range of classes:

- `.post-id`
- `.post`
- `.attachment`
- `.sticky`
- `.hentry` (hAtom microformat pages)
- `.category-ID`
- `.category-name`
- `.tag-name`
- `.format-name`

Therefore, on your site that has the different color site title for the "special" page template, you might also have color-coded categories. You could style the title of any post in the "special" category like so:

```
article.category-special .entry_title a {
  color: #b22400;
}
```

I've touched on the `.sticky` class already; it's a useful one for styling—and the following example demonstrates how you could use a combination of conditional CSS and conditional tags. For example, say you wanted to add some text highlighting sticky posts. You could do this in two ways:

- Using a CSS pseudo-element with the `.sticky` class:

```
.sticky:before {
  content: "Read this post! It's really great.";
}
```

  You'd need to add some extra CSS to style it but you get the drift.

- Alternatively, if you added a check in the loop for sticky posts, you could add content before the post there. You would add the following to the loop, before `<?php the_content();?>`:

```
<?php
if ( is_sticky() ){ ?>
 <h3>Read this post! It's really great.</a></h3>
<?php }
?>
```

  You could then either keep the default `<h3>` styling for your alert or use `.sticky h3`. This has the advantage of both using existing classes and working in legacy browsers, unlike the pseudo-element approach.

Menus and Widget Core CSS

When registering menus and widgets, you code these in a way that tells WordPress to generate classes and IDs for these. You can then use these to style menu items, widget areas and widgets within them conditionally.

Menus

Beginning with version 3.0, WordPress incorporates menu functionality that uses the WordPress admin to create menus, displaying them using the function `wp_nav_menu`:

```
<?php wp_nav_menu( $args ); ?>
```

You can pass a number of arguments to this function, including the menu to be displayed, the container class and menu class, and more.

When outputting the menu using this function, WordPress adds classes to each item within it. The list of potential classes is long (and listed at `http://codex.wordpress.org/Function_Reference/wp_nav_menu#Menu_Item_CSS_Classes`), but some of the more useful ones for conditional styling include the following:

- `.menu-item-object-category`
- `.menu-item-object-page`
- `.current-menu-item`
- `.current-menu-parent`
- `.current-menu-ancestor`
- `.menu-item-home`

The most common use of these is to highlight the current page in the menu or to highlight its parent or ancestors, as shown in the following example:

```
.menu li.current-menu-item,
.menu li.current-menu-parent {
  text-decoration: underline;
}
```

You could also use it, however, to add an icon next to the home page in the menu:

```
.menu li.menu-item-home {
  padding-left: 20px;
  background: url([icon location]);
}
```

Or, returning to the example of the magazine site, you could use it to style static pages differently from your posts:

```
.menu li.menu-item-object-page {
  color: #000;
}
```

Unfortunately, the number of classes generated isn't as great as that for `body_class` or `post_class`, so you can't target listings from specific categories, for example, but because most menus don't list individual posts, you wouldn't want to—you might be more likely to do this if you were listing recent posts in a widget, using `get_posts` and `post_class`.

Widgets

The way widgets work is a little different. Instead of WordPress automatically generating a host of CSS classes and IDs for you to work with, you have to specify them when registering widget areas. Individual widgets and widget areas have their own IDs and classes, which are created based on the way you code the `register_sidebar()` function, which creates widget areas.

Here's the code for registering a widget area. This example creates a sidebar called "Before Header Widget Area," designed to display anything that needs to appear above the site's header:

```php
<?php
 register_sidebar( array(
  'name' => __( 'Before Header Widget Area' ),
  'id' => 'before-header-widget-area',
  'description' => __( 'The header widget area - widgets placed here
   appear above your header' ),
  'before_widget' => '<div id="%1$s" class="widget-container %2$s">',
  'after_widget' => '</div>',
  'before_title' => '<h3 class="widget-title">',
  'after_title' => '</h3>',
 ) ); ?>
```

The arguments you use when registering your sidebar are important and are as follows:

- `name`—The name displayed in the Widgets admin screen

- `id`—The sidebar's ID, which generates the `#before-header-widget-area` ID in this case, which you can then target using CSS. You also use this ID to call the sidebar from your template files.

- `description`—This appears in the Widgets admin screen and is particularly useful if you'll be releasing your widgets to the public or have other developers creating the widgets.

- `before-widget`—The wrapper code generated before each widget in your widget area. The preceding code generates a `<div>` with a unique ID based on the name of the widget and the instance of its use (if you use it twice, you get two unique IDs, each with a number at the end—1 the first time you use it, 2 the second time you use it, and so on). It also generates a class in the same way.

- `after-widget`—The closing `</div>` tag

- `before-title`—The HTML to output before the widget title, in this case an `<h3>` tag with the class `.widget-title`.

- `after-title`—The closing `<h3>` tag

If you don't specify the `before-widget` and `after-widget` arguments, WordPress will automatically add a `<li>` around each widget. This can be a pain when styling, as you need to remove any default list styling from around your widgets.

The widget created by the previous code is shown in the Widgets admin screen in figure 8-2.

Figure 8-2 The widget area in the Widgets admin screen

Conditional Content in Action: Case Study

Now you'll take a look at an example which uses the template hierarchy to style different areas of a site in different ways and include different content. In an earlier incarnation of the site for my agency, Compass Design, I built the site with three separate areas to reflect the three main areas I was targeting at the time: Design, Mobile, and Social. This new site design replaced three separately existing sites, enabling the blog posts from all three parts of the business to be listed together. Figure 8-3 shows the home page of the site, and Figures 8-4 through 8-6 show the three incorporated sites. Note that each section retains its own branding and sidebar content.

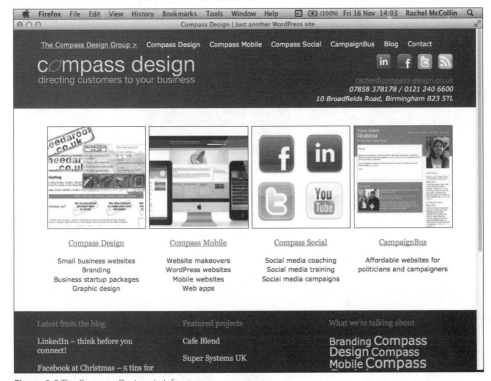

Figure 8-3 The Compass Design site's front page

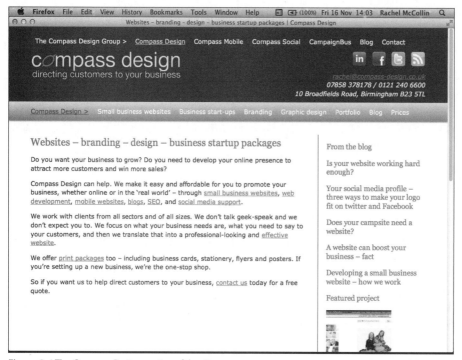

Figure 8-4 The Compass Design section of the site

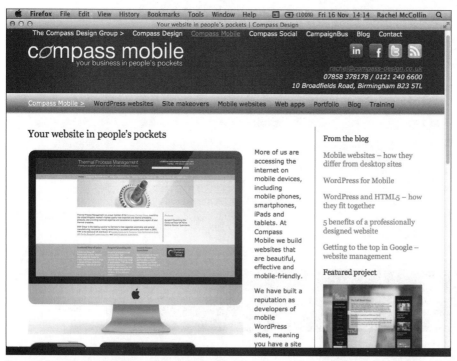

Figure 8-5 The Compass Mobile section of the site

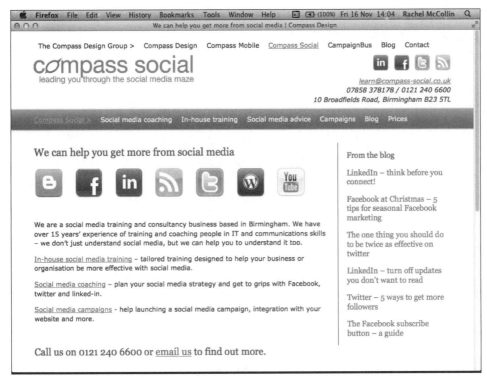

Figure 8-6 The Compass Social section of the site

This site used a combination of conditional tags, template files, and targeted CSS, so I will use it to illustrate the three different methods covered in this chapter. I've added a copy of this site at `http://wp-ptl.rachelmccollin.co.uk/conditional-content` so you can see how it works. The theme used for the site included several template files, as shown in Figure 8-7.

The theme works as follows:

- It uses one version of `page.php` and `single.php`, with conditional tags used where relevant to call the necessary include. Static pages all have the default includes, whereas single posts and archives have section-specific includes.

- It uses a different version of the header and sidebar includes (`header.php` and `sidebar.php` for each area of the site) with different content.

- It targets the body classes generated by WordPress to style the different areas of the site appropriately.

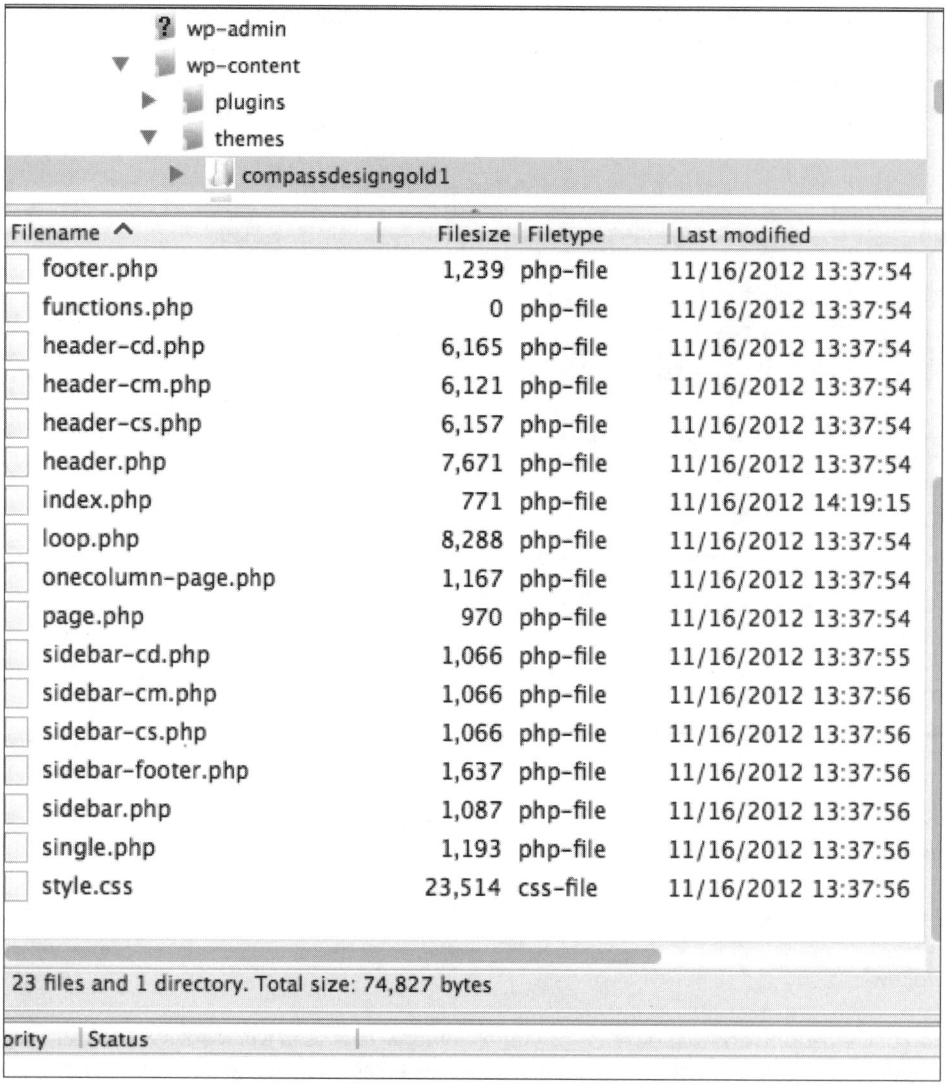
wp-admin
wp-content
plugins
themes
compassdesigngold1
Filename
Filesize
Filetype
Last modified
footer.php 1,239 php-file 11/16/2012 13:37:54
functions.php 0 php-file 11/16/2012 13:37:54
header-cd.php 6,165 php-file 11/16/2012 13:37:54
header-cm.php 6,121 php-file 11/16/2012 13:37:54
header-cs.php 6,157 php-file 11/16/2012 13:37:54
header.php 7,671 php-file 11/16/2012 13:37:54
index.php 771 php-file 11/16/2012 14:19:15
loop.php 8,288 php-file 11/16/2012 13:37:54
onecolumn-page.php 1,167 php-file 11/16/2012 13:37:54
page.php 970 php-file 11/16/2012 13:37:54
sidebar-cd.php 1,066 php-file 11/16/2012 13:37:55
sidebar-cm.php 1,066 php-file 11/16/2012 13:37:56
sidebar-cs.php 1,066 php-file 11/16/2012 13:37:56
sidebar-footer.php 1,637 php-file 11/16/2012 13:37:56
sidebar.php 1,087 php-file 11/16/2012 13:37:56
single.php 1,193 php-file 11/16/2012 13:37:56
style.css 23,514 css-file 11/16/2012 13:37:56
23 files and 1 directory. Total size: 74,827 bytes
ority
Status

Figure 8-7 Template files used in the example website

The Header: Conditional Content and Styling

Now you look at the site header.

Single Posts

The include code for the header used in `single.php` is as follows:

```
<?php
if ( in_category( '49' ) ) {
  get_header( 'cd' );
 } elseif ( in_category( '51' ) ) {
  get_header( 'cm' );
```

```
 } elseif ( in_category( '50' ) ) {
  get_header( 'cs' );
 } else { get_header(); }
}
?>
```

This code identifies whether the post is in a given category (relating to the sections of the site) and calls the relevant include—if it isn't in any of the relevant categories, the `else` statement calls the default header. The different headers are similar except for the site name and description, logo, and contact details displayed. For example, the function `get_header( 'cm' )` calls the template part `header-cm.php`. By naming your header, sidebar, and footer files in this way, WordPress will look for the file with the contents of the brackets appended to its filename.

Static Pages and Archives

The default header used by static pages and archive listings (`header.php`) uses conditional tags to display the correct logo and link it to the home page for that section of the site. The following code demonstrates the conditional tags used—the image sources and `<alt>` tags have been edited for brevity:

```
<!--get correct logo based on category-->
<?php if ( in_category( '49' ) ) { ?>
 <a href="<?php bloginfo( 'url');?>/compass-design/" title="home" >
 <img src="/compass-design-logo-web.png"  alt="" /></a>
<?php } elseif ( in_category( '51' )) { ?>
 <a href="<?php bloginfo( 'url');?>/compass-mobile/" title="home" >
 <img src="/compass-mobile-white.png"  alt="" /></a>
<?php } elseif ( in_category( '50' )) { ?>
 <a href="<?php bloginfo( 'url' );?>/compass-social/" title="home" >
 <img src=" /compass-social-logo-web.png"  alt="" /></a>
<?php } else { ?>
 <a href="<?php bloginfo( 'url');?>" title="home" ><img src="/
 compass-design-logo-web.png"  alt="" /></a>
<?php }
?>
```

Navigation: Same Content, Different Styling

The navigation bar's content is the same across the site but it's styled differently according to what's being displayed, using CSS targeting the body classes generated by the `body_class` function. The two classes targeted are `.page-template-name` and `.category-name`. This means that the styling is applied when a given page template is being used or when a post of a given category is being displayed. The code (with extra browser-targeted gradient styling removed for brevity) is as follows:

```
.category-compass-social .nav-strip {
 background: linear-gradient(top, #e48ed6 0%,#cc0099 100%);
}
.category-compass-design .nav-strip {
 background: linear-gradient(top, #aaffff 0%,#12acac 100%);
}
.category-compass-mobile .nav-strip {
 background: linear-gradient(top, #ffffff 0%,#666666 100%);
}
```

(continued)

```css
#access a,
.category-compass-social #access a,
.category-compass-design-php #access a {
 color: #fff;
}
.category-compass-mobile #access a {
 color: #000;
}
.category-compass-social #access li:hover > a,
.category-compass-social #access ul ul :hover > a,
.category-compass-social #access ul li.current_page_item > a,
.category-compass-social #access ul li.current-menu-ancestor > a,
.category-compass-social #access ul li.current-menu-item > a,
.category-compass-social #access ul li.current-menu-parent > a {
 color: #e48ed6;
 text-decoration: underline;
}
.category-compass-design #access li:hover > a,
.category-compass-design #access ul ul :hover > a,
.category-compass-design #access ul li.current_page_item > a,
.category-compass-design #access ul li.current-menu-ancestor > a,
.category-compass-design #access ul li.current-menu-item > a,
.category-compass-design #access ul li.current-menu-parent > a {
 color: #366;
 text-decoration: underline;
}
.category-compass-mobile #access li:hover > a,
.category-compass-mobile #access ul ul :hover > a,
.category-compass-mobile #access ul li.current_page_item > a,
.category-compass-mobile #access ul li.current-menu-ancestor > a,
.category-compass-mobile #access ul li.current-menu-item > a,
.category-compass-mobile #access ul li.current-menu-parent > a {
 color: #fff;
 text-decoration: underline;
}
```

The Sidebar

In this site, the sidebar works in the same way as the header. Therefore, on static pages and archive listings, the default sidebar is displayed; but on single post listings, a conditional tag includes the correct sidebar:

```php
<?php if ( in_category( '49' ) ) {
  get_sidebar( 'cd' );
  } elseif ( in_category( '51' )) {
  get_sidebar( 'cm' );
  } elseif ( in_category( '50' )) {
  get_sidebar( 'cs' );
  } else { get_sidebar();
}
?>
```

Each sidebar includes two widget areas—one that is site-wide and one that is location-specific, as shown in the following code for `sidebar-cd.php`:

```php
<?php
//Primary sidebar for widgets.
if ( is_active_sidebar( 'primary-widget-area' ) ) : ?>
 <aside id="primary" class="widget-area" role="complementary">
  <?php dynamic_sidebar( 'primary-widget-area' ); ?>
 </aside><!-- #primary .widget-area -->
<?php endif; ?>
<?php
// A second sidebar for section-dependant widgets.
if ( is_active_sidebar( 'cd-widget-area' ) ) : ?>
 <aside id="cd" class="widget-area" role="complementary">
  <?php dynamic_sidebar( 'cd-widget-area' ); ?>
 </aside><!-- #secondary .widget-area -->
<?php endif; ?>
```

An alternative way of doing this would be to replace the different include files with some conditional code in `sidebar.php`, as follows:

```php
<?php
//Primary sidebar for widgets
if ( is_active_sidebar( 'primary-widget-area' ) ) : ?>
 <aside id="primary" class="widget-area" role="complementary">
  <?php dynamic_sidebar( 'primary-widget-area' ); ?>
 </aside><!-- #primary .widget-area -->
<?php endif; ?>
<?php
// A second sidebar for section-dependant widgets.
// cd sidebar
if ( in_category( '49' ) && is_active_sidebar( 'cd-widget-area' )) : ?>
 <aside id="cd" class="widget-area" role="complementary">
  <?php dynamic_sidebar( 'cd-widget-area' ); ?>
 </aside><!-- #secondary #cd .widget-area -->
// cm sidebar
<?php elseif ( in_category( '52' ) && is_active_sidebar( 'cm-widget-area'
  )) : ?>
 <aside id="cm" class="widget-area" role="complementary">
  <?php dynamic_sidebar( 'cm-widget-area' ); ?>
 </aside><!-- #secondary #cm .widget-area -->
// cs sidebar
<?php elseif ( in_category( '51' ) && is_active_sidebar( 'cs-widget-area'
  )) : ?>
 <aside id="cs" class="widget-area" role="complementary">
  <?php dynamic_sidebar( 'cs-widget-area' ); ?>
 </aside><!-- #secondary #cs .widget-area -->
<?php endif; ?>
```

As mentioned earlier, the approach you take depends on whether you are more comfortable maintaining multiple template files or includes, or one file with more code. It also depends on how you anticipate the site or theme changing in the future.

> When deciding on the best way to display conditional content, always ask yourself, "How is this site or theme likely to change in the future? Will that affect the conditional content needed and the best way to display it?"

Taking Styling Further

This site has several static pages that all have the default styling. However, you might be working on a similar site with static pages that need different styling and header content. You could achieve this in one of two ways:

- By using a conditional tag to call the relevant includes in `page.php`, as demonstrated here for `single.php`

- By creating template files for each area of the site to display the correct header and sidebar; and, if necessary, to display the content differently in the main content area, perhaps by adding some text to the page title or by including different widget areas in the content area as well as the sidebar. The template files and their header includes for this site would be as follows:

  - `page-compass-social.php`: `<?php get_header( 'cs' ); ?>`

  - `page-compass-mobile.php`: `<?php get_header( 'cm' ); ?>`

  - `page-compass-design.php`: `<?php get_header( 'cd' ); ?>`

  - `page.php`: `<?php get_header(); ?>`

  This has the advantage of providing more control, but the disadvantage of creating more template files to manage.

In addition, you could run the loop differently in different template files, or create multiple versions of the loop using `loop.php` with conditional tags within it or alternative loops for different parts of the site using multiple loop files as shown earlier in the chapter.

Of course, this just scratches the surface of how template files can display different content in each part of the site—you could do more with archive template files and/or post type and taxonomy template files.

Summary

As demonstrated in this chapter, you can take three different approaches to displaying and styling conditional content in WordPress: using conditional tags, template files, and targeted CSS. Each of these approaches provides a variety of techniques you can use to achieve your objectives—for example, in your template files you can use includes for conditional content or simply use multiple template files.

The possibilities using these approaches, especially when combined with your own functions, are virtually endless. The biggest challenge is probably deciding which approach is best for you and your project, as once you have begun it's a lot of work to backtrack and adopt a different approach. When deciding on which approach is best for your site or theme, consider the following:

- How is the site or theme likely to evolve in the future? How would the potential approach keep up with that?

- What are the preferred working methods of your team? A team accustomed to managing multiple template files but unfamiliar with conditional tags may not appreciate having to work with a single `index.php` file crammed full of conditional code, to give an extreme example!

- Is your approach consistent? Try to use the same approach throughout your site, finding the one that works best across all the instances where you need to display conditional content.

- Are you releasing your code to the public? If your theme will be used by other WordPress users, it makes sense to keep your code as simple as possible. Avoid long, complicated conditional tags that check for multiple conditions, or multiple layers of includes, for example.

Whatever approach you adopt, ensure that everyone working on the project understands why and how you're using the approach you've chosen, and don't forget to comment your code liberally.

Further Resources

Conditional Tags

WordPress conditional tags: an explanation and list of the tags available
`http://codex.wordpress.org/Conditional_Tags`

PHP conditional statements: syntax and examples
`http://php.net/manual/en/control-structures.if.php`

Justin Tadlock on disabling widgets from functions.php
`http://justintadlock.com/archives/2009/03/06/disable-widget-areas-without-touching-theme-templates`

Template Files and Includes

The WordPress template hierarchy
`http://codex.wordpress.org/Template_Hierarchy`

Include tags
`http://codex.wordpress.org/Include_Tags`

The WordPress loop
`http://codex.wordpress.org/The_Loop`

The query_posts function
`http://codex.wordpress.org/Function_Reference/query_posts`

The WP_Query class
http://codex.wordpress.org/Class_Reference/WP_Query

The get_posts tag
http://codex.wordpress.org/Function_Reference/get_posts

The pre_get_posts hook
http://codex.wordpress.org/Plugin_API/Action_Reference/pre_get_posts

Conditional Styling

The body_class template tag
http://codex.wordpress.org/Function_Reference/body_class

The page or post ID template tag
http://codex.wordpress.org/Function_Reference/the_ID

The wp_nav_menu function
http://codex.wordpress.org/Function_Reference/wp_nav_menu

The register_sidebar function
http://codex.wordpress.org/Function_Reference/register_sidebar

Justin Tadlock on registering widget areas correctly
http://justintadlock.com/archives/2010/11/08/sidebars-in-wordpress

Chapter 9

Custom Functionality in Theme Functions and Plugins

WordPress is designed to be added to. A vanilla WordPress installation gives you a great deal you can use to build a website, such as the ability to add pages with a hierarchical structure, posts, category and tag archives, menus, widgets, and more. But if you want to take it further (for example, by adding your own custom post types or taxonomies or linking to external APIs such as Google and Twitter), you'll need to include additional functionality. Most sites you build will likely need functionality that isn't included in the core WordPress installation. There are three ways you could do this:

- Use an off-the-shelf plugin, either by downloading a free one from the WordPress plugins repository at `http://wordpress.org/extend/plugins/` or by buying a premium one. You can use any plugins you download as is, or you can edit them to meet the needs of your project. But if you do edit a third-party plugin, you won't be able to take advantage of automatic updates for that plugin.

- Write your own plugin.

- Add functionality via the theme's `functions.php` file.

This chapter assumes that you need to code your own functionality, so you will be using the functions file or your own plugin. The method you choose doesn't affect the result—it's largely the same code, after all; but it does affect the maintainability and flexibility of any site you build, or the scope of a theme or theme framework you're developing.

The first part of this chapter describes when you might choose to write a plugin versus using the functions file, and then you'll walk through both scenarios, looking at each approach by way of some examples.

Theme Functions vs. Plugins

One of the themes of this book is that WordPress always provides more than one way to crack an egg. That is, there are multiple approaches to most aspects of WordPress development, each of which has its place. In this case, when adding functionality to a site you have a choice—functions file or plugin? This section looks at the rationale for using each.

The code you add to a plugin or to your functions file might be identical and achieve the same result in the site you're building, but the longer term implications will be different. The best use of each approach can be summarized as follows:

- Use the theme functions file when the functionality you are adding is specific to the theme, not the site. Therefore, if you're adding a theme options screen that amends the layout of a theme, or you're building functionality into a theme framework, use the functions file.

- Use a plugin when the functionality you're adding will still be needed if the site changes themes, or when you want to add the same functionality to more than one site. Therefore, if you're manipulating data in any way, or adding content that will be output by WordPress regardless of the theme being used, use a plugin.

Following are some examples that generally hold true (but not always, I'm afraid!):

- If you're registering custom post types, use a plugin.

- If you're registering menus or widget areas, use the functions file (because you'll need to add them to the template files of your theme as well).

- To build widgets for populating your widget areas, use a plugin (you don't want to lose these if the theme is changed).

- To add a shortcode, use a plugin.

- To add a form, use a plugin.

- To add theme layout and styling options, use the functions file.

- To give users the option of adding data to be displayed on the site (such as a contact number and e-mail address), use a plugin.

Sometimes the best approach is dictated by what you're trying to achieve:

- If you're building a theme framework, use the functions file, or additional files in the theme.

- If you're building themes for release to the public, use the functions file.

- If you're building plugins for release to the public, obviously you'll have to use a plugin.

Building your own framework or parent theme can be a good way to add functionality—you can add bespoke functionality to the parent theme's functions file and that functionality will then be available to all projects using a child theme. For more details about this, see Chapter 7.

> You may be wary of creating a lot of small plugins, having heard that plugins can cause performance issues. It's a misconception. Well-written plugins don't add any more code than if you were adding similar functionality via your functions file, and shouldn't slow your site down. Matt Mullenweg's personal site at `http://ma.tt` runs dozens of small plugins, and it ran pretty smoothly the last time I checked. In this chapter you'll learn how to code plugins that run like a dream.

Working with the Theme Functions File

When you are adding theme-specific functionality, you'll need to work with the theme functions file, and possibly with additional files that you call from it.

The theme functions file sits in the theme's root directory and is always named `functions.php`. A theme doesn't need a functions file to work—you may not need additional functions for a theme, or you may have added them all via plugins. However, if you're going to add theme-specific functionality, this is where you do it.

Uses for the Functions File

Common functionality you would add via the functions file includes the following:

- Adding theme support for WordPress features such as the Theme Customizer, post thumbnails, post formats, and navigation menus, using the `add_theme_support()` function
- Registering widget areas and menus using `register_sidebar()` and `register_menu()` (or `register_sidebars()` and `register_menus()`)
- Hooking into WordPress actions and filters (or your own) to make use of them in your theme
- Adding actions that aren't related to specific locations in your template files, such as actions when the theme launches
- Adding a theme options page or parameters for the Theme Customizer
- Defining your own functions to add extra functionality to your theme

For a simple theme, you would add all of your functions in the one file, using commenting to identify what each chunk of code does. For a more complex theme, or situations in which you want to be able to separate code that performs different tasks, you can add include files for those functions and call them from your main functions file—I'll cover this shortly.

Coding a Robust Functions File

Adding functionality to the functions file seems easy enough—you simply drag and drop whatever you can find in there, right? Well, not quite. In order for your functions file to run smoothly and not give you any headaches, you need to approach it with the same care and attention you would bring to writing a plugin:

- Every piece of functionality you add to the functions file should be wrapped in a function and then actioned by attaching it to an action or filter hook. It's important to understand how the hook you're accessing works and why you're using it.
- Your function names should be prefixed in order to avoid conflict with WordPress core functions or plugins you've downloaded. For a theme functions file, it's a good idea to use the theme name as the prefix—for example, all the functions in my compass framework theme's functions file begin with `compass_`. *Never* use `wp_` as a prefix, and don't use those used by any third-party themes on your site.
- Each function should perform just one operation and do that simply, with as little code as possible. Use comments for the benefit of other developers and for yourself when you revisit the code in the future. You can always write more than one function, using `add_action()` or `add_filter()` more than once.

■ Ensure that your functions file is tidy. Code functions in the order in which they fire, and group together those functions that are run together or do similar things. For example, at the beginning of your functions file, add all the theme setup functions attached to the `after_setup_theme()` hook, such as adding theme support for thumbnails, feeds, and so on. Then register any sidebars, menus, and so on. After doing all that, add any other functions that are more specific to the theme, but in a logical order.

■ The functions file must begin with `<?php` and end with `?>`, with nothing outside these tags. If you add anything, even white space, the file won't work—PHP isn't as forgiving as HTML, unfortunately.

Be sure you understand any functions you're adding to your functions file so you can work with them and ensure that they are doing what's needed for your theme. If you are working with code you've found elsewhere (such as in the WordPress codex), take the time to pick the code apart, edit it if necessary, and ensure that it works as needed.

Adding Include Files for Functions

If your functions file is becoming unwieldy, or you want to separate out functions that do different things, you can add them all to different files. You then call each of these files from your main `functions.php` file using an include, in much the same way you call template includes in your template files or additional stylesheets in your main `style.css` file.

For example, suppose you have created a functions file that registers menus and widget areas for your theme. You want to use this file in exactly the same way in other themes, but you can't use a plugin because you'll be releasing this theme to the public. To do this, follow these steps:

1. Create a file to contain the widgets and sidebars functions. Call it `wpptl-sidebars-menus.php`.

2. Save this file either in the theme's directory or in a subdirectory. Using a subdirectory makes sense if you're adding more than one include file in this way. In this case, create a directory called `/includes`.

3. Add your functionality to the new file. This file must be set up in the same way as the main functions file and use all the same best practice tips listed earlier. If you will be using this file again in different themes, you may choose to use a different prefix, or you may edit it each time you copy it into a new theme. If you're adding includes to a theme for release to the public, use the same prefix throughout.

4. Call the include file from the main functions file using the following code:

   ```php
   <?php include( get_template_directory() . '/function-filename.php' ); ?>
   ```

5. `get_template_directory()` fetches the full path to the current theme's main directory, so in this case the code would be as follows:

   ```php
   <?php include( get_template_directory() . '/includes/wpptl-sidebars-menus.php' ); ?>
   ```

This then includes the `wpptl-sidebars-menus.php` file at the point in the functions file where it is called—so functions called in the included file will be run before any functions called after them in the main functions file. For this reason, it's important to be careful about where you add your includes. It's also important to check the functions in your includes when you're adding functions to the main `functions.php`, to avoid any conflicts or duplication.

Functions Files and Child Themes

If you're building child themes, either for your own parent themes or framework or for a third-party framework, you should understand how the functions files in the two themes interact. Sometimes you may need to override functionality from the parent theme in your child theme, for example if you want to remove comments functionality, change the way pagination works or alter the page title display. This means that understanding how to override parent theme functions is important to ensure that you get it right.

Order in Which Functions Are Run

The child theme's functions file is loaded immediately before the parent theme's functions file. This means that all functions in your child theme will run first, followed by all the functions in the parent theme. This is different from the way in which parent and child theme stylesheets work—generally, you call the parent theme's stylesheet using an @include tag at the beginning of the child theme's stylesheet, meaning the parent theme's styles are loaded first and can therefore be overridden by the child theme's styles.

So if you write a function in your child theme intended to replace functionality in the parent theme, it won't work, as the function in the parent theme will be defined after your function in the child theme. This doesn't mean you can't override parent theme functionality, you just need to know how to do it.

There are three main ways to override functions in the parent theme:

- Code the parent theme in a way that makes it pluggable, so functions can be overridden in the child theme. Obviously, this if possible only if you're building your own parent theme.

- Remove the action or filter that executes the function from the relevant hook. You would do this if you wanted to remove the function altogether and not replace it.

- Add a new action or filter with a higher priority than the one in the parent theme.

> If you want to remove a function from a parent theme, *don't* just delete it or comment it out. Parent themes are not for touching!

Coding Pluggable Parent Themes

To allow child themes to override functions in your parent theme, you code the functions in a way that makes them pluggable, using a conditional function to determine whether they are already defined:

```php
<?php
if ( ! function_exists( 'wpptl_pluggable_function' ) ) {
 function wpptl_pluggable_function() {
 // code for your pluggable function
 }
}
?>
```

Because the parent theme's functions file is loaded after the child theme's functions file, this checks whether the function has already been defined. If so (i.e., it is defined in the child theme), it doesn't get defined it. If the child theme doesn't include a function with this name, it defines the function as normal. Coding all your parent theme functions in this way is time-consuming but if you anticipate needing to override some of them on a frequent basis, you can make them pluggable and then code a new version in your child themes.

Some functions provided by the WordPress core are pluggable. **For a list, see** `http://codex.wordpress.org/Pluggable_Functions`. **New functions added in future won't be pluggable; they'll make use of filters instead.**

Removing a Parent Theme Function from the Relevant Hook

If you're working with a preexisting parent theme whose functions aren't pluggable, you need to find another way to remove the functionality. This can be done using the `remove_action()` or `remove_filter()` functions. You need to know the action or filter hook to which the function is attached in the parent theme, plus the specifics of how it's coded.

Using an Action Hook

To remove a parent theme function that is attached to an action hook, you use the `remove_action()` function. For example, suppose you are building a child theme using Twenty Twelve as its parent. One of the functions in Twenty Twelve is `twenty_twelve_content_width()`, which specifies the width of the content area of the layout in certain circumstances:

```php
<?php
function twentytwelve_content_width() {
  if ( is_page_template( 'page-templates/full-width.php' ) ||
  is_attachment() || ! is_active_sidebar( 'sidebar-1' ) ) {
   global $content_width;
   $content_width = 960;
  }
}
add_action( 'template_redirect', 'twentytwelve_content_width' );
?>
```

To remove this functionality in your child theme so you can use CSS to set the width of this area instead, you would use the following:

```php
<?php
function wpptl_remove_content_width() {
  remove_action( 'template_redirect', 'twentytwelve_content_width' );
}
add_action( 'after_setup_theme', 'wpptl_remove_content_width' );
?>
```

Note the use of two hooks here:

- `template_redirect`—The action hook from which you want to remove the `twentytwelve_content_width()` function

- `after_setup_theme`—A WordPress action hook that fires when the current theme is activated, which you use to attach to your `wpptl_remove_content_width()` function in your child theme

Four things are happening here, in the following order:

1. The child theme uses `add_action()` to attach the `wpptl_remove_content_width()` function to the `after_setup_theme` action hook.

2. Twenty twelve (the parent theme) uses `add_action()` to attach the `twentytwelve_content_width()` function to the `template_redirect` action hook.

3. WordPress calls `do_action()` to run these two action hooks.

4. Finally, the child theme uses `remove_action()` to remove the `twentytwelve_content_width()` function from the `template_redirect` action hook, which overrides that functionality.

Using a Filter Hook

Filter hooks can also be used to change content from a parent theme. Instead of `remove_action()`, you use `remove_filter()` to remove the filter specified in the parent theme. For example, suppose you were developing a child theme with Twenty Twelve as the parent and you wanted to override its `twentytwelve_wp_title()` function, which is attached to the `wp_title()` filter.

The function in Twenty Twelve amends the output of `wp_title()` as follows:

```php
<?php
function twentytwelve_wp_title( $title, $sep ) {
 global $paged, $page;
 if ( is_feed() )
  return $title;
 // Add the site name.
 $title .= get_bloginfo( 'name' );
 // Add the site description for the home/front page.
 $site_description = get_bloginfo( 'description', 'display' );
 if ( $site_description && ( is_home() || is_front_page() ) )
  $title = "$title $sep $site_description";
 // Add a page number if necessary.
 if ( $paged >= 2 || $page >= 2 )
  $title = "$title $sep " . sprintf( __( 'Page %s', 'twentytwelve' ),
  max( $paged, $page ) );
 return $title;
}
add_filter( 'wp_title', 'twentytwelve_wp_title', 10, 2 );
?>
```

Action Hooks and Filter Hooks: A Refresher

Action hooks (sometimes referred to as hooks) make something happen—an action. When you add an action hook to a parent theme or framework, you don't specify what it will contain—this is coded separately in a function which you attach to that action hook.

Filter hooks (sometimes referred to as filters) change the way data is output. When adding a filter hook to a parent theme or framework, you specify the data that will run through that filter, and then attach a function to the same filter hook in the child theme to override or alter it.

For more information about action hooks and filter hooks, see Chapter 7 and the "Building Functionality into a Plugin" section later in this chapter.

This uses the parameter `$title` to specify what the title tag will be in different scenarios, using conditional statements to identify where in the site the user is located. However, suppose you want to fall back to the standard `wp_title()` filter—you would do that by removing the `twenty_twelve_wp_title()` function from that filter in your child theme's functions file as follows:

```php
<?php
function wpptl_restore_wp_title() {
 remove_filter('wp_title', 'twentytwelve_wp_title', 10, 2 );
}
add_action( 'after_setup_theme', 'wpptl_restore_wp_title' );
?>
```

This simply removes the function in the parent theme, returning `wp_title()` to its default. Note that you must include the priority and `accepted_args` parameters in the `remove_filter()` function (in the preceding example, `10` and `2` respectively)—if you simply name the filter and the function without including those too, the filter isn't removed.

Using Priorities to Override Functions

If your child theme has a function attached to a hook and you want it to be defined or run after a similar function in the parent theme attached to the same hook, another way to do that is to simply code it into your child theme's functions file and give it a higher priority than that in the parent theme's file. You can use this to effectively override the function in the parent theme.

Returning to the earlier examples using Twenty Twelve, let's revisit the one that removed the filter for content width in your child theme. Recall that it removed the following action from Twenty Twelve:

```php
<?php
function twentytwelve_content_width() {
 if ( is_page_template( 'page-templates/full-width.php' ) || is_
attachment() || ! is_active_sidebar( 'sidebar-1' ) ) {
  global $content_width;
  $content_width = 960;
 }
```

```
}
add_action( 'template_redirect', 'twentytwelve_content_width' );
?>
```

In your child theme, you used `remove_action()` to prevent this function from executing. If you wanted to add your own function to provide alternative functionality, you could use `remove_action()` and then code your own afterward, but a quicker and more efficient solution is to add your new function and give it a higher priority than the one from the parent theme when attaching it to the action hook. The default priority for any action or filter is `10`, so assigning `11` to your new action ensures that it will fire after the one on the parent theme:

```
<?php
function wppt1_content_width() {
  if ( is_page_template( 'page-templates/full-width.php' ) ||
   is_attachment() || ! is_active_sidebar( 'sidebar-1' ) ) {
   global $content_width;
   $content_width = 980;
  }
}
add_action( 'template_redirect', 'wppt1_content_width', 11 );
?>
```

The new function, called `wppt1_content_width()`, is almost identical to the original one on Twenty Twelve, but it specifies a new width of `980`. Running this after the function from the parent theme effectively overrides it (to be strictly accurate, it doesn't override it but runs after it, but the effect is the same). This works in a similar way to the CSS in the child theme being read after that in the parent theme—the difference here is that unless you use priorities in this way, it won't happen.

Function-Specific Removal

For some functions, there is an alternative to removing actions and filters. In the case of `register_sidebar()`, for example, you can use the `unregister_sidebar()` function to remove sidebars from the parent theme in your child theme.

For example, I'm working with my compass framework parent theme that has widget areas already defined using `register_sidebars()`. I want to remove this and define a new set of widget areas in my child theme. The `register_sidebars()` function is executed via the `widgets_init()` action hook as follows:

```
<?php
function compass_widgets_init() {
  // Area 0, located above the header.
  register_sidebar( array(
   'name' => __( 'Before Header Widget Area', 'compass' ),
   'id' => 'before-header-widget-area',
   'description' => __( 'The header widget area', 'compass'),
   'before_widget' => '<div id="%1$s" class="widget-container %2$s">',
   'after_widget' => '</div>',
   'before_title' => '<h3 class="widget-title">',
   'after_title' => '</h3>',
  )
);
```

(continued)

```
// Area 1, located at the top of the sidebar.
register_sidebar( array(
  'name' => __( 'Primary Widget Area', 'compass'),
  'id' => 'primary-widget-area',
  'description' => __( 'The primary widget area', 'compass'),
  'before_widget' => '<div id="%1$s" class="widget-container %2$s">',
  'after_widget' => '</div>',
  'before_title' => '<h3 class="widget-title">',
  'after_title' => '</h3>',
  )
 );
}
add_action( 'widgets_init', 'compass_widgets_init' );
?>
```

To remove the sidebars, the following is added to the child theme:

```
<?php
function wpptl_remove_sidebars() {
  unregister_sidebar( 'before-header-widget-area' );
  unregister_sidebar( 'primary-widget-area' );
  }
add_action( 'widgets_init', 'wpptl_remove_sidebars', 11 );
?>
```

By specifying a priority of 11 when uasing `add_action()` to attach the `wpptl_remove_sidebars()` function to the `widgets_init` hook, you can ensure that this function is defined after the one in the parent theme, which uses the default priority of 10. This means that the widgets are added first by the parent theme, and then removed by the child theme. You can then add your own sidebars in a fresh function with a different name than what is used in the parent theme, actioning it via the `widgets_init()` action hook.

Building Functionality into a Plugin

If you want to retain the functionality you are adding should a site's theme later be changed, then you need to code a plugin instead of using the functions file. This section describes how to do that and looks at some example types of plugin such as creating widgets and shortcodes.

> Plugin development is a huge topic and therefore beyond the scope of this chapter. An excellent book with comprehensive coverage of plugin development is *Professional WordPress Plugin Development*, by Brad Williams, Richard Ozh, and Justin Tadlock (Wrox, 2011).

Plugins Overview

In addition to themes, plugins are one of the main building blocks of WordPress. Most users new to WordPress create their first site using a few plugins to achieve the functionality required by the site. This could range from simply using Akismet (`http://wordpress.org/extend/plugins/akismet/`) to control spam to buying a premium plugin such as Gravity Forms (`http://www.gravityforms.com`) to create complex forms. Indeed, with more than 22,000 plugins currently available, finding what you need can seem overwhelming. This section offers some perspective, provides some guidelines for their use, and includes many resources for more information.

Uses for Plugins

The uses for plugins are almost limitless and they can be used to achieve anything you can achieve with code using WordPress. Following are some of the most common types of plugin:

- **Widgets**—Plugins that provide a widget, enabling users who can't (or don't want to) code to add content to widget areas
- **Shortcodes**—Plugins that run functionality such as displaying content or inserting conditional tags from within post or page content by inserting text such as `[shortcode]` between square brackets
- **External content or APIs**—Plugins that display content from external sites or services, such as social media feeds, iframes, and RSS feeds
- **Gallery plugins**—Plugins that enable users to manage and display images, and customize them
- **SEO**—Plugins that enhance SEO in a variety of ways, including editing meta tags, creating `robots.txt` files, creating sitemaps, or providing analytics data
- **Forms**—Plugins to add forms to a site without having to code them from scratch
- **Performance**—Plugins designed to enhance site performance, such as by minifying code or cashing pages
- **Mobile**—Plugins designed to make a site mobile-friendly or to add mobile functionality such as responsive menus or images

This is just a selection of the most popular uses for plugins; in addition to these you're likely to code your own simple plugins that perform functions specific to your own site. These might include registering custom post types or taxonomies or creating an options page that isn't specific to the theme. Anything you can do in the functions file can also be done via a plugin.

Don't Reinvent the Wheel

Before you write your own plugin, it's a good idea to check whether an existing plugin does the same job or a very similar one. It's tempting to dive in and code because you know exactly what you need, but downloading a well-written third-party plugin can save you a lot of work. Alternatively, you may be able to find a third-party plugin that will do what you need with some modifications.

The best starting point is the WordPress plugin repository (`http://wordpress.org/extend/plugins/`). If you're looking for free plugins, I don't recommend looking anywhere else, as you may not be able to trust the code. If you're planning to buy a premium plugin, confirm that it meets the following requirements:

- It has robust, bug-free code.
- It comes from a trustworthy source.
- It has a GPL license so you can extend it for your own projects if necessary (to find out about the GPL license, see `http://wordpress.org/about/gpl/`).

- It reliably does what you need it to do.

- Other developers whose opinion you trust rate it favorably.

- You can't achieve the same results with a free plugin (maybe with some customizations).

Interacting with WordPress APIs

If you do decide to write your own plugin, you will need to make use of a few WordPress APIs such as the following:

- Plugins API (http://codex.wordpress.org/Plugin_API), which includes action hooks and filter hooks

- Widgets API (http://codex.wordpress.org/Widgets_API), which enables you to create widgets for use in the Widgets Dashboard screen and use them in multiple places in a theme

- Shortcode API (http://codex.wordpress.org/Shortcode_API), which enables you to create shortcodes for inserting functionality into a page or post's content

- Settings API (http://codex.wordpress.org/Settings_API), which enables you to add settings pages for your plugins

- Options API (http://codex.wordpress.org/Options_API), which enables you to store data in the wp_options table. This table isn't attached to any of the other database tables and is used to store data relating to the site as a whole. For more information on the database and its tables, see Chapter 3.

- Transients API (http://codex.wordpress.org/Transients_API), which is very similar to the Options API but enables you to specify expiration times for data, so it can be stored temporarily

- Dashboard Widgets API (http://codex.wordpress.org/Dashboard_Widgets_API), which enables you to create Dashboard widgets for users. This is covered in Chapter 4.

- HTTP API (http://codex.wordpress.org/HTTP_API), which enables you to send HTTP requests—for example, to pull in data from external sources.

- Metadata API (http://codex.wordpress.org/Metadata_API), which enables you to retrieve and manipulate metadata relating to posts, comments, and users from the wp_postmeta, wp_commentmeta, and wp_usermata tables.

- Rewrite API (http://codex.wordpress.org/Rewrite_API), which enables you to specify rewrite rules for permalinks

Each API has a number of functions associated with it, and some relate to database tables. Because the APIs differ, and your plugins will interact with them in different ways—it's well worth reading the relevant codex pages to get a solid understanding of the ones you'll be using. The preceding WordPress APIs are those you are most likely to interact with when writing plugins; for a full list of the APIs, see http://codex.wordpress.org/WordPress_API's.

Pluggable Functions

Plugins are loaded before theme files, which affects when the functions coded into your plugins run compared to similar ones that might be part of the active theme. Figure 9-1 shows a flowchart illustrating the order of file loading when WordPress is activated.

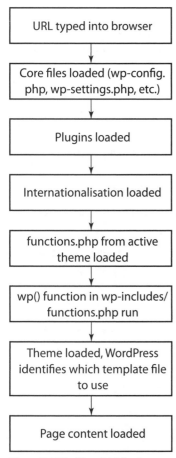

URL typed into browser

↓

Core files loaded (wp-config.
php, wp-settings.php, etc.)

↓

Plugins loaded

↓

Internationalisation loaded

↓

functions.php from active
theme loaded

↓

wp() function in wp-includes/
functions.php run

↓

Theme loaded, WordPress
identifies which template file
to use

↓

Page content loaded

Figure 9-1 WordPress initialization—
the order in which things happen when
a page is loaded

For this reason, some functions are pluggable, meaning if you code a new version of them into your plugin, this will overwrite the pluggable function. Pluggable functions are among core WordPress functions or they could be coded into a theme.

Pluggable functions, as you've seen already in this chapter, use a conditional statement:

```php
<?php
if ( ! function_exists( 'wpptl_example_function' ) ) {
 function wpptl_example_function() {
 // code for your pluggable function
 }
}
?>
```

Pluggable functions will become less common in WordPress over time, as the use of hooks replaces them. For a list of the current pluggable functions, see `http://codex.wordpress.org/Pluggable_Functions`.

Must-Use Plugins

If you're developing plugins to use with a site you're building, or you're adding third-party plugins to the site, you have the option to make those plugins *must-use* (or *mu*), which means they are always activated and cannot be deactivated or deleted via the Dashboard by any user with any role.

Must-use plugins have some advantages:

- They can save time, as you don't have to enable them manually.
- If you have a set of plugins that you use on all the sites you build, you can quickly upload them and they're active instantly.
- They reduce the risk of clients or less experienced users or developers switching them off.
- They can be enabled simply by uploading the file to the mu- directory without logging in, which can be helpful if you don't have access to the Dashboard for some reason.
- They are loaded before normal plugins, so any hooks added to a must-use plugin are available to other plugins.

However, they do have their disadvantages:

- WordPress does not check must use plugins for updates so you will receive no notifications about new versions in the Dashboard.
- When they are uploaded and activated, activation hooks are not executed for them, meaning any installation code attached to these hooks will not run; and if you remove the plugin, any code for cleaning up after the plugin is deleted won't be run either.

For these reasons, when working with third-party plugins it's advisable to check if they're suitable for use as a must-use plugin with the developer.

To upload and activate must-use plugins, you simply upload the plugin to the `wp-content/mu-plugins` folder (or create one if you don't already have one). To deactivate them, you remove them from the folder.

Coding Robust Plugins

As with themes, your WordPress plugins should be well-coded, efficient, and robust. I'll describe some important coding practices specific to plugins, but here are some tips for coding robust plugins:

- Use the WordPress coding standards (`http://codex.wordpress.org/WordPress_Coding_Standards`).
- Use valid code (PHP and HTML, but especially PHP or the plugin won't run!) and debug it using `WP_DEBUG` (`http://codex.wordpress.org/WP_DEBUG`).
- Ensure that your plugin is written securely and won't present any security risks.
- Ensure that your plugin has accessibility built in, both in the way you code options or settings pages and the HTML output by the plugin.

- Ensure that your plugin is compatible with the latest version of WordPress and doesn't cause any conflicts when activated alongside some of the most popular third-party plugins (or your own plugins that you may be using alongside it).

- Use unique names for your plugin and its files and functions, ensuring that they don't clash with names from WordPress core or your themes. As a best practice, use the name of your plugin as a prefix before every function and file it contains. If your plugin has a function with the same name as another function, it will break a site running the two plugins.

- If you're releasing your plugin to the public, include useful information in the header, and provide a readme file and a support page on your website. For more details about this, see Chapter 12.

- Make sure your plugin is efficient—minimize code bloat, don't overuse HTTP requests, and only load the scripts and stylesheets needed.

- Include an uninstallation function to tidy up when your plugin is uninstalled.

- Prepare your plugin for translation—details describing how to do this are in Chapter 12.

The Plugin Header

The one essential thing that every plugin needs is a header. This is similar to a theme header and contains information about the plugin. Later in the chapter you'll walk through the process of creating a widget plugin, and the header is as follows:

```php
<?php
/*
Plugin Name: WordPress Pushing the Limits Widget Plugin
Plugin URI: http://rachelmccollin.co.uk/wordpress-pushing-the-
   limits/example-plugin
Description: Plugin used for demonstration in the book 'WordPress Pushing
   the Limits'. This plugin adds functionality for a 'Thought for the day'
   widget.
Version: 1.0
Author: Rachel McCollin
Author URI: http://rachelmccollin.co.uk
License: GPLv2
*/
?>
```

As you can see, the plugin header contains information about the plugin, including its name, its author, and a description. The description is important, as it will appear in the Plugins screen in the Dashboard, as shown in Figure 9-2.

As you can see, the screen also displays the author of the plugin, a link to the author's website, the version number, and a link to the plugin's site, which can be anything you want—a support page on your blog or main site, a dedicated website, or support pages at wordpress.org. If you're releasing plugins to the public, it's a good practice to have a support page or site outside wordpress.org that tells users a bit more about your plugin.

Figure 9-2 The plugins screen shows the name and description of your plugin

File Structure

My plugin currently has one file, `wpptl-widget-plugin.php`. I can stick to just one file or I can add more if necessary, either additional PHP files (or includes) or assets such as stylesheets, scripts, or media. If you are using multiple files, you should store everything (including the main file) in a folder and use subdirectories to store each type of asset, like so:

- `/wpptl-widget-plugin`
  - `/wpptl-widget-plugin.php` (the main plugin file)
  - `/uninstall.php` (an uninstall file for the plugin)
  - `/includes/` (folder for other PHP files used by the plugin)
  - `/images/` or `/media/` (folder for images or media)
  - `/css/` (folder for stylesheets)
  - `/js/` (folder for scripts)

Obviously, you use only the folders you need depending on the plugin's requirements.

PHP Includes in Plugins

One of the types of assets listed in the preceding folder structure is PHP includes. These are useful for large, complex plugins that incorporate several different elements for their functionality. Using more than one file can help you work with your code, as it organizes it more clearly than if you just use one very large main file. It can also help other users who work with your code.

Accessing these files for a plugin is done in the same way as it is in the functions file:

```php
<?php include( plugin_dir_path(__FILE__) . '/filename.php'); ?>
```

TEMPLATEPATH represents the full path to the current file (i.e., the main plugin file), so to call an include called `shortcode.php` (for example) from my `/includes` folder, I would use the following:

```php
<?php include( plugin_dir_path(__FILE__) . '/includes/shortcode.php'); ?>
```

This would define all the functions contained in the `shortcode.php` file at the point in the main plugin file where the include is located, before continuing with the rest of the code in the main plugin file, as described earlier in the chapter.

WordPress Version Compatibility

I've already mentioned that it's a good practice to ensure that your plugin is compatible with the current version of WordPress and the one before it, as those are the versions most of your users will have installed. See "Planning for the Future" in Chapter 6 for more information about how to detect the WordPress version running on a site, and how to deactivate a plugin if it isn't compatible.

Plugin Security

Ensuring that your plugin is secure is fundamental, whether you are using it in sites you and your team develop or you are releasing it to the public. Failing to do so is a sure recipe for disaster—in the first case, your clients won't appreciate being exposed to security risks, and in the second you are likely to incur the wrath of developers and users.

Securing a plugin is similar to securing a site as a whole, as covered in Chapter 6. Aspects of security specific to plugins include the following:

- Checking permissions, in scenarios in which users are adding or editing data or making changes to the output of template files
- Using nonces to prevent logged-in site administrators from clicking malicious links that could, for example, delete a post
- Validating and sanitizing data as it is added via the plugin's interface

The following sections describe each of these and provide an example.

Checking Permissions

User permissions are related to roles and capabilities. Each role in WordPress (e.g., administrator, editor) has a corresponding set of capabilities that users with that role are allowed to perform. For example, administrators have the capability `activate_plugins` but editors and other roles below that don't.

To check the capabilities of the user, you use the `current_user_can()` function (http://codex.wordpress.org/Function_Reference/current_user_can), which can be used by passing the capability you wish to check along wth any relevant data. You then prevent the plugin from running using `wp_die()`.

To check a specific capability for the current user, you use something like the following example, which checks if the user can install plugins:

```php
<?php
if ( !current_user_can( 'install_plugins' ) )
 wp_die( 'You have insufficient permissions to install this plugin' );
?>
```

The `current_user_can()` function has one parameter, the name of the capability you are checking for—you can also pass it an array of capabilities to check for more than one at a time. The `wp_die()` function has three arguments, only the first of which is required:

```php
<?php wp_die( $message, $title, $args ) ?>
```

- `$message`—The message displayed if the function is activated (in this case, 'You have insufficient permissions to install this plugin').
- `$title`—The error title, for use if you use a `WP_Error` object.
- `$args`—Optional arguments to specify how the error should be handled.

The `wp_die()` function halts execution of the current request and displays the HTML output by the `$message` parameter. Therefore, in this instance, if someone without the proper permissions tries to install a plugin (which has to be from outside the plugins admin screen, as only administrators have access to that), they would simply be presented with an error message and the request would not be completed.

Nonces

A nonce serves a similar purpose to checking capabilities, as it can prevent a user from doing something, but it differs in that the user may have permission to do something you want to prevent.

For example, someone might create a malicious link that when clicked by a logged-in user with the correct authorization deletes a post or page on the site. This isn't difficult to do, as someone knowledgeable about WordPress would be able to figure out the URL generated if a user tried to do this genuinely. By using a nonce, you tell WordPress to add some unique text at the end of a URL which is only valid within certain very tight parameters, and can't be faked by someone creating a malicious link.

Nonce stands for "number used once," and in WordPress it's a short string such as a password that applies only to the following:

- One user
- One action (e.g., deleting, saving, updating, etc.)
- One object (e.g., a post, a page, a setting, etc.)
- One 24-hour time frame

For example, the link to delete post ID 44 in my site could be `http://wp-ptl.rachelmccollin.co.uk/wp-admin/post.php?post=44&action=trash&_wpnonce=a5927066a4`. Note that this includes `&_wpnonce=a5927066a4` at the end, a unique number that can only be used for this action, on this post, within 24 hours, and by me.

Using the incorrect nonce results in an error—so if I change the preceding link to `http://wp-ptl.rachelmccollin.co.uk/wp-admin/post.php?post=44&action=trash&_wpnonce=d6923466a4`, I get the error page shown in Figure 9-3.

Figure 9-3 The error page that results from using an incorrect nonce to delete a post

> **For more detailed information about nonces, see** `http://markjaquith.wordpress.com/2006/06/02/wordpress-203-nonces/`.

Creating a Nonce

To create a generic nonce , you use the `wp_create_nonce()` function (`http://codex.wordpress.org/Function_Reference/wp_create_nonce`), which takes one parameter:

```php
<?php wp_create_nonce( $action ); ?>
```

The parameter, `$action`, is the nonce action, a string that makes the nonce specific to one action and one object. You can name this string whatever you want, but it's a good practice to make it meaningful, referring to the action to which it refers. For example, if your nonce related to updating a field in a widget, you might use the following:

```php
<?php wp_create_nonce( 'wpptl_update_widget_field1' ); ?>
```

In addition to this function, WordPress also has functions to generate nonces in specific contexts, such as the following:

- `wp_nonce_url()`—Generates an URL with a nonce appended
- `wp_nonce_field()`—Generates a nonce field in a form
- `check_admin_referrer()`—Checks whether the current request was referred from an admin page and whether it is using a valid nonce

For details about nonce functions, see `http://codex.wordpress.org/WordPress_Nonces`.

Verifying a Nonce

Having created a nonce, you need to verify it when carrying out the action to which it relates. To do this, you use `wp_verify_nonce()` (`http://codex.wordpress.org/Function_Reference/wp_verify_nonce`):

```php
<?php wp_verify_nonce( $nonce, $action ); ?>
```

The `wp_verify_nonce()` function has two parameters:

- `$nonce`—The nonce being verified (optional)
- `$action`—A required parameter that specifies the name of the action as defined when creating the nonce

Therefore, to verify the nonce shown earlier, you would use the following:

```php
<?php wp_verify_nonce( $nonce, 'wpptl_update_widget_field1' ); ?>
```

You call this in a conditional statement or assign the result to a variable and then take action based on the result. If the nonce is invalid, and the error screen shown in Figure 9-3 is displayed, no further action will be possible.

Validation and Sanitization

As well as checking that users have the correct permissions to carry out actions in your plugin and that their request has a valid nonce, it's important to validate and/or sanitize any data they add to the database via the plugin. The former prevents malicious individuals from using your plugin's interface to add malicious code to the site, and the latter tidies up any inputs and ensures that it is in the correct format:

- Validation is the simple process of ensuring that data input by users is in the correct format, such as numerical or alphanumeric, or is contained within a predefined range of values.
- Sanitization doesn't check what kind of data has been input, but rather cleans it—for example, stripping out HTML tags.

Whether you simply complete validation on a given input or use sanitization as well depends on the nature and location of that input and the level of risk associated with not doing so.

WordPress can validate and sanitize data both on input and output, and it has a range of functions to do this, including the following:

- `esc_attr()`—A sanitization function which encodes < > & " ' as HTML attributes; demonstrated in the example widget plugin later in this chapter
- `esc_url()` —Sanitizes URLs, confirming that they use a whitelisted protocol and don't contain any dangerous characters
- `strip_tags()` —Santiizes inputs by stripping HTML tags from them, and enables you to specify any tags that are not to be removed
- `sanitize_text_field()`—Sanitizes text input into a field, stripping tags, removing line breaks, checking for invalid code, and more
- `is_email()`—Validation function which returns `true` if the input is a valid e-mail address, `false` if not

For a full list of relevant functions, see `http://codex.wordpress.org/Data_Validation`, and for advice on how they are used, see `http://codex.wordpress.org/Validating_Sanitizing_and_Escaping_User_Data`.

Hooking Your Plugin to WordPress

In order for your plugin to be useful—to yourself, your team, and possibly other users or developers—it needs to not only fulfill a need, but also work effectively. This means making use of WordPress APIs to integrate effectively with core functionality.

All plugins need to hook into something to work, and what they hook into are action hooks and filter hooks (also referred to as hooks and filters, respectively).

Hooks and filters are covered in detail in Chapter 7, so here I'll recap how they work and look at the different types of actions and filters to help you determine which are appropriate for your plugins.

Action Hooks

Action hooks make something happen. WordPress includes more than 200 action hooks (listed at `http://codex.wordpress.org/Plugin_API/Action_Reference`). They are categorized as follows:

- **Actions run during a typical request**—Actions called when a user opens the site's home page. These include theme setup, data retrieval and display, and much more.
- **Actions run during an admin page request**—e.g. actions called when a logged-in user opens the Posts Dashboard screen
- **Post, page, attachment and category actions (admin)**—Actions called when posts, pages, attachments, and categories are added, edited, deleted, or published
- **Comment, ping, and trackback actions**—Actions called when comments, pings, and trackbacks are posted or managed
- **Feed actions**—Actions relating to the blog's RSS feed

- **Template actions**—Actions relating to theme setup and those called from the template files, such as `get_footer()` and `wp_head()`

- **Administrative actions**—Actions triggered when changes are made in the Dashboard, such as plugin or theme activation, user setup and editing, login, and actions related to the Right Now Dashboard pane

- **Advanced actions**—Actions related to the queries WordPress uses to identify what content to display, which plugins to activate, and use of the loop

When coding a plugin, you need to identify which actions (or filters) you should use to run the functions in your plugin. Start by identifying the type of function it is (for example, a Dashboard plugin), and then look at the list of actions in that category. It's also helpful to know in which order actions are run, as that might be important if your function should run before or after something else. You can find more information about this on the Action Reference page in the codex.

To attach a function in your plugin to an action, you use `add_action()`. For example, you would use the following code attached a function to the wp_head action hook, which comes just before the closing `</head>` tag in most themes:

```php
<?php
function wpptl_example_function() {
  //function goes here
}
add_action( 'wp-head', 'wpptl_example_function' );
?>
```

You'll look at using `add_action()` in the example plugins shortly.

Filter Hooks

Filter hooks work differently. Instead of enabling you to run your function when the action is triggered, they are used to amend the way data is output. They're also used for styling, by changing the classes or IDs attached to content. Each filter has a default value—when you attach your function to a filter, you are overriding that default with the value specified in your function.

Many filters relate to data that is read or written by a particular function, and they often have the same name as that function. It's important to check the name of a filter before using it, and be clear about which function it relates to in case you need to work with that as well.

A list of filter hooks is available at `http://codex.wordpress.org/Plugin_API/Filter_Reference`. They are categorized as follows:

- **Post, page, and attachment (upload) filters**—Filters related to reading or writing posts, pages, and attachments in the `wp_posts` database table, such as `the_content`, which reads the content of a post, or `status_save_pre`, which is applied to a post's status before it is saved to the database

- **Comment, trackback, and ping filters**—Filters related to the reading and writing of comments, trackbacks, and pings, such as `get_comment_text`, which is applied to the text of a comment when it's read from the database, or `pre_comment_content`, which is applied to a comment's content before it is saved

- **Category and term filters**—Filters related to categories and to the terms you specify when registering taxonomies, such as `wp_list_categories`, which is applied to the list of categories generated by the `wp_list_categories()` function

- **Link filters**—Filters related to links for posts, comments, and so on, such as `post_link`, which is applied to the generated permalink for a post as specified in the Permalinks screen, or `post_type_link`, which does the same for custom post types

- **Date and time filters**—Filters related to the display of data and time data, such as `the_date()`, which is applied to the post date as output by the `the_date()` function

- **Author and user filters**—Filters related to logins and the writing of author data for posts and comments to the database, as well as the reading and display of author data

- **Blog information and option filters**—Filters related to data about the blog or site stored in the `wp_options()` table, such as `bloginfo()`, which relates to the blog data returned with the `get_bloginfo()` function

- **General text filters**—There are only two filters in this category as of WordPress 3.5: `attribute_escape`, which relates to content for which characters are being changed into HTML attributes, and `js_escape`, which is applied to JavaScript code before it's sent to the browser by the `js_escape()` function.

- **Administrative filters**—Filters related to the display and functionality of the Dashboard and site administration, such as filters applied to e-mails sent out by WordPress, and those related to default content and settings and to the content and layout of Dashboard screens

- **Rich text editor filters**—Filters related to the configuration and display of the TinyMCE rich text editor

- **Template filters**—Links related to themes, template files, and stylesheets, such as `stylesheet_uri`, which is applied to the URL of the stylesheet by the `get_stylesheet_uri()` function

- **Advanced filters**—Advanced filters related to queries, rewrite rules, internationalization, and other fundamental functions

- **Widgets filters**—Filters added by the bundled WordPress widgets

- **Admin Bar**—There is just one filter in this category, `wp_admin_bar_class`, which enables changing the default `WP_Admin_Bar` class.

Within many of these categories, you'll find that filters can be divided into two subcategories:

- **Database reads**—Filters related to the reading and display of data from the database

- **Database writes**—Filters related to the editing, saving, and deleting of data in the database

As with hooks, the filters you use will depend on your plugin's functionality, but knowing the main categories can help you narrow things down.

Creating Settings, Parameters, and Controls

Some simple plugins serve their purpose as soon as they are activated and don't require any further attention from the site administrator, such as the simple plugin built in Chapter 3 to register custom post types and taxonomies. More complex plugins, or those that allow users to display and manipulate content, layout, or data, however, need their own settings screens.

In order for users of your plugin (including yourself and your team) to be able to interact with it, you need to create one or more of the following:

▪ One or more widgets or Dashboard widgets

▪ One or more menu items for your settings page(s)—and for a plugin with multiple pages, a menu to hold them

▪ One or more settings pages

▪ Meta boxes in your settings page or the Post or Page editing screens

You also need to consider how to style your plugin's settings page(s), making use of standard styling and assets so that users can work with a familiar interface.

Creating a Widget

Some plugins don't have a settings page—all of their parameters can be set via a widget, which also enables users to place that widget in a widget area to display its contents in their theme.

To create a widget, you need to interact with the Widgets API (`http://codex.wordpress.org/Widgets_API`). This API includes the functions necessary to build widgets as well as those used in themes to register and display them. To create a widget, you use a class called `WP_Widget`.

Classes are used in PHP for object-oriented programming. A class defines a set of functions and data, while an object is an instance of a class. The `WP_Widget` class incorporates a number of functions that make the class work.

> **For more information about classes and objects, see** `http://en.wikipedia.org/wiki/PHP#Objects`.

The `WP_Widget` class looks like this:

```php
<?php
class Wpptl_Widget extends WP_Widget {
 function Wpptl_Widget() {
  // code to process the widget
 }
 function form( $instance ) {
  // displays the form for the widget in the Widgets dashboard screen
 }
 function update( $new_instance, $old_instance ) {
  // processes widget options to be saved
 }
 function widget( $args, $instance ) {
  // outputs the content of the widget
 }
}
?>
```

This code constructs the class which includes the function `Wpptl_Widget()`, which you then use to create the widget itself. Note that this function should have the same name as the class.

You then register your widget using `register_widget()`, attaching this to the `widgets_init()` action hook:

```php
<?php
function wpptl_register_my_widget() {
 register_widget( 'wpptl_widget' );
}
add_action( 'widgets_init', 'wpptl_register_my_widget' );
?>
```

Earlier in the chapter you looked at the header for a plugin to create a "Thought for the day" widget. We'll use this example to demonstrate how to create the widget.

First, here's the header again:

```php
<?php
/*
Plugin Name: WordPress Pushing the Limits Widget Plugin
Plugin URI: http://rachelmccollin.co.uk/wordpress-pushing-the-
   limits/example-plugin
Description: Plugin used for demonstration in the book 'WordPress Pushing
   the Limits'. This plugin adds functionality for a 'Thought for the day'
   widget.
Version: 1.0
Author: Rachel McCollin
Author URI: http://rachelmccollin.co.uk
License: GPLv2
*/
?>
```

Coding the Widget Class and Registering It

Below this, you add the class to define the widget:

```php
<?php
class Wpptl_Thoughtfortheday_Widget extends WP_Widget {
 function Wpptl_Thoughtfortheday_Widget() {
 }
 function form( $instance ) {
 }
 function update( $new_instance, $old_instance ) {
 }
 function widget( $args, $instance ) {
 }
}
?>
```

Below this, add the function to register the widget:

```php
<?php
function wpptl_register_thoughtfortheday_widget() {
 register_widget( ' Wpptl_Thoughtfortheday_Widget' );
}
add_action( 'widgets_init', 'wpptl_register_thoughtfortheday_widget' );
?>
```

This gives you a structure for the widget code in your plugin. Now you need to write the functions inside the widget class.

Constructing the Widget

The next step is to define the function that processes your widget, namely `wpptl_widget_plugin()`:

```php
function __construct(
 $id_base = 'wpptl_tftd_widget',
 $name = 'Thought for the Day',
 $widget_options = array(
  'classname' => 'wpptl_tftd_widgetplugin',
  'description' => 'Display your thought for the day using a simple
  widget.',
  ),
 $control_options = array()
 ) {
 parent::WP_Widget( $id_base, $name, $widget_options, $control_options );
}
```

This constructs the widget as follows:

1. It opens a `__construct` function,.

2. It sets the arguments for the `construct` function:

   * `$id_base`—A unique id for the widget

   * `$name`—The name displayed in the Widgets Dashboard screen

   * `$widget_options`—An array of up to two optional parameters, including the class generated by the widget and its description in the Widgets Dashboard page. These are passed to the `wp_register_sidebar_widget()` function.

   * `$control_options`—Specifies the height and width of the widget if needed and is passed to the `wp_register_widget_control()` function. In this case, there is nothing to specify so an empty array is used.

3. It defines the current class (`$this`) as the `WP_widget` class with the parameters you have defined—and these must be listed in the correct order. Again, translation is enabled. Note that this is where the function's braces are opened, as this is what WordPress executes.

After defining the widget, you need to code the form that displays it in the Widgets Dashboard page.

Building the Widget Form

The next function defines the form used in the Widgets screen to edit the widget's contents and settings:

```php
function form( $instance ) {
 $defaults = array(
 `title' => `Thought for the Day',
 `thought' => `',
);
 $title = $instance[ `title' ];
 $thought = $instance[ `thought' ]; ?>
 <p>
 <label for="<?php echo $this->get_field_id( `title' );
?>">Title:</label>
 <input type ="text" id="<?php echo $this-
>get_field_id( `title' ); ?>" name="<?php echo $this->get_field_name(
`title' ); ?>" value="<?php echo esc_attr( $title ); ?>" />
 </p>
 <p>
 <label for="<?php echo $this->get_field_id( `thought' ); ?>">Your
thought:</label>
 <input type ="text" id="<?php echo $this->get_field_id(
`thought' ); ?>" name="<?php echo $this->get_field_name( `thought' );
?>" value="<?php echo esc_attr( $thought ); ?>" />
 </p>
<?php }
```

This does the following:

1. It defines the default content for the form, using `$instance` as a paramater to the function (this will be used again in the next function). It also outputs the form fields and their labels, using functions form the Widgets API including `get_field_name()`.

2. It sets the value of the `$title` variable as `$instance[ 'title' ]` and does the same for the `$thought` variable.

3. It then defines the markup for the form itself:

   - The `Title` input field, with a value of `$title`
   - The `Your thought` input field, with a value of `$thought`

Currently, the form has little in the way of styling, but you'll revisit that shortly.

Enabling the Widget to Update

The next step is to sanitize and save the data added to the widget. This is done using the `update` function:

```php
function update( $new_instance, $old_instance ) {
 $instance = $old_instance;
 $instance[ 'title' ] = strip_tags( $new_instance[ 'title' ] );
 $instance[ 'thought' ] = strip_tags( $new_instance[ 'thought' ] );
 return $instance;
}
```

This function takes the old values ($old_instance) and replcaes them with the new values input by the user ($new_instance). Before doing this it strips out any tags to sanitize the data.

> These values are saved to the wp_options database table, which means if your plugin is deleted, the data will still be there. Although this ensures that any data isn't lost—if the plugin is updated, for example—it does mean that you have to add an uninstall function to remove the data if the plugin is deleted. In some cases you may not want to do this—for example, if you are building a plugin to enable users to add or update data that needs to remain whether the plugin is there or not, such as a plugin to register custom post types.

Displaying the Widget on the Site

The final function in your class ensures that the widget can be displayed on the front end of your site, in the widget area to which it has been added in the Dashboard:

```
function widget( $args, $instance ) {
 extract($args);
 echo $before_widget;
 $title = apply_filters( 'widget_title', $instance[ 'title' ] );
 $thought = empty( $instance[ 'thought' ] ) ? 'No deep thoughts today,
 come back tomorrow!' : $instance[ 'thought' ];
 if ( !empty( $title ) ) {
  echo $before_title . $title . $after_title;
 };
 echo '<p>' . $thought . '</p>';
 echo $after_widget;
}
```

This function includes the markup and PHP to display the widget in the browser. The extract() function imports variables from an array into the current symbol table, in this case as local variables to this functions. These are defined by the register widgets() function in the theme's functions file (see Chapter 7 for more details). The $title variable is defined by applying the widget_title() filter hook to $instance['title'], which was defined in the previous function. Applying the filter hook means other developers can use this filter to amend the title of the widget if necessary. The definition of the $thought variable includes a simple conditional tag to identify where no thoughts for the day have been added.

That's the final function required to define your widget class. Figure 9-4 shows how it now looks in the Widgets Dashboard screen. The layout isn't ideal, so amend the HTML to display the form, inside the function for the widget form:

```
<p>
 <label for="<?php echo $this->get_field_id( `title' );
?>">Title:</label>
 <input class="widefat" type ="text" id="<?php echo
$this->get_field_id( `title' ); ?>" name="<?php echo $this-
>get_field_name( `title' ); ?>" value="<?php echo esc_attr( $title );
?>" />
</p>
<p>
 <label for="<?php echo $this->get_field_id( `thought' ); ?>">Your
thought:</label>
 <input class="widefat" rows="10" type="text" id="<?php
echo $this->get_field_id( `thought' ); ?>" name="<?php echo $this-
>get_field_name( `thought' ); ?>" value="<?php echo esc_attr( $thought
); ?>" />
</p>
```

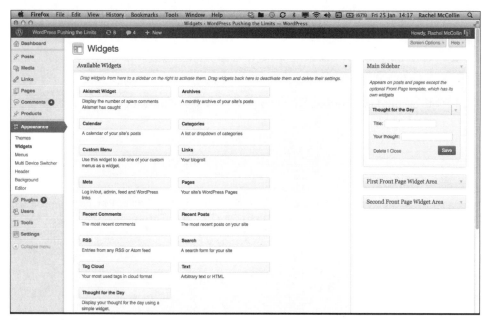

Figure 9-4 The new widget displayed on the Widgets Dashboard screen

This adds the `widefat` class to both inputs, and changes the input for the thought to a `textarea` with 10 rows, giving users some more space to record their thoughts. Now it looks like Figure 9-5.

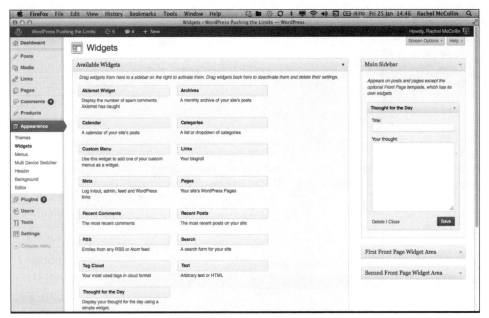

Figure 9-5 The widget form with layout improvements

Here's the full plugin code, with all four functions plus the action hook to register the widget:

```php
<?php
/*
Plugin Name: WordPress Pushing the Limits Widget Plugin
Plugin URI: http://rachelmccollin.co.uk/wordpress-pushing-the-
   limits/example-plugin
Description: Plugin used for demonstration in the book 'WordPress Pushing
   the Limits'. This plugin adds functionality for a 'Thought for the day'
   widget.
Version: 1.0
Author: Rachel McCollin
Author URI: http://rachelmccollin.co.uk
License: GPLv2
*/

class Wpptl_Thoughtfortheday_Widget extends WP_Widget {
 //widget constructor function
 function __construct(
  $id_base = 'wpptl_tftd_widget',
  $name = 'Thought for the Day',
  $widget_options = array(
    'classname' => 'wpptl_tftd_widgetplugin',
    'description' => 'Display your thought for the day using a simple
    widget.',
  ),
  $control_options = array()
  ) {
 parent::WP_Widget( $id_base, $name, $widget_options, $control_options );
```

```php
}

 //function to define the form in the Widgets screen
 function form($instance) {
  $defaults = array(
    'title' => 'Thought for the Day',
    'thought' => '',
  );
  $title = $instance[ 'title' ];
  $thought = $instance[ 'thought' ]; ?>
  <p><label for="<?php echo $this->get_field_id( 'title' );
  ?>">Title:</label><input class="widefat" type ="text" id="<?php echo
  $this->get_field_id( 'title' ); ?>" name="<?php echo $this-
  >get_field_name( 'title' ); ?>" value="<?php echo esc_attr( $title );
  ?>" /></p>
  <p><label for="<?php echo $this->get_field_id( 'thought' ); ?>">Your
  thought:</label><input class="widefat" rows="10" type="text" id="<?php
  echo $this->get_field_id( 'thought' ); ?>" name="<?php echo $this-
  >get_field_name( 'thought' ); ?>" value="<?php echo esc_attr( $thought
  ); ?>" /></p>
<?php }

 //function to define the data saved by the widget
 function update( $new_instance, $old_instance ) {
  $instance = $old_instance;
  $instance[ 'title' ] = strip_tags( $new_instance[ 'title' ] );
  $instance[ 'thought' ] = strip_tags( $new_instance[ 'thought' ] );
  return $instance;
 }

 //function to display the widget in the site
 function widget( $args, $instance ) {
  extract($args);
  echo $before_widget;
  $title = apply_filters( 'widget_title', $instance[ 'title' ] );
  $thought = empty( $instance[ 'thought' ] ) ? 'No deep thoughts today,
  come back tomorrow!' : $instance[ 'thought' ];
  if ( !empty( $title ) ) {
   echo $before_title . $title . $after_title;
   };
  echo '<p>' . $thought . '</p>';
  echo $after_widget;
 }
}

//function to register the widget
function wpptl_register_thoughtfortheday_widget() {
    register_widget( 'Wpptl_Thoughtfortheday_Widget' );
}
add_action( 'widgets_init', 'wpptl_register_thoughtfortheday_widget' );
 //hooks the registration function to the appropriate WordPress action
 hook
?>
```

This simple plugin gives you an overview of the process to create a widget. Of course, there are many more uses for widgets, but this is a good starting point and demonstrates the structure of the `WP_Widget` class.

Creating a Shortcode

Another common use for plugins is to create shortcodes, which enable users to add functionality provided by your plugin to the content of posts or pages by typing in some text surrounded by square brackets—for example, `[shortcode]`. To create a shortcode, you need to interact with the Shortcode API (`http://codex.wordpress.org/Shortcode_API`). This enables you to create a handler function, which works similarly to a filter—it accepts parameters and provides an output.

Shortcode Naming

Within the square brackets, shortcodes generally use a short string, which must be unique. Some shortcodes are already registered by WordPress, so it's important that you don't use these:

- `[gallery]`
- `[caption]`
- `[wp_caption]`
- `[embed]`

In addition, because you don't want your shortcode to clash with any shortcodes provided by other plugins that the site may be running, use a unique prefix in your shortcode to distinguish it, such as `[wpptl_shortcode]`. Although you can theoretically use any text you like as the string, it's a good practice to use short, simple strings in lowercase.

Uses for Shortcodes

Shortcodes can be incredibly useful. Here are just a few of their possible uses:

- Output some lengthy text or a link that you use repeatedly in your site.
- Output the content of a widget within a post or page's content.
- Output some static HTML, such as a call to an action box.
- Run a query on the database and output its results—for example, outputting a list of related posts, or posts in the same category.
- Display a custom gallery with additional parameters besides the built-in `[gallery]` shortcode.
- Display the featured image for the post (which gives you the flexibility of using it in different places in each post, which you can't do if you code it into the template file).
- Embed content from an external source.

The list is endless—basically, anything you can achieve with PHP in WordPress can be put into a shortcode.

Registering a Shortcode

To register a shortcode, you use the `add_shortcode()` function, as follows:

```php
<?php
function my_shortcode() {
 //code for the shortcode's content
}
add_shortcode('wpptl_shortcode', 'my_shortcode' );
?>
```

In this case, if the user types `[wpptl_shortcode]` into a post, the value output by the `my_shortcode()` function would be inserted into the post at that point.

Shortcode Attributes

In some cases, you might have similar content you want to output using a shortcode. You can do this either by creating multiple shortcodes or by creating attributes for your shortcode. Suppose you want to create a shortcode that echoes the name of a color of the rainbow and styles the text in that color. You could start by creating a shortcode for the color red:

```php
<?php
function wpptl_rainbow_shortcode() {
 return '<span class="rainbow red">red</span>';
}
add_shortcode('rainbow', 'wpptl_rainbow_shortcode' );
?>
```

You would then use CSS to style the `red` class:

```css
.rainbow.red {
 color: #ff0000;
}
```

You can take this further by adding a color parameter:

```php
<?php
/*
Plugin Name: WordPress Pushing the Limits Rainbow Shortcode Plugin
Plugin URI: http://rachelmccollin.co.uk/wordpress-pushing-the-
limits/rainbow-plugin
Description: Plugin used for demonstration in the book 'WordPress Pushing
the Limits'. This plugin adds functionality for a [rainbow] shortcode
with a color parameter.
Version: 1.0
Author: Rachel McCollin
Author URI: http://rachelmccollin.co.uk
License: GPLv2
*/
```

```
function wpptl_rainbow_colors( $atts ) {
 extract(shortcode_atts(array(
   'color' => 'red',
   ), $atts ));
 return '<span class="rainbow ' . $color . '">' . $color . '</span>';
}
add_shortcode('rainbow', 'wpptl_rainbow_colors' );
?>
```

This uses the `extract()` function on the `shortcode_atts()` array to define and extract a series of attributes for the shortcode—in this case, a `'color'` parameter with a default value of `'red'`. Therefore, if you add `[rainbow color="blue"]` to a post, the word "blue" would be output in blue—as long as styling for the `.rainbow.blue` class is in the theme's stylesheet. However, you can save your users the bother of doing this by simply adding styles to your plugin.

Adding Styling to a Plugin's Output

The preceding plugin is very limited because it requires the user to have styling specified in their stylesheet, which is far from ideal. A better solution is to add styles to your plugin.

To do this, you create a stylesheet, save it to a `/styles/` subdirectory in your plugin, and then use the `wp_enqueue_scripts()` function to call the stylesheet.

You first create a directory for your plugin called `wpptl-rainbow-shortcode`, saving the main plugin file in this directory. You then create a stylesheet called `wpptl-rainbow-styles.css` and save it to a directory called `/css/` within the `wpptl-rainbow-shortcode` directory.

The following adds the styles to your stylesheet:

```
/*
stylesheet to accompany the wpptl-rainbow-shortcode plugin
adds styling for the shortcode output depending on the parameters
specified
*/
.rainbow.red {
 color: #ff0000;
}
.rainbow.blue {
 color: #0000ff;
}
.rainbow.green {
 color: #00ff00;
}
```

Having done this, you need to attach the stylesheet to your plugin, which you do using two functions and an action hook:

- `wp_register_style()`—The function which registers your stylesheet and tells WordPress where it's located. It takes up to five parameters: the name of the stylesheet, its location relative to the plugins directory, any other stylesheets it's dependant on, the version number of the stylesheet where relevant, and the media for which the stylesheet is defined.

- `wp_enqueue_style()`—This function enqueues (or adds) the stylesheet to the list of stylesheets attached to the page. This has just one parameter—the name of the stylesheet.

- `wp_enqueue_scripts`—The action hook that is used to attach functions enqueing styles or scripts.

The function looks like this:

```php
<?php
function wpptl_add_rainbow_stylesheet() {
 wp_register_style( 'wpptl-rainbow-styles', plugins_url('/css/wpptl-
rainbow-styles.css', __FILE__) );
 wp_enqueue_style( 'wpptl-rainbow-styles' );
 }
add_action( 'wp_enqueue_scripts', 'wpptl_add_rainbow_stylesheet' );
?>
```

Having added this to your plugin along with the stylesheet, you can use the following content in your post:

```
Jane's favourite colour is [rainbow color="red"].
Paul's favourite colour is [rainbow color="blue"].
Siobhan's favourite colour is [rainbow color="green"].
```

The page output by this is shown in Figure 9-6.

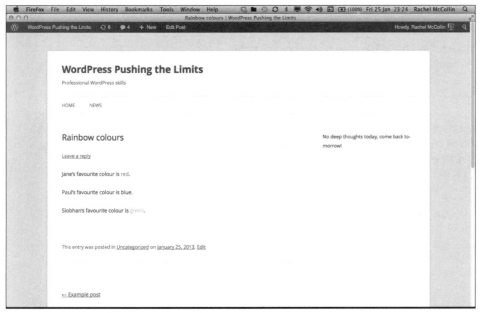

Figure 9-6 The output of the shortcode, including its parameters

As in the previous example, this gives you a taste of what can be done with parameters—the options are limitless, especially if you combine shortcodes with settings screens.

Creating a Settings (or Options) Screen

The plugins added so far use the content of the shortcode or the form for a widget to amend their output; but in many cases you will need to give users more control, making the interface as user-friendly as possible. This is where settings screens come in.

To create a settings screen, you interact with the Settings and Options APIs. These help you to define options and settings and save them to the `wp_options` table. You also need to set up menus and create and style your settings screen—fortunately, WordPress provides built-in classes to ensure that your user interface is consistent with the rest of the Dashboard.

> Chapter 4 covers how to create menus and settings screens in detail, and includes examples of plugins with settings screens. It also describes how to create Dashboard widgets, which your plugins may need to use.

Creating an Uninstall File

Although some plugins are created only to provide an interface for data entry or import, in which case the plugin itself might be deleted but data saved to the database is wanted long-term, in many cases data isn't needed after your plugin is removed. It's a good practice to ensure that your plugins tidy up after themselves. To do this, you create an uninstall function, which is typically stored in a separate uninstall file.

> It's important to understand the difference between deactivating and uninstalling a plugin—your uninstall function should only be triggered upon uninstallation (i.e., deletion) of the plugin, not deactivation.

The following example creates an uninstall file for the widget plugin to remove any data it added to the `wp_options` table. First, you create an `uninstall.php` file and save it in the plugin's main directory along with the main plugin file. Add the following to this file:

```php
<?php
/* Uninstall file - activated when the wpptl-sidebar-widget plugin is
deleted
*/
if( !defined( 'WP_UNINSTALL_PLUGIN' )
 exit();
delete_option( 'wpptl_widget_plugin_options' );
?>
```

This does two things:

1. It confirms that the `uninstall.php` file is being called by WordPress, in which case the `WP_UNINSTALL_PLUGIN` constant is defined. If this is not the case, the uninstall function is not activated and the file is exited.

2. If everything is OK, it deletes any options stored by the plugin and removes any untidy data hanging around on the site after the plugin is deleted.

All plugins that write to the database should include an uninstall file; otherwise, you risk cluttering up your users' databases or leaving behind data that might cause problems later.

Summary

Being able to add custom functionality to your projects using functions and plugins is essential to creating advanced WordPress sites. In this chapter you have learned about the various uses of both the theme functions file and plugins, and how they overlap and differ. You worked through some examples demonstrating the use of the functions file, such as sidebar registration, and you learned some ways to override functions from a parent them in its child theme.

You have also learned how to develop robust and secure plugins. By working through two example plugins, you learned how to create a widget plugin and a shortcode plugin, and how to ensure that your plugin tidies up after itself using an uninstall file.

Further Resources

Plugins vs. Themes

Plugins vs. themes
`http://wp.tutsplus.com/articles/general/functionality-plugins-vs-themes/`

Functions file explained (including the difference between functions files and plugins)
`http://codex.wordpress.org/Functions_File_Explained`

Theme Functions File

WordPress theme functions files—best practices
`http://justintadlock.com/archives/2010/12/30/wordpress-theme-function-files`

Overriding parent theme functions in a child theme
`http://ottopress.com/2010/wordpress-protip-child-themes/`

Pluggable functions
`http://codex.wordpress.org/Pluggable_Functions`

The `remove_filter()` function
`http://codex.wordpress.org/Function_Reference/remove_filter`

The `remove_action()` function
`http://codex.wordpress.org/Function_Reference/remove_action`

Debugging
`http://codex.wordpress.org/Debugging_in_WordPress`

Plugins Overview

WordPress plugins
```
http://codex.wordpress.org/Plugins
```

Codex guidance on writing a plugin
```
https://codex.wordpress.org/Writing_a_Plugin
```

Plugin repository
```
http://wordpress.org/extend/plugins/
```

Plugins API
```
http://codex.wordpress.org/Plugin_API
```

Query overview (including information on what aspects of the query plugins can modify)
```
http://codex.wordpress.org/Query_Overview
```

WordPress initialization overview
```
http://humanshell.net/2011/08/14/wordpress-initialization/
```

Plugins best practices
```
http://wp.tutsplus.com/tutorials/7-simple-rules-wordpress-plugin-
development-best-practices/
```

WordPress APIs

WordPress APIs
```
http://codex.wordpress.org/WordPress_API's
```

Plugins API
```
http://codex.wordpress.org/Plugin_API
```

Widgets API
```
http://codex.wordpress.org/Widgets_API
```

Shortcode API
```
http://codex.wordpress.org/Shortcode_API
```

Settings API
```
http://codex.wordpress.org/Settings_API
```

Options API
```
http://codex.wordpress.org/Options_API
```

Transients API
```
http://codex.wordpress.org/Transients_API
```

Dashboard Widgets API
```
http://codex.wordpress.org/Dashboard_Widgets_API
```

HTTP API
```
http://codex.wordpress.org/HTTP_API
```

File Header API
```
http://codex.wordpress.org/File_Header_API
```

Metadata API
http://codex.wordpress.org/Metadata_API

Rewrite API
http://codex.wordpress.org/Rewrite_API

Plugin Security

Roles and capabilities
http://codex.wordpress.org/Roles_and_Capabilities

The `current_user_can()` function
http://codex.wordpress.org/Function_Reference/current_user_can

The `wp_die()` function
http://codex.wordpress.org/Function_Reference/wp_die

Detailed explanation of nonces
http://markjaquith.wordpress.com/2006/06/02/wordpress-203-nonces/

Using nonces in plugins
http://www.prelovac.com/vladimir/improving-security-in-wordpress-plugins-using-nonces

Capabilities and nonces
http://wp.tutsplus.com/tutorials/creative-coding/capabilities-and-nonces/

Data validation
http://codex.wordpress.org/Data_Validation

Building Widgets

PHP classes and objects defined
http://en.wikipedia.org/wiki/PHP#Objects

The `register_widget()` function
http://codex.wordpress.org/Function_Reference/register_widget

Documentation for `WP_Widget`
http://phpdoc.wordpress.org/trunk/WordPress/Widgets/WP_Widget.html#$control_options

Creating Shortcodes

The Shortcode API
http://codex.wordpress.org/Shortcode_API

Guide to shortcodes
http://wp.smashingmagazine.com/2012/05/01/wordpress-shortcodes-complete-guide/

Plugin Styling

The `wp_enqueue_style` function

http://codex.wordpress.org/Function_Reference/wp_enqueue_style

Including scripts and styles in themes and plugins

http://wp.tutsplus.com/articles/how-to-include-javascript-and-css-in-your-wordpress-themes-and-plugins/

Chapter 10

Making Your Site Soar: HTML, JavaScript, and CSS

As you know, WordPress is built on PHP. To push the limits of the platform in terms of querying and outputting data, building complexity into your themes, customizing the Dashboard, writing plugins, and more, PHP is the language you need to be familiar with. But WordPress also needs other languages to function—HTML provides the markup used to display page content, CSS styles your site, and JavaScript enables you to create more complex animations, transitions, and interactions.

Obviously, this chapter cannot provide a comprehensive guide to these languages—many excellent resources are available if that's what you need (you can find a list of some I find especially useful in the "Further Resources" section at the end of this chapter). What you will learn here is how to identify scenarios in which you'll need to work in different languages; how to optimize your markup, styles, and scripts for performance, accessibility, and standards compliance; and how to use CSS and JavaScript in particular to create visual and interactive effects on your site. You'll also learn about some of the applications of your code—forms, animations, galleries, and navigation—and some approaches to improving and working with them.

Choosing Your Approach

This chapter also emphasizes a common theme of this book—that there is more than one approach to solving many of the challenges you are likely to encounter when you're working with WordPress, or indeed with web design in general. Some examples include the following:

- **Animations and effects**—CSS3 provides the capability to add animations that previously would have required JavaScript. For more complex animations, you may prefer to use a JavaScript or JQuery approach, or (where possible) to work with advanced CSS.

- **Markup**—CSS pseudo-elements enable you to add markup that isn't in the template file, but rather the stylesheet. This has its uses, particularly for styling, but it shouldn't be used for anything that's in the flow of the document, as it will have accessibility implications.

- **Mobile and responsive design**—In some cases you might choose to use CSS to display content on specific devices, or to display it differently. In other cases—for example, to enhance performance—you might use PHP or a combination of PHP and JavaScript to prevent content from being sent to certain devices altogether. This is covered in more detail in Chapter 11.

In all of these cases, there isn't a blanket approach that is always right—the most appropriate method will vary according to the needs and constraints of your project. Choosing the best approach will depend on an understanding of what you need to achieve and the skills and experience of your team.

Optimizing Your Code

Whatever code you're using, it's important to optimize it. It should be tidy, fast, standards-compliant, and accessible. Make sure you stick to the WordPress coding standards (`http://codex.wordpress.org/WordPress_Coding_Standards`) as well as the tips described in this chapter.

HTML

HTML may not be the language you're primarily coding in when working in WordPress, as you'll be working mainly in PHP. However, browsers will use your PHP to output HTML so it's important that you ensure that HTML is valid and standards-compliant.

Most modern themes are written in HTML5, and I recommend that yours should be too. HTML5 offers several significant benefits:

- It provides a number of semantic elements that improve the accessibility of your site and improve its SEO.

- It gives you access to numerous APIs such as geolocation, video, audio, and drag and drop.

- It gives you access to offline data storage, which is particularly useful if you're developing web apps whose users may not be online while accessing your app's data.

- It has a much simpler `DOCTYPE` declaration, making coding quicker.

HLTM5 Elements and WordPress Templates

There has been some debate about how the HTML5 semantic elements fit into the structure of a WordPress template (or the page that's output by it), but there's no denying that some of the elements in particular correspond closely to content types and page elements used by WordPress:

- `header`—For use in headers or banners. Most of the content of `header.php` is contained inside a `header` element.

- `article`—For use with the post's content. Each post listing output by the loop should be in an `article` element.

- `section`—Used with part of a page or a post listing. Instead of being a self-contained article or post, `section` is used to divide either the page or the article into sections. For example, within a post listing, `<div class="postmeta">` can become `<section class="postmeta">`. Sections can also be used to break up the page, but they shouldn't be used to replace `div`s unless there is a semantic reason for doing so.

- `aside`—This is used for content that is outside the main flow of the page, such as the sidebar. In a WordPress template you might use this for widget areas and blockquotes if they aren't part of the flow of the article.

- `footer`—Used within another element or the page as a whole to denote "a footer for its nearest ancestor," according to the HTML5 spec. This can mean the page footer (in `footer.php`) or a footer within an article, such as navigation to the next post or a link back to the archive listing. The footer doesn't have to appear after the rest of its ancestor's content, but it usually does.

- `nav`—Use this for your main navigation menu and possibly for additional navigation in the template, such as a menu in the sidebar or footer. There is a debate about whether `nav` should be used for navigation elements other than the main menu—my advice is to consider the semantics of your template when coding it. If a `nav` element will help screen readers and browsers to identify important navigation within the page, then use it, but don't overdo it. Advertising links for example, should definitely not be in a `nav` element.

- `hgroup`—This is used for headings and subheadings grouped together, such as your site name and description in the header. In HTML4, you may have coded this as follows:

```
<h1>My amazing site</h1>
<h2>Lots of fantastic things for you to read</h2>
```

Alternatively, you may have used a `p` or `span` element for the site description.

In HTML5, you can make it more obvious that these two elements are grouped together, using `hgroup`:

```
<hgroup>
 <h1>My amazing site</h1>
 <h2>Lots of fantastic things for you to read</h2>
</hgroup>
```

This structure makes it abundantly clear to browsers, search engines, and screen readers that these two elements are grouped together, with the `hgroup` element acting as a wrapper to distinguish them from other page elements, such as the title of a page further down in the markup.

Many more new semantic elements are offered by HTML5, and you'll probably be using a lot of them in your templates; these are just some of the key ones that are particularly relevant to many WordPress themes.

Standards Compliance

A well-written WordPress theme or site will be standards-compliant and use valid markup. Adhering to web standards mean the following:

- Your code is accessible to all—for example, it doesn't use plugins or add-ons that might not be installed on all machines or used by people with disabilities (by this I don't mean WordPress plugins, but software plugins such as Flash).

- Your site (or a site running your theme) will be faster and more efficient.

- Search engines and screen readers will be better able to understand your code, enhancing SEO and accessibility.

- Your code will have greater long-term viability as web standards evolve over time but aren't drastically changed.

Ensuring that your code is standards-compliant means writing valid HTML and CSS, only using freely available technologies for your content, and using the DOM (Document Object Model) correctly.

For more information about web standards, see `http://www.webstandards.org/` and `http://www.w3.org/standards/`. To learn about developing with web standards in depth, you can work through the WaSP curriculum, developed by the web standards project, at `http://interact.webstandards.org/curriculum/`.

Accessibility

Hopefully you don't need me to point out the benefits of accessibility, but if you do need a business case for it, then the W3C has a list of great resources on the topic at `http://www.w3.org/WAI/bcase/resources.`

Making your code accessible isn't difficult. It involves some simple best practices:

- Write standards-compliant code, using semantic elements and the document structure correctly.

- Ensure that any important content (i.e., not just for presentation) is included in your markup and not via CSS or other means.

- Consider accessibility in visual design and user experience (UX)—your users might not be using assistive technologies, but they could have poor eyesight or learning disabilities, for example. Examples of good practices include making text large enough to read easily and providing sufficient contrast between adjacent colors.

- Provide clear, intuitive signals and feedback to users as they interact with your site, such as making links and hover states obvious and providing feedback when users have completed a process such as submitting a form.

- Provide text alternatives for nontext-based content such as images and video.

- Don't include functionality that's only accessible using a mouse—keyboard users should be able to access all areas of your page in a logical order.

- Make navigation clear and use navigation styles and positioning that people will easily recognize.

- If you are designing for touchscreens, make links and inputs large enough to be tapped easily.

These guidelines are by no means exhaustive; for a fuller list, see `http://www.w3.org/WAI/WCAG20/quickref/`.

Accessibility is not only relevant for developing sites and themes—if you're customizing the WordPress admin or developing plugins, you need to ensure that the markup in your admin screens is accessible and standards-compliant too.

Optimizing Stylesheets and Scripts

All WordPress themes use stylesheets, and a large number use scripts, so you need to know how to access these effectively from within your themes or plugins to enhance performance and make life easier for your users.

Calling Stylesheets Correctly

A WordPress theme won't work without a stylesheet, so you'll need to call one from the `header.php` file. In addition, if you're using a child theme, multiple stylesheets, or calling a stylesheet from within a plugin, you need to make an additional call to extra stylesheet(s). There are two ways to do this: using `link` or `@import`:

```
<link href="style.css" type="text/css" />
```

or

```
@import url("style.css");
```

Each of these does a similar job but they work slightly differently:

- The `link` method is used in the `<head>` of the page and is normally the faster of the two methods.

- The `@import` method is used within a stylesheet to import an additional stylesheet or within a PHP file in a plugin to import a stylesheet used by the plugin.

Stylesheets should always be called first, as they are loaded by the browser before it renders the page content—so if you are coding them into your theme, add the link to the `<head>` section; if you're adding them via a hook, use `wp_head()`.

Alternatively, you can use the `wp_enqueue_style()` function:

```php
<?php
wp_enqueue_style( $handle, $src, $deps, $ver, $media );
?>
```

This has five parameters, of which only the first is required:

- `$handle`—the name of the stylesheet
- `$src`—the stylesheet URL, which you shouldn't hardcode—instead use `plugins_url()` (for Plugins) and `get_template_directory_uri()` or `get_stylesheet_uri()` (for Themes) to get a proper URL
- `$deps`—any other stylseets which this one is dependant on
- `$ver`—the version number of the stylesheet
- `$media`—the media for which the stylesheet is defined, such as `print` or `screen`.

You attach this function to the `wp_enqueue_scripts` action hook as follows:

```php
<?php
function wpptl_enqueue_styles() {
  wp_enqueue_style( 'wpptl-style', get_stylesheet_uri() );
}
add_action( 'wp_enqueue_scripts', 'wpptl_enqueue_styles' );
?>
```

You can add as many styles (and scripts, as you'll see in the next section) to this, saving you having to edit the `header.php` file.

Calling Scripts Correctly

Scripts are called in HTML files in only one way, using the `<script>` tag:

```
<script src="myscript.js" type ="text/javascript"></script>
```

You add this at the end of the file, as scripts can prevent other content from loading. Therefore, add them immediately before the closing `</body>` tag or using the `wp_footer()` hook.

It's better practice in WordPress to use the `wp_enqueue_script()` function instead of hardcoding script calls into your template files. This is particularly important if you're using a library, because if the library is also being used by another plugin or by the active theme, it could be loaded multiple times.

```php
<?php
wp_enqueue_script( $handle, $src, $deps, $ver, $in_footer );
?>
```

The parameters for this function are as follows:

- $handle—The name of the script, in lowercase
- $src—The script's URL. This is optional and should only be included when WordPress doesn't already know about the script.
- $deps—An array of handles (i.e., names of other scripts) that this script is dependant on and must be loaded first in order for this one to work
- $ver—The script's version number
- $in_footer—A Boolean operator that defaults to false, placing the script in the header. To place your script in the footer, set this to true.

In many cases, you'll be calling a script that is bundled with WordPress, so you only need to name the script, as shown in the following example function to call the JSON library and place it in the <head>:

```php
<?php
function wpptl_call_scripts() {
 wp_enqueue_script( 'json2' );
}
add_action( 'wp_enqueue_scripts', 'wpptl_call_scripts' );
?>
```

If you were calling a script you had added to your theme's /scripts directory and this script were dependent on JSON, you would need to include the source URL and the dependency:

```php
<?php
function wpptl_call_scripts2() {
 wp_enqueue_script( 'example_script', get_template_directory_uri() .
'/js/example_script.js', 'json2' );
}
add_action( 'wp_enqueue_scripts', 'wpptl_call_scripts2' );
?>
```

To reference a script from a plugin and place it in the footer, you would use this:

```php
<?php
function wpptl_call_scripts3() {
 wp_enqueue_script( 'example_script', plugins_url('/js/example-
script.js', __FILE__),array() ,'version' , true );
}
add_action( 'wp_enqueue_scripts', 'wpptl_call_scripts3' );
?>
```

Note that if you're populating the $in_footer paramater, you can't leave the ones before it empty, which is why the example above uses an empty array for dependencies followed by 'version' to denote the current version.

These methods ensure that the script is being called from the correct URL relative to the theme (get_template_directory_uri()) or plugin (plugins_url(..., __FILE__))).

For a list of the scripts bundled with WordPress, see `http://codex.wordpress.org/Function_ Reference/wp_enqueue_script#Default_scripts_included_with_WordPress`.

Slimming Down File Sizes

As well as calling scripts and stylesheets in the right place and using the correct method, you can also improve performance by reducing the size of these files as follows:

- Write clean code and avoid repetition or duplication.

- When building child sites, ensure that declarations in the parent theme's stylesheet aren't duplicated in the child theme—adding only the styling you need in the child theme.

- Minify your code using a minifying plugin such as WP-Minify (`http://wordpress.org/extend/ plugins/wp-minify/`) or W3 Total Cache (`http://wordpress.org/extend/plugins/ w3-total-cache/`), which also caches content for performance. These plugins reduce the size of stylesheets and scripts by removing unnecessary characters and spaces. The degree to which this improves performance varies by site but it's worth testing, especially if you're managing a large site with a lot of scripts.

Working with JQuery

JQuery is probably the most popular JavaScript library. It speeds up the process of JavaScript development and provides a slew of resources that you can use to incorporate JavaScript in projects.

WordPress is already bundled with jQuery, so you use `wp_enqueue_script()` as shown earlier to load the correct version.

Calling jQuery is incredibly simple—just add the following function to your functions file or plugin:

```php
<?php
function wpptl_call_jquery() {
 wp_enqueue_script( 'jquery' );
}
add_action('wp_enqueue_scripts', 'wpptl_call_jquery' );
?>
```

In some cases you will want run a script that uses the jQuery library:

```php
<?php
function wpptl_call_jqueryscript() {
 wp_enqueue_script( 'example_script', get_template_directory_uri() .
'/js/example_script.js', array( 'jquery'),'version' , true );
}
add_action('wp_enqueue_scripts', 'wpptl_call_jqueryscript' );
?>
```

This adds your script to the footer of each page and tells WordPress that it's dependent on jQuery—simple!

Practical Applications

At this point, you know how to include stylesheets and scripts in your projects, and you have looked at some examples demonstrating when each of these might be useful, or when an alternative approach using PHP or HTML is appropriate. This section includes some practical examples that demonstrate common scenarios in which you might want to use CSS and JavaScript (as well as PHP) to make your site soar: forms, animations, media and galleries, and navigation.

Creating Forms

Forms enable you to turn a bland, infrequently updated site from static *brochureware* into something interactive that lets users complete processes, provide feedback, make purchases, contribute content, and much more. Forms aren't just for contact pages—they can be the backbone of a site.

If you code your forms well, then they will be easier for users to interact with, reducing the number of people who abandon a process before completing the form or forms it uses. If you already use forms, the chances are good that you use a forms plugin such as the free Contact Form 7 (`http://wordpress.org/extend/plugins/contact-form-7/`) or the premium Gravity Forms (`http://www.gravityforms.com`). However, it pays to understand how form code is generated so you can optimize it for performance and the user experience (UX), and choose the best plugin for your project. A poorly written forms plugin often results in forms that are overly long and frustrating to users, who will give up and never make it to the Submit button.

UX, Accessibility, and Standards

A good user experience is all-important in forms, and this applies especially to assistive technologies, touchscreens, or small screens. By carefully considering the UX you will code highly accessible forms that conform to web standards. Some examples of best practices include the following:

- **Content**—Keep the content of your forms and the number of inputs requested (not just required) to an absolute minimum. Every field you add potentially increases the number of users who don't complete the process.

- **Layout**—Make your form logical and ensure that tabbing between fields occurs smoothly in the correct order—that is, as the forms are laid out on the page. Consider where you place your labels—labels above the fields speed up response time but take up more vertical space (see `http://static.lukew.com/webforms_lukew.pdf`).

- **Inputs**—Code inputs to include a `type` attribute, so browsers and devices will know what kind of input it is. This enables autofilling of contact forms, and on mobile devices it ensures that the most appropriate keyboard is provided. Use select boxes instead of text fields where possible to reduce user error and speed up the process, and make use of date pickers where these are provided by the device or via JavaScript.

- **Required inputs**—Keep these to an absolute minimum, requiring only data that you or your client truly needs to complete the process for which the form is designed. Excessive requests for data, especially personal data, reduces user trust in the site.

- **Styling**—Ensure that your forms look familiar to others like it, and that they are easy to read and interact with. Avoid the temptation to create a fancy Submit button that doesn't look like something users might expect.

■ **Feedback**—Always provide obvious feedback to users after they have completed a form, so that they know the process is complete. This could be either a message on the existing page (not just a paragraph at the bottom) or a redirect to a new page.

The majority of a form's content will be inputs. By observing some simple best practices, you can create clear, inviting forms that users can easily interact with.

Type Attributes for Inputs

The first and most simple best practice is to add a `type` attribute to your forms. This is an attribute added in HTML5, so it won't be recognized by all browsers; but it is recognized by smartphones, where it is typically used. Four types are provided:

■ `<input type="text">`—For text-based input (you can also just use `<input>` for this as text is the default)

■ `<input type="number">`—For numerical input

■ `<input type="email">`—For e-mail addresses

■ `<input type="url">`—For URLs

All of these are supported by Gravity Forms, which includes the `"text"` and `"number"` types in its Standard Fields pane, and the `"email"` and `"url"` types in its Advanced Fields pane, as shown in Figure 10-1. Contact Form 7 supports the e-mail type only.

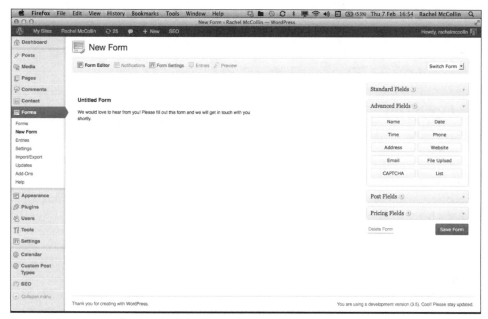

Figure 10-1 Input types offered by the Gravity Forms plugin

Select Boxes

In scenarios in which users must select from a limited number of options, it's a good practice to replace text fields with select boxes. For example, in the mobile version of the Carborelli's site (`http://rachelmccollin.co.uk/carborellis/`), a demonstration site of mine, users can select the number of ice-cream scoops they want to add to an ice cream sundae:

```
<select>
  <option value="One">One</option>
  <option value="Two">Two</option>
  <option value="Three">Three</option>
</select>
```

This minimizes the potential for invalid input and provides a more user-friendly interface, particularly on mobile devices, as shown in Figure 10-2.

Figure 10-2 The select box input on an iPhone

Textareas

Sometimes users need to input more than one line of text, in which case you should use a `<textarea>` element, which is supported by both Gravity Forms and Contact Form 7 (the latter is shown in Figure 10-3).

Date Pickers

Where users need to input a date, you want to make the process as simple as possible and minimize errors, which is why a date picker is helpful.

On desktops, a date picker must be added with JavaScript. The Gravity Forms plugin includes a date picker that is activated for all date fields. Contact Form 7 doesn't have a date picker itself but one can be added with the Contact Form 7 Datepicker plugin (`http://wordpress.org/extend/plugins/contact-form-7-datepicker/`). Both of these use the jQuery UI datepicker (`http://jqueryui.com/datepicker/`), as shown on its demo site in Figure 10-4.

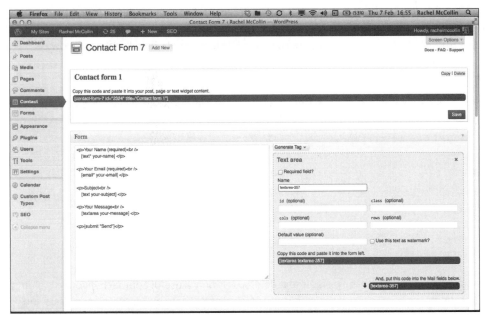

Figure 10-3 Creating a textarea with Contact Form 7

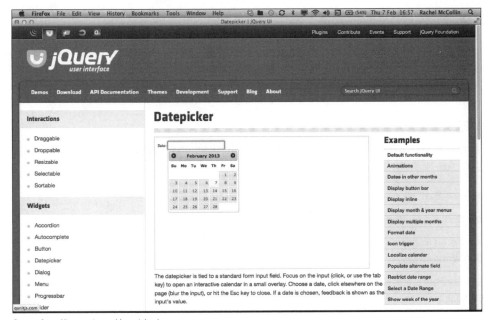

Source: http://jqueryui.com/datepicker/
Figure 10-4 The jQuery UI datepicker

On mobile devices, it's possible to access the device's native date picker. Unfortunately, this isn't provided by the major forms plugins out of the box, but you can add it if you're coding your own input fields or by using a hook with Gravity Forms, as demonstrated in the next section. The basic HTML for a date field type is as follows:

```
<input type="date">
```

Using this gives users access to the date picker on mobile devices—for example, as displayed on an Android device using the Chrome browser, as shown in Figure 10-5.

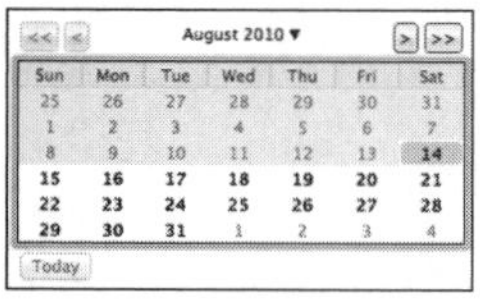

Figure 10-5 The Google Chrome date picker on an Android device

However, on the desktop this simply works as a default text field, so it is only a useful approach if you're building a mobile-specific site or theme, or if you choose to display one version of the date picker to desktop users and another to mobile users.

Beefing Up Form Plugins

If, like the majority of WordPress users and developers, you're using a third-party plugin to add forms, it's helpful to understand how you can customize and extend those plugins. Contact Form 7 has some tips for customizing the plugin at `http://contactform7.com/docs/`, but users of Gravity Forms have access to a range of action hooks and filters, which you can use to customize the way the plugin works in your site and add extra functionality.

The Gravity Forms API

Gravity Forms has its own API, which includes dozens of hooks (mainly filters) that enable you to make changes such as the following:

- Change the form fields that are displayed and their properties, such as tags and classes.
- Change the labels displayed within forms—for example, where translation is not possible.
- Manipulate data entered in a form—for example, feeding data to a third-party application or using it to perform a function within the site.
- Customize the Gravity Forms admin screens, including adding new form fields or submenus or changing the default input masks.

The list of filters is long and well worth exploring if you need to build custom forms or a customized form admin—you'll find the list at `http://www.gravityhelp.com/documentation/page/Developer_Docs`.

Example: Adding a Custom Field with Gravity Forms

Earlier in this chapter I mentioned the advantages of adding a `type` attribute to form fields. By default, Gravity Forms doesn't add any specific attribute to date fields: They are simply text fields with a jQuery datepicker attached to them. By using a filter, however, you can add a field to the Gravity Forms form creation screen, and then add the attribute to it.

The Gravity Forms website recommends adding custom functions and filters to your theme's `functions.php` file, but the following example creates a plugin because the form field created isn't theme-specific (for more details about when to use a plugin versus when to use the functions file, see Chapter 9).

The plugin begins like so:

```php
<?php
/*
Plugin Name: WordPress Pushing the Limits Gravity Forms Extension Plugin
Plugin URI: http://rachelmccollin.co.uk/wordpress-pushing-the-limits/
Description: Plugin used for demonstration in the book 'WordPress Pushing
the Limits.' This plugin extends Gravity Forms by adding an additional
field type. Requires the gravity forms plugin.
Version: 1.0
Author: Rachel McCollin
Author URI: http://rachelmccollin.co.uk
License: GPLv2
*/
?>
```

To add the new field type, use the `gform_field_input()` filter documented at `http://www.gravityhelp.com/documentation/page/Gform_field_input`. You also need to add a new field using the `gform_add_field_buttons()` filter documented at `http://www.gravityhelp.com/documentation/page/Gform_add_field_buttons`.

Firstly add the new button to the Advanced Fields pane:

```php
<?php
function wpptl_add_date_field($field_groups){
  foreach($field_groups as &$group){
    if($group["name"] == "advanced_fields"){
      $group["fields"][] = array(
        "class"=>"button",
        "value" => __("Date (HTML5)","gravityforms" ),
        "onclick" => "StartAddField( 'text' );"
      );
    break;
    }
  }
  return $field_groups;
}
add_filter( 'gform_add_field_buttons', 'wpptl_add_date_field' );
?>
```

Working through the preceding function:

1. The plugin looks at each field group (`$field_groups`) and checks whether it's the Advanced Field group.

2. The new field is to the arary of fields using `$group["fields"][]` to specify the attributes of the button being added to the admin and the action that should occur when it's clicked using `onclick` (namely, adding a text field).

3. The updated array of `$field_groups` is returned, as is required for a filter.

As shown in Figure 10-6, you can see the new date field in the admin screen.

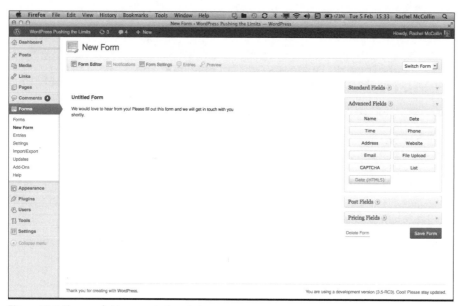

Figure 10-6: The new field appears in the admin screen.

Gravity Forms doesn't let you add the `type` attribute directly to this new field type; instead, you need to use a specific field that you create using the form builder which is part of Gravity Forms, so your next step is to create a simple form, as shown in Figure 10-7.

Now you use the ID of the form and the relevant field to specify additional attributes for fields displayed using this form and field, using the `gform_field_input()` filter:

```php
<?php
function wpptl_date_field_type( $input, $field, $value, $lead_id,
$form_id ) {
  if ( $form_id == 1 && $field["id"] == 1 ) {
    $content = '<input type="date" class="datepicker">';
  }
    return $content;
}
add_filter( 'gform_field_content', 'wpptl_date_field_type', 10, 5);
?>
```

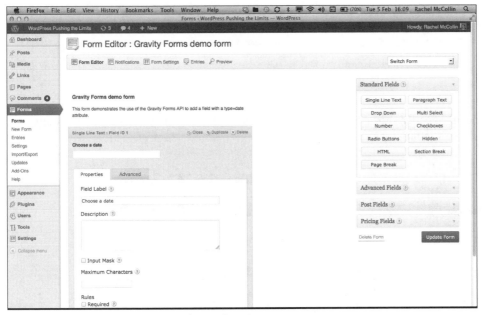

Figure 10-7: The next step is to create your form and save it.

Note that the preceding example uses 1 as the id for the form and field, you would need to amend this according to the form and field you're targetting. This specifies the HTML that will be output when the field is displayed. On desktops, this simply appears as a standard text field; but on a smartphone it gives users access to the date picker, as shown in Figure 10-8.

Figure 10-8 The field now uses the native date picker on the iPhone.

This is just one example using the Gravity Forms API to add and customize a form field—there are many more possibilities, but I'll leave you to explore them!

> The WordPress Pushing the Limits Gravity Forms Extension Plugin is available for download from this book's web page at `www.wiley.com/go/ptl/wordpress`.

Media and Galleries

The WordPress 3.5 media uploader, shown in Figure 10-9, has been greatly improved, offering a much more user-friendly and intuitive interface than previous versions.

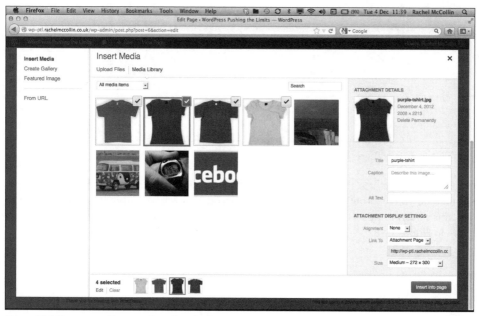

Figure 10-9 The new and improved media uploader

This is great news for WordPress users and any clients you have, as it will simplify the process of uploading media to posts and pages and reduce the risk of errors. In particular, the interface for creating galleries is much more intuitive, making it easier to identify which images should be in a gallery, both from within the post and elsewhere on the site, and to set the gallery up.

The way WordPress stores and accesses images can be hugely helpful when you are designing and developing complex image-based sites, enabling you to insert galleries that you can then customize with a jQuery plugin or with CSS, or to use featured images to list posts and make them look great, as well as giving you access to a number of file sizes for each image you upload. You'll work through an example of a thumbnail post listing shortly, but first a short detour to look at how WordPress stores and retrieves images.

Media Storage: A Refresher

In Chapter 3 you learned about how WordPress stores media and other attachments in its database. Rather than repeat the full details here, a quick recap of the main points would be useful to this discussion:

- Metadata on attachments (or media) is stored in the `wp_posts` table in the same way as data relating to posts and pages.

- The physical media itself is stored in the uploads folder in the `wp-content` directory, in a subdirectory associated with the year and month when the media was uploaded (for example, an image you upload in April 2013 will be stored in `wp-content/uploads/2013/04`). Multiple versions of the image are saved at different sizes. This is slightly different for Multisite installations, which since version 3.5 store media in `wp-content/uploads/`, with a subdirectory for each site in the network whose name will be a number corresponding to the ID of that site. Within each of those subdirectories, the file structure is the same as for a standard installation.

- Media (and other attachments) that have been uploaded via a page or a post (versus using the Media menu) will have a value in the `post_parent` field that equates to the `ID` of the post or page to which the media is attached.

- The `wp_postmeta` table holds additional data about attachments such as their alt text and caption, linked via the ID of the attachment itself, which is stored in both the `wp_posts` and the `wp_postmeta` tables.

- Galleries work slightly differently beginning with version 3.5, as explained in the section "The WordPress Gallery" later in this chapter.

> **For more information on media in WordPress, see** `http://codex.wordpress.org/Media_Library_Screen`.

Post Thumbnails and Featured Images

The "Featured Images" section in Chapter 3 describes in detail the terminology related to thumbnails and featured images, as this is sometimes confusing to new users. If you're unsure of the differences, I suggest you have a quick look at that chapter.

Featured images have some great uses, both within posts and pages and on archive pages. Before using them in a site, however, you need to enable them in your theme with the following line in `functions.php`:

```php
<?php
add_theme_support( 'post-thumbnails' );
?>
```

This makes the Featured Image pane visible in post editing screens so that users can upload featured images (or post thumbnails, same thing!) to their posts.

Post Thumbnails in Posts

Displaying a post thumbnail in a post or a page is done with the `the_post_thumbnail()` template tag, which you add in the loop:

```php
<?php
the_post_thumbnail( $size, $attr );
?>
```

Its parameters are:

- `$size`—The size of the image to be displayed, as defined in the Media settings screen or in `functions.php`. These include `thumbnail`, `medium`, `large`, and `full size`, and defaults to thumbnail or to the size defined using `set_post_thumbnail_size()`.

- `$attr`—An optional array of attributes such as `class`, `alt`, and `title`

For example, to display a post thumbnail at medium size and give it a title corresponding to the post excerpt, you would use the following:

```php
<?php
the_post_thumbnail( 'medium', array (
  'title' => esc_attr( $the_excerpt() )
  )
);
?>
```

This might be a bit lengthy for a title, but it could be useful if you know your posts will have short excerpts or if you've redefined the length of automatic excerpts. Alternatively, you could trim the excerpt manually.

To alter the size of thumbnail images across your site, you can use `set_post_thumbnail_size()` instead of manually defining a size in each loop. Add the `set_post_thumbnail_size()` function to the `functions.php` file (in this the functions file is more appropriate than a plugin, as the functionality *is* theme-specific):

```php
<?php
set_post_thumbnail_size( $width, $height, $crop );
?>
```

The parameters of the `set_post_thumbnail_size()` function are:

- `$width`—The post thumbnail width in pixels

- `$height`—The height in pixels

- `$crop`—A Boolean value, defaulting to `false`. If set to `false` (or omitted), a soft proportional crop is made; if set to `true`, a hard crop is made to the precise pixels.

I'll demonstrate how the crop works with a couple of examples. First, a soft crop, added via a function attached to the `after_setup_theme` action in `functions.php`:

```php
<?php
function wpptl_thumbnail_support() {
  add_theme_support( 'post-thumbnails' );
  set_post_thumbnail_size( 100px, 75px, false);
}
add_action( 'after_setup_theme', 'wpptl_thumbnail_support' );
?>
```

This would resize all images to ensure they fitted into a box 100px by 75px, with no cropping. An image 400px square, for example, would be resized to 75px by 75px. Figure 10-10 shows the resized image at 75px square inside an imaginary crop area of 100px by 75px.

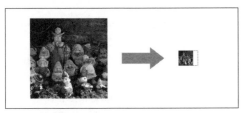

Figure 10-10 A soft crop

A hard crop works quite differently:

```php
<?php
function wpptl_thumbnail_support2() {
  add_theme_support( 'post-thumbnails' );
  set_post_thumbnail_size( 100px, 75px, true);
}
add_action( 'after_setup_theme', 'wpptl_thumbnail_support2' );
?>
```

This would resize all images to 100px by 75px, making any crop necessary to preserve the aspect ratio. Cropping a 400px square image would create an image 100px by 75px with some of the image cropped on either side. Figure 10-11 shows the image created by this crop with the parts of the image cropped off shaded at the top and bottom.

Figure 10-11 A hard crop

Having set this, you would just need to use the simplest form of the call for the post thumbnail in the loop as follows:

```php
<?php
the_post_thumbnail();
?>
```

This would then display all your thumbnails at the size and crop specified in `functions.php`.

Post Thumbnails in Archives

Besides displaying post thumbnails in posts and pages, it's also possible to display them in archive pages or elsewhere in the page such as in the sidebar—also by including them in the main loop or an additional loop. This uses the exact same function used in a post—namely, `the_post_thumbnail()`.

The "Featured Images" section of Chapter 3 contains example code to display post thumbnails on archive pages, and you'll work through a case study using this approach shortly.

The WordPress Gallery

The way that galleries work changed in WordPress 3.5. Prior to that, a gallery consisted of all the images uploaded to the page or post on which the gallery was displayed, and it would be included in the page or post's content using the `[gallery]` shortcode or by using the Add Gallery screen.

Beginning with 3.5, you have more control over your galleries. You can specify exactly which images will be included in a gallery, either in the Create Gallery screen or by adding the attachment IDs to the shortcode.

This gives you a few extra possibilities:

- You can include a subset of the images on a page within a gallery.
- You can include images uploaded to one page (or via the media menu) in a gallery on another page.
- You can include images in multiple galleries around the site.

Creating a gallery via the Create Gallery screen is very simple—you just select the images you want to include, add a caption, title, and alternative text to each image as required, and click "Create a new gallery." As shown in Figure 10-12, you can specify whether to select from all media items uploaded to the site or just those added to the current page.

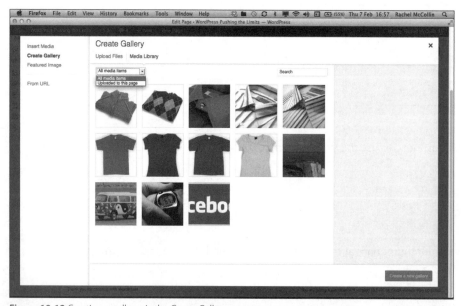

Figure 10-12 Creating a gallery via the Create Gallery screen

Adding a gallery containing specific images via the shortcode is also very simple—just include the IDs of the images you want to include within the shortcode:

```
[gallery ids="39,41,43,55,60"]
```

Finding the ID of an image is a matter of visiting its attachment page and getting it from the URL or doing the same from the media manager. For example, the URL of the screen shown in Figure 10-13 is `http://wp-ptl.rachelmccollin.co.uk/wp-admin/post.php?post=39&action=edit`, which means that the ID of the image is 39.

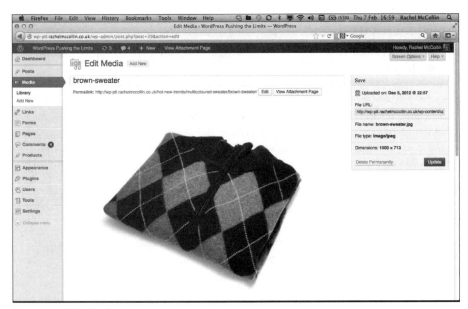

Figure 10-13 Edit Media page

Optimizing Media Performance

Like stylesheets and scripts, discussed earlier, images also need to be optimized. Images are large, heavy files for which the browser has to send an HTTP request. Therefore, displaying any image at all slows down performance slightly, and using large images slows things down even more. The following sections provide some tips for optimizing the images in your site or theme for performance.

HTTP Requests

Minimizing HTTP requests will improve a site's performance. Each request is work for the browser, which has to create a connection, send out an HTTP request to access the resource (in this case an image), and render the image in order to display it. To minimize HTTP requests, try to do the following:

- Use code instead of images for design where possible—for example, making use of CSS3 properties such as `box-shadow`, `corner-radius`, and `gradient` where in the past you might have used images.

- Never use an image for text—this adds an HTTP request, which affects accessibility. I've redesigned a few sites for which the menu or buttons originally took the form of images with text. Not only is this poor for accessibility (not to mention SEO) and potentially slow, it also requires a lot more work to edit those buttons and links when their content needs to change.

- Don't request multiple versions of an a image when you only need one. For example, in a responsive site, use a server-side solution to display variously sized images for different devices, to avoid downloading unwanted images. This is covered in more detail in Chapter 11.

Reducing File Size

It's likely that the original version of any image you need to upload to your sites and themes is large. I always recommend resizing them in Photoshop or another image editor prior to upload to save server space and upload time; but if you can't, WordPress has built-in functionality to display the correct image file for the size being displayed. For best results, try to observe the following guidelines:

- Ensure that your image sizes are set correctly in your site's Media settings screen of the theme's functions file. This is a better practice than using CSS to resize images, as CSS has no effect on the image file downloaded by the browser. To include extra image sizes in addition to the standard thumbnail, medium, and large, you can use the `add_image_size()` function in your `functions.php` file. Refer to the earlier section "Post Thumbnails on Posts" for more information about using this function.

- When adding images in the loop or within a post or page, always use the appropriate image size, not a larger one. Don't expect CSS to do the resizing for you.

- For sites where images are important (such as photography sites), consider using smaller or lower-resolution images on gallery pages or in slideshows, with a link to the full-size image. People will still be able to see what a great photo it is without having the benefit of the full size.

Responsive Images

Responsive images is the term used to describe the process of resizing image files for mobile devices so that only the required size file will be downloaded. There is some debate regarding to what degree users of mobile devices face performance issues, given that an increasing proportion of mobile use is done over Wi-Fi and not 3G (or even 4G, which can be faster than Wi-Fi). However, it makes sense to avoid sending to small screens images that are larger than they need to be.

Techniques for handling responsive images are covered in detail in the "Responsive Images" section of Chapter 11, which looks at mobile-first responsive images, images for retina displays, and server-side responsive images.

Case Study: CSS for a Post Thumbnail Listing

The Morija Museum website (`http://www.morija.co.ls`), which I worked on in 2012, includes a section showcasing the museum's collections. This section uses custom post types and taxonomies; for each post, the post thumbnail is displayed and rollover text appears when the user hovers their mouse over the image. This effect is created with CSS—you can see an example at `http://www.morija.co.ls/museum/ collections/basotho-objects/`.

Each archive page uses the museum taxonomy and the `archive-museum.php` template file. The loop within the template file is as follows. Because this is a fairly long block of code, it includes comments:

```
<div class="museum-item">
  <!-- start off by displaying the post's featured image -->
  <?php the_post_thumbnail('thumbnail'); ?>
 <div class="item-meta">
  <!-- display the post's title followed by the excerpt -->
  <div class="item-thumbnail-text">
   <h2 class="item-thumbnail-title"><?php the_title(); ?></h2> <?php
the_excerpt(); ?>
  </div>
  <div class="clear"></div>
  <!-- next check that the post has a featured image and if so, fetch its
ID and URL -->
  <?php if ($image !='') {
   $image_id = get_post_thumbnail_id();
   $image_url = wp_get_attachment_image_src($image_id,'large', true);
  ?>
  <!-- add a link to zoom the image will use the lightbox plugin
installed on the site. -->
  <a rel="lightbox[archive]"
   class="thickbox-link"
   href="<?php echo $image_url[0]; ?>"
   rel="nofollow"
   target="_blank" title="&lt;h5&gt;<?php the_title();?
  >
 <!-- Special characters are used for the HTML within the link title,
which is used by the lightbox along with the excerpt -->
   &lt;/h5&gt; <?php the_excerpt();?> &lt;a href=&quot;<?php
the_permalink();?>&quot; class=&quot;link-more&quot;>Read
more&lt;/a&gt;">
   ZOOM
  </a>
  <?php } ?>
  <!-- Finally, add a 'more' link to the post permalink -->
  <a class="link-more"
   title="<?php the_title();?> - read more"
   href="<?php the_permalink() ?>" >
   MORE
  </a>
 </div><!--.item-meta-->
</div><!--.museum-item-->
```

The preceding outputs the following HTML, which is an abbreviated example of the Lerumo Spear (I've taken out the lengthy URLs, excerpts, and titles to save space):

```html
<div class="museum-item">
 <img width="175" height="175" src="..." class="attachment-thumbnail wp-
post-image" alt="Lerumo Spear" title="Lerumo Spear" />
 <div class="item-meta">
  <div class="item-thumbnail-text">
   <h2 class="item-thumbnail-title">Lerumo Spear</h2>
   <p>...</p>
   </div>
   <div class="clear"></div>
   <a rel=" lightbox[archive]" class="thickbox-link" href="..."
rel="nofollow" target="_blank" title="...">ZOOM</a>
   <a class="link-more" title="Lerumo Spear - read more" href="..."
>MORE</a>
  </div>
 </div>
```

I then added CSS both to hide the text content until the user hovers over the image and to style the links.

First, here is the styling for the image and the meta box when the page is loaded:

```css
/* styling for items-list and the image including relative positioning
and z-index */
.items-list .museum-item {
 list-style-type: none;
 float: left;
 position: relative;
 overflow: none;
}
.items-list img {
 overflow: hidden;
 position: relative;
 z-index: 20;
}

/*item meta including styling that is needed for the mouseover effect to
work */
.items-list .item-meta {
 text-align: left;
 left: 0;
 top: 0;
 position: absolute;
 z-index: 50;
 -moz-opacity:0;
 filter:alpha(opacity=0);opacity:0;
 opacity: 0;
 font-weight: 400;
 visibility: visible;
}
```

This uses a few key bits of styling:

- Relative positioning for the `.museum-item` div
- Absolute positioning for the image, with a `z-index` of 20
- Absolute positioning for the metabox, with a `z-index` of 50 to place it on top of the image, and `opacity` at zero to hide it

The result looks like Figure 10-14.

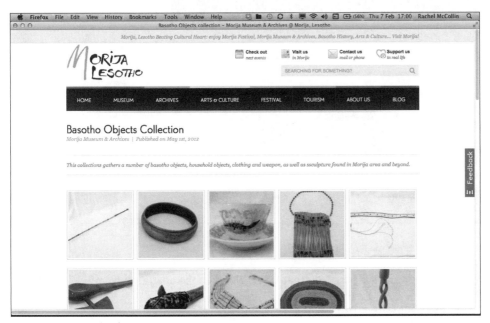

© 2012 Morija Museum & Archives
Figure 10-14 The collections archive when it's first loaded

The next part of the CSS creates the hover effect, displaying the text over the image:

```
/*add the hover effect on mouseover*/
.museum-item .item-meta:hover,
.museum-item:hover .item-meta {
 display: block;
 -moz-opacity:1;
 filter:alpha(opacity=100);
 opacity:1;
 visibility:visible;
 border: 1px solid #999999;
 margin-left: -3px;
 margin-top: -3px;
}
```

In addition to changing the `opacity` to 1 to display the `div`, this also gives it a margin and border, which make the text box larger than the original image and encloses it in its own border. As shown in Figure 10-15, when users hover over an image, they see the text.

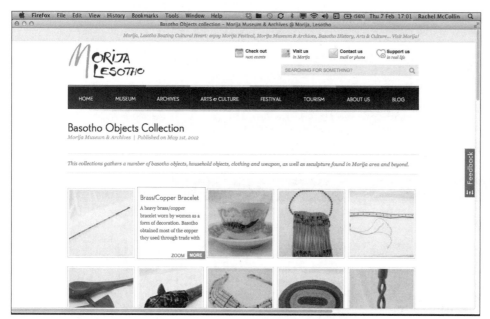

© 2012 Morija Museum & Archives

Figure 10-15 The effect when users hover their mouse over an image

Finally, the CSS is added to position and style the links that are visible when the image is hovered over:

```
/* style the links to the lightbox and the post */
.item-meta a.thickbox-link,
.item-meta a.link-more {
 display: block;
 position: absolute;
 z-index: 100;
 bottom: 0;
 width: 46px;
 height: 16px;
}
.item-meta a.thickbox-link {
 background: none;
 color: #C63C2A;
 right: 50px;
}
.item-meta a.link-more {
 background: #999999;
 color: #fff;
 right: 0;
}
```

```
/* hover effects on the links */
.item-meta a.thickbox-link:hover,
.item-meta a.thickbox-link:active {
 color: #C63C2A;
 font-weight: bold;
}
.item-meta a.link-more:hover,
.item-meta a.link-more:active {
 color: #fff;
 background: #666666;
}
```

These have their own hover effects, achieved using the a:hover pseudoclass and a z-index of 100, which places the links on top of the meta box.

The effect used here adds some interactivity to the post thumbnail listing and means that more information can be displayed in a smaller space. It also includes a shortcode to access JavaScript functionality provided by a lightbox plugin that was added to the site. You could adapt this effect and use it for galleries or in a sidebar, using the image listing code from Chapter 3.

Approaches to Animations

As well as outputting images in galleries and archive listings, you'll undoubtedly work on projects for which some kind of animation is needed. For images, this will be mainly focused on slideshows, carousels, and lightboxes, but it may be relevant for content other than images, such as drop-down boxes, accordions, and navigation display.

With increasing browser support for CSS3, many of the animations for which we previously used JavaScript can now be achieved in CSS. Which approach you decide to take will depend on the complexity of the effect required, the amount of code involved for each approach, the availability of plugins and libraries to speed up the process, and your own (and your team's) experience and preference.

> **Warning:** Animations aren't always a good thing. They can distract users from the main content of the page; cause difficulties for people with certain visual impairments; and, when handled badly, look very amateurish. When a client requests an animation, first determine why they want it and what they hope it will achieve. If it's simply a way to squeeze more content onto the home page, you might be able to work with them to find a better solution.

CSS Animations and Effects

CSS3 includes all sorts of goodies for animations and effects, which can be grouped under the following headings:

▨ Transforms—These include methods for transforming the size, position, and shape of elements in two or three dimensions. They are documented at http://www.w3.org/TR/css3-transforms/.

- Transitions—These enable you to animate changes in the state of an object, such as color or opacity. They are documented at `http://www.w3.org/TR/css3-transforms/`.

- Animations—These are similar to transitions but work differently. Instead of defining a state change, you define property values for the beginning and end of the animation using `@keyframes` blocks, and then apply these animations to any element you want. The animations are coded independently from the elements themselves and then applied to each. Animations are documented at `http://www.w3.org/TR/css3-animations/`.

Example: CSS Transition

In the "Case Study: CSS for a Post Thumbnail Listing" section earlier in this chapter you saw how you can use CSS to achieve a mouseover effect, making a meta box appear over a thumbnail image when the user hovers over the image.

In its current form, the example simply makes the box appear as soon as users hover their mouse over it, but you could make this more attractive by using a transition. To do this, you use new declarations relating to transitions and apply them to `opacity`.

To add this transition to the meta box, you would add the following CSS:

```
.museum-item .item-meta:hover,
.museum-item:hover .item-meta {
  transition-property: opacity;
  transition-duration: 1s;
  transition-timing-function: ease;
}
```

You can make this even easier by combining the `transition-property` and `transition-duration` declarations into one `transition` declaration:

```
.museum-item .item-meta:hover,
.museum-item:hover .item-meta {
  transition: opacity 1s ease;
}
```

It's as simple as that. This would now create an effect that transitioned the opacity of the meta box from 0 to 1 in a period of 1 second when the user hovers over the image, using a timing function of `ease` (the default), which makes the transition start quickly and gradually slow down.

> **For a list of possible properties for the transition-timing-function declaration, see** `http://www.w3.org/TR/css3-transitions/#transition-timing-function-property`.

Obviously, there are many more transitions, transforms, and animations, but as they aren't specific to WordPress it's beyond the scope of this book to cover them all. For more information, see the "Further Resources" section at the end of this chapter; and if you are looking for a book with step-by-step examples demonstrating how to code each type of effect, see *Practical CSS3: Develop and Design,* by Opera's Chris Mills (Peachpit Press, 2012, `http://amazon.com/0321823729`).

CSS Effects and Browser Support

When using CSS effects in your projects, you need to consider browser support. Generally, CSS effects are supported by modern browsers but not by legacy browsers. In addition, some effects are supported by some browsers but not others; for example, two-dimensional transforms are supported by more browsers than three-dimensional transforms. For a current list of supporting browsers, see `http://caniuse.com`.

> If you want to use CSS3 effects in browsers that don't support them, you can use a library such as **Modernizr** (`http://modernizr.com`). **Modernizr doesn't detect browsers themselves but instead identifies supported features and uses JavaScript to fill in the gaps for you.**

JQuery Animations

Over time, the WordPress core has been shifting from using PHP to JavaScript in its interface, such as in the new media manager and the Theme Customizer. WordPress lead developer Andrew Nacin has said that this trend will continue (`http://wpcandy.com/reports/a-shift-from-php-land-to-JavaScript-land`).

As mentioned earlier, WordPress is bundled with the latest version of jQuery, which means you shouldn't be overriding that with an alternative version—indeed, there is talk of making that impossible in future releases. You can access jQuery to add animations (and more) to your projects, including themes, sites, and plugins; and of course myriad plugins are already using jQuery.

The jQuery library includes a range of methods for creating animations, documented at `http://api.jquery.com/category/effects/`. Some of these can also be achieved using the CSS3 effects you learned about in the previous section, but jQuery does have its own advantages:

- **Browser compatibility**—jQuery is compatible all the way back to IE6.

- **Flexibility**—With jQuery you can animate what you want when you want, such as animating one element when the state of another element is changed (e.g., the user clicks or hovers over it or an animation applied to it ends). With CSS you can only animate the element that is clicked or hovered over.

- **Extensibility**—CSS3 effects have their limitations, whereas with jQuery you can do pretty much anything you like. It's not dissimilar to the benefits you get from working in PHP over HTML.

On the flip side, jQuery has the disadvantage of often being slower than CSS to achieve the same effect (`http://dev.opera.com/articles/view/css3-vs-jquery-animations/`)—although for more complex animations, the opposite may sometimes be true. Whether you choose to use javascript or CSS for some of these effects may come down to these factors or to the degree of familiarity you have with the two languages.

Example: jQuery Animation

Returning to the earlier example of animating the transition of an element from transparent to opaque, which was achieved with the CSS transition effect, you can also do this with jQuery. To do so, you remove the relevant code for the element's hover state, as you'll be setting that using jQuery instead. Therefore, the following is removed from the stylesheet:

```
/*add the hover effect on mouseover*/
.museum-item .item-meta:hover,
.museum-item:hover .item-meta {
 display: block;
 -moz-opacity:1;
 filter:alpha(opacity=100);
 opacity:1;
 visibility:visible;
 border: 1px solid #999999;
 margin-left: -3px;
 margin-top: -3px;
}
```

Then change the initial status of the `div` to be transitioned to `hidden` instead of setting its opacity:

```
.items-list .item-meta {
 visibility: hidden;
}
```

Finally, add the jQuery `.animate()` effect to achieve the animation, inside a jQuery wrapper:

```
<script>
 jQuery(document).ready(function($) {
  $(".items-list img").hover(function(){
  $(".museum-item .item-meta").animate({
    opacity: 1,
    border: "1px solid #999999",
    margin-left: "-3px",
    margin-top: "-3px",
    } , 1000);
  });
 });
</script>
```

This animates the `.item-meta` element when the `.items-list img` element is hovered over, setting it to change to the defined CSS properties over a duration of 1,000 milliseconds (one second). If you only wanted to change the opacity of the element, you could use the `.fadein()` effect instead, which avoids defining the CSS; but this example also changes the margins and border, so `.animate()` is used.

> One chapter can only skim the surface of what you can achieve with jQuery—for more details, including practical examples, see *JQuery: Novice to Ninja* by Earle Castledine and Craig Sharkie (O'Reilly, 2012, `http://shop.oreilly.com/product/9780987153012.do`).

Improving Navigation

The final topic of this chapter is integral to almost every site, and crucial to large, complex sites. Navigation will be the method by which most users move around your site (other methods include searching and clicking internal links), and making it user-friendly is essential.

You can add effects to navigation areas (such as drop-down lists) by using CSS or jQuery—for example, making a list swipe in, moving content below a "mega menu," or expanding an accordion-style menu—as described in the previous section on animations. This section covers navigation itself, and how you can manipulate navigation in WordPress to achieve the desired effect.

Navigation and Accessibility

Coding your navigation with accessibility in mind will greatly enhance the experience of users who access your site with assistive technology. If you're using animated or disappearing navigation, you should make sure your code is valid and accessible, to help users with visual impairments or learning disabilities. Bear the following main points in mind:

- Enable screen readers to skip to navigation, going straight to the content, using a link to an anchor later in the text. The following example shows how this is handled in the Twenty Twelve theme:

```
<a class="assistive-text" href="#content" title="<?php esc_attr_e( 'Skip
to content', 'twentytwelve' ); ?>"><?php _e( 'Skip to content',
'twentytwelve' ); ?></a>
```

  This provides a "Skip to content" link that is hidden using the `assistive-text` class and links to the element with the `#content` ID further down the page.

- Use semantic elements for your navigation. If you're coding in HTML5, you have access to the `nav` element, used for main navigation such as the main menu and any sidebar menus. This will aid accessibility for those suers of assistive technology whose software does understand HTML5, which at present is a relatively small proportion but will grow over time.

- For each navigation item, use a `li` element within a `ul`. This helps screen readers to spot links that are part of a list, highlighting them as a list to the user.

- The `nav` element isn't enough to provide screen readers with `ARIA` role information, so code your `navs` as `<nav role="navigation">`. For more on ARIA roles see `http://www.w3.org/WAI/intro/aria`.

Multiple Navigation Areas

WordPress makes it easy to add multiple navigation areas to a site or a theme. You can register as many navigation areas as you need in the Menus admin page, as shown in the example of the Compass Design site (see Figure 10-16), which is discussed in detail in Chapter 8.

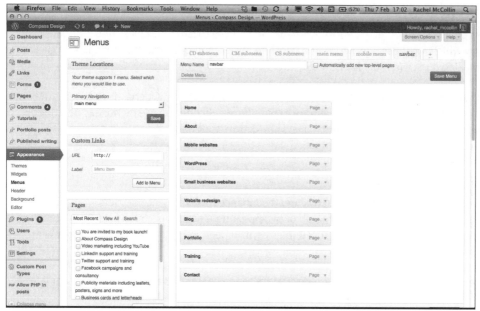

Figure 10-16 The Menus screen with multiple menus added

There are a number of ways to use multiple menus in a site or a theme:

▪ The quickest (but least tidy in terms of code generated) is to use the Custom Menu widget to add a menu to a widget area.

▪ You can specify alternative menus in different template files—for example, using a different menu or submenu in different sections of the site. This is covered in Chapter 8.

▪ You can display different menus according to the conditions by using a conditional tag, as demonstrated in Chapter 8.

▪ You can display different menus according to the device, as demonstrated in Chapter 11.

▪ You can add multiple menus to your themes using template includes—for example, adding the main menu in `header.php` and a submenu in `sidebar.php`.

> Registering navigation menus isn't covered here, as I'm assuming it's a topic with which readers are familiar. For a primer, see `http://codex.wordpress.org/Function_Reference/register_nav_menus`.

Auto-Generated Navigation

In my opinion, introducing the Navigation admin screen in WordPress 3.0 was a key step in moving WordPress from a blogging platform to a CMS. Having the flexibility to order your menu in any way you need and to include custom links and post types in the menu, as well as enabling clients and users to edit menus without having to code, greatly improves WordPress's menu handling.

However, in some cases you might not want your client to touch the menu, but nor can you anticipate how the menu will need to evolve over time. In these cases you need to code the menu content within the template file instead of calling a menu using `wp_nav_menu()`.

Using the basic e-commerce website demonstrated in **Chapter 3** (`http://wp-ptl.rachelmccollin.co.uk`), suppose the menu needs to display all the categories and/or terms assigned to posts without these being manually added via the Menus screen. The menu will need the following links:

- Home—the site's home page, a ststic page in this case

- News—a link to the main blog listing

- Departments—with submenu listing the terms in the "departments" taxonomy

- Ranges—with submenu listing terms in the "clothing types" taxonomy

To achieve this, the following is added to the theme's `header.php` file:

```
<nav role="navigation">
 <a class="assistive-text" href="#content" title="<?php esc_attr_e( 'Skip
to content', 'wpptl' ); ?>"><?php _e( 'Skip to content', 'wpptl' );
?></a>
 <ul class="nav-menu">
  <li><a href="<?php bloginfo('url'); ?>" title="home">Home</a></li>
  <li><a href="<?php
   // check if front page has posts or is static
   if( get_option( 'show_on_front' ) == 'page' )
   // if static front page, link to post listing page
    echo get_permalink( get_option('page_for_posts' ) );
   else
   // if posts on front page, link to front page
    echo bloginfo('url');
   ?>">News</a></li>
  <li><a href="">Departments</a>
   <ul>
    <?php
    // fetch the list of terms for the department taxonomy and echo
these inside a link
    $terms = get_terms( 'department' );
     foreach ( $terms as $term ) {
      echo '<li><a href="'.get_term_link( $term->slug, 'department'
).'">'.$term->name.'</a></li>';
     } ?>
   </ul>
  </li>
  <li><a href="">Ranges</a>
   <ul>
     <?php
     // repeat the process for the clothingtype taxonomy
     $terms = get_terms( 'clothingtype' );
      foreach ( $terms as $term ) {
       echo '<li><a href="'.get_term_link( $term->slug, 'clothingtype'
```

(continued)

```
    ).'">'.$term->name.'</a></li>';
        } ?>
    </ul>
    </li>
    </ul>
</nav><!-- #site-navigation -->
```

I've added comments to describe what's going on here, but I'll step through it to show what the code does:

1. A `nav` element is opened.

2. It includes a link to the main content for screen readers.

3. It opens an unordered list with the `nav-menu` class for styling. The first link is to the home page. The second link is to the post listing page. The next link to a list of departments is empty, as this page doesn't exist yet—it would need to be set up to list the terms in the relevant taxonomy using either a custom page template or a custom loop include.

4. Inside the list item for departments, another unordered list is opened for the submenu.

5. Each of the terms for the taxonomy is retrieved using `get_terms('department')`. These are echoed inside a link to the permalink for the term's archive page.

6. This is repeated for the `clothingtype` taxonomy.

7. The list items and lists are closed, as is the `nav` element.

This creates a menu that automatically includes links to all the terms for the relevant taxonomies, as shown in Figure 10-17.

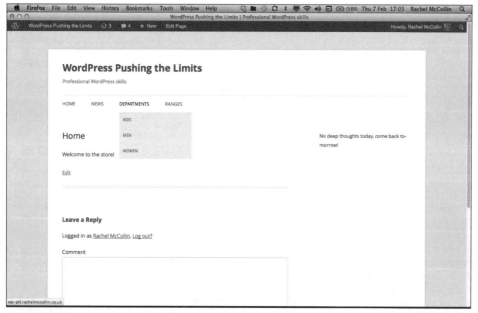

Figure 10-17 The automatic menu in action

Now, if site editors add any terms to those two taxonomies, the terms will automatically be listed in the menu, which is much more efficient than expecting editors to manually add these via the Menus screen each time.

Summary

PHP is the core language used by WordPress and it's what you'll be using to generate and display content, as well as to perform custom functions and manipulate data; but with CSS and jQuery, you can add more to a site's front end, making it look modern and beautiful.

In this chapter, you learned how to extend WordPress with CSS and JavaScript (particularly jQuery), and some techniques for coding HTML in a way that is semantic and accessible. Because it is important to create effects without sacrificing performance, you also saw how you can include JavaScript and CSS in a way that doesn't negatively impact your site's speed or your users' experience.

By working through some examples of these languages in action in WordPress, you have seen how they can be combined with images, animations, forms, and navigation to push WordPress further. Finally, in accordance with the rest of this book, you've seen that most of the time there isn't one "best" approach, but multiple possible approaches that vary according to the circumstances and the requirements of the project.

Further Resources

Optimizing Performance

CSS Wizardry guide to front-end performance (including stylesheets, scripts, and images)
`http://csswizardry.com/2013/01/front-end-performance-for-web-designers-and-front-end-developers/`

HTML5

WordPress coding standards
`http://codex.wordpress.org/WordPress_Coding_Standards`

The HTML5 specification
`http://www.w3.org/html/wg/drafts/html/master/Overview.html`

HLMTL5 Rocks—tutorials and resources on HTML5
`http://www.html5rocks.com/`

HTML5 Doctor, with useful resources to help you implement HTML5 (including a list of HTML5 elements)
`http://html5doctor.com`

Introducing HTML5 by Bruce Lawson and Remy Sharp (published by Peachpit)
`http://introducinghtml5.com`

WordPress and HTML5
`http://rachelmccollin.co.uk/blog/wordpress-and-html5/`

Web Standards

W3C web standards page
`http://www.w3.org/standards/`

Web standards project
`http://www.webstandards.org`

Web standards—WaSP InterACT curriculum
`http://interact.webstandards.org/curriculum`

W3C validator
`http://validator.w3.org`

Designing with Web Standards, Third Edition, by Jeffrey Zeldman and Ethan Marcotte (New Riders, 2009)
`http://www.zeldman.com/dwws/`

Accessibility

Resources for making an accessibility business case
`http://www.w3.org/WAI/bcase/resources`

The W3C web accessibility initiative (WAI)
`http://www.w3.org/WAI/`

Accessibility techniques
`http://www.w3.org/WAI/WCAG20/quickref/`

Stylesheets and Scripts

Why you shouldn't use `@import` in an HTML file
`http://www.stevesouders.com/blog/2009/04/09/dont-use-import/`

Stylesheets, scripts, and performance (plus much more)
`http://csswizardry.com/2013/01/front-end-performance-for-web-designers-and-front-end-developers/`

Scripts included with WordPress
`http://codex.wordpress.org/Function_Reference/wp_enqueue_script#Default_scripts_included_with_WordPress`

The `wp_enqueue_script()` function
`http://codex.wordpress.org/Function_Reference/wp_enqueue_script`

The jQuery site
`http://jquery.com`

Forms

Contact Form 7 plugin
`http://wordpress.org/extend/plugins/contact-form-7/`

Gravity Forms plugin
`http://www.gravityforms.com`

Contact Form 7 documentation
`http://contactform7.com/docs/`

Gravity Forms API—developer documentation
`http://www.gravityhelp.com/documentation/page/Developer_Docs`

Mini guide to the Contact Form 7 plugin
`http://wp.tutsplus.com/tutorials/plugins/mini-guide-to-contact-form-7/`

Best practices for form design
`http://static.lukew.com/webforms_lukew.pdf`

Guide to web form usability
`http://uxdesign.smashingmagazine.com/2011/11/08/extensive-guide-web-form-usability/`

Media and Galleries

Codex page on the media library
`http://codex.wordpress.org/Media_Library_Screen`

Codex page on post thumbnails
`http://codex.wordpress.org/Post_Thumbnails`

The `the_post_thumbnail()` function
`http://codex.wordpress.org/Function_Reference/the_post_thumbnail`

The `set_post_thumbnail_size()` function
`http://codex.wordpress.org/Function_Reference/set_post_thumbnail_size`

A guide to resizing post thumbnails

`http://markjaquith.wordpress.com/2009/12/23/new-in-wordpress-2-9-post-thumbnail-images/`

The `gallery` shortcode
`http://codex.wordpress.org/Gallery_Shortcode`

The Morija Museum website (used in the case study)
`http://www.morija.co.ls`

CSS Animations

CSS transforms
`http://www.w3.org/TR/css3-transforms/`

CSS transitions
`http://www.w3.org/TR/css3-transforms/`

CSS animations
`http://www.w3.org/TR/css3-animations/`

Properties for the transition-timing-function declaration
`http://www.w3.org/TR/css3-transitions/#transition-timing-function-property`

Practical CSS3: Design and Develop by Chris Mills (Peachpit, 2012)
`http://amzn.com/0321823729`

CSS transitions tutorial
`http://net.tutsplus.com/tutorials/html-css-techniques/css-fundametals-css-3-transitions/`

Examples of CSS 3D transforms
`http://www.netmagazine.com/features/20-stunning-examples-css-3d-transforms`

A guide to CSS animation
`http://coding.smashingmagazine.com/2011/09/14/the-guide-to-css-animation-principles-and-examples/`

Browser support for CSS 2D transforms
`http://caniuse.com/#feat=transforms2d`

Browser support for CSS 3D transforms
`http://caniuse.com/#feat=transforms3d`

Browser support for CSS transitions
`http://caniuse.com/#feat=css-transitions`

Browser support for CSS animations
`http://caniuse.com/#feat=css-animation`

JQuery Animations

jQuery and the future of WordPress
`http://wpcandy.com/reports/a-shift-from-php-land-to-JavaScript-land`

List of jQuery animations
`http://api.jquery.com/category/effects/`

CSS vs. jQuery animations
`http://dev.opera.com/articles/view/css3-vs-jquery-animations/`

jQuery: Novice to Ninja by Earle Castledine and Craig Sharkie (SitePoint, 2010)
`http://shop.oreilly.com/product/9780987153012.do`

Navigation

Navigation and accessibility
`http://www.jimthatcher.com/webcourse4.htm`

Using the HTML5 nav element
`http://www.w3.org/WAI/GL/wiki/Using_HTML5_nav_element`

The `get_terms()` tag
`http://codex.wordpress.org/Function_Reference/get_terms`

Registering navigation menus
`http://codex.wordpress.org/Function_Reference/register_nav_menus`

The `wp_nav_menu()` tag
`http://codex.wordpress.org/Function_Reference/wp_nav_menu`

Chapter 11

Device Compatibility: Responsive and Mobile Development

If you're developing themes for release to the public or for use on client sites, a solid grasp of responsive design is essential. As the use of mobile devices, and the range of available devices, continues to grow, your clients will expect you to be well versed about the latest technologies and how to get the most from them.

There is some debate among responsive developers regarding whether responsive design should be considered extra to a website build, to be charged separately, or whether it should be considered a core part of development, in the same way that progressive enhancement might be. As the mobile browser market share overtakes the market share of older browsers, I believe that responsive design is not an add-on, but just as important as, if not more important than, accounting for legacy browsers. For example, in February 2012, the number of visitors to my website using Internet Explorer (all versions combined) was less than the combined number of visitors on Safari for iPad and iPhone (see `http://compass-design.co.uk/are-you-testing-your-website-in-the-right-browsers/` for the figures). Based on analytics such as these, it's clear that designing for mobile browsers is just as important as accommodating IE and its layout eccentricities.

These days, responsive design is becoming less about layout and media queries, and more about content—including delivering smaller files to mobile devices to improve speed, as well as identifying where mobile-specific content might be required. It's also about the user experience (UX)—the considerations for navigating a site using a touch interface, for example, are different from those when using a mouse.

The great news is that WordPress makes this process easier. In particular, it facilitates the delivery of different content to different devices. This can be anything from sending smaller image files to mobile devices to using a mobile-specific theme to create a web app. Moreover, a wide range of plugins geared toward responsive and mobile designs are available, and 2013 is likely to see an acceleration of such plugin development.

This chapter looks at the current landscape in responsive design and development, and demonstrates how you can harness WordPress to build impressive fast and user-friendly mobile sites.

WordPress As a Responsive Platform: Trends and Advances

WordPress is great for responsive design. It can help you with a range of mobile and responsive development tasks, from using a plugin to quickly make a site mobile-friendly to developing a mobile-first theme or a mobile web app.

The number of plugins that support responsive and mobile design is growing all the time. In January 2012 I did a search for the word "mobile" in the WordPress plugin repository (`http://wordpress.org/extend/plugins/`) and got 466 results. In November 2012, the same search yielded 652 results. A search for "responsive" returned 703 plugins—295 of which are for responsive images. Of course, there will be overlap between the results of these two searches, but it demonstrates how developers are responding to the demand for responsive WordPress sites.

The main advance over the last couple of years has been the move away from plugins that merely add a simple theme to your site for display on mobile devices, such as WPTouch and WordPress Mobile Pack. These plugins have their place, but the development of new plugins to do this job has tapered off, with more focus now on plugins to support more advanced responsive design, sometimes called *adaptive design* or *reactive design*—which is the process of creating a responsive site that also uses server-side scripting to deliver a different experience or different content for mobile users. In addition, the number of responsive themes is growing, and the major theme and framework vendors have either started to release responsive themes or increased their stock of responsive themes in 2012. Of course, the default Twenty Twelve theme and its predecessor Twenty Eleven are responsive, too.

Also changing are the assumptions that developers can safely make about the so-called context, or the circumstances, in which users will be viewing your site on different devices. When mobile development was in its early stages, and responsive design was first introduced, it was widely assumed that users on mobile devices would have a slower connection and less time for browsing than desktop users—based on the idea that such users would be out and about, rather than sitting at a desk leisurely browsing through your site.

This assumption has been turned on its head in the last year or so. As high-end smartphones become cheaper and more widely available, and more people buy a tablet for home use instead of a laptop, mobile devices are becoming more powerful and enabling faster connections. Indeed, mobile users on 4G can find their connection speed faster than their home broadband. The way that people use their mobile devices to surf the web has also changed—no longer is it a few snatched moments while commuting or waiting in line. Instead, it's now common for mobile usage to occur in the evening as people sit on their sofa—with one eye on their mobile browser and the other on their TV, sometimes even communicating with other household members! This phenomenon will only increase as more people use their mobile device as their sole means of accessing the Internet, and don't bother with a home PC (or never had one in the first place).

In other words, while the old assumptions no longer apply, you *can* make some new assumptions:

- All users, regardless of platform or device, will benefit if your site runs as fast as it can while delivering a great user experience. This goal has an impact on image size—users on small, low-resolution screens don't need to be sent large, high-resolution images, so you can speed up their particular experience by delivering a smaller image file.

Mobile users have different challenges when it comes to UX. They are grappling with an unwieldy set of buttons or scroll wheels, or they are using a touchscreen, which means using fingers or thumbs, rather than a nice, accurate mouse, to navigate your site. You need to ensure that if nothing else changes in your mobile design, the usability of links and other tappable elements is good enough to ensure that users can reliably navigate and interact with your site.

This chapter examines both of these issues and demonstrates methods you can use in WordPress and using CSS and PHP to optimize the speed and usability of your responsive sites.

WordPress Makes Responsive Design Easier

As mentioned earlier, there are hundreds of WordPress plugins that you can use for mobile and responsive design and development. In addition, however, by using one of the available methods for detecting devices, you can then serve up different themes or content according to the device—and of course the WordPress apps make it easier for you and your clients to manage their sites.

Some of the ways in which WordPress makes responsive design easier include the following:

- Numerous responsive themes, including the default theme, which you can use off the shelf or as a starting point
- Plugins to help you deliver responsive images, navigation, and more
- Using PHP to deliver different content to different devices
- The capability to build multiple themes for multiple devices if necessary, in order to "skin" your content in various ways

Of course, how you actually use WordPress to develop a responsive theme or site depends on what you and your clients are trying to achieve.

Identifying the Best Approach for Your Clients

Your approach to mobile and responsive development will depend on schedules, budgets, and resources; but more important, it will depend on the needs of the site owner and users. It's very likely that your clients' understanding of mobile development will be limited—therefore, your job is to ask them the right questions and help them understand how the different approaches will meet their needs. Some clients insist that they need an app for no reason other than that it's the cool thing to do; but by understanding their site, its functionality, and its target audience, you can identify what's truly needed—whether it's an app, a web app, or a simple responsive site.

Table 11-1 summarizes the the scenarios in which different development approaches are most relevant and includes some of the disadvantages of each.

Table 11-1: Choosing a Development Approach

Approach	Best if...	Disadvantages
Quick-fix mobile plugin	You need to make an existing site mobile quickly, with no budget or a limited budget. The design or branding of the mobile version of the site is less important than its usability. The site is content-driven, often a blog or news site, with limited use of static pages and no custom post types. The site makes little or no use of widgets.	The mobile site will look nothing like the desktop site. This approach may not take tablets into account. Depending on the plugin you use, widgets may not be displayed on the mobile site. Images and graphics won't be displayed. The mobile site may not be as fast as it could be (WPTouch, for instance, can actually make a mobile site slower than the desktop site).
Off-the-shelf responsive theme	You have no existing theme and want to create a responsive site quickly. You can find an off-the-shelf responsive theme that meets your needs or customize one. The site's functionality and design don't require a high level of customization.	You have little or no control over the design. You have little or no control over the code and functionality. You may have to pay for a premium responsive theme if you can't find a free one appropriate for the site.
Child of an off-the-shelf responsive theme	You want to use an off-the-shelf responsive theme but need to customize it more extensively than the theme options allow. You've found a responsive theme that works for your content but need to change the layout, colors, or use of template files. You want a responsive theme without the trouble of coding your own from scratch.	You need to avoid adding CSS to your child theme that could override the contents of the parent theme's media queries—see "Child Themes and Responsive Design," later in the chapter.
Custom responsive theme (or making an existing theme responsive)	You have an existing desktop theme and need to retain the design while adding responsiveness. You are developing a theme from scratch and need custom functionality. You are developing a "core" theme to use as your own parent theme for various sites. You are developing a theme for release to the public.	This takes more time (and potentially money) than the options that use off-the-shelf themes or plugins.

Approach	Best if...	Disadvantages
Mobile-only theme powering a web app	You are developing a web app to support an existing WordPress site. There will be data shared by the main site and the web app. The user experience for mobile visitors is more transactional than on desktop, and the web app is more about completing a process than consuming content. You want to make your app available on a wide range of mobile devices without having to build multiple versions of it. You don't need to sell your app (but may want to sell via the app). Your app includes functionality that is available in the more widely used smartphone browsers. You may need to build in a fallback for users on lower-end phones.	Building and maintaining two themes takes more work than one (although generally not twice as much). You can't sell a web app as easily as a native app. Mobile browser functionality is restricted compared to the functionality you can access with a native app, so this approach is less suitable for richer applications such as games (although this is constantly improving). Users expecting to see your app in the app store may not think of looking online instead. Users tend not to store shortcuts to web apps on their mobile home screens, so the easy accessibility of a native app may be lost.
Native app	You need access to device functionality such as local storage and integration with the calendar, address book, or game center. Your app is resource-intensive and would run too slowly over an Internet connection. Your users need access to the app when they don't have Internet access. You want to sell your app. You want to target one or more specific devices and have the budget and resources to do so.	You cede a lot of control to the relevant app store, including the decision to actually release your app at all. The phone or browser vendors take a cut of your income from the app. Whenever you need to update the app, you need to do so for all the platforms supported, and rely on users to download the update.

Using plugins and off-the-shelf responsive themes is a simple process of installation and configuration. I'm assuming you know how to do this, so these approaches are not covered here.

Assuming you have decided to develop a responsive theme or a web app in WordPress, what tools and techniques are at your disposal?

The following sections describe three techniques in detail:

- Developing your own responsive theme, including mobile-first themes and responsive parent and child theme combinations
- Delivering different content to different devices to enhance speed and UX
- Using mobile-specific themes to build web apps in WordPress

Developing a Responsive Theme Using CSS

Building a responsive WordPress theme or making an existing one responsive isn't difficult. At its most basic, it's simply a case of adjusting the layout and optimizing links for better UX.

If you're working on an existing theme that has been up and running for a while, you may want to take the opportunity to review its markup, make any improvements, and maybe update to HTML5. A slim, tightly written theme will be much easier to make responsive than a bloated, out-of-date one.

Fluid Layout and Media Queries for Layout

If you're an old hand at responsive design and know media queries inside out, feel free to skip this section; but I have met advanced WordPress developers who don't know how to do this, so it's worth a brief look.

Basic responsive design consists of two things:

- A fluid layout
- Media queries to adjust the layout according to screen width

> This section first covers the desktop scenario in case you're adapting an existing desktop theme. The mobile-first approach is covered next, as it's arguably better practice.

Fluid Layouts

The first step is simple. Imagine your site width is styled like so:

```
body {
 width: 940px;
}
```

Obviously, the width of your site will stay the same regardless of the width of the screen or browser window. Now change the styling to the following:

```
body {
 width: 90%;
}
```

This sets the width of your site to be 90% of the width of the screen, regardless of screen size. On very wide screens, however, this results in a stretched site, as shown on my own blog in Figure 11-1.

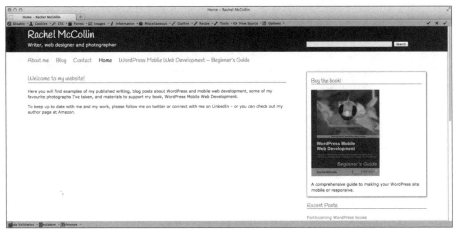

Figure 11-1 A site resized to 90% width on a very wide screen

This is easily corrected, as shown in Figure 11-2, using `max-width`:

```
body {
 width: 90%;
 max-width: 940px;
}
```

Figure 11-2 Adding a max-width value prevents a site from getting too wide on large monitors

After you have made the width of your entire site fluid, you also need to amend all your layout styling to use percentage widths instead of pixels.

For each element, you need to convert its absolute width in pixels to a percentage width. You do this by dividing its pixel width by the pixel width of its containing element, using the following calculation:

$$\frac{\text{pixel width of element}}{\text{pixel width of containing element}} \times 100 = \text{percentage width of element}$$

Why Not Calculate Percentage Heights?

Responsive design is all about adjusting layout in line with the width of the browser window. Percentage heights don't work very well in CSS because it's impossible to know the height of the full page, given that content will vary and so will browser rendering. Therefore, stick with pixels for element heights and vertical margins and padding.

This might result in some very long figures containing numerous decimal points. Don't worry about that; just round everything to the nearest whole number. After all, these values represent pixel perfection only at one browser width, and a large proportion of your users will be viewing at different widths anyway. The important thing is to ensure that your rounding up doesn't result in elements floated side by side with combined widths (including padding and margins) greater than the width of their containing element, as that will break any floats.

After calculating the percentage widths of every element, now you need to update your stylesheet to incorporate them. Remember to include horizontal margins and padding in the percentages too.

After you have done all this you'll have a theme that resizes itself when the browser resizes, but it won't exceed 940px in total width. If you ever need to change the maximum width in the future, this is the only declaration you'll need to change—all the other widths will adjust automatically because they are percentages.

Defining Media Queries

Creating a fluid layout is all well and good, but it won't look so great on narrow screens, as illustrated in Figure 11-3, which shows my site viewed on a 320px wide screen.

Figure 11-3 My fluid layout on a 320px wide screen

The layout needs to be adjusted so that it isn't squeezed in so tightly. You do this by adding media queries to your stylesheet, which relate to the different screen widths for which you need to adjust the layout. Most WordPress themes have four main layout areas:

- Header
- Content
- Sidebar
- Footer

On the desktop, the header and footer tend to be full width, with the content and sidebar side by side in between. On very narrow screens (e.g., smartphones), this layout needs to be adjusted so all these elements are stacked, as illustrated in Figure 11-4.

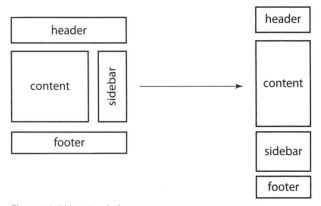

Figure 11-4 Mapping desktop content to very narrow screens

On wider screens such as tablets in portrait mode, it can be helpful to place the main containing elements above each other but have content within them side by side, as illustrated in Figure 11-5.

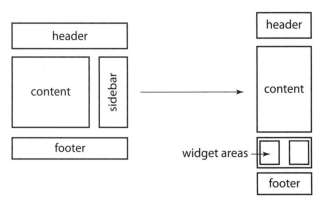

Figure 11-5 Placing widget areas side by side on tablet devices

In order to make this happen, you need to assign some media queries specifying breakpoints at which the layout needs to change. Most developers use the widths of the most common devices to define media queries, so the empty media queries would be as follows:

```
/* tablets in landscape mode or small desktops*/
@media screen and (max-width: 1024px) {
}

/* tablets in portrait mode*/
@media screen and (max-width: 768px) {
}

/* smartphones in landscape mode*/
@media screen and (max-width: 480px) {
}

/* smartphones in portrait mode*/
@media screen and (max-width: 320px) {
}
```

An alternative approach is to define your breakpoints according to the design—so instead of targeting devices, set your media queries at the screen widths where the wider design starts to break, either because text strays outside its containing element, images are squeezed, or navigation is difficult to read or use.

This means your media queries aren't based on the current set of devices, so they won't become obsolete. You can find out more about this approach on my blog at `http://rachelmccollin.co.uk/blog/iphone5-does-it-break-your-responsive-design/`.

After defining the media queries you need, add the width settings for your content. I won't go into detail about the specifics because they'll differ from site to site, but the following sections cover some of the basic settings that most sites will have in common.

Adjustments for Medium-Size Screens

If you're developing desktop-first and setting media queries for smaller screens, you need to start with the next widest screen. I don't tend to make any layout changes for screens of 1,024px width, as they have enough space to fit a desktop layout. The changes I do tend to make, however, involve navigation, which I'll return to in the next section.

For tablets in portrait mode, you can place the widgets side by side below the content, instead of one above the other next to it, using floats and percentage margins.

For example, in the case of a widget area with two widgets side by side, you would use the following CSS:

```
@media screen and (max-width: 768px) {
 .sidebar {
  width: 100%;
 }
 .sidebar .widget-container {
  float: left;
  width: 48%;
```

```
  margin-right: 2%;
 }
 .sidebar .widget-container:last-child {
  margin-right: 0;
 }
}
```

This sets the right margin of each widget at 2% except for the last one. If you're targeting browsers that don't read CSS3 and therefore won't understand the `:last-child` pseudo-element, you can add `overflow: none` to the containing `.sidebar` element, to ensure that if the combined widths of the sidebars and their margins does overflow their container, this won't be displayed.

Figure 11-6 shows the effect on the widgets in my blog.

Figure 11-6 Widgets side by side on my blog

The code used here assumes that there will be two widget containers—if there were three you would adjust the width and margins accordingly. When calculating the values for your margins and widths, you use the following calculation:

Total % width = (no. of widgets ´ (% width of each widget + % padding for each widget)) + ((no. of widgets-1) ´ % right margin for each widget)

If that sounds complicated, here are some examples:

For three widgets:

- Total width and padding for each widget = 32% - multiplied by 3 = 96%
- Right margin for each widget = 2% - multiplied by 2 = 4%
- Right margin for last widget = 0%
- Total = 100%

For four widgets:

- Total width and padding for each widget = 23.5% - multiplied by 4 = 94%
- Right margin for each widget = 2% - multiplied by 3 = 6%
- Right margin for last widget = 0%
- Total = 100%

I don't advise exceeding four widgets side by side; in fact, in most cases four widgets would look better in a two-by-two grid, using the preceding code for two widgets side by side.

You might then need to make some more tweaks to your layout depending on how much you want to tailor it for tablet devices—this can be anything from simply adjusting the size of navigation links to completely rethinking the layout to make the best use of touch gestures.

Adjustments for Small Screens

On small screens, typically mobile phones and the iPod Touch, it's likely that your content will need to be displayed in a vertical column. To achieve this, you simply need to add some width settings to your main layout elements:

```
@media screen and (max-width: 480px) {
  body {
   width: 90%;
   margins: 0 5%;
  }
  header, nav.main .main, .content, .sidebar, footer {
   width: 100%;
  }
}
```

The classes will vary but the ones I've used should be self-explanatory. This allows for a small margin on either side of the body, to avoid the layout butting up to the edges of the screen, and then sets everything else at 100% of the body width to line everything up next in a column. You may also need to remove some floats.

This results in a long narrow layout with elements below one another, as shown in Figure 11-7 (on my blog).

Figure 11-7 All elements laid out in a column on small screens

If you had already set the width of any of those elements to 100% for a larger screen, such as tablet screens, you don't have to do it again—as media queries apply to screens of a certain width and below, any smaller screen will use the same styling unless you overrode it in the next media query.

This layout means a lot of scrolling for users, which will affect ease of navigation—for example, users will have to scroll all the way back up the page to get to the menu after reading a long blog post. You'll see how you can optimize that in the section "Responsive Navigation."

Resizing Images

You might find that some of the images in your theme start to encroach on the space outside their container, or even outside the width of the screen—obviously, an undesirable user experience. Fortunately, you can quickly fix this in CSS, by adding the following declaration either in your desktop styling or in the first media query:

```
img {
 max-width: 100%
}
```

Enabling Zoom

I occasionally come across responsive sites that disable zoom on mobile devices. Zoom enables users to employ whatever means the device provides to zoom in on the content, and it is particularly useful on nonresponsive sites to make the content large enough to read. You might disable zoom, however, assuming that because you have made your site responsive, users won't want to do this. My advice is to leave zoom enabled—there may be users who need to zoom in even on your optimized text in order to read it, or who want to zoom in on images to get a better look at them. This is particularly the case with infographics. Therefore, leave well enough alone and don't change the zoom settings!

This tells the browser to display images only at the maximum width of their container, so they won't stray outside and break your design. This still sends the same image file to mobile devices, and won't do anything to optimize file size—we'll come back to that later.

So that's the basics of making your layout responsive. You've just taken a whistle-stop tour through the process, because plenty of other resources are available that deal with it in more detail. It gets more interesting when you look at site performance and UX, which we'll do next.

Adding the Viewport Meta Tag to Make Your Media Queries Work

You may find that having set your media queries, some smartphones are still displaying the desktop view. This is because mobile browsers render web pages in a virtual window, the *viewport*, which is displayed as if the screen were 1,024px wide. To override this, you need to add the `meta name="viewport"` tag to the `<head>` section of your pages:

```
<meta name="viewport" content="width=device-width">
```

If you were having any problems, this should fix them.

Media Queries for Larger Screens

There's nothing to stop you from using media queries to alter the layout on large screens and make use of that extra desktop real estate. For example, you could add a media query *above* the others to target screens wider than 1,600px:

```
/*styling for very wide screens */
@media screen and (min-width: 1600px) {
}
```

In my blog I have used this to move the navigation to the left of the main content as shown in Figure 11-8, but you could use it to display images in a carousel, to place widgets or articles side by side in a wider row, or to include "hidden" content only visible to large screens.

Figure 11-8 A layout for very large desktop screens

Mobile-First Themes

The approach you just looked at is how responsive design started—take an existing desktop layout and add media queries to make it responsive. Most responsive sites and themes are still built this way, even if they have responsiveness worked into them from scratch.

This section describes another method, the mobile-first approach, first popularized by Luke Wroblewski, which turns the stylesheet on its head. It involves styling the smallest screen first and then adding media queries to accommodate increasingly large screens—that means thinking about the essential content that mobile users will need and building and styling that, and then considering what else should be added for desktops. It can lead to some drastically different decisions in terms of content and site structure—designing this way encourages you to question whether the content you have in your desktop site is there because it is needed or just because you have the space.

Mobile-First Media Queries

The media queries you would use for this approach are different, because you are looking for browsers of a *minimum* width, not a *maximum* width. Therefore, the equivalent of our media queries in the earlier example would be as follows:

```
/* smartphones in landscape mode*/
@media screen and (min-width: 321px) {
}

/* tablets in portrait mode*/
@media screen and (min-width: 481px) {
}
```

(continued)

```
/* tablets in landscape mode or small desktops*/
@media screen and (min-width: 769px) {
}

/* medium desktop browsers*/
@media screen and (min-width: 1025px) {
}

/*styling for very wide screens */
@media screen and (min-width: 1600px) {
}
```

Notice that only one of these media queries remains unchanged: the one for very wide screens, because that already uses `max-width`. Its contents won't need to change either, because by the time you reach that media query, all the styling for medium desktop screens would have been applied in the same way that they would have been for a desktop-first design.

Thinking Mobile First

Adding CSS to a mobile-first stylesheet requires a different approach. The steps are as follows:

1. Code everything that's needed for the mobile version and style it. You should find that this is simpler than coding a desktop-first site—for example, because large background images probably won't be needed, mobile devices can simply ignore the media queries that load them.

2. Add styling for each screen size, working your way up. Add in additional styling, background images, and content as needed. Where necessary, use CSS or PHP as appropriate to display conditional content (you'll learn more about this shortly).

It's a bit like progressive enhancement versus graceful degradation—start with what's necessary on all devices, including very small ones, and then add extras as needed for each larger screen size. Thinking about your site this way is likely to change the way you approach your design, and it should make your sites and themes faster on mobile devices.

Child Themes and Responsive Design

If you're building parent and child themes, you'll need to tread carefully when setting up media queries, for one simple reason: Any styles in your child theme's main stylesheet area that clash with styling in your parent theme's stylesheet will override the parent theme.

Obviously, this is generally a good thing, but with responsive theming it can complicate things. If you make your parent theme responsive, and then add any styling to the layout in the child theme that clashes with this, the responsiveness will be lost and your layout could break.

Luckily, it's a simple issue to resolve. You have two ways around it—one involves a responsive parent theme and the other involves a responsive child theme.

Using Object-Oriented CSS to Make Your Parent Theme Responsive

The first solution is to code the full layout into your parent theme, including responsiveness, and don't alter it at all in your child theme. Assuming you need your parent theme to work with a number of child themes that have different layouts, this method works only if you take an object-oriented approach to your layout styling.

For example, assume the styling you were applying to your layout elements used percentages for each main element, as shown in this very simplified example:

```
header, footer, nav.main, .content-container {
 width: 100%;
}
.content {
 width: 66%;
 float: left;
}
.sidebar {
 width: 30%;
 float: right;
}

@media screen and (max-width: 480px) {
  body {
   width: 90%;
   margins: 0 5%;
  }
  header, nav.main .main, .content, .sidebar, footer {
   width: 100%;
  }
}
```

You would replace the preceding with a set of classes with percentage styling:

```
.full-width {
 width: 100%;
}
one-third {
 width: 33%;
}
.two-thirds {
 width: 66%;
}

@media screen and (max-width: 480px) {
  body {
   width: 90%;
   margins: 0 5%;
  }
.full, two-thirds, .one-third {
   width: 100%;
  }
}
```

This would set up styling for object-oriented CSS classes, rather than classes that applied to specific areas of the page layout.

> Note that here I'm using the term **object-oriented** as it applies to CSS, and not to PHP—for more on this see http://coding.smashingmagazine.com/2011/12/12/an-introduction-to-object-oriented-css-oocss/.

When building child themes, you would then assign these classes to the elements in your theme's template files as required, as shown in this example:

```
<body>
 <header class="full">
  <!--header content-->
 </header>
 <section class="container full">
  <div class="content two-thirds">
   <!--PHP to display the content - normally the loop-->
  </div>
  <aside class="sidebar one-third">
   <!--PHP to display widget areas and any other sidebar content-->
  </aside>
 </section><!—end of .container-->
 <footer class="full">
  <!—footer content-->
 </footer>
</body>
```

Obviously, the preceding code is a highly simplified example and wouldn't all be contained in the same template file, but it gives you a general idea.

This approach can be useful if you are using parent themes essentially as a grid system, to power a range of child themes with different layouts—and you won't need to make any layout changes to your child themes that aren't covered by the grid. You would need to add a lot more object-oriented classes to make it future-proof, such as half width, quarter width, and more. You would also need to do the math to ensure that all margins and padding worked at all screen sizes and with all combinations. The advantage, however, is that once you've done this, you would never need to add layout styling again, just insert classes into your HTML.

If you want to have more flexibility with your child themes, there is another approach.

Using Element-Targeted CSS to Make Your Child Themes Responsive

This approach involves using a parent theme that isn't responsive—it's either styled for small mobile screens or for desktops, depending on whether you're using the mobile-first approach. It involves using the approach outlined earlier in this chapter to add layout to your media queries in each child theme you create.

The advantage is that you don't need to code quite so much CSS, as you won't need all those "just-in-case" object-oriented classes and their styling. This may speed your site up slightly. It also gives you more control over the exact layout of your child themes.

The disadvantage is that you have to code media queries into every single child theme you build. You can make this easier by creating some starter child themes, which is what I do. I use a collection of starter themes with the characteristics shown in Table 11-2.

Table 11-2: My Starter Child Themes

Starter Theme	Responsive?	Includes Blog Functionality (e.g., comments, metadata)?
Responsive CMS-type theme	yes	no
Responsive blog theme	yes	yes
Nonresponsive CMS-type theme	no	no
Responsive CMS-type theme	no	yes

Using this approach, each responsive theme has some standard media queries added to adjust the layout, to which you then add more specific styling according to the needs of each project. This approach covers a lot of bases for many types of sites, but you could introduce several variations into your child starter themes—for example, by including different functions in the `functions.php` file or using custom loops.

Responsive Navigation

Earlier, I mentioned that for tablets in landscape view, I don't adjust the layout but rather the size of navigation links. This enables users who navigate the site with their fingers or thumbs, rather than a mouse, to reliably tap the correct link every time.

There are a few approaches to this you could use:

- Keep navigation as it is but enlarge links.
- Restyle the navigation to make it look better on smaller screens, as well as enlarge the links.
- Move navigation so it isn't dominating the screen when users first access the site—for example, move it below the content and add a link to it at the top of the page.
- Hide navigation and create a button that users tap to access it.

The first approach is the simplest but it involves some care to ensure that the navigation links don't encroach outside their container, or outside any background image. The following section looks at an example of the second and third approaches, which I have implemented on my agency's site, `http://compass-design.co.uk/`.

Responsive Design Case Study – Compass Design

The Compass Design website is responsive, desktop-first, and includes media queries targeting tablets and smartphones. For smartphones in landscape mode it isn't changed from the desktop view, as this works fine for users (see Figure 11-9).

However, in portrait mode, as shown in Figure 11-10, the narrower width of the screen forces three of the navigation links to a second line, overflowing the background image, which looks messy.

Figure 11-9 The Compass Design website as seen on an iPad in landscape mode

Figure 11-10 The Compass Design website on an iPad in portrait mode before restyling the navigation

If you were to make the links smaller to fit in the available space, they would be way too small to tap. Therefore, a better solution is to style the links to be narrower and deeper, as shown in Figure 11-11.

Figure 11-11 The Compass Design website on an iPad in portrait mode after restyling the navigation

This is achieved by doing something controversial—using CSS to lay the links out as table cells, which is the only way to do this given the current technology.

The CSS is as follows:

```
@media screen and (max-width: 780px) {
  .nav-strip {
    background-image: url(images/nav-background-tablet.png);
    height: 67px;
  }
  .menu li {
    width: 7%;
    padding: 1%;
    margin: 0;
```

(continued)

```
    border-left: 1px solid #fff;
    border-right: 1px solid #333;
    display: table;
}
.menu li:first-child {
    border-left: none;
}
.menu li:last-child {
    border-right: none;
}
.menu li a {
    margin: 0;
    padding: 0 0 0.2em 0;
    line-height: 1.1em;
    text-align: center;
    height: 3.8em;
    display: table-cell;
    vertical-align: middle;
}
.menu ul ul {
    top: 67px;
}
.menu ul ul li {
    display: block;
}
.menu ul ul li a {
    text-align: left;
}
```

This styling does a few things:

1. It sets a different, deeper background image for the `.nav-strip` element, which is a full-width element containing the menu.

2. It resizes each list item in the menu, assigning each `width: 7%`, which accommodates the number of links, and adds a border to each on the left and right. It then uses `first-child` and `last-child` to remove the relevant border from the first and last links. It also adds `display: table` to make the layout work.

3. It adds styling for each link, including the use of `display: table-cell` and `vertical-align:middle` to display the links correctly, including text wrapping.

4. It adds styling for second-level navigation links, changing the `display` declaration back to `block` and the alignment back to `left`.

Moving on to small screens, this layout wouldn't work at all, as it would create links that are much too small to tap and whose contents wouldn't fit. The approach I've adopted here, as shown in Figures 11-12 and 11-13, is to move the navigation below the page content and add a link to the top of the page to access it.

Figure 11-12 For small screens, the navigation can be replaced by an anchor linking to navigation at the bottom of the page.

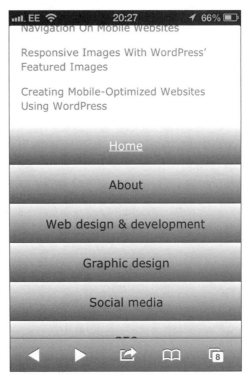

Figure 11-13 When users tap the link, they are taken to the navigation, now moved below the widget area.

Handling this involves the use of a snippet of HTML to display the anchor. Insert this above the markup for the main navigation:

```
<a class="menu-link" href="#menu">Menu</a><!--menu link for small
screens-->
<div class="nav-strip"><!--for styling-->
 <span class="menu-anchor" name="menu">
 <nav id="access"><?php wp_nav_menu( array( 'container_class' => 'menu-
header', 'theme_location' => 'primary' ) ); ?></nav>
</div><!--.nav-strip-->
```

This adds an element(span class="menu-anchor" name="menu") with a link to it (a class="menu-link" href="#menu"). The position of the menu on small screens is styled using absolute positioning with CSS, as follows:

```
/* styling for small screens e.g. smartphones in landscape mode */
@media screen and (max-width: 568px) {
 /* reposition the menu*/
 .container {
 padding-bottom: 522px;
 position: relative;
 }
```

(continued)

```
.nav-strip {
 position: absolute;
 bottom: 0;
}
.menu-link,
.menu-anchor {
 display: block;
}
.menu-link {
 display: block;
 width: 100%;
 margin: 0;
 border-top: 1px solid #fff;
 border-bottom: 1px solid #333;
 background: linear-gradient(top, #ffffff 0%,#666666 100%);
 font-size: 16px;
 padding-top: 10px;
 height: 34px;
 color: #000;
 text-align: center;
}
.menu-link:hover, .menu-link:active {
 color: #fff;
}
.menu-anchor {
 height:0;
 }
}
```

Working through the code:

1. It sets `padding-bottom` on the `.container` element to `522px`, which creates the space for the menu. This `.container` contains the navigation menu itself plus the content and sidebar—it needs to contain the navigation for the absolute positioning to work.

2. It gives absolute positioning to `.nav-strip`, which contains the menu, and places it at the bottom of its container.

3. It ensures that the `.menu-link` and `.menu-anchor` links are displayed—in the main section of the stylesheet these are set to `display: none`.

4. It styles `a.menu-link` in exactly the same way as each link in the navigation menu itself is styled for this screen size (also included in this media query but not shown here).

5. It assigns `height:0` to `a.menu-anchor` to make the anchor invisible.

This is just one way of achieving the result, adding minimal extra markup but a lot of extra styling. Other alternatives include the following:

- Code two menus and display the relevant one in the right place using PHP (the topic of the next section).

- Leave the menu at the top and hide it until the user taps a button.

- Change the display of the menu to a select field.

Conditional Content for Devices

Using CSS as a client-side solution for responsive design is great. It enables you to adjust layout and styling for different devices, and by using `display: none` it provides some capability to display or hide elements according to screen width. Using CSS for this purpose has its limitations, however. Any content you hide with CSS will still be delivered to the device, so a lot of content or an image, for example, could slow things down. Fortunately, because WordPress is based on PHP, it offers a server-side solution to ensure that content not needed on a device isn't sent to it.

When to Send Different Content to Different Devices

The extent to which you send device-specific content can range from one element, such as a large image or the navigation menu, to the entire content of the site. If you're sending a huge amount of different content, the best approach is probably to use a mobile-specific theme, which is covered in section "Mobile-Only Themes" later in the chapter.

This section looks at scenarios in which you might want to send limited amounts of different content to different devices, and describes the available techniques to accomplish that.

Following are the three most common reasons why you would send different content to different devices:

- **Images**—If your desktop site contains large images, you don't need to send full-size versions to mobile devices. Methods for sending different image files to different devices are being worked on by many developers right now, with various solutions being proposed, including the adoption of new standards and elements for images.
- **Navigation**—If your navigation includes a lot of links, you may want to reduce their number, by adding a mobile-specific menu with links to the most commonly accessed content. A word of warning, however: Your mobile navigation should still give users access to all parts of the site. You should either add second-level links directing users to the rest of the site or create a second menu further down on the page that provides access to the same content as the desktop menu.
- **Device-dependent content**—This is also a topic of some debate, with some commentators arguing that sites should create content targeted at devices, and others arguing that content should be the same regardless of device. Another consideration is that managing two sets of content involves twice as much work (and budget).

Targeting content at devices, therefore, will depend on three things: the need to optimize site performance, the differing needs of mobile and desktop users, and the devices your site is actually being accessed on.

A Note on Context

At the beginning of this chapter I talked about context, the circumstances and manner in which people use different devices. It's important to remember that mobile users won't necessarily have slower connections or shorter attention spans. What is certain is that they have a smaller screen to work with—which is why it makes sense to optimize images. That is, don't send images that are larger than they need to be, and review content to ensure that it fits well and is easy to interact with on small screens.

Techniques for Identifying Device Types

There are two commonly used ways of detecting device types:

- Detecting screen width using CSS
- Detecting User Agents with PHP

Using CSS to Detect Screen Width

As mentioned earlier, this approach should only be used for small items that won't slow a site down. The simple way to use CSS to display or hide content is to style device-oriented classes and display or hide them within each media query:

```css
.tablet, .mobile {
 display: none;
}
.desktop {
 display: block;
}

/* tablets in landscape mode or small desktops*/
@media screen and (max-width: 1024px) {
 .desktop, .mobile {
  display: none;
 }
 .tablet {
  display: block;
 }
}

/* smartphones in landscape mode*/
@media screen and (max-width: 480px) {
 .desktop, .tablet {
  display: none;
 }
 .mobile {
  display: block;
 }
}
```

Then you would simply assign the relevant class (.desktop, .tablet, or .mobile, or a combination of two), to each element you wanted to display on only one type of device. This is the approach used earlier to set up a menu anchor.

Detecting User Agent with PHP

This is the method that most existing mobile or responsive plugins use, from theme switchers to the majority of responsive image plugins.

Detecting User Agents has two main disadvantages. First, if you're setting variables based on the User Agent, you must factor in a huge number of potential values that could be returned by the server, which will be changing all the time. For example, at the time of writing, the iPad mini doesn't have its own unique UA string, but rather shares one with the iPad—a pain if you want to target its smaller screen.

Second, it can be unreliable. For example, whatever the browser, the UA string will always contain "Mozilla"—not just in Firefox.

The code to detect the User Agent is as follows:

```php
<?php echo $_SERVER['HTTP_USER_AGENT'] . "\n\n"; ?>
```

In Safari for Mac, for example, this outputs what is shown in Figure 11-14.

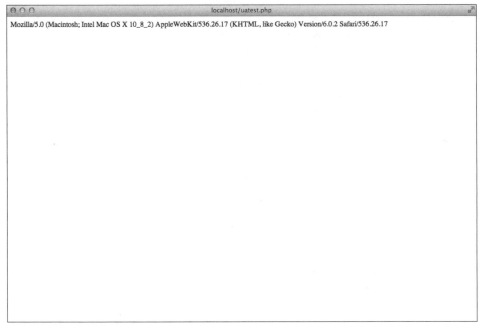

Figure 11-14 The UA string for the latest version of Safari for Mac OSX at time of writing

The UA string shown in Figure 11-14 is as follows:

```
Mozilla/5.0 (Macintosh; Intel Mac OS X 10_8_2) Apple WebKit/536.26.17
(KHTLM, like gecko) Version/6.0.2 Safari/536.26.17
```

As you can see, the UA string shown includes "Mozilla," despite being for the Safari browser, not Firefox. Similarly, if you run this in Chrome, the string returned includes "Safari"—very misleading! However, we're not concerned with desktop browsers—the important thing here is to detect mobile User Agents.

To do this, you would define a function similar to the following extract of the function used in the Mobble plugin (`http://wordpress.org/extend/plugins/mobble/`):

```php
$useragent = isset($_SERVER['HTTP_USER_AGENT']) ?
  $_SERVER['HTTP_USER_AGENT'] : "";
```

(continued)

```
/*****************************************************************
* Function is_iphone
* Detect the iPhone
*****************************************************************/

function is_iphone() {
 global $useragent;
 return(preg_match('/iphone/i',$useragent));
}
```

This assigns the UA string to a variable $useragent, and then defines a function called is_iphone that searches for iphone in the UA string, returned when the page is being viewed on an iPhone. As you can imagine, you would have to define a lot of functions to detect each possible mobile device! That's why I tend to use a plugin to do this, such as Mobble or another plugin that works with specific content if I need to do that.

Because UA detection can be unreliable, you may need to include a fallback, or at least use it only when the results aren't crucial—therefore, ensure that anything that might be sent in error won't break on the devices for which it's not intended.

Using Responsive Images

Responsive images is currently a hot topic in web development circles. The rationale behind responsive images is that it makes no sense to send large image files to devices with small screens that will have to scale those images down anyway. Of course, as I've already mentioned, you can't assume that your mobile users will be on a slow connection; but it still makes sense to avoid sending to a device image files that are larger than the device's screen size.

There are two ways to make your images responsive:

- **Using CSS**—Earlier in the chapter, the max-width property was added to the media queries, which makes the images look smaller but has no effect on file size. If you're developing mobile-first, another alternative is to use small images inline and then use CSS to display larger images as background images on larger screens.

- **Using PHP**—This option enables you to tell the server which image file to deliver depending on the device. You can do this by using a plugin or by adding conditional tags to your theme combined with User Agent detection.

Creating Mobile-First Responsive Images with CSS

This technique involves adding images in your markup at their smallest resolution, then using CSS to hide them and replace them with background images at the correct resolution. However, you can only use it for images you have some control over, such as banner images—there's no way to use it for images added via the media uploader, as you have no way of knowing the filenames of those images in advance, so you can't use them in your stylesheet.

To do this for a banner image, you would add the image to your header.php file and then style it using CSS. Suppose you have uploaded three versions of the image at different sizes. The following would display your image at its smallest size in the markup, meaning this image is sent to *all* devices:

```
<div class="banner-box">
<img class="banner" src="<?php bloginfo( 'stylesheet_directory'
);?>/images/banner-small.jpg" alt="banner image">
</div>
```

Next, in your media queries you would add the following:

```
img.banner {
 width: 100%;
}

/* tablets in portrait mode*/
@media screen and (min-width: 481px) {
 img.banner {
  display: none;
 }
 div.banner-box {
 background: url(images/banner-med.jpg);
 height: 225px;
 }
}

/* medium desktop browsers*/
@media screen and (min-width: 1025px) {
img.banner {
  display: none;
div.banner-box {
  background: url(images/banner-large.jpg);
  height: 350px;
 }
}
```

This technique takes a lot of work—it requires the addition of a background image in CSS for every image you want to make responsive, so it's only appropriate for a few key images in your site such as the banner image or a background image. Some other techniques are more appropriate for other images.

Creating Responsive Images with PHP and Featured Images

This approach uses PHP to detect the UA, and then based on the result it displays a different version of the featured image for each post or page. I've used this technique on a few sites and I tend to use the Mobble plugin, which includes some conditional tags for mobile devices and saves me the trouble of setting up my own UA detection. The technique involves adding a featured image to each post or page (versus inline images).

In the loop in the relevant template file(s), you add a call to the featured image wrapped in a conditional tag:

```
<?php
 if (is_mobile()) {
  the_post_thumbnail('medium');
 } else {
  the_post_thumbnail('large');
 } ?>
```

The main disadvantage of this technique is that it relies on featured images being used instead of inline images, which might not be the case if your site will be maintained by editors who aren't familiar with featured images. However, where this *is* the case and posts won't include a lot of other images, it can be useful. For a complete tutorial about this method, see `http://mobile.smashingmagazine.com/2012/06/14/responsive-images-with-wordress-featured-images/`.

Responsive Images Plugins and Other Techniques

There is a range of plugins and techniques aside from the ones I've described to make your images responsive. Among the good WordPress plugins is WP Responsive Images (`http://wordpress.org/extend/plugins/wp-responsive-images/`), which uses JavaScript to detect screen width with UA detection as a fallback.

Outside WordPress, `php-mobile detect` (`http://code.google.com/p/php-mobile-detect/`) is a PHP class that detects mobile devices. Mat Wilcox's Adaptive Images (`http://adaptive-images.com`) uses a combination of JavaScript and PHP to automatically resize image files on the fly, but it can be tricky to combine with WordPress because of the way it requires your file structure to be set up.

Responsive Images and Retina Displays

The advent of Retina Display complicates responsive design a bit. Before Apple released these high-resolution wonders, we were used to defining our media queries at the pixel density reported by the browser.

Retina Display work differently. The value of the actual pixels used to display content (the device pixels) is twice the pixel value the browser uses for the purpose of rendering content according to your CSS (CSS pixels). This means if your CSS specifies that an element is 320px square, for example, the browser will actually use 640px by 640px to display it, although the physical size on the screen would be the same as a non-Retina Display using 320px by 320px to display it. In other words, the element is displayed at the same size but double the resolution.

You can add a media query to target Retina Display devices, which can be useful for a site on which images are important and you want to send high-resolution versions:

```
@media
  (-webkit-min-device-pixel-ratio: 2),
  (min-resolution: 192dpi) {
  /* Retina-specific styling here */
}
```

If you're using PHP to detect Retina Display (or HiDPI display on other devices), you have to identify the UA of devices with it.

Warning: Although images look great on Retina Displays, remember that twice the resolution equals four times the actual size—so these could be very large files. An image optimized for the iPad's Retina Display, for example, will be larger than the same image optimized for the desktop. Consider download speeds before making all your images high resolution.

The Future of Responsive Images

The W3C has responded to the efforts of developers to find a robust solution for responsive images, proposing a new `picture` element that would allow multiple source files for one element, each to be used on different screen resolutions.

The `picture` element would contain a `p` element within it for accessible text, replacing `alt` attributes, and can be combined with the `screen` attribute to link it to media queries. The following code works on a mobile-first basis and shows how it could be used:

```
<picture>
    <source media="(min-width: 1024px)" srcset="large-1.jpg 1x, large-
2.jpg 2x">
    <source media="(min-width: 768px)" srcset="med-1.jpg 1x, med-2.jpg
2x">
    <source srcset="small-1.jpg 1x, small-2.jpg 2x">
    <img src="small-1.jpg" alt="">
    <p>Accessible text</p>
</picture>
```

However, this element is in its very early stages. It hasn't been adopted by any browsers yet and how exactly it would work is still being discussed, if indeed it is introduced at all. It also has the downside of requiring each image to have the media query and alternative images coded into it, which would be time-consuming—but it would probably be possible to write a function to specify the media queries and size images to be used in each case, using `wp_get_attachment_image`. You can find out more about the `picture` element at `http://picture.responsiveimages.org`.

Conditional Navigation

Earlier, you looked at an example using CSS to move the menu further down the page, to avoid having it take up too much space on the screen; but in some cases you may want to use a different menu for different devices. This can be useful if the following apply:

- You want mobile users to access specific content quickly, because mobile users tend to interact with the site differently from desktop users. This might be the case for an airline website, for example, where most bookings are made on desktops while checking in is done on mobile. Of course, you'd still want to make both processes available to both groups of users; otherwise, you might confuse people or lose potential customers.

- You want a short, easy to tap navigation menu at the top of your page and a longer one at the bottom, which leads to the rest of the site's content.

There are two ways of doing this:

- Using CSS, simply hide each menu from the relevant devices, as shown earlier. This isn't ideal if the menus are long, as that's more content to download on all devices. Also, any users with CSS turned off (for example, screen reader users) will be confronted with multiple menus, which may be confusing.

- Use PHP to display the correct menu according to the device being used. This is what I did for the Centenary Lounge website, described in the following section.

Conditional Navigation Case Study: Centenary Lounge

Centenary Lounge is a coffee shop whose website includes a lot of information about its location and history, as it's located in a heritage railway station and has Art Deco décor. The site is responsive. The owner wanted it to be as easy as possible for mobile users to access the most frequently accessed information about her business, so conditional navigation was used to achieve this.

First, two menus were set up in WordPress, one for mobile and one for desktop. The mobile menu includes all the same links as the desktop menu but with many fewer top-level links.

Using the Mobble plugin, the menus were wrapped in a conditional tag:

```
<nav class="main">
 <?php
 if ( is_mobile() ) {
 wp_nav_menu( array('menu' => 'mobilenav', 'container_class' =>
'menu-header', 'menu-class' => 'mobilenav' ));
   } else {
   wp_nav_menu( array( 'container_class' => 'menu-header',
'theme_location' => 'primary' ) );
   } ?>
</nav><!--.main -->
```

By using the `mobilenav` class added by the `wp_nav_menu()` function, you can then style the mobile menu differently from the desktop version.

The result is a very different navigation menu when viewed on different screens, as shown in Figures 11-15 and 11-16.

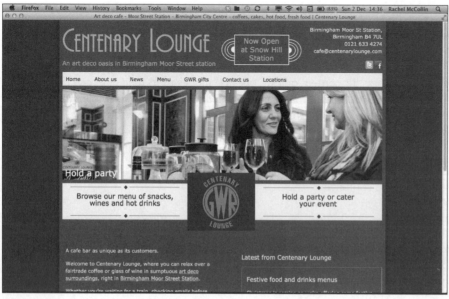

© 2011 Centenary Lounge

Figure 11-15 The Centenary Lounge menu as viewed on desktops

© 2011 Centenary Lounge
Figure 11-16 The Centenary Lounge menu as viewed
on mobiles

Mobile-Only Themes

It used to be that the only way to make your WordPress site mobile-friendly was to use a mobile theme—this is how plugins such as WP Mobile Pack and WPTouch work. With the advent of responsive design, that's changed—the number of mobile plugins is decreasing while the number of responsive themes increases.

There is a place for mobile themes, however. When your mobile content is so different from the desktop content that managing the differences within one theme becomes unwieldy, a mobile theme is probably the answer—but why limit yourself to the ones provided by the plugins when you can build your own?

Uses for a Mobile Theme

If your desktop and mobile sites will be structured in the same way and prioritise the same content, it makes sense to use a responsive theme—there's only one theme to manage and maintain, which can save time and money. But what if your client needs a mobile site that will perform quite a different function from the main site?

Examples of this might include the following:

- Single-page mobile sites directing visitors to call the site owner
- Sites with different versions of the content for different devices
- Sites that take advantage of touchscreen interactivity—for example, gallery or e-commerce sites using touch-enabled carousels
- Web apps—sites with a process-based interface on mobile but a content-based interface on desktop

All these scenarios (and others) are valid reasons to develop a different theme on mobile devices.

Mobile Theme Best Practices

It's important to ensure that your mobile theme doesn't result in a diminished experience for mobile users. After all, with more people accessing the Internet on a mobile device, sometimes exclusively, you need to ensure that all of your site's content is available to everyone.

- Always make it possible for users to switch to the main site, usually via a link in the footer.
- Make your main site responsive, so that if users switch to it they will get an optimized mobile experience.
- Don't force mobile users to download an app instead of browsing the mobile site—even a pop-up advertising the app can be irritating and may cost you some visitors.
- Be aware of accessibility issues—not all mobile users will be using touch to interact with your site or will even be able to see it. Be sure you include all the accessibility options you would include in a desktop site.

Displaying a Different Theme Based on Device

After you or your client has determined that a different theme is needed on different devices, the easiest way to do that is to use a *theme switcher*, a plugin that detects the UA of the device accessing the site and then switches to a different theme according to the settings you've specified.

A good theme switcher is the Multi Device Switcher plugin, available at `http://wordpress.org/extend/plugins/multi-device-switcher/`. This plugin includes a Settings page that enables you to specify the theme for different kinds of devices—the defaults are smartphones, tablets, mobile phones, and gaming devices. You can add your own categories and specify the User Agents to which they apply, as well as edit the User Agents detected for the default device types. For example, if you wanted to develop a theme for the iPhone only, you would type "iPhone" in the Custom Device Switcher field and then add "iPhone" to the list of devices targeted by that switcher, remembering to remove it from the default list for smartphones. The various settings are shown in Figure 11-17.

Building Your Mobile Theme

The approach you use to build your mobile theme will depend on the extent to which you need it to differ from the main theme, and whether you already have code you can use from the main theme. For example, if the theme is responsive, this is a starting point—even better if it's responsive and mobile first.

Figure 11-17 The Settings page for the Multi Device Switcher plugin

If the site content isn't wildly different, I suggest using the following approach, which should be most efficient in terms of both effort and code:

- Build your main theme, using mobile-first responsiveness.
- Duplicate the main theme and remove any styling and content for devices not supported by the mobile theme (or duplicate it during development, before you add any desktop content or styling).
- Edit the new mobile theme to restyle it and include the content needed.

This is the approach I took with the Carborelli's site, detailed in the section "Mobile Commerce Case Study: Carborelli's," later in this chapter.

Exploring the Possibilities: WordPress Web Apps

As mobile browsers evolve, you will be able to pack more and more functionality into a WordPress web app. This section looks at three examples to demonstrate some of the possibilities: geolocation, file upload, and mobile commerce.

Geolocation

Geolocation is a great feature for web apps. Assuming that your users could be anywhere on earth, being able to locate them in order to provide location-specific data can be useful for all kinds of services. Examples include the following:

- Apps for a chain of restaurants or stores, enabling users to find the local branch
- Apps for an event, enabling users to get directions to the event or see different locations involved in the event
- Social apps, enabling users to see where other users are currently located

There are two main ways of identifying user location: identifying their IP address and using the HTML5 geolocation API, which uses JavaScript and passes that to the page's markup.

Identifying IP addresses can be useful when you want to match a number of location areas to a set group of locations. In the case study that follows, IP addresses are used to match a user's location against an office location. Because the app had to identify just one office, this was the best approach. The Geolocation API may have resulted in two results, and it would have been difficult for the app to determine which one to choose.

The Geolocation API, however, is generally more reliable, as it avoids the potential issue of browsers misreporting IP addresses for whatever reason. It also means you don't have to store data relating to IP addresses and how they match your app's data.

The HTML5 Geolocation API

The Geolocation API uses a script to determine the user's latitude and longitude. You can then use this information to place a marker on a map or get directions.

Before retrieving the location, you need to determine whether the browser supports geolocation with the following script:

```
<script type="text/javascript">
 //Check if browser supports Geolocation
 if (navigator.geolocation) {
  navigator.geolocation.getCurrentPosition(successFunction,
errorFunction);
 } else {
  //code to run if Geolocation not supported
}
</script>
```

This calls a JavaScript function, `successFunction`, which you would then define in order to specify what should happen if geolocation is supported. For example, to display the user's location to them, you would use the following (inside your `<script>` tags):

```
function successFunction(position) {
 var lat = position.coords.latitude;
 var long = position.coords.longitude;
 alert('Your latitude is :'+lat+' and longitude is '+long);
}
```

As it stands, however, this isn't hugely useful—most users won't find their latitude and longitude very helpful! What you really need to do is get that information and plot it on a map, for example. To do this, you need to use a mapping API, which can generate maps based on latitude and longitude values. This example uses the Google Maps API (`https://developers.google.com/maps/`).

To include the Google Maps API script in your page, you need to enqueue the script in your functions file using `wp_enqueue_script()` as detailed in Chapter 10.

```php
<?php
function wpptl_enqueue_maps() {
 wp_enqueue_script( 'google-maps', 'http://maps.google.com/maps/api/
js?sensor=false' );
}
add_action( 'wp_enqueue_scripts', 'wpptl_enqueue_maps' );
?>
```

Next, to create a marker for your user's location, you would add the following to your geolocation script (instead of the previous example):

```javascript
//Load Google Map
var latlng = new google.maps.LatLng(mylat, mylong);
    var myOptions = {
      zoom: 15,
      center: latlng,
      mapTypeId: google.maps.MapTypeId.ROADMAP
    };

var map = new google.maps.Map(document.getElementById("map_canvas"),
myOptions);

//Add marker
var marker = new google.maps.Marker({
      position: latlng,
      map: map,
      title:"You are here"
  });
}
```

In order to display this on the page, you need to add the map to your HTML, in the relevant place in the page:

```html
<div id="map_canvas"></div>
```

Finally, you need to style the map. Use percentages for this, rather than pixels, to avoid pixelation on devices with Retina Display:

```css
#map_canvas {
      height: 85%;
      width: 100%;
    }
```

This creates a map with a marker displaying the user's position, as shown in Figure 11-18, from the Opera developers' website, `http://dev.opera.com`.

The next step is to add the coordinates of your client's business, such as store, restaurant, or whatever location users will need to find. You could do this manually, but a better way to do it is by using another API that stores locations, such as the Google Maps API or the Foursquare API. Which one you use will depend on what geolocation-enabled services your client is using. I recommend using the Google Maps API, as you can use it to either retrieve data from the Google Places API or to display a marker for an address you define in your script. (Details about how to do this are beyond the scope of this chapter, and could be the topic of an entire book!)

Figure 11-18 A Google Map with place marker displayed –
example from the dev.opera.com website

If you want to add multiple markers on a map in your web app, wptuts+ has a useful tutorial demonstrating how to do so at `http://wp.tutsplus.com/tutorials/creative-coding/use-geo-location-to-give-your-customers-driving-directions/`

File Upload

Until quite recently, file upload wasn't possible on mobile browsers—if you wanted your users to be able to upload files, you had to develop an app. Since the release of Mobile Safari 6 with iOS6, that is now possible on iOS devices at least, and it shouldn't be long before Android and other platforms catch up.

I built a personal site with an image gallery over the summer of 2012, with most of the users accessing the site from mobile devices (including me). To upload photos, they had to send them to me, and I uploaded them via the WordPress app—a convoluted and not very convenient process.

With Safari 6, the file upload process couldn't be simpler. Just insert the following into your HTML:

```
<input type=file>
```

You can also let the user upload multiple files at once:

```
<label>Multiple files:</label>
<input type="file" multiple>
```

When users access the page, they see the relevant button(s) for file upload, as shown in Figure 11-19.

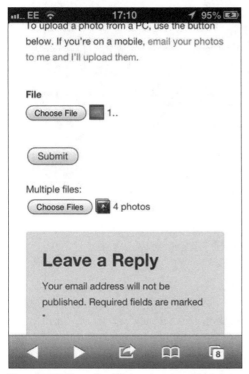

Figure 11-19 The upload file buttons on mobile Safari

After tapping the button for a single file, the file upload options shown in Figure 11-20 appear.

By tapping the button for multiple file upload, users can select as many images as needed from their photo library, as shown in Figure 11-21.

Note that at present the only file types users can upload are images and videos, because there's no way to access any other file type on an iOS device. Using the following, you can stipulate which kind of file users can upload:

```
<input type=file accept="video/*">
<input type=file accept="image/*">
```

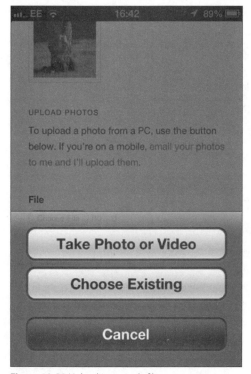

Figure 11-20 Uploading a single file

Figure 11-21 Uploading multiple files

This case study is a very simple use of file upload, but you can imagine the possibilities, For example, for social sites or photo gallery sites, users can upload their own profile image, shots of what they've been doing, or portfolio photos. For a site supporting an event, a museum, or a band, for example, you could encourage users to upload related photos.

Mobile Commerce

Mobile commerce can take a number of forms. From the simple purchase of downloads to a full-blown mobile shop, the advantages of making any form of e-commerce mobile are significant.

Research undertaken by IBM following Black Friday, the day after Thanksgiving, in 2012 (`http://www.prnewswire.com/news-releases/early-promotions-drive-record-online-sales-for-thanksgiving-fuels-black-friday-retail-surge-reports-ibm-180691231.html`) showed that the proportion of online sales made that day from mobile devices increased from 9.8 percent in 2011 to more than 16 percent in 2012. The dominant device was the iPad, which accounted for nearly 10 percent of online shopping, more than any other mobile device.

Black Friday is a big day for retailers, and a day when a lot of shoppers may be away from home and their desktop computer. If your client runs an online shop, they don't want to miss out on this growing market.

You can approach mobile commerce in a number of ways:

- Use a responsive shopping theme such as those provided by JigoShop (`http://jigoshop.com`).

- Make your own e-commerce theme responsive.

- Build a web app designed to optimize the mobile shopping experience.

- Build a native app.

A web app using a separate theme gives shoppers the best possible user experience and may actually be easier to work with than a responsive theme. Your e-commerce site will include images and product descriptions that need to be laid out quite differently on different devices—and these differences may be significant enough that it's actually easier to build a separate mobile theme, especially for smaller screens. Tablets may benefit from the use of a layout with side-to-side swiping instead of vertical scrolling, or the use of tabs to keep everything "above the fold." Creating media queries aimed at tablets can help you optimize the design, layout, and UX for these devices, giving shoppers a better shopping experience—and one that makes them more likely to come back for more.

An example wireframe for an e-commerce site for the desktop might look as shown in Figure 11-22.

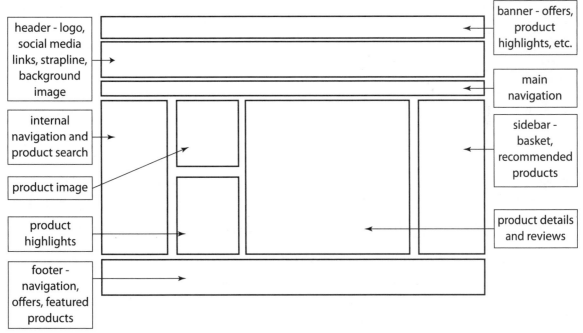

Figure 11-22 E-commerce wireframe for the desktop

As shown in Figure 11-23, for tablets the wireframe would look considerably different, using a swipable grid to display featured images for a range of products, and displaying product details in a pop-up window when a product is tapped.

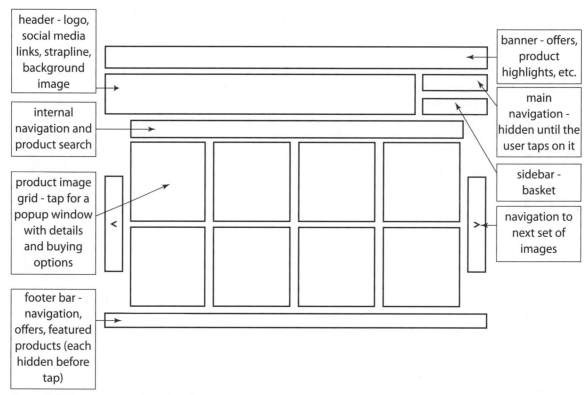

Figure 11-23 E-commerce wireframe for tablets

On mobile devices the wireframe would also be different, using collapsing menus and buttons to minimize use of screen space, removing the top banner and moving other content lower down the page, as shown in Figure 11-24.

The mobile device wireframes could be realized using responsive design, but it would be tricky for a few reasons:

- Content appears in different places in the page on different devices.
- Menus are managed in very different ways on different devices, and may have a different structure.
- The image grid on tablets is unique to that device type and would need to incorporate swipable navigation, using code that would be redundant on other devices.

For these reasons, it might be easier to develop a theme for each type of device, possibly basing each on a common parent theme that used code common to all three themes.

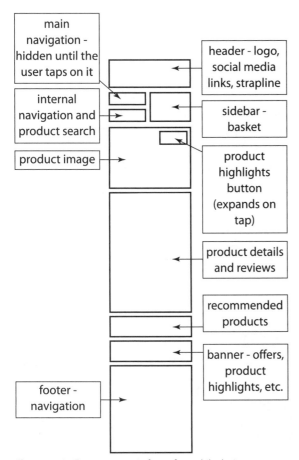

Figure 11-24 E-commerce wireframe for mobile devices

Mobile Commerce Case Study: Carborelli's

The Carborelli's site (a site for a fictitious ice cream parlour that I built to test some mobile development techniques) makes use of a very different theme on mobile devices to create a web app.

The main site includes e-commerce but is also built around content such as information about the store's products, location, history, and services. The web app is focused on one process—building your own ice-cream sundae and then ordering it either to eat in the store or to have the necessary ice creams and accompaniments delivered to you.

The following process was used to achieve this:

1. Build a responsive theme for the main site.

2. Take the elements of the responsive theme targeted at mobile devices (including styling and content) and place these in a new theme.

3. Add functionality to the mobile theme aimed at creating an app-like experience. The home page consists of buttons enabling the user to do something, rather than navigation directing them to content, for example. Also added are a map and directions to the store, using the location of the user's device if available.

4. Add a "switch to main site" link to the web app theme and a "switch to web app" link to the main site when viewed on mobiles, to give users the option to switch between the two.

The main site, as viewed on small screens, looks like Figure 11-25.

Figure 11-25 The Carborelli's responsive site

With the mobile theme in place and the switcher activated, the web app looks like Figure 11-26.

The app uses an ordering form to enable users to build their sundae—users work through a series of options, choosing their preferred flavor of ice cream or topping, and then are taken to PayPal to pay. The form uses select boxes extensively to minimize the amount of typing required by users and to improve accuracy:

```
<label for="input_1_3">Choose your first flavor </label>
<select id="input_1_3" tabindex="2 ">
 <option value="Strawberry cheesecake">Strawberry cheesecake</option>
 <option value="Chocolate dream">Chocolate dream</option>
 <option value="Vanilla heaven">Vanilla heaven</option>
 <option value="Blueberry tart">Blueberry tart</option>
 <option value="Coffee whip">Coffee whip</option>
</select>
```

Figure 11-26 The Carborelli's web app home page

When the user taps on one of these boxes, the device's native select functionality is triggered, as shown in Figure 11-27, improving the user experience.

After users build their sundae, the order is placed and they are shown a map of the store—they can then get directions, which automatically use their location if this functionality is enabled, as shown in Figure 11-28.

I did this using the MapPress Easy Google Maps plugin (`http://wordpress.org/extend/plugins/mappress-google-maps-for-wordpress/`), but you could the HTML5 Geolocation API, described earlier in this chapter.

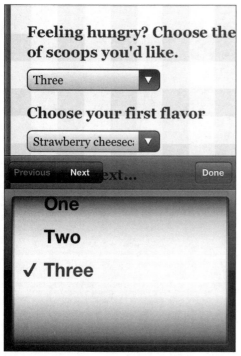

Figure 11-27 The select functionality seen on the iPhone

Figure 11-28 Directions using the MapPress plugin

Mobile Forms Best Practices

This case study revolves around a form, which is an important part of any web app or mobile commerce site. Interacting with forms is much harder on mobile devices if they haven't been optimized for such devices. Following are some tips for optimizing your mobile forms:

- Ensure that you're accessing the correct virtual keyboard using `<input type="#">`. On many devices, you can access four separate keyboards as follows:
  - `<input type ="text">`—For the default, text keyboard
  - `<input type ="number">`—For the numerical keyboard
  - `<input type="email">`—For the e-mail keyboard
  - `<input type ="url">`—For the URL keyboard

- Style your buttons and fields so they're large enough to comfortably tap—Apple's mobile UX guidelines recommend at least 44px square.

- Use select fields to avoid typing where possible.

- Use date pickers whenever a date is needed, to avoid typing and the inevitable errors that result.

Summary

Responsive and mobile development is no longer an optional feature but a core aspect of delivering sites that are available to the widest possible audience. If you're developing for clients, many of them will demand a mobile-optimized site. If you're developing themes, then developing responsive ones gives you an edge. As you have seen in this chapter, there are a lot of things to take into consideration when developing a mobile or responsive WordPress theme, but the starting point is always the need. Once you have a solid grasp of what your client or your theme's users need, WordPress has the tools to help you develop the right responsive or mobile site or theme.

Further Resources

Responsive Design

Responsive Web Design by Ethan Marcotte (A Book Apart, 2011)
`http://www.abookapart.com/products/responsive-web-design`

Mobile First by Luke Wroblewski (A Book Apart, 2011)
`http://www.abookapart.com/products/mobile-first`

WordPress Mobile Web Development by Rachel McCollin (Packt, 2012)
`http://www.packtpub.com/wordpress-mobile-web-development-beginners-guide/book`

Setting device-agnostic media queries
`http://rachelmccollin.co.uk/blog/iphone5-does-it-break-your-responsive-design/`

Conditional Content for Mobile

Getting the User Agent with `'HTTP_USER_AGENT'`
`http://www.php.net/manual/en/reserved.variables.server.php`

Responsive Images

Using featured images for responsive images
`http://mobile.smashingmagazine.com/2012/06/14/responsive-images-with-wordress-featured-images/`

WP Responsive Images plugin
`http://wordpress.org/extend/plugins/wp-responsive-images/`

`php-mobile detect`
`http://code.google.com/p/php-mobile-detect/`

Adaptive images
`http://adaptive-images.com`

The W3C on the proposed `picture` element
`http://picture.responsiveimages.org`

WordPress Web Apps

Google Maps API
`https://developers.google.com/maps/`

How to use the Geolocation API from dev.opera.com
`http://dev.opera.com/articles/view/how-to-use-the-w3c-geolocation-api/`

Tutorial on using Google Maps to display directions to a location
`http://wp.tutsplus.com/tutorials/creative-coding/use-geo-location-to-give-your-customers-driving-directions/`

Black Friday 2012 mobile shopping statistics
`http://www.prnewswire.com/news-releases/early-promotions-drive-record-online-sales-for-thanksgiving-fuels-black-friday-retail-surge-reports-ibm-180691231.html`

Chapter 12
Releasing Your Code to the Public

WordPress is more than just the core installation. For millions of users, the only way they can build a site that meets their needs or the needs of their clients is by using third-party themes and plugins, either from the WordPress repository or via commercial vendors.

In this chapter you'll learn about the process for releasing your themes and plugins so that other users and developers can make use of them. Releasing your code for free via wordpress.org is a great way to hone your WordPress skills, get feedback on your code, and give something back to the WordPress community. If your code is good enough and meets a market need, you might even decide to sell premium themes or plugins.

Sharing Your Code

Sharing your themes or plugins with other WordPress users may seem daunting at first but it has many benefits:

- It supports the WordPress community—like all WordPress users, you get the platform (and other developers' code) for free and it's good to give something back.

- It gives you an opportunity to get feedback on your code. WordPress developers are a supportive bunch and tend to be constructive when pointing out flaws in themes and plugins released via wordpress.org.

- It gives you access to other developers who can help you improve your code—either directly or indirectly.

- It enhances your standing in the WordPress community and possibly with clients.

- It can make money (although this isn't easy to do).

However, sharing your code isn't all clear sailing. You need to ensure your code is robust and meets the WordPress standards, and you need to support it and keep it updated. In particular:

- Ensure that you're using the correct license.

- Your code should be tidy, valid, and bug-free, and work across browsers and platforms.

- You'll need to provide documentation, at minimum in the form of a readme file (for plugins) but also (for more complex themes and plugins) on your own website.

- When WordPress is updated, you need to ensure that your code still works on multiple installations, and release updates if necessary.

- You may need to provide support for users of your code.

- You should provide translation support for your code, for people developing in different languages.

Additionally, if you want to make money by releasing your code, you'll have to do all of this to a higher standard and very promptly—people who have paid for a plugin will expect it to work with WordPress updates as soon as they are released, and expect quick responses to support questions.

If you can take all this on and have an idea for a great theme or plugin that fills a gap in the market, read on!

Filling a Gap in the Market

As of February 2013, the WordPress plugin repository had 23,631 plugins and 1,691 themes—and counting! As you can imagine, these plugins and themes meet a range of user needs and vary from simple plugins that add a shortcode, for example, to complex plugins with their own APIs, such as BuddyPress. Add to this the huge range of premium themes and plugins sold outside wordpress.org, and you're looking at a very crowded marketplace.

However, this doesn't mean there isn't a market for new themes and plugins. New code is released all the time—in response to a new need from users, or a development in WordPress itself, or in the field of web development; the growth in responsive themes and mobile plugins is a good example of the latter.

Therefore, there may be a place for your theme or plugin—but before you start coding, it's a good idea to confirm that there isn't already something out there that does the same job just as well (or maybe better):

- **Find out what's going on in the area you're working in.** For example, if your plugin uses an API (Geolocation, for example), familiarize yourself with development in that area—both in the WordPress community and outside it. Talk to other developers, find out what they're doing and what opportunities there are for collaboration, and where work is already being done that makes yours redundant.

- **Keep abreast of developments in WordPress itself that affect your theme or plugin.** For example, you wouldn't want to have developed a plugin enhancing the Media Manager immediately prior to the release of WordPress 3.5. Keep an eye on the trac site at `http://core.trac.wordpress.org/` and use that to spot changes to WordPress that suggest a need for a new plugin or theme.

- **Talk to potential users of your code.** Find out what they need, and what they're currently using and whether it meets those needs. If it isn't, find out why. Familiarize yourself with the products they are currently using and any planned updates that may coincide with what you have got in mind. Know your competition!

- **Identify ways in which you can develop code to complement other themes or plugins already available.** For example, you may have a great idea for a plugin to enhance BuddyPress or to make use of the Gravity Forms API. If your code will support a community plugin like BuddyPress, get involved in the community of developers working with that plugin and find out what they're doing. Your code isn't competing—it's contributing!

- **Start small.** I've talked to a lot of developers who have launched startups over the years—both in the WordPress community and elsewhere—and the one thing that's most likely to result in failure is being overly ambitious at the beginning. If you have a great idea for a huge, complex plugin, start by releasing a lean version of it, make sure that it does its job as well as possible, grow your user base, and then build on it over time. By being too ambitious too soon, you run the risk of having nothing at all to release until you've done months of development, which may mean giving up before you've even started, or someone else beating you to it. Conversely, if your early efforts on a theme or plugin don't work or aren't adopted, you won't have wasted all that time.

Free vs. Premium Themes and Plugins

Whether you develop free or premium themes and plugins is up to you, but it's a good idea to start out by developing free code, as it gives you a chance to develop your skills and get to know what's involved in supporting users and maintaining your code.

You'll learn more about the considerations for developing premium themes and plugins later in this chapter, but a few things you'll have to consider when deciding which route to take include the following:

- **Is your idea solid enough for people to want to pay for it?** If something very similar is already available free, then it's unlikely anyone will pay for your product.

- **Do you have the time to provide support to your users?** Users of premium themes and plugins expect prompt support—this isn't something you can do in your spare time.

- **Will you be able to maintain your code so it is compatible with new versions of WordPress as soon as they're released?** If users' sites are breaking because of your code, they will be much less tolerant if they paid for that code.

- **Will your code be released under the GPL license?** Some theme vendors use a different license—if you want to stick with GPL, you'll need to find alternative distribution channels.

- **What payment and distribution models will you use?** There are a variety of ways to distribute and take payment for your code; these are covered in the section "Selling Premium Themes and Plugins."

Releasing Your Code on wordpress.org

Most plugin and theme developers start out by releasing free themes and plugins on wordpress.org, even if they're planning to sell their code later.

Reassuringly, there are standards your code has to adhere to before it will be accepted—which is just why wordpress.org is the best place to download free themes and plugins.

> If you're planning to release your code free, I always recommend doing this via wordpress.org. This gives you access to a community of developers, helps users find your product, and ensures that your code won't be altered in a way that causes problems for users. Some developers use GitHub, which is a valid place to share your code but not as robust (or as user-friendly) as wordpress.org.

The Theme Review Guidelines

Themes submitted to wordpress.org are reviewed by the Theme Review Team (`http://make.wordpress.org/themes/`) to ensure that they meet the following minimum standards:

- **Code quality**—Your code should meet the WordPress Coding Standards (`http://codex.wordpress.org/WordPress_Coding_Standards`) and must not generate any deprecated function notices, warnings, or errors.

- **Presentation vs. functionality**—Themes are for presentation, so if your theme is functional, it should be a plugin instead.

- **Theme features**—Your theme should support all core WordPress features, regardless of whether it has its own additional features.

- **Template tags and hooks**—These should be implemented correctly.

- **WordPress-generated CSS classes**—Your theme must use these where relevant.

- **Template files**—Your theme must use these correctly.

- **Security and privacy**—Themes must ensure data security and user privacy.

- **Licensing**—Your theme must be licensed under a GPL-compatible license.

- **Naming**—Your theme's name must not include "WordPress" and it should be unique, to avoid confusing users.

- **Credit links**—Your theme should use these appropriately.

- **Documentation**—At a minimum, you should provide a readme.txt file.

- **Theme Unit Tests**—Your theme must pass these (`http://codex.wordpress.org/Theme_Unit_Test`).

- **Theme obsolescence**—You should keep your theme current after it is accepted.

> **For full details of these standards and what each involves, see** `http://codex.wordpress.org/Theme_Review`.

Reviewing WordPress Themes

Anyone can become a member of the WordPress Theme Review Team. If you want to get involved in reviewing themes, you'll need to meet their guidelines and be able to set up a WordPress theme testing environment where you can review submitted themes according to the guidelines. This is a great way to learn about how themes are coded and to give something back to the community—find out more at `http://make.wordpress.org/themes/`.

Theme Unit Test

When reviewing submitted themes, the Theme Review Team uses the Theme Unit Test (`http://codex.wordpress.org/Theme_Unit_Test`). You can run this test on your theme before submitting it, to ensure that you won't have any problems.

To do so, you follow these steps:

1. Download an `xml` file containing test data from `https://wpcom-themes.svn.automattic.com/demo/theme-unit-test-data.xml`.

2. Using the Import menu, import the `xml` file to your theme.

3. Set `WP_DEBUG` to `'true'` in `wp-config.php`.

4. Install a list of plugins, available at `http://make.wordpress.org/themes/about/how-to-join-wptrt/`, all of which can be installed via the Developer Plugin (`http://wordpress.org/extend/plugins/developer/`).

5. Perform a theme review using the process outlined at `http://www.chipbennett.net/2011/04/20/a-guide-to-reviewing-themes-for-the-wordpress-theme-repository/`.

If your theme passes this review when you do it, hopefully it will also get past the Theme Review Team.

Plugin Submission Guidelines

Plugins have their own set of guidelines that you must conform to before your plugin is accepted for distribution at wordpress.org:

- **Licensing**—The plugin's license must be compatible with the GPL license version 2 or later. If you don't specify a license, it will be assumed that you're releasing your plugin under GPLv2.

- **Subversion**—You must use the Subversion repository in order for your plugin to be available at `http://wordpress.org/extend/plugins/`. This means your plugin is hosted at wordpress.org, not just listed there.

- **Obfuscated code**—This isn't permitted. Encoded code such as PayPal donation buttons aren't considered obfuscated but may be questioned before your plugin is accepted.

- **Trialware**—Plugins must not disable functionality after a trial period or require payment to unlock functionality. You can create a "pro" version of your plugin that you sell outside wordpress.org, but the free version must be a genuinely useful plugin.

- **Serviceware**—Serviceware plugins, which provide an interface to a third-party service such as a video hosting site, are allowed as long as they meet the other guidelines. They must be useful.

- **Data collection**—Plugins must not collect user data without authorization. Collection of data is allowed as long as it requires authorization.

- **Hosting**—Plugins must not use code such as images and scripts hosted outside the plugin, or include banner or link advertising. All of the plugin's content must be contained within the plugin's files.

- **Executable code**—Plugins must not send executable code via third-party systems, as this may present a security risk.

- **Illegality**—Plugins must not do anything illegal or morally offensive, including spamming.

- **Links**—Plugins must not embed links on the public site (such as a "powered by" link) without asking permission—any options must default to not show the link. The plugin page (as coded in the `readme.txt` file) must not include sponsorship links.

- **Admin**—Plugins shouldn't "hijack" the admin or include "nagging." Adding Dashboard widgets is acceptable as long as they can be turned off and are of a standard size.

- **Commits**—Limit commits and avoid frequent blank commit messages, as these may confuse users.

- **Updates and submission**—A complete version of the plugin must be submitted for review. Each update must result in the version number being upgraded.

- **Trademarks**—Don't use "wordpress" or "WordPress" in your plugin's name or your website URL—use "wp" or be more imaginative!

That's a long list of standards, but a necessary one, as it protects users from plugins that could break their WordPress installation, introduce malicious code, or act unexpectedly. It also provides legal protection to developers, such as by not accepting plugins that do anything illegal or infringe on copyright.

If you have developed a plugin that you want to submit to wordpress.org, you'll need to work through that list to ensure your plugin meets the guidelines. Some of these are examined in more detail in the next section.

Preparing Your Code for Release

In order to meet the guidelines, and provide a theme or plugin that will meet your users' needs and be easy to interact with, you need to prepare your theme or plugin for release.

Coding Standards

The first and most obvious check is to ensure your code meets the WordPress coding standards. I won't go into this in detail here because it's covered in Chapter 1; but before submitting your code, you should make some checks:

- **Ensure that your code syntax won't cause conflicts with other themes or plugins or with WordPress core.** For example, name all files correctly and give your plugin files and functions unique names, using the name of your plugin or theme as a prefix. Don't use `wp_` as a prefix for any functions or files, to avoid conflicts with the core.

- **Validate your code.** Use a validation service such as the W3C's validation site at `http://validator.w3.org/` (for HTML) and `http://jigsaw.w3.org/css-validator/` (for CSS) to ensure that your code validates. In some cases your code may not validate for good reasons (e.g., you're using HTML5 or CSS3, which aren't part of the spec yet)—if this is the case, be sure that you understand why the code isn't validating and fix it so that it won't cause any problems.

- **Debug your code.** Use `WP_DEBUG` to verify that your code doesn't throw any errors, including deprecated function notices, PHP errors, warnings, or other notices.

- **If your theme or plugin uses JavaScript, test it using the JavaScript console in your browser.** Make sure you're using the latest version of any JavaScript libraries; and if you're using jQuery, do this by accessing the version of jQuery bundled with WordPress.

- **Browser-test your code.** Confirm that your theme or plugin works across the major browsers, and avoid using browser hacks to achieve browser compatibility where possible—it's far better to write clean code that supports multiple browsers and then add "extras" such as CSS3 goodies that aren't necessary for effective use of a site running your theme or plugin.

- **Test your code on multiple devices.** As more and more users access WordPress sites on mobile devices, your code should work across these. Consider whether your theme should be responsive and ensure that any interactions in your plugin work across devices and don't break the layout.

- **Test your code on multiple WordPress installations, including installations on different server platforms and those running Multisite.** It's also helpful to test on installations running other popular plugins such as BuddyPress and some of the big theme frameworks if you can, to ensure there are no incompatibilities. Ask other developers to help you with this so you have as wide a range of testing environments as possible.

Licensing

Your theme or plugin *must* be compatible with the GPL license to be accepted for release on wordpress.org. This is because any theme or plugin released in this way is considered to be a derivative of WordPress itself, which is released under GPLv2. You don't have to use GPLv2 itself—you can use a compatible license or a later version of the GPL license, but in most cases it's simpler to use GPLv2.

If you release a commercial or "pro" version of a free theme or plugin (known as *freemium*), it must also be sold under the GPL license, or your free theme or plugin won't be accepted.

If your code is a derivative of someone else's code (i.e., it's based on an existing theme or plugin but with added functionality or changes, which is entirely acceptable), you must credit the developer of the original theme or plugin. Any theme you release must not clone the design of a past or present website—so if you're developing a BuddyPress theme with Facebook-like features, don't clone the Facebook interface!

If you're developing premium themes and selling them via a theme vendor, there may be different licensing requirements. Make sure you understand what's involved and any consequences this may have in terms of releasing derivative code to wordpress.org. This is covered in more detail later in this chapter, in the "Selling Premium Themes and Plugins" section.

For a full version of the GPL license, see `http://www.gnu.org/licenses/gpl-2.0.html`.

Documentation and Readme Files

All plugins and themes must have a `readme.txt` file, as this provides the content that will be visible to users on the theme or plugin's main page at wordpress.org. In addition, it's helpful to provide extra documentation, either bundled with the theme or plugin or online, on a page on your website, or in a dedicated site for the theme or plugin. The better your documentation, the less support questions you will have to field—and the better the feedback you're likely to receive about your code.

Documentation can be provided via one or more channels:

- Information in the header of the main plugin file or stylesheet (commented out)
- A `readme.txt` file (for plugins)
- Inline documentation or comments
- Instructions or help text in the WordPress admin, added via meta boxes
- A WordPress help menu
- A page for your plugin or theme on your website
- A dedicated website
- Written manuals (or even a book!)

It can also take many forms:

- A reference guide
- A glossary

- A list of functions, filters, or hooks in your code

- A tutorial on using your code

- A screencast

- Any combination of these

How and where you provide documentation depends on the nature of your code and your users—for example, inline documentation won't be of much help if your users are unlikely to be developers and may never open your theme or plugin files. Documentation is essential, but it isn't a substitute for a poorly coded interface. For example, if your theme or plugin has settings screens, make sure they are intuitive, and include clear labeling and help text where relevant.

Header Information

Both themes and plugins must include information about them in the correct file—the stylesheet for themes, and the main plugin file for plugins. Without this information, WordPress won't recognize that a theme or plugin is present at all; with it, the information will appear in users' admin screens and help them understand how the theme or plugin works. For themes, this information is particularly important, as it also appears in the theme repository.

A theme needs to contain the following:

- Theme name and theme URI—from where it can be downloaded and where any documentation is held

- Author and author URI

- Description

- Version

- License and license URI

- Tags

All of this information will appear in the Themes admin screen when the theme is installed. For example, the header information for the Twenty Twelve theme (`http://wordpress.org/extend/themes/twentytwelve`) is as follows:

```
/*
Theme Name: Twenty Twelve
Theme URI: http://wordpress.org/extend/themes/twentytwelve
Author: the WordPress team
Author URI: http://wordpress.org/
Description: The 2012 theme for WordPress is a fully responsive theme
that looks great on any device. Features include a front page template
with its own widgets, an optional display font, styling for post formats
on both index and single views, and an optional no-sidebar page template.
Make it yours with a custom menu, header image, and background.
```

```
Version: 1.1
License: GNU General Public License v2 or later
License URI: http://www.gnu.org/licenses/gpl-2.0.html
Tags: light, gray, white, one-column, two-columns, right-sidebar,
flexible-width, custom-background, custom-header, custom-menu, editor-
style, featured-images, flexible-header, full-width-template,
microformats, post-formats, rtl-language-support, sticky-post, theme-
options, translation-ready
Text Domain: twentytwelve

This theme, like WordPress, is licensed under the GPL.
Use it to make something cool, have fun, and share what you've learned
with others.
*/
```

This is then displayed in the Manage Themes screen, as shown in Figure 12-1.

Figure 12-1 The Themes admin screen displaying theme header information for the Twenty Twelve theme

The list of tags is particularly useful, as it helps users to find your theme in the theme repository at `http://wordpress.org/extend/themes/`. There is a list of tags currently in use at `http://wordpress.org/extend/themes/tag-filter/`—it helps to use these if possible.

The information from the header is also used by the WordPress theme repository, as shown in the wordpress.org Themes Directory screen in Figure 12-2.

Figure 12-2 The theme repository page for the Twenty Twelve theme

A plugin also contains header information, which is also displayed in the relevant admin screen. For example, Akismet (`http://wordpress.org/extend/plugins/akismet/`) has the following header text:

```
/*
Plugin Name: Akismet
Plugin URI: http://akismet.com/?return=true
Description: Used by millions, Akismet is quite possibly the best way in
the world to <strong>protect your blog from comment and trackback
spam</strong>. It keeps your site protected from spam even while you
sleep. To get started: 1) Click the "Activate" link to the left of this
description, 2) <a href="http://akismet.com/get/?return=true">Sign up for
an Akismet API key</a>, and 3) Go to your
<a href="plugins.php?page=akismet-key-config">Akismet configuration</a>
page, and save your API key.
Version: 2.5.4
Author: Automattic
Author URI: http://automattic.com/wordpress-plugins/
License: GPLv2 or later
*/
```

As shown in Figure 12-3, note that text in the `Plugin URI` and `Author URI` descriptions automatically shows up as links in the admin screen, whereas if you want links within your description text, you need to code them in the markup.

Creating a readme.txt File for a Plugin

In addition to adding header information, for plugins you should also create a `readme.txt` file for users. The `readme.txt` file contains the information displayed on that plugin's page in the repository.

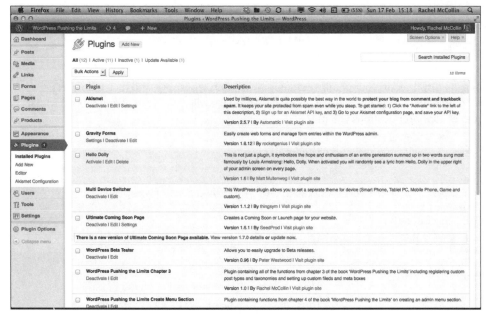

Figure 12-3 The Plugins admin screen displaying theme header information for the Akismet plugin

There is a very handy example of a plugin `readme.txt` file provided at `http://wordpress.org/ extend/plugins/about/readme.txt`. A plugin's `readme.txt` file is split into sections, each of which is identified with the section title as follows:

```
===Plugin Name===
// information relevant to section
```

The file should include the following sections:

- **Plugin Name**—Contributors, tags, compatibility information, license information, plus a short description of what the plugin does and any other essential information

- **Description**—An explanation of what your plugin does, which can be any length

- **Installation**—How to install the plugin and get it working

- **Frequently Asked Questions**—Common questions users have, with answers

- **Screenshots**—Links to screenshots, which should be stored in the plugin's /assets directory. Include descriptions for your screenshots.

- **Changelog**—A list of changes made in each version of the plugin

- **Arbitrary sections**—Additional sections, with names you define, for information that doesn't fit into the preceding sections

Save your `readme.txt` file to the plugin's main directory.

> **You can use markdown in all sections of the** `readme.txt` **file except the first - for more on markdown, see** `http://en.wikipedia.org/wiki/Markdown`

The contents of this file are displayed in your plugin's pages in the plugin repository, and they help users understand what your plugin does and how to use it. A good readme file will make your plugin more popular and reduce the number of support questions you get.

For example, the `readme.txt` file for Akismet is as follows:

```
=== Akismet ===
Contributors: matt, ryan, andy, mdawaffe, tellyworth, josephscott,
lessbloat, automattic
Tags: akismet, comments, spam
Requires at least: 3.0
Tested up to: 3.3.1
Stable tag: 2.5.4
License: GPLv2 or later

Akismet checks your comments against the Akismet web service to see if
they look like spam or not.

== Description ==
Akismet checks your comments against the Akismet web service to see if
they look like spam or not and lets you
review the spam it catches under your blog's "Comments" admin screen.

Major new features in Akismet 2.5 include:

* A comment status history, so you can easily see which comments were
  caught or cleared by Akismet, and which were spammed or unspammed by a
  moderator
* Links are highlighted in the comment body, to reveal hidden or
  misleading links
* If your web host is unable to reach Akismet's servers, the plugin will
  automatically retry when your connection is back up
* Moderators can see the number of approved comments for each user
* Spam and Unspam reports now include more information, to help improve
  accuracy

PS: You'll need an [Akismet.com API key](http://akismet.com/get/) to use
it.  Keys are free for personal blogs, with paid subscriptions available
for businesses and commercial sites.

== Installation ==
Upload the Akismet plugin to your blog, Activate it, then enter your
[Akismet.com API key](http://akismet.com/get/).
1, 2, 3: You're done!
== Changelog ==
= 2.5.4 =
```

```
* Limit Akismet CSS and Javascript loading in wp-admin to just the pages
  that need it
* Added author URL quick removal functionality
* Added mShot preview on Author URL hover
* Added empty index.php to prevent directory listing
* Move wp-admin menu items under Jetpack, if it is installed
* Purge old Akismet comment meta data, default of 15 days

= 2.5.3 =
// etc.
```

In the plugin repository it appears as shown in Figure 12-4.

Figure 12-4 The plugin repository page for Akismet

Providing Online Documentation

As you may have noticed, your theme or plugin contains a link to the theme or plugin URI. This can be its page at wordpress.org or it could be a page on your own website or a dedicated site. For large, popular, or complex themes and plugins, it is helpful to provide additional support outside the repository.

Documentation you might include on your website includes the following:

- A list of theme/plugin features
- Documentation on functions, filters, and hooks—and how they're used
- Documentation on any settings or options and how to enable or disable them

- Notes on any incompatibilities with other plugins or themes (although this isn't an excuse to let these happen!)

- Version notes

- A support page (maybe using bbPress or similar)—but be aware that doing this yourself can confuse users, who won't know if they should be using the support pages on wordpress.org or your own

- Screencasts or tutorials helping users to get the most from your theme or plugin

- Somewhere users can provide feedback or make suggestions for improvements, such as a contact page, form or email link

- A link to the theme or plugin's page on wordpress.org

- The facility to download the theme or plugin files—or you may want to skip this and just provide the link to wordpress.org

- A bulletin board or similar for users of your theme or plugin—some plugins such as BuddyPress have their own community pages

If your theme or plugin is premium, and therefore not available via wordpress.org, obviously all of this will be unnecessary because your own website will be the only place you can provide it.

An example of a popular plugin that has its own dedicated website is WordPress SEO by Yoast (`http://wordpress.org/extend/plugins/wordpress-seo/`), which has a dedicated site at `http://yoast.com/wordpress/seo`, shown in Figure 12-5.

© 2003-2013 Joost de Valk

Figure 12-5 Support site for the WordPress SEO plugin by Yoast

Submitting Your Theme or Plugin

At this point, you have confirmed that your theme or plugin meets the requirements, you've tested it thoroughly, and you have your documentation in place. The next step is to submit it.

Creating an Account

In order to submit a theme or plugin, you must have an account at wordpress.org—if you don't have one already, you can create one at `http://wordpress.org/support/register.php`. You'll need access to this account to submit code and participate in the support forums—either as a WordPress user asking questions or as a developer providing support for your code.

Submitting a Theme

To submit a theme, you upload a zip file containing all of your theme's files at `http://wordpress.org/extend/themes/upload/`. It will then be reviewed, and if accepted placed on the theme repository.

Submitting a Plugin

To submit a plugin, you need to zip it, upload your zip file to somewhere outside wordpress.org (which could be your own site or a hosting service such as GitHub or Dropbox), and submit it via `http://wordpress.org/extend/plugins/add/`. You need to provide the following information:

- Plugin name
- Plugin description
- Plugin URL—the link to your zip file

After your plugin has been reviewed and accepted, you'll be given access to the Subversion repository, which you use to manage versions of your plugin.

Maintenance and Support

After you have submitted your code and it has been accepted, your work isn't over. You need to maintain your code to ensure it continues to work with newer versions of WordPress, you need to fix bugs and make improvements where necessary, and you may also need to provide user support.

Supporting Your Theme or Plugin

If users run into problems with your theme or plugin, they may ask questions in the support forums. Sometimes these questions can be answered by another user, but it's much better to keep an eye on the forums and provide support yourself. Alternatively, you may choose to provide support via your own website.

Supporting a theme or plugin isn't mandatory, but if you don't offer support, you should explicitly state that in the description of your code—in plugins, this will be in your `readme.txt` file; in themes, this will be in your stylesheet.

WordPress Support Forums

The WordPress support forums are at `http://wordpress.org/support/`. Hopefully you've used them before, either as a user looking for help or as a developer assisting other users. The support forums are a great way to get involved with the WordPress community and learn more about WordPress.

When your code is added to the repository, a support page is automatically created for it at `http://wordpress.org/support/plugin/xxx` or `http://wordpress.org/support/theme/xxx`, where *xxx* is the slug of your theme or plugin. This will be linked to by one of the tabs in your plugin's page or theme's page in the repository.

Try to respond to support queries as quickly as possible, especially if they relate to problems with your code. If a user points out that your plugin or theme is breaking for some reason, it's important to at least acknowledge the issue and indicate when you'll fix it; otherwise, you'll lose your users' trust.

Updates and Maintenance

From time to time you'll need to release a new version of your theme or plugin, for a variety of reasons, including the following:

- Bug fixes
- Updates for compatibility
- Improvements and enhancements

You do this using Subversion, which is covered in detail shortly.

Compatibility with WordPress Releases

When WordPress itself is updated, it's important to check whether your own code still works, and to test this on multiple installations, browsers, and platforms—as you did before submitting the code in the first place. Keep an eye on the trac site at `http://core.trac.wordpress.org/` to anticipate upcoming releases and test your code on an installation running the beta version of an upcoming release—that way, you can identify any problems in advance of the release and prepare a new version that users can update to as soon as possible after the new release.

In the case of plugins, users are provided with compatibility information via your plugin's `readme.txt` file. Having tested your plugin against a new release and found that it still works, update your `readme.txt` file to reflect the compatibility—this will be displayed in the plugin's page on the plugin repository and in the pop-up that users see when they download the plugin from their WordPress admin.

This compatibility check will also enhance users' trust in your code when they're downloading it for the first time—users are less likely to download themes or plugins that aren't compatible with the version of WordPress they're running.

Maintaining compatibility with WordPress is covered in detail in Chapter 6.

Version Control Using Subversion

You submit new releases using Subversion, which is described at `http://wordpress.org/extend/plugins/about/svn/`. Managing plugin version control using Subversion means you can upload new versions of your plugin files and they will be stored correctly. It also enables users to access an earlier version of your plugin if necessary. Subversion uses a process of checking in and checking out—users of your plugin can check out code, but only you can check it in.

To start out with your new plugin, you do the following:

1. Check out the blank repository that will have been set up for you, i.e. download a version from the repository to your local machine.

2. Add your plugin files to the `/trunk` directory of that repository, including the `readme.txt` file.

3. Check the new files back in, which tells Subversion that you've made chnages (i.e. added files).

> Checking in and out is a process you carry out in Subversion to let the system know that you've made changes, such as downloading, uploading or changing files.

When making changes to your code, you follow a similar process:

1. Edit your local files (or a copy that you've checked out from SVN).

2. Check in your changes.

However, if you're releasing a new version of your code, you also need to edit your `readme.txt` file to reflect the new version number and add a copy of the old version to a subdirectory in `trunk/tags/`; for example, if you were creating version 1.1, you would create a directory called `trunk/tags/1.0` and save the previous version to that. You would then do the following:

1. Move your existing plugin files to the new directory.

2. Update the the main directory with the latest version of your files, with the new version number in your main plugin file's header text.

3. Check in the new files in the `/trunk` directory and the new subdirectory.

Using Subversion isn't complicated as long as you work methodically and make sure you cover all the steps. Make backups on your local machine before you start, just in case!

Selling Premium Themes and Plugins

If your theme or plugin serves a purpose that is extremely valuable to WordPress users and developers, or you have been supporting a free version that is becoming popular but difficult for you to maintain because of other commitments, you may decide to sell your code.

Commercial Development Expectations

Selling themes and plugins isn't easy. Users of premium products won't be anywhere near as forgiving as users of free code if they encounter any problems, and they'll expect excellent levels of support and documentation, as well as extremely robust code that is easy to work with and customize if needed. Nor is selling themes and plugins a way to get rich quickly—you'll have to put a lot of effort into marketing your product, updating it, and providing support and documentation. Even if you decide to let a third party such as a theme vendor do some of the work for you, you'll still need to update your code and possibly provide support.

To successfully market and sell your code, you need to do the following:

- Fill a gap in the market by producing a product that doesn't already exist and will meet a clear and real need—you'll need to do extensive market research to identify this, not just talk to your WordPress developer friends!

- Build a product that does enough for people to want to pay for it. Plugins should provide advanced functionality that is easy to configure via admin screens, and themes should be original and thoroughly coded, and offer more than just a nice design.

- Raise the profile of your product in the most appropriate way, ensuring that WordPress users are aware of it and want to buy it. This is the aspect of selling premium themes and plugins that's often the most challenging for developers.

- If you choose not to do your own marketing, identify a third-party vendor that can sell your theme, and be sure you understand what they expect of you, their licensing requirements, and the percentage of sales revenue you will receive. There are many vendors of WordPress themes and plugins out there and it's beyond the scope of this book to recommend any; however I would always advise asking other developers for their recommendations and experiences of vendors.

- Provide prompt, easy to understand support that will be helpful to both novice users and advanced developers, tailoring your support appropriately.

- Provide clear, thorough, and easy to understand documentation (possibly in multiple languages) that will be helpful to users at all levels. For premium products, this needs to be available via a clear interface such as a professional-looking website, which novice users in particular will be happy interacting with.

The Practicalities

If after reading the preceding section you still want to proceed and you think there's a market for your code, you need to consider some practicalities—licensing, payment, and distribution.

Licensing

It's a legal requirement to release premium themes and plugins under the GPL license. Reputable theme vendors will sell only GPL themes, and if you release a free version of your plugin via wordpress.org, the "pro" version that people pay for must also be GPL-compliant.

The Meaning of "Free"

All code released under the GPL license is free in the sense that it's open source—users are free to copy it, customize it, and tweak it as they wish. However, this does not necessarily mean "free" in the monetary sense. Open-source code can still be sold for profit. The important thing is that anyone who buys your code must have complete access to it—it must not be locked down in any way. Access to the code is restricted to those who have paid for it; but once users have paid for it, they will have full access to all the code in your theme or plugin and will be able to copy it and edit it as needed.

Protecting Your Work

If users need to pay for your plugins or themes, you'll need to provide a way to ensure people can't use them without paying first. The most common way to do this is by using a key, sometimes called an API key, activation key, or license key. This means users can upload your plugin or theme to their WordPress installation using a zip file, but in order to activate it or access updates to it they need to enter the key. An example of a plugin with an API key is Akismet—the key is free for personal users but paid-for for commercial use.

As your code is open source, an API key will only affect its functionality if your plugin needs to interact with your own servers in order to work—if it doesn't, users could hack your files to remove the API key requirement. However, most users won't do this—either because they're honest or because they don't have the technical know-how. Akismet is an example of a plugin that needs to interact with the provider's servers, as this is where the processing takes place to manage spam.

Payment Models and Distribution Channels

The different methods for distributing, and accepting payment for, premium themes and plugins is continually increasing as developers come up with more inventive ways to market their code. Table 12-1 outlines several common options.

Table 12-1: Payment and Distribution Models for Themes and Plugins

Payment/ Distribution Model	What It Involves	Example(s)	Pros	Cons
Subscription	Users pay a regular subscription fee (normally annually). If the fee is not paid they may lose access to either updates or a plugin's functionality.	WPMU DEV (multiple plugins, `http://premium.wpmudev.org`)	Regular income	Users may decide to stop paying or resent the regular payment.
One-off payment	Users pay a one-off fee for lifetime access to the theme or plugin.	Gravity Forms (`http://www.gravityforms.com`)	Guaranteed up-front income	May not generate as much income over its lifetime as a subscription model; users may be reluctant to pay up front

(continued)

Table 12-1 *(continued)*

Payment/ Distribution Model	What It Involves	Example(s)	Pros	Cons
Affiliate programs	Users are encouraged to promote your theme or plugin and receive an affiliate fee when people buy via a link you provide.	Genesis framework (`http://www.studiopress.com/`)	Others are doing your marketing for you.	Reduction in income for each sale; sometimes users don't trust links to products using this scheme, as they may not be genuine recommendations
Paid support and/or installation	The theme or plugin is free, but users who want support or help with installation or customization must pay for it.	Hybrid theme (`http://themehybrid.com/`), WordPress SEO by Yoast (`http://wordpress.org/extend/plugins/wordpress-seo/`)	Your user base will be higher because your plugin or theme is free and (optionally) available via wordpress.org.	Not enough people pay for additional services to cover your development costs.
Free plugin, premium themes to power it	Premium themes are sold specifically to power a free plugin.	Jigoshop (`http://wordpress.org/extend/plugins/jigoshop/`)	Your user base will be higher because your plugin is free and (optionally) available via wordpress.org.	Not enough people might buy premium themes to cover your development costs.
Theme and/ or plugin vendors	A third-party theme vendor sells your themes via their site and you get a percentage of the revenue.		You don't have to spend time marketing; the theme vendor will already have a user base.	Theme vendors receive a proportion of revenue—in some cases this is very high.

Payment/ Distribution Model	What It Involves	Example(s)	Pros	Cons
Free and "pro" versions (or *freemium*)	A free version is available via wordpress.org, while a paid version offers premium features and extra support.	WPTouch (`http://wordpress.org/extend/plugins/wptouch/`)	Your user base will be higher because your plugin is free and (optionally) available via wordpress.org.	Not enough people might upgrade to cover your development costs.
Per-installation fee	Users pay for a set number of installations and access is controlled via an API key; alternative pricing plans often available.	Gravity Forms (`http://www.gravityforms.com`)	Additional income from large-scale users; cheaper pricing for small-scale users	Users may be reluctant to pay if they don't feel they are getting value for their money.

For more examples of different freemium models, see `http://wp.smashingmagazine.com/2012/01/13/commercial-plugin-developers-wordpress-repository/`.

Preparing for Translation

A good plugin or theme, whether it's free or premium, will be translation-ready. This means coding it in such a way that users who access WordPress in a language other than your own will have the text translated for them, both in the public site and on any admin screens you create or customize. By doing this you make both the front-end of your site and the back-end administration screens accessible to users speaking a wide range of languages, which will increase the size of your audience.

Why Translate Your Code?

Translating your code makes your theme or plugin accessible to a much wider audience. According to Wikipedia (`http://en.wikipedia.org/wiki/Languages_used_on_the_Internet`), currently 56.6% of websites are in English, while 27% of Internet users are English speakers, with Chinese a very close second, at 25%. In contrast, only 4.5% of websites are in Chinese. A scan of past WordCamps at `http://central.wordcamp.org/schedule/past-wordcamps/` shows that WordPress developers are located in many places worldwide—including Europe, India, Nepal, and Japan.

Although many non-English-speaking developers and Internet users are accustomed to coding or reading in English by necessity, this is by no means ideal. By making your code available for translation, you are making your plugins and themes, and your clients' websites, available to a vast and fast-growing international audience. It's not even as if translation is difficult—it simply involves the use of a few functions that WordPress provides.

> You shouldn't translate your code—that will always be in American English, as that's what browsers read. What you'll be translating is the text that appears on public sites using your themes and plugins, and on any admin screens you create or modify.

Internationalization and Localization

It's easy to get confused between the two terms used in translation—localization and internationalization, and many tutorials and articles online use the terminology incorrectly. The two terms can be defined as follows:

- **Internationalization**—The process of making your code available for translation using the relevant WordPress functions
- **Localization**—The process carried out by a translator on your code, to translate it into the user's language (as well as making other changes such as switching text from left-to-right to right-to-left, for example)

In this section you'll learn how to internationalize your code. This is sometimes referred to as *i18n*, because there are 18 letters between the "i" and the "n" in internationalization.

Preparing your code for translation involves three steps:

1. Create a language file.
2. Load a text domain.
3. Use WordPress functions to internationalize text messages.

Language Files

WordPress uses three kinds of language files for translation:

- A `.pot` file contains a list of all the translatable messages in a theme or plugin.
- A `.po` file is created when the `.pot` file is translated (i.e., when localization takes place).
- A `.mo` file is a binary file created from the `.po` file. This is in machine-readable text and contains the strings and their translations—you could say it caches the translations and therefore speeds things up when WordPress is being translated.

The file you create for your theme or plugin is the `.pot` file.

To create a `.pot` file, you use a utility such as Poedit (`http://www.poedit.net/`). When creating this file, you have to provide the tool with the following information:

- Project information, including the name, the charset, and the language you're working in
- The path to the folder where your `.pot` file will be located (the /languages directory)
- The WordPress functions used to translate text (which are listed shortly)

Once you've provided this information, the tool will scan your source files and locate text you've identified for translation using these functions. You then save the `.pot` file it creates for you in your /languages directory, giving it the same name as your text domain.

> **For a detailed tutorial on using Poedit, see** `http://wp.smashingmagazine.com/2011/12/29/` `internationalizing-localizing-wordpress-theme/`.

Text Domains

The functions you use to translate your text will include a text domain, which should be unique—normally you use the name of your theme or plugin. Before using these functions in your theme or plugin, you need to register the text domain, either in `functions.php` or in your plugin. To do this, you use either `load_theme_textdomain()` or `load_plugin_textdomain()`.

Following is the code for the `load_plugin_text_domain()` function:

```php
<?php
 load_plugin_textdomain( $domain, $path_from_abspath, $path_from_plugins_
folder );
?>
```

This function takes the following parameters:

- `$domain`—The unique identifier for the text domain
- `$path_from_abspath`—The relative path to the translation file; this is deprecated since WordPress 2.7, so use `false` here
- `$path_from_plugins_folder`—The relative path to the folder containing the translation file from the plugin directory

The function is then attached to the `plugins_loaded` action hook.

For example, to load a text domain in one of my plugins I would use the following function:

```php
<?php
function wpptl_plugin_textdomain() {
 load_plugin_textdomain( 'wpptl', false, dirname( plugin_basename( __
FILE__ ) ) . /'languages' );
}
add_action( 'plugins_loaded', 'wpptl_plugin_textdomain' );
?>
```

This accesses the `wpptl.pot` file that I've added to the `/languages` subdirectory in my plugin's directory.

The `load_theme_textdomain()` function is similar, but fired via the `after_setup_theme` action hook:

```php
<?php
load_theme_textdomain( $domain, $path );
?>
```

Its parameters are as follows:

- `$domain`—The unique identifier for the text domain, normally the name of the theme
- `$path`—The relative path to the translation file

For example, to add a text domain to my theme, I would add the following to `functions.php`:

```php
<?php
function wpptl_theme_textdomain(){
  load_theme_textdomain('my_theme', get_template_directory() .
  '/languages' );
}
add_action( 'after_setup_theme', 'wpptl_theme_textdomain' );
?>
```

This loads the text domain using the `wpptl.pot` translation file in the `/languages` subdirectory of my theme directory.

As well as defining text domains using your own language files, you can also use the default translation file bundled with WordPress, by loading the default text domain. You do this using `load_default_textdomain()`, which has no parameters:

```php
<?php
load_default_textdomain();
?>
```

This loads the `.mo` translation file located in the `WP_LANG_DIR` constant path from the root of your WordPress installation. If you are using the default text domain, you don't include a reference to the text domain in your translation functions.

WordPress Translation Functions

The three translation funcitons used most commonly by WordPress are as follows:

- `__( 'message' )`—Translates the content of the message
- `_e( 'message' )`—Echoes the content of the message
- `_n( 'message' )`—Used for singular and plural text

In addition you will find the `printf()` and `sprintf()` functions useful, which don't relate directly to tranlsation but are often wrapped aorund translation functions, as you'll see later in this section.

Translating a Message

The `__()` function is as follows:

```php
<?php
__ ( $message, $textdomain );
?>
```

It has two parameters:

- `$message`—The message to be translated

- `$textdomain`—The text domain, as defined earlier by one of the text domain loading functions (if you want to use the default WordPress translation and have called `load_default_textdomain()`, you don't include this parameter).

To translate the content of a `<h3>` tag output by a function in my theme or plugin, I would add the following:

```php
<?php
echo '<h3>' . __( 'Hello', 'wpptl' ) . '</h3>';
?>
```

This would output the following HTML if English were being used:

```
<h3>Hello</h3>
```

If the site were being translated into French, however, it would output this:

```
<h3>Bonjour</h3>
```

Echoing Translated Text

WordPress has a specific function for echoing translated text. In the preceding example, I used `echo` to echo the h3 tags and the text to be translated, but this can be simplified using the `_e()` function, which takes the same parameters as the `__()` function:

```
<h3>
<?php _e( 'Hello', 'wpptl' ); ?>
</h3>
```

This would output the same HTML but is used whenever you're using `echo` to output PHP.

Translating Placeholders

Things get a little more complicated when you're translating placeholders. Let's say, for example, you're writing a function to display the number of comments for a post:

```php
<?php
function wpptl_comment_count() {
 $comments_count = wp_count_comments( $post->ID() );
 $count = $comments_count->total_comments;
 echo '<p>This post has $count comments</p>';
}
?>
```

You might assume that the way to translate this would be to use the following:

```php
<?php
function wpptl_comment_count() {
 $comments_count = wp_count_comments( $post->ID() );
 $count = $comments_count->total_comments;
 echo '<p>' . __( 'This post has $count comments', 'wpptl' ) . '</p>';
}
?>
```

However, that won't work, as WordPress wouldn't translate $count, but simply output it in the text as follows:

```
<p>This post has $count comments</p>
```

To translate this proeprly you need to output a formatted string, which is what the `printf()` and `sprintf()` functions do. In this case you use `sprintf()` because you are using `echo`. Here you use the message and the `%d` placeholder as the parameters for your function:

```php
<?php
function wpptl_comment_count() {
 $comments_count = wp_count_comments( $post->ID() );
 $count = $comments_count->total_comments;
 echo '<p>' . __( 'This post has $count comments', 'wpptl' ) . '</p>';
 echo '<p>' . sprintf(__( 'This post has %d comments', 'wpptl' ), $count )
.'</p>';
}
?>
```

This uses the parameter $count to populate `%d`, outputting the following HTML:

```
<p>This post has 12 comments</p>
```

...and the relevant equivalent in other languages!

If the text has more than one placeholder, you use %1$s, %2$s, and so on for each value, with each placeholder listed in order as a parameter of `sprintf()`:

```php
<?php
function wpptl_postmeta() {
 $author = the_author( $post->ID() );
 $comments_count = wp_count_comments( $post->ID() );
 $count = $comments_count->total_comments;
 echo '<p>' . sprintf(__( 'This post has %1$s comments and was written by
%2$s', 'wpptl' ), $count, $author ) . '.</p>';
}
?>
```

Using the numbers ensures the placeholders are output in the correct order.

Note that because `printf()` doesn't translate the text, it must surround the ___() function. This outputs the correct HTML:

```
<p>This post has 12 comments and was written by Rachel McCollin.</p>
```

Working with Singular and Plural Text

Translating singular and plural text is a little trickier, as you need to tell WordPress how to translate both versions.

In the preceding example that translated the comment count for the current post, this would be displayed oddly if the post had only one comment:

```
<p>This post has 1 comments</p>
```

To fix this, you use the _n() function, which is placed inside the `printf()` function and has four parameters:

```php
<?php
_n( $singular, $plural, $number, $textdomain );
?>
```

Therefore, to fix the function, it would be changed to the following:

```php
<?php
function wpptl_comment_count2() {
  $comments_count = wp_count_comments( $post->ID() );
  $count = $comments_count->total_comments;
  echo '<p>' . sprintf( _n( 'This post has %d comment', 'This post has %d
comments', $count, 'wpptl' ), $count ) . '</p>';
}
?>
```

All those nested brackets can get confusing. This is how they work, from the inside out:

▨ The _n() function is on the inside, with four parameters:

  • `'This post has %d comment'`, the singular message

  • `'This post has %d comments'`, the plural message

  • `$count`, the runtime count which allows the correct message (singular/plural) to be selected

  • `'wpptl'`, the textdomain

  The _n() function which is used to translate singular and plural text.

▨ The next layer out is the `printf()` function, which has two parameters:

  • The _n() function, which defines the message to be printed

  • `$count`, the number of comments

This outputs the correct HTML:

```
<p>This post has 1 comment</p>
```

Summary

For any developer releasing themes or plugins to the public, it's essential to do this properly. This includes ensuring that your code meets WordPress standards and submitting your code in the right way. Preparing your code for translation ensures that it can be used by as wide an audience as possible; and as the use of WordPress extends to non-English-speaking parts of the world, this will become increasingly important.

In addition, if you want to sell your themes or plugins, you'll have to do a lot of work researching your market, developing a product that meets a real need, and determining exactly how you're going to sell it. This will all take time; but if you plan properly and know what you're getting into and why you're using a particular model to sell your code, you'll have a better chance of success.

Having done all this, all that remains is for you to provide support for your users and maintain your code, ensuring that it's compatible with WordPress updates, fixing bugs, and making enhancements. No easy task, but it can be a hugely rewarding way to develop your coding skills and give something back to the WordPress community.

Further Resources

Theme and Plugin Guidelines

Theme Review
`http://codex.wordpress.org/Theme_Review`

Theme Review team
`http://make.wordpress.org/themes/`

Theme upload page
`http://wordpress.org/extend/themes/upload/`

Plugin submission and promotion
`http://codex.wordpress.org/Plugin_Submission_and_Promotion`

Plugin submission page
`http://wordpress.org/extend/plugins/add/`

Plugin developer FAQ
`http://wordpress.org/extend/plugins/about/faq/`

Plugin guidelines
`http://wordpress.org/extend/plugins/about/guidelines/`

Theme Unit Testing

Codex page on Theme Unit Testing
`http://codex.wordpress.org/Theme_Unit_Test`

The `xml` file containing test data
`https://wpcom-themes.svn.automattic.com/demo/theme-unit-test-data.xml.`

The Developer Plugin
`http://wordpress.org/extend/plugins/developer/`

Guide to reviewing themes
`http://www.chipbennett.net/2011/04/20/a-guide-to-reviewing-themes-for-the-wordpress-theme-repository/`

Theme Unit Testing tutorial
`http://wp.tutsplus.com/tutorials/creative-coding/the-beginners-guide-to-unit-testing-what-is-unit-testing/`

Preparing Your Code for Release

GPL license
`http://www.gnu.org/licenses/gpl-2.0.html`

WordPress coding standards
`http://codex.wordpress.org/WordPress_Coding_Standards`

W3C HTML validation service
`http://validator.w3.org/`

W3C CSS validation service
`http://jigsaw.w3.org/css-validator/`

Codex page on `WP_DEBUG`
`http://codex.wordpress.org/WP_DEBUG`

Documentation

Documentation tutorial
`http://wp.smashingmagazine.com/2012/07/04/writing-effective-wordpress-documentation/`

Improving your plugin's readme.txt file
`http://wp.smashingmagazine.com/2011/11/23/improve-wordpress-plugins-readme-txt/`

Dummy readme file
`http://wordpress.org/extend/plugins/about/readme.txt`

Theme tags
`http://wordpress.org/extend/themes/tag-filter/`

Support and Maintenance

WordPress support forums
`http://wordpress.org/support/`

Using Subversion
`http://wordpress.org/extend/plugins/about/svn/`

Premium Themes and Plugins

How commercial plugin developers are using the WordPress repository
http://wp.smashingmagazine.com/2012/01/13/commercial-plugin-developers-wordpress-repository/

Building WordPress themes you can sell
http://wp.smashingmagazine.com/2011/11/01/building-wordpress-themes-you-can-sell/

Translation

Languages used on the Internet
http://en.wikipedia.org/wiki/Languages_used_on_the_Internet

Translating WordPress
http://codex.wordpress.org/Translating_WordPress

Internationalizing your plugin
http://codex.wordpress.org/Writing_a_Plugin#Internationalizing_Your_Plugin

Internationalization for WordPress developers
http://codex.wordpress.org/I18n_for_WordPress_Developers

Poedit
http://poedit.net

Index